PROGRAMMING
FUNDAMENTALS
USING MATLAB®

PROGRAMMING FUNDAMENTALS USING MATLAB

MICHAEL C. WEEKS, PHD

(Georgia State University)

MERCURY LEARNING AND INFORMATION
Dulles, Virginia
Boston, Massachusetts
New Delhi

Publisher: David Pallai
MERCURY LEARNING AND INFORMATION
22841 Quicksilver Drive
Dulles, VA 20166
info@merclearning.com
www.merclearning.com
(800) 232-0223

Michael Weeks. *Programming Fundamentals Using MATLAB.*
ISBN: 978-1-68392-555-2

The publisher recognizes and respects all marks used by companies, manufacturers, and developers as a means to distinguish their products. All brand names and product names mentioned in this book are trademarks or service marks of their respective companies. Any omission or misuse (of any kind) of service marks or trademarks, etc. is not an attempt to infringe on the property of others.

Library of Congress Control Number: 2020939910

202122 321   Printed on acid-free paper in the United States of America

Our titles are available for adoption, license, or bulk purchase by institutions, corporations, etc. For additional information, please contact the Customer Service Dept. at (800) 232-0223(toll free).

Digital versions of our titles are available at: www.academiccourseware.com and other electronic vendors. *Companion files are available from the publisher by writing to info@merclearning.com.* The sole obligation of MERCURY LEARNING AND INFORMATION to the purchaser is to replace the book and/or disc, based on defective materials or faulty workmanship, but not based on the operation or functionality of the product.

I dedicate this book to my son, Samuel.
I hope that he finds the same joy
in mathematics that I have found.

CONTENTS

LIST OF FIGURES

LIST OF TABLES

PREFACE

People use MATLAB in many different fields, such as the growing field of bio-informatics. There are many applications in biology, chemistry, mathematics, engineering and physics, which could benefit from scientists who can program. Given the volume of data for these applications, and the ease of use of MATLAB, this is a natural match.

WHY A BOOK ON MATLAB

This book grew out of an Introduction to MATLAB Programming class. There are other MATLAB books available, but they are often either encyclopedic or version dependent. In the first semester that I taught it, Fall 2006, I found that my students did not have the same software. The classroom had version 6.1, the main lab where students could do homework had version 6.5, while I demonstrated code on my laptop with version 7.0. Some had a student edition of the software, in either version 7.0 or the brand-new 7.2. In other words, there were at least five different versions of the software. A conversation with some students drove this point home. As I talked to a group of three people who were working on a project together, they explained that they split the work into three sets of tasks, and would work on each task one at a time. I asked why they did not work on them together, or go in a different order. Their response was that they could not go backwards, because each person in sequence had a newer version than the previous one.

Standardizing the versions available across the university (at that time) was not feasible. Copies were purchased by different departments at different times. Some even had different toolboxes available; what the math department needed was different than the computer science department. And one biologist might need to work with images, while another needs to do signal acquisition.

Another issue is the amount of material that can be covered in one semester. My class involves a laboratory component, meaning it emphasizes problem solving. Class time includes both lecture and the time to work on the computer, at roughly a 3 to 1 ratio. Students who have already studied a programming language pick up MATLAB quickly. In fact, several classes for computer science majors use MATLAB without requiring previous experience with it. For people who have never programmed a computer before, it takes a while before the concepts "sink in." They need a solid foundation in the basics, with plenty of practice.

This text is meant to get across the basics of MATLAB programming to form that foundation. Chapters are meant to be stand-alone as much as possible. The first chapter covers concepts and terminology that appear again and again. It should be a quick read for people who already have programming experience, but sufficient to get everyone else up and programming.

COMPANION FILES

This book comes with companion files and supplementary materials. For example, many of the figures are available in full color. The example code, functions and programs shown in the text, images, sound, and other data files are also available. All of the full-color figures in the book can be found on the disc (or on the downloadable companion files). *The files are also available from the publisher by writing to info@merclearning.com.*

INSTRUCTOR ANCILLARIES

Solutions to the end of chapter exercises and slides are available to instructors upon adoption.

ACKNOWLEDGMENTS

This book was only possible with the support of many people. I could not have written it without the support and understanding of my wife and family.

M.C.Weeks
June 2020

THE MATLAB ENVIRONMENT AND PROGRAMMING TERMINOLOGY

```
disp('helloworld!');
```

One of the first things a person writes in a new computing language is often a "hello world!" program. The computer responds with something that the programmer told it to do, demonstrating a small victory in control. The programmer gives the computer a command, the computer executes the command and responds with the message showing that it did it. Better yet, it has an absence of warnings and error messages. Many languages have several lines of code that must be typed exactly, even for such a simple task. Fortunately, MATLAB® does not, and the line above is all that you need.

If you are an experienced programmer, you should note that MATLAB uses single quotes to mark the beginning and ending of strings. Recent MATLAB releases allow doubles-quotes to delineate strings, also. If you are not an experienced programmer, do not worry, this book is written for everyone.

MATLAB will calculate the result of an expression that you enter, so you could use it as a calculator. Suppose that you are ordering food to be delivered to your home, and want to include a tip based on the amount of the order. If the order comes to $23.17, and you want to know how much a 15% tip is, you can type 23.17 * 15/100, where the 15/100 is literally 15 percent, i.e., 15 divided by 100. The expression 23.17 * 0.15 would work, too. Entered into a MATLAB command window, you will see the following. The >> is MATLAB's command prompt, which it displays when it waits for you to type something.

```
>> 23.17 * 15/100
ans =
    3.4755
```

The world of programming involves *abstractions*, where we summarize the behavior of code, then use that code as a building block. In the preceding example, we could summarize it as a 15% tip calculator for a $23.17 order, although it would be even better if we could make it work for any given order amount. This will be addressed in later material. To understand abstractions, first we need some experience, so when you see code or an equation, put your own numbers in. With example code in this text, type it in a MATLAB session at the command prompt, and see that it matches what you expect. Many of the included examples have arbitrarily chosen values. For example, what if you repeat the previous example with 15/100*23.17? Or 10*20/30? To understand how things work, put a number in. When experimenting with code, it does not usually matter what values you choose, since we simply desire a "concrete" example. If the number does not work, the computer may indicate that. Or it might carry out the command, and give you an unexpected result, such as when instructed to find 15/0.

```
>> 15/0
ans =
    Inf
```

Some computer languages give an error when asked to divide by zero. In this case, MATLAB simply returns "infinity" as the answer.

To remember a value that we use again and again, we use a *variable*. A common analogy is to think of variables like post office boxes, where you can put a value in each one. To keep track of variables, perhaps when trying to figure out what a program does, write down the name and a box next to it. Inside the box, put whatever value it has. It can only have one value at a time, so erase any old value when giving it a new one. You may have noticed that MATLAB stores the answer to the last expression as the "ans" variable.

Technology changes over time. Just as you cannot imagine how your parents lived without cell phones, television, and the Internet, people 20 years from now will consider today's latest developments crude by comparison. For us, the computer is a lightweight device that fits in a briefcase; for them, the computer may be as heavy as a credit card, although not as large, and may be carried in the wallet.

FIGURE 1.1 A sketch of the MATLAB user interface. The command window is on the left.

Note: This figure and all of the full-color figures in the book can be found on the disc (or on the downloadable companion files).

As technology changes, so too do the tools we use. This document is about one such tool, used by scientists and engineers all over the world. It changes over time, as the developers add new features. Things that made users in the past say, "Why won't this work? It should work" have been made to work. The user's job becomes easier since the tool does more, while the necessary information about the tool increases. In a sense, the user is expected to know more!

This guide is not meant to teach you everything about this tool. Instead, the goal is to teach the fundamentals, the issues that will always be there as the tools we use come and go. You will learn everything you need to know to solve your problems. If a built-in feature will do the job, that is nice. But if no such feature exists, you should be able to program your own solution. Use what works. We will start with terminology, and build up to programming syntax: the instructions that we give to the computer, and the form that we use so that it understands what we want.

Note that this text contains examples that sometimes include the prompt >>. If you try these examples yourself, which is highly recommended, you do not type the >>. If you have an "educational" version of MATLAB, made for students, you will see EDU>> as the prompt. It is not an important difference. The examples in this text are meant to be general enough that they will work on any recent version of MATLAB.

Lines can be broken up with three periods in a row (...). You will see this occasionally in this text, mainly to make the examples fit nicely within the margins, and still have them work. There will be times when you have questions about how things work. For example, in a = 5, are the spaces around the equal sign necessary? Try it and see!

1.1 ALGORITHMS

An *algorithm*, at least in the every-day sense of the term, means a plan to accomplish a task. It is a list of abstract steps to take, in the order given. These steps are "abstract" in the sense that they may be quite complex themselves. Formally, computer scientists describe an algorithm in terms of a *Turing Machine*, a simple, theoretical device that works on a tape, moving left and right, reading and replacing symbols, according to a set of states (conditions) and instructions. It can lead to an accept state, a reject state, or run forever. Loosely, a state keeps track of the step, with transitions that lead to other states, based on the input. An algorithm is a decidable process for doing something, where *decidable* means that it ends in the accept or reject state.

To illustrate the informal idea of an algorithm, let's consider a set of driving directions. Suppose you have a set of instructions that say:

```
1. Go straight 1 mile, then take a left.
2. At the third light, take a right.
3. When you cross the railroad tracks, take a right directly
   after them.
4. Stop at the fifth house on your left.
5. If you see a dead-end sign, then you have gone too far.
   Back up about 500 feet.
```

Obviously, you must do these steps in order, or you will not get to the destination. Also, a human will understand what each step means, without further explanation. Humans are also great at detecting a problem. For example, what if the railroad tracks were paved over? What if we drive for a long time but never see the railroad tracks? A human would know that something is not correct, and take action (e.g., call the person who gave directions).

Algorithms are specified in an English-like way, called *pseudo-code*. When we write an algorithm, we are primarily concerned with getting the idea across, and we care about conforming to a machine-understandable pattern to a lesser extent. For example, what if the second line begins with a lower-case character, and the fourth line does not end in a period? While we like consistency, any human would still understand the algorithm.

A *loop* is when a set of directions repeat, and each repetition is called an *iteration*. For example, cooking instructions could say to "chop the carrots and set aside. Repeat this with the onions." If we follow directions that say to do something several times, we might count on our fingers, or perhaps count out loud. The *index* keeps track of the number of iterations, where a variable stores this value. We start at one, add one to the count every time we repeat, and stop when we reach the maximum. Of course, we could start at the maximum and count down, as some people do with exercises as a motivational trick. We do not even need to count by whole numbers; imagine if you run laps on a quarter-mile track. If you plan to reach a daily goal of 5 miles, and you already ran 2.5 miles this morning, you might start with 2.5 and add 0.25 every time you get back to the starting place. That type of loop iterates for a set number of times, known in advance. Other loops repeat until a condition is met.

Pseudo-code statements are written by humans, for other humans to read. They conform to standards so that they can be directly expressed in a programming language, such as numbering each step, and contain certain keywords like `for`. Many computer languages have a loop structure invoked by the keyword `for`, although they differ in specific syntax (how the statement is expressed). Pseudo-code statements are not meant for a computer to understand directly. They are precise about the instruction sequence and control flow, and yet intentionally vague about how some things may be accomplished, such as "display the result." Whether that result is displayed as text on a screen, printed onto paper, or shown on a high-resolution monitor, does not matter. The programmer who implements the algorithm will determine the best way to display the result with the specific computer language.

1.2 PROGRAMS

A *program* is a list of instructions for a computer to follow. Some people confuse this with an algorithm, but the intended audience for each is different. Algorithms are for humans, while programs are primarily for computers. Programs must be much more detailed than algorithms, since they must specify what to do in a way the computer can understand, as opposed to saying things in a way that a fellow human would follow. Programs must conform to a *syntax*, the rules of how a programmer specifies commands to the computer. Different computer languages have different syntaxes.

Suppose that we translate the above algorithm to a program, and give it to a computer. It will do exactly what it is told to do. If it does not detect the railroad crossing, it may keep looking for it, forever. We need to test it. We need to provide commands to deal with unexpected conditions, like unused train tracks being paved over.

When we write a program, we call it *source code*. Most programming languages have a special program called a *compiler*, meaning that the program will be translated (*compiled*) into a form that the computer's microprocessor (also called a central processing unit, or CPU) can use. The compiled code is specific to that computer's type of CPU, i.e., a program compiled on a PowerPC-based Mac is incompatible with a Sun SPARC processor, as well as an Intel-based personal computer. For that matter, a program compiled on a PowerPC-based Mac is not compatible with the recent Intel-based Macs. The compiler generates an *executable* program that other people can use on their computers, and may even pay for. Most people mean the executable program when they say the word *software*. In contrast, *hardware* means the physical computer. To *run* a program means to execute it; to tell the computer that it should follow the directions specified by the program. By the way, "app" is just a trendy word for application, and it means the same thing as software, although often it is software made specifically for a mobile device.

In some companies, the executable programs are sold while the source code used to make them are carefully guarded secrets. An analogy is the recent news item from Coca-Cola: while millions of people buy Coke products every day, an employee allegedly obtained the secret formula and tried to sell it to rival Pepsi for over a million dollars [1]. Needless to say, the plot was discovered and the people involved were arrested. Similar to the way soft drink makers sell their products but do not disclose exactly how they make them, a software company may write a useful program, and sell only the executable version of it. We call this *closed source*. The average (home) user would not know what to do with the source code if they had it, but a programmer could examine it for errors or add features and potentially make it better. Of course, an unscrupulous programmer could change it just enough to make it appear to be their own work, then sell the executable code. Or they could find weaknesses in the code, and use them for malicious purposes, like taking over someone else's machine.

A different approach is the *open source* movement, where source code is available (usually for free). An obvious question is, "How do you make money by giving something away for free?" One answer is convenience. Consider an oil-change for your car. If you have ever changed the oil in your car, it was probably not difficult, but it was a messy experience. Why bother to get dirty when you can drive to a quick-change facility and (for a reasonable fee) have someone else do it in only a few minutes? Similarly, a technical person may find the nominal cost for a CD-ROM (or other media) of software to be well worth the expense, instead of spending an evening downloading code, configuring it, compiling it, etc. Also, service is a potential area of revenue for an open-source software company, as many users will pay a yearly fee for the ability to call a technician who is very familiar with the software. Users will also pay to subscribe to automatic updates. But what if an unscrupulous person finds problems in the software that they can exploit? Of course this is a potential problem, but what the open-source community found is that many good people will spot potential problems, and updates are quickly disseminated.

Related to open-source software is the open standard. A good example of this is the portable document format (PDF), associated with the Adobe Acrobat program. While Acrobat is closed source software, the portable document format standard is an *open standard*; it is available on the Internet. (Actually, the portable document format standard is based on postscript, another open standard.) This means that while you are not going to have access to the source code for Acrobat, you can still write your own program to read or write portable document format files. Not all standards are open, and the use of closed standards has become an area of debate. The state of Massachusetts recently passed a law requiring state employees to use an open standard for documents, based on the idea that their citizens have a right to public information in an open format [2].

MATLAB is a product of The MathWorks, a company based in Massachusetts. MATLAB is a program that provides an environment for programming. (Take a deep breath—it is really not that complicated!) Programs written according to the MATLAB syntax are read and *interpreted* by the MATLAB programming environment. Or, you could say that MATLAB programs are read and executed by the MATLAB program. Since this results in confusion, we will take care to call the MATLAB program the "MATLAB programming environment" or simply "MATLAB," and use "MATLAB program" to mean a program written in the syntax that MATLAB understands.

While it is closed source software in the sense that you are not going to have access to the source code, you will find that many MATLAB functions are available for inspection. Programs are stored in an open standard, called the "MATLAB syntax" above. MATLAB programs are text files that have ".m" for the extension. For example, you might name a program to calculate your taxes "`mytaxes.m`" if you wrote it in MATLAB. By the way, the Objective-C language also uses ".m" for its extension. If you click on a file with a ".m" extension, your computer may call up a different programming environment than MATLAB. See Section 2.10 for other common file extensions used in the MATLAB environment.

With MATLAB, you can interact with the command window, typing commands one by one, getting feedback, and revising the commands as needed. You might have a series of commands that you would like to save and use again later. In the command window, typing "`edit`" calls up MATLAB's editor, similar to other text-processing software that you have used. From here, you can copy and paste the commands into the editor, then save it under a name ending in `.m`, although the editor will likely take care of that detail for you. That file is a program, also called other names like code, source-code, and *script*. Later, we will cover *functions*, although for the moment, you can tell scripts and functions apart by the `function` keyword. If a MATLAB file contains the word `function` at the start of the first line of commands, then it is a function. Otherwise, it is a script.

1.3 COMPILERS AND ERRORS

The compiler translates the entire program all at once. A *syntax error* (similar to the missing period in the above algorithm) would stop a computer from understanding the directions. It would essentially say, "I do not understand these directions, so I cannot follow them." It may stop trying at this point. If it keeps going, any further errors reported might be a result of the first one, so it is good practice to examine the error messages in order. Syntax errors will be fixed by the programmer. A different type of error called a *logic error* occurs when the program does something that the programmer did not intend. The commands may make sense individually, but not when considered together. A computer does not make judgment calls (unless we specifically tell it how to do this). It will perform each command, doing precisely what we tell it to do. But it may not do what we want it to do! We also call a logic error a *bug*, coming from a story about the computing pioneer Grace Hopper discovering a moth that had short-circuited a computer, causing an error.

Here is an example of a logic error. Suppose you write down the steps to calculate employees' gross pay. Some work part-time, some work full-time. Many of them work overtime, and they are paid a "time and a half" bonus for overtime. Your instructions may look like this:

```
1. if the number of hours worked < 40,
   then pay=(hours worked)*(pay rate)

2. if the number of hours worked > 40,
   then pay=(hours worked)*1.5*(pay rate)
```

If a computer were to process those directions, many people would receive weird paychecks, perhaps even negative amounts! The instructions specify what to do when someone works less than 40 hours, and the instructions also specify what to do when someone works more than 40 hours. But these instructions say nothing about what to do when a person works exactly 40 hours. Thus, we have a logic error. Depending on the computer language, the amount stored in pay might not have been initialized, so the value there is whatever value happened to be there before. One person may receive an automatic payment of negative billions of dollars, while someone else may be credited millions.

MATLAB provides an *interpreter*. It works a bit differently from a compiler in that it translates line-by-line. We have an interactive environment with MATLAB: you type a command, and it performs it. It gives you immediate feedback (unless you tell it to do something very time-consuming). You can experiment until you have it just right. This *iterative approach* to programming means to make small changes to a program, test them out, and repeat. It allows us to build a program one step at a time. MATLAB provides a good environment for this approach, since we can enter commands one at a time, and correct them when we make mistakes.

1.4 VARIABLES

A variable is a label for a piece of data. Like the name implies, a variable's value can be changed. Variables in a computer program are similar to variables used in mathematics. A mathematician may write "Let $x = 1$." Similarly, a computer programmer may write $x = 1$, an example of an *assignment* statement. It assigns the value 1 to the variable x, so the computer can substitute any future references to x with the value 1, at least until we assign another value to x. The short example below demonstrates this idea. Everything on the line after >> is the command as you would type it.

```
>> x = 1;
>> disp(x);
      1
>> x = 5;
>> disp(x);
      5

>>
```

If you enter these lines in the MATLAB command window, it responds with 1 the first time that it displays x, and 5 the second time, since the third command reassigns the value of x.

Variables in MATLAB are flexible. You can store a whole number, called an integer, like 1, or 14, or –937. You can store a real number, called a float (for floating point) or double (for double the precision of a float), like 1.0, or 14.6, or –937.7259. The difference in precision comes up when you need to store numbers with a wide range of values. In many computer languages, the programmer must "declare" a variable in advance, that is, specify the data type as well as the variable name, before it can be assigned a value. MATLAB allows you to assign a variable without declaring it first. The default data type for MATLAB is the double. You can also store a character, or a bunch of characters, called a string, like 'a', 'abc', or 'My address is 246 Oak Street'.

The pattern for an assignment statement is variable = expression, where the variable gives a label, like x or x1 or address. More generally, you can think of everything to the left of the equal sign as where to store the result. The expression can be as simple as a number, or something complex like a formula. Here are some examples of assignment statements.

```
x = 14.6;
address = 'My address is 246 Oak Street';
y = x * 7 + 5;
```

The last line recalls the value for x, multiplies it by 7, and adds 5. The variable y will have the value 107.2 if you type in the above three lines. Strings are started and ended with the single quote ', although now MATLAB allows double quotes, too. To have a single quote within a string, use two single quotes together, as in mystr = 'don''t have a cow';

An assignment statement differs from an equation. For example, in mathematics, the equation

$$x = x + 2$$

leads to an inconsistency, since x could be removed from both sides, resulting in 0 = 2. Clearly, this cannot be true under any circumstance. However, the statement x = x + 2 is perfectly valid as an assignment. The computer evaluates the right-hand side of it, x + 2, retrieving the current value of x, and adding 2 to it. (Note that x must already have a value, otherwise how could the computer know what x + 2 should be?) Then it stores the result in the variable given on the left-hand side, x. So x = x + 2 does not work as an equation in mathematics, but it is perfectly acceptable as an assignment in a computer language. As a counter-example, an equation like

$$2y = 4$$

is valid in mathematics, but does not work as an assignment statement since the left-hand side contains more than just a variable name. We can modify it to make it work by solving for y; that is, the statement y = 4 / 2 works.

We use variables to keep track of things. Suppose that you want to figure out how much money you made at work. You would need to know how many hours you worked, how much per hour you are paid, what percent you pay in income taxes, and any other expenses, such as pre-tax charges for parking. If you write these things down, it might looks something like this:

```
I worked 60 hours this month.
My pay rate is $18.75 per hour.
Income tax is 20%.
I pay $30.00 per month for parking, pre-tax.
Before taxes, my pay subtotal will be 60*18.75 - 30.00.
Taxes will be the above subtotal * 0.20 .
My pay will be subtotal - taxes.
```

We can re-write this information, storing everything in variables. The text below actually works as a simple program.

```
hoursWorked = 60;
payRate = 18.75;
taxRate = 0.20;
```

```
parking = 30;
subtotal = hoursWorked * payRate - parking;
taxes = subtotal * taxRate;
pay = subtotal - taxes;
disp(pay);
```

Above we see examples of assignment such as "hoursWorked = 60;", and arithmetic like "subtotal = hoursWorked * payRate - parking;". Notice how each line ends with a semi-colon ";". This is not a requirement of MATLAB, but it shows a typical example of program syntax—we use the semi-colon much like we use the period in the pseudo-code (English) version. Using a semi-colon in a MATLAB command means that it will not echo back the result[1]. Also notice that the variable names do not contain spaces. Some do not need them, like taxes, while other variable names are two words run together, as in payRate. Spaces are not allowed in MATLAB variable names.

Characters that are allowed include all alphabetic characters, including upper-case as well as lower-case. But MATLAB is case-sensitive; to it the variable payRate is a different variable than payrate. Numbers are allowed in variable names, as long as they are not the first character. For example, tax1 and t1ax are acceptable, but 1tax is not. You can also use the underscore "_" in a variable name, again only if it is not the first character. So pay_rate would be fine, as would p_a_yRate. The names for variables can be as long as you want, but MATLAB ignores anything after the 63rd character.

Sometimes we may want to define a value once, and keep its value the same throughout. We call this a *constant*. Many computer languages have a way to define a constant, such that your program cannot later change it. Aside from the Constant property in the definition of a class, covered in Chapter 5, *Grouping Data*, MATLAB does not. Of course, you can always define a variable and simply not change it. When doing this with MATLAB, a common convention is to use all capital letters, such as FULL_TIME = 40; which defines a variable for the number of hours that a full-time employee would expect to work. Naming the variable in all capital letters like this signals to programmers that the value should not be changed. Assignments like this often appear at the top of a program, so that they can be easily altered in the future. While we do not expect a constant to change while a program runs, there may be times when we want to alter the value. For example, some

---

[1] Try entering x = 5 and y = 5; to see the difference.

companies classify an employee who works 35 hours as full-time. Defining the value only once, in all capitals, at the top of a program allows us to know that that variable should be treated as a constant.

By the way, you might forget what variables you have defined. If your MATLAB interface shows the "Workspace" window, you can view them there. Alternatively, you can use the who command to print the names of the variables currently defined.

```
>> who

Your variables are:

hoursWorked    parking    pay    payRate    subtotal
taxRate        taxes
```

A similar command, whos, shows the names along with some other information.

```
>> whos
Name            Size    Bytes    Class      Attributes

hoursWorked     1x1         8    double

parking         1x1         8    double

pay             1x1         8    double

payRate         1x1         8    double

subtotal        1x1         8    double

taxRate         1x1         8    double

taxes           1x1         8    double
```

As we see in the preceding example, the size is expressed in rows and columns, the data type (class), and the amount of memory, in bytes, that the variables reserve. Occasionally, the data type can give you unexpected results, as we will see in a later chapter. You may also want to inspect the amount of memory used, especially if your program runs slowly. If you can reduce the amount of memory your program uses, it may give a faster response. Finally, you can specify the name of one or more variables with who and whos. The following example shows that we can request information about two particular variables.

```
>> whos pay taxes
Name            Size     Bytes    Class        Attributes
pay             1x1          8    double
taxes           1x1          8    double
```

Can we store the returned information? Yes, the next example sets a with the result of the whos command for the variable pay.

```
>> a = whos('pay')
a =
            name: 'pay'
            size: [1 1]
           bytes: 8
           class: 'double'
          global: 0
          sparse: 0
         complex: 0
         nesting: [1x1 struct]
      persistent: 0
```

We call variable a a *structure*, and accessing the different pieces of data associated with a variable like this is covered in Chapter 5, *Grouping Data*.

As you proceed through this chapter, try out the different commands. When the command window fills up with things you have typed and the computer's response, it will start to scroll. If you want to clear the command window, the command clc does this. At some point, you might want to start over. Typing exit or quit at the command prompt causes MATLAB to stop, and closes all windows. You can always restart it. When you do so, the previous commands will appear on the command history window, but not the computer's responses. If you want to keep a copy of what you type as well as the response, use the diary command, as in the following example.

```
diary('logFromOctober3');
```

The diary command causes commands entered after this point, along with the responses, to be stored in a file called "logFromOctober3," although you can call it something else, of course.

Suppose that we store a value in a variable, then realize that we want to remember more than one value. Perhaps we are trying to establish a budget, so we use gas to represent the amount we spent refueling the car, as in the following line.

```
gas = 23.64;
```

This works well at first, but at some point we will return to the gas station and buy more gas, and then have a new value for the variable. A single data point is not very telling, so it makes sense to keep both values. A simple solution is to change the name slightly, for example, the following variable assignments keep track of two values.

```
gas1 = 23.64;
gas2 = 35.78;
```

We can even find the average, as follows:

```
gas_average = (gas1 + gas2) / 2;
```

This works when we have just a few values. But what do we do for more than a few values? If you discover a box full of gas station receipts, and want to enter them, you quickly realize that this naming scheme is unworkable. Typing in the equation for the average would be a chore. When we need to store many data values, a natural solution is to use an array. The following code looks like the preceding variable assignments but it has a crucial difference: the numbers 1 and 2 are not part of the name, they are indices into a list of values.

```
gas(1) = 23.64;
gas(2) = 35.78;
```

If you write down how much you spend at the gas station in a list, you can refer to the values by their position. You might ask yourself "Why did I spend so much the seventh time?" The advantage of using an array is that the computer can reference the values more abstractly. For example, consider the following code.

```
x = 7;
gas(x)
```

Assuming that gas(7) has a value, the computer will replace the x in the line gas(x) with the index 7, then look up that value. We can use a loop, discussed later, to process all of the values in the array. Another refinement, also discussed later, is that we can store all the values in a file.

What if we want to add another value to the array, 42.13, but we are not sure how long the array is? We can use the following commands to accomplish this.

```
x = length(gas);
gas(x+1) = 42.13;
```

The first line looks up how many entries are in the array gas, and stores the result in variable x. The second line uses x+1 as an index, that is, however long the array is, plus one. It stores the number 42.13 at that location. We could shorten the lines above down to one line, as follows:

```
gas(length(gas)+1) = 42.13;
```

However, compact code is not necessarily good code, especially when it degrades readability.

In the example above, we use the function length. A *function* is a predefined instruction that may have parameters, such as gas in the example, and gives us one or more values when it finishes.

It is possible to give a variable (or function) a pre-defined name. We call this *overloading*, which can be useful in some programming languages. With MATLAB, it is generally a bad idea. As long as the new variable or function name exists, you cannot use the original (unless you use the function builtin), however, programs that you run may use the original, and have a problem with the redefined one. Consider the following example.

```
>> disp = 4      % this is a bad idea
disp =
    4
>> disp(disp)
Index exceeds matrix dimensions.
'disp' appears to be both a function and a variable. If this is
unintentional, use 'clear disp' to remove the variable 'disp'
from the workspace.
```

While we can set disp to a value, doing so causes problems for subsequent lines that use disp as a function.

Most programming languages will not create a variable until you specify what *type* it has first, that is, what kind of thing you will store in it. For example, a number like 3 is an integer, while 3.1 is a floating point number, and "3" is a character (similar to "a" or even "@"). The computer treats them differently, and stores each of them in a different manner. In fact, your computer likely uses 4 bytes to store 3, 8 bytes to store 3.1, and 1 (or 2) bytes to store "3". The internal representations look nothing alike. In most programming languages, the programmer must specify the type to use for each variable, which says a lot about how it will be used. MATLAB, however, does its best to figure out the correct type to make a variable, and creates the variables as needed. By default, MATLAB makes variables a `double` type, meaning that it will be stored as a floating point number with 64 bits of precision. In other words, the number 3 would be stored as the binary equivalent of $+3.0 \times 2^0$. In the case of `'3'`, the single quotes let MATLAB know that it should not store this with the default type. By *precision*, we mean the number of binary digits ("bits") used. Think of this in terms of a gas pump: the display showing how much gas you have pumped typically has 3 digits for the dollars, then 2 digits for the cents. So it has 5 decimal digits of precision.

MATLAB provides ways to change data (and variables) from one type to another, as do other languages. It is very flexible with variables, and allows the easy creation and manipulation of arrays and matrices.

1.5   DATA TYPES

Values default to the double data type, meaning that the computer represents each one internally as a sign bit (0 for positive or 1 for negative), a binary significand (52 bits), and a binary exponent (11 bits), for a total of 64 bits. Just as we can write a floating point number in scientific notation, we can express a binary number, including a fractional part, in notation like $+1.X \times 2^Y$, where X and Y stand for groups of binary values. For example, the number $125.125 = 1.25125 \times 10^2$, while $1.111101001 \times 2^{0110} = 1111101.001$. The binary value 1111101 means $1 \times 2^7 + 1 \times 2^6 + 1 \times 2^5 + 1 \times 2^4 + 1 \times 2^3 + 1 \times 2^2 + 0 \times 2^1 + 1 \times 2^0$, which equals 125. Meanwhile, 0.001 equals $0 \times 2^{-1} + 0 \times 2^{-2} + 1 \times 2^{-3}$, or 0.125. So we can represent a number containing a fractional part in decimal, or equivalently in binary. The data type double means that it stores a binary number containing a fractional part using a total of 64 bits.

The name "double" might sound odd. Is there a "single"? Yes, there is a single data type, that MATLAB supports, with 32 bits per value. If we double the precision that a single data type has, we get the double data type, thus the name.

MATLAB supports several other data types, and we will focus on the most popular ones. The "logical" data type stores either a one or a zero, corresponding to true or false. In fact, you can assign variables as `true` or `false`, as the following lines do.

```
>> a = true
a =
     1
>> b = false
b =
     0
```

These values take up a byte (8 bits) worth of memory, since anything smaller than a byte introduces more overhead than it saves. We call these Boolean values, by the way.

While we refer to values as integers, they may not be stored as integers. Consider the lines below.

```
>> c = 5
c =
     5
>> whos
  Name      Size      Bytes     Class      Attributes
   c         1x1         8       double
```

Variable c holds the value 5, yet it has the double data type. This means that the computer stores it as a floating-point value, even though all fractional bits are 0. MATLAB does provide integer data types, in fact there are several of them, according to the number of bits they use. These include int8, int16, int32, and int64. By definition, an integer must be a whole number, and it can be positive, negative, or zero. An unsigned integer allows you to store numbers twice as large, since the most significant bit represents another bit as part of the magnitude, instead of the sign. The unsigned types are uint8, int16, int32, and uint64, again distinguished primarily by the number of bits they use. Of these, uint8 comes up frequently, especially when working with image data.

The cast function allows you to convert a value of one data type to another. The following example shows that we can convert a double to an integer.

```
>> c = 5;
>> d = cast(c, 'int16')
d =
     5
```

```
>> whos
   Name        Size      Bytes     Class        Attributes
    c          1x1          8      double
    d          1x1          2      int16
```

Both c and d hold the value 5, although you could say that c holds the value 5.0. Variable d cannot have a fractional part. Watch what happens when we add 0.1 to each variable's value.

```
>> c = c + 0.1
c =
     5.1000
>> d = d + 0.1
d =
     5
```

With the variable c, the change occurred. Variable d cannot, by definition, have a fractional part. Therefore, the attempt to add 0.1 to d failed. To make this work, we must change the value to another type. The next example does that.

```
>> double(d) + 0.1
ans =
     5.1000
```

Here, we convert d to the double data type, meaning that the computer stores it as a double precision floating point number, at least for that line. It can then add 0.1 to it, and return that result. Note that this does not change the data type of d itself; we must re-assign d if we want that.

1.6 A PREVIEW OF BASIC MATLAB COMMANDS

There are a few basic MATLAB commands that we will use repeatedly, and this section provides a preview. The following chapter gives more details, along with usage examples. First, we have the *assignment* statement, which uses an equal sign (=). Whatever appears on the right side of the equal sign will be evaluated, then stored in the variable that appears on the left side. We can include arithmetic or logical operations on the right side.

MATLAB allows you to work with a list of numbers (an *array*, also called a *vector*), just like you would with a single number (a *scalar*). In fact, you work with *matrices* of values often as easily as you can work with scalars. We also use the word *element* to mean a value of an array or matrix.

Arithmetic operations include the familiar addition, subtraction, multiplication, and division. Logic operations include comparisons, such as greater than or equal to, less than, equal, not equal, etc. We use two equal signs (==) to test for equality. Additionally, we can also specify complex logic operations with and, not, and or.

Programming languages provide a way to do *conditional flow*, typically with an if statement. We saw this with the driving directions above; if you see a dead-end sign... Except for simple examples, programs need a way to deviate from doing some steps. In MATLAB, we accomplish this through the if .. else .. end blocks. A *block* is a group of programming lines that the computer executes in sequence. The keyword if starts the block and the keyword else or end finishes the block. The if statement precedes a *condition*, an expression that may (or may not) evaluate to true. Often, a comparison will be tested, such as (a < 3). When the condition evaluates to true, the block under the if will be executed. But when the condition is not met, the else block will execute instead, when one is specified.

The switch .. case .. end statements provide another way to do conditional flow. Sometimes when programming, we have several possible things to do based upon a variable. For example, we might prompt the user for input, such as "should we save your changes?" and read a character from the keyboard. If the key is "Y" or "y", we want to carry out the save; if the key is "N" or "n", we want to go on without the save; if the key is "?", we might print some helpful information; if the key is anything else, we might print that we expected a "y" or "n". We could encode all of this with if statements, but the switch statement potentially makes the program easier to understand.

Often times, a programmer will repeat the same block of code over and over again. While copying and pasting the code would work, this will be cumbersome. You might make a correction in one spot, but forget to correct the problem in the other spot(s). A *loop* is a programming construct where the same commands can be repeated as many times as needed. MATLAB provides the for .. end statements to do a loop, especially when you know how many times the loop should occur (e.g., "do this 10 times"). A similar set of instructions, the while .. end statements will keep looping (repeating the block of commands) as long as a given condition is met. A search exemplifies this; while we have not yet found (what we are looking for), keep going through the data.

Programs carry out tasks that sometimes fail. A prominent example is working with a file. If a person specifies a filename, and the program attempts to read the file, the program may crash if the file does not exist. For this reason, the `try .. catch .. end` statements allow the program to gracefully handle operations like this, and recover when errors occur. The computer executes the commands in the block after `try`, and jumps to the `catch` block upon running into an error. If everything works, it by-passes the `catch` block.

MATLAB also provides many useful functions, such as `length`, which returns the number of elements in an array. Also, you can create your own functions. This allows for abstraction, which helps people to understand programs as well as maintain them. For example, suppose that you want to sort a list of numbers. MATLAB includes a function called `sort`, which will sort an array in increasing order by default. Does it use bubble sort, insertion sort, merge sort, or some other algorithm? As long as it works well, do you care? By the way, if you are familiar with the bubble sort, you probably do care because it is particularly inefficient. A function allows for abstraction—we know what it does, and we do not know exactly how it does it, unless a problem causes us to investigate.

1.7 KEY SHORTCUTS

You can use the up-arrow key to recall the previous command(s). Also, if you type part of a command, then press the up-arrow, it will recall the last command that began with what you typed. For example, suppose that you type a `length` command, then later type `le` and press the up-arrow. MATLAB should display the `length` command. If there are multiple commands that begin with `le`, they will be recalled in reverse order as the up-arrow is pressed. The down-arrow key recalls the next command entered, effectively allowing you to cycle through the earlier commands in either direction.

When a command is on the input line, you can use the left-arrow and right-arrow keys to move the cursor left or right, respectively. For example, suppose that you type `lenght(myarray);` then the RETURN key[2]. This command will not work, since `length` is misspelled. To fix it, type the up-arrow key, then the left-arrow key repeatedly, until the cursor is over the `t`. Then press the DELETE key twice, then press the `t` and `h` keys. You can then press ENTER (without moving the cursor to the end of the line). If you prefer, you can use the mouse to move the cursor.

---

[2] Some keyboards have a key marked ENTER instead. These keys are equivalent.

Recent versions of MATLAB will suggest a command in cases where the function cannot be found. In the following code, we define the `gas` array to have two values, like in a previous example.

```
>> gas(1) = 23.64;
>> gas(2) = 35.78;
>> lenght(gas)
Undefined function 'lenght' for input arguments of type 'double'.
Did you mean:
>> length(gas)
ans =
     2
```

Typing `lenght(gas)` caused the interpreter to say that no function by the name `lenght` exists, and it automatically put `length(gas)` at the prompt as if the user typed it. In this case, after typing the function incorrectly, the user simply presses ENTER to accept the auto-corrected line.

The TAB allows for completion, just like at the operating system's command prompt, such as the `Terminal` program located under "Utilities" on an Apple Macintosh®. The Linux operating system also provides a `Terminal` program. Under Microsoft Windows®, the `command` utility program has built-in shortcuts like this, depending upon its configuration.

1.8   WRITING PROGRAMS THAT ARE EASY TO READ

Most people think that programmers spend their time writing code. This is true to an extent, but a large amount of time will be spent maintaining code, along with other tasks involving communication. A company will have a set of programs that do what they need done. But if a bug is found, or new features are required, someone has to change the code to fix it or add new code to it. People come and go, so the person who maintains the code is often not the one who wrote it. As a result, a good programmer will write code that others can easily read, understand, and maintain. Several conventions help. Program readability allows for good maintenance.

First, you must document your code. Use the percent sign (`%`) to add comments. Anything on the line after this character will be ignored by the computer. Always make sure to include pertinent details at the top: who you are, what the date is, what you plan to do (especially if you make changes to old code). Your comments should explain what your program does, both at the top (which appears as a result of the `help` command), as well as within the body of the program. You might wonder who the comments are for, and that answer varies. Have you ever written a program so long ago that you forgot you wrote it? You will! First and foremost, make comments throughout your code for your future self. You may try something one way, discover that it does not work well, and change it to something better. If you do not document what you did, you might someday revisit the program and think "why did I do it like that? I'll change it..." and re-introduce a problem you already solved. Use comments to explain what you are doing to yourself and others. Documenting your code should also help solidify your ideas.

Be sure to give other people credit where it is due, as in the following comment.

```
% The next 4 lines are from Sally Smith.
...
```

If you include code from the Internet, make sure you put in as much detail as you can (who wrote it, the company, a book that shows it, when you got it, the URL, etc.). Be sure to say where the borrowed code starts, and where it stops, e.g.,

```
% Begin: code from King's "C Programming: A Modern Approach"
%        2nd ed, 2006, page 300
```

followed later by a comment like this.

```
% End: code from page 300 of King's book.
```

Obviously, just because you find someone else's code does not give you the right to use it. You should make sure that you have permission (which may be implied by where and how you found the code). You should be certain that it is legal and ethical for you to use the code, and check with your instructor or employer. If you use someone else's code, you are still responsible for knowing what it does.

To clarify this, suppose you get 3 lines from another source, and put it in the middle of your code. You should include it only if you understand exactly what those lines do, and if you could have done it yourself given the time. Now suppose that you find a function that does something complex for you, such as read in and decode an `.ogg` sound file, and return an array of double values from –1 to 1. In this case, your knowledge of how each line works is not necessary. Your code calls the function that someone else wrote, as if their code was part of MATLAB. You understand what it does without knowing how it does it. As long as you could break it down line-by-line given enough time, do not worry about knowing the details.

You can also use `%{` and `%}` to indicate multi-line comments. That is, the computer will ignore everything between these two, as in the following example.

```
%{
    All of these lines are comments,
    meant for a human to read,
    so the computer ignores them.
%}
```

If you have a program with several lines that you want to comment-out, you can select them in the editor and click the comment button, or you can simply use `%{` and `%}` around the lines.

MATLAB gives special meaning to two percent signs in a row, "`%%`", which define a *code cell* up to the next pair of percent signs. You can run the code in such a section with the "evaluate cell" button on the editor window. When writing code and testing it periodically to get it just right, this feature allows you to focus on a subset of a program.

Compactness is good, but taking it to an extreme is not. Clever code that is not understandable is not maintainable. Keep in mind that someone else may have to understand and maintain your code, and if enough time has passed, the person struggling to understand your code could be you. Use parentheses to make meaning clear. Use *whitespace* such as spaces and blank lines to provide structure. A common convention is to indent code in the same block. The computer does not care; it will figure out the code with or without whitespace. But it makes the code easier to read. Be consistent with this! If you include four spaces to the left of each line in a block, you should not later use three spaces. MATLAB's built-in editor will help, and it will automatically indent your code. However, you should get into the habit of indenting code for the sake of clarity even without the editor. You can use any editor that you like, however the built-in one provides features that other editors do not, such as commenting out a selection of lines, or color-coding the commands.

Give variables (and programs) sensible names. If you store someone's rate of pay, names like `rateOfPay`, `rate0pay`, `payRate`, or `pay_rate` get the idea across. Names like `p`, `PR`, and `thing` should be avoided. Use one-letter variables like `i` or `n` if it makes sense and is well localized. For example, `payRate(i)` would be acceptable. By "well localized," a one-letter variable should not be assigned a value once, then used hundreds of lines later.

Consider using a variable for any constant value, because you may want to change it later. Some constants, like `pi` (π), never change. Often, however, a program will have constant values according to choices that make sense at the time, like expecting to work with 100 images, and show them for 100 seconds each. It might be tempting to use the value 100 wherever it needs to go, but how do you change it later, conceivably if you want to work with 150 images, and show them for 80 seconds each? You would have to carefully replace some instances of 100 with 150, and other instances of it with 80. A much better solution is to assign variables for these values, such as the following.

```
numberOfImages = 100;
secondsToShow = 100;
```

With these lines at the top of the program, changing them to different values becomes easy.

Document your assumptions, using comments. For example, suppose that we ask the user for their age. Should our program reject any age below 18? Should it reject any age above 100? If we do not use these minimum or maximum ages, should it ever reject an age? Is zero OK? Could we use a byte value to store the age, i.e., between 0 and 255? Are negative numbers acceptable? Are fractions, such as 4.5 OK, or should the number be an integer? What about complex values, characters, or strings? Would a matrix of values make sense (e.g., in a function where the age is passed as a parameter)? We should specify exactly what we expect in the code comments. Making this clear to the user is a good idea, too.

Like other programming languages, MATLAB includes *keywords* which are reserved for special use. As an example, the word `for` can only be used as part of a `for` loop. A command like `for = 4` results in an error. The keywords include the programming constructs that you would expect, i.e., `while`, `switch`, `end`, `try`, `if`, etc. These words already have a specific meaning, so they cannot be redefined.

We call *embedded systems* the broad area of hardware and software development for specific products. These are computers in the sense that they have processors, programs, memory, inputs, and outputs, yet these parts are embedded in the product to the degree that we do not think of them as computers. For example, wearable fitness tracking devices, microwave ovens, and cell phones are all embedded systems. Many such systems are designed and prototyped with MATLAB and Simulink, even though MATLAB is not normally the programming language used to control them. This text uses the term embedded system often as a contrast to more traditional computers.

Whatever convention(s) you use for names, be consistent throughout. In embedded systems, some programmers use a lower-case letter to indicate the variable type, like `iCounter` to indicate a counter with the integer data type. Other programmers use all capitals for *constants*, values that do not change, like π. Or the first letter is capitalized if it names a function, but lower-case when used for a variable. You may even find that different companies have different styles. Whatever style you use, be consistent with it.

Use one entry and one exit for your code, except when handling errors. This is no longer the issue it once was, back in the days of "goto" statements that allowed a flow-chart (a graphical depiction of the program's order of execution) to look like a plate of spaghetti. Today, this means you should avoid using the `break` statement to end a loop in the middle, unless you have a good reason to do this.

Use encapsulation. If one page of code does a particular task, you should consider moving it to its own separate file. You can also standardize it, so that you can use it again in the future. While MATLAB allows global variables, meaning that they can be viewed and changed by any function, use local variables as much as possible. By default, the variables that you create will be local variables.

When you print your code, use a monospaced font (Courier is a good one). It makes the printout easier to read, and the whitespace stands our better. Compare the two lines below:

This sentence is not monospaced.

```
This sentence is monospaced.
```

The second line, using a monospaced font, resembles what you will see in the MATLAB command window, and in the editor.

Be professional about your code. Make things explicit with your comments, and do not abbreviate as if you are sending a text message. Clean up your code when you are done. You may comment and uncomment blocks of code while getting it to work correctly. When the program is "finished," you should get rid of commented-out code that is no longer needed. Try not to misspell words, and watch out for other grammatical errors. Yes, the computer will not care. However, if you do communicate well, the other programmers or managers who see your work are likely to be impressed with your thoroughness and attention to detail.

When writing code, try to make it *robust*, referring to the quality of a program to work even with bad inputs or under poor conditions. It should work without generating an error when possible. Sometimes, there can be a problem that your program cannot handle, such as if an important data file does not exist. In that case, it should pass along an error message. However, if the user gives the program bad data, such as values outside of the expected range, the program should handle it gracefully. It could display a message about the data being out of range, and returning back to the prompt.

Another good quality for code is making it *modular*, where it is self-contained. It should have everything it needs, although it may specify any required parameters. Like a building block, a well-written program or function can be included as a small piece of a large design. With modularity, each piece can be tested to ensure that it works as expected.

Remember that we can split a command into multiple lines. When a line becomes long, use an ellipsis (three periods) to specify that it continues on the next line. This allows us to make the code more readable.

```
>> disp(sprintf('Using 10 places, pi has value %2.8f,\n%s', ...
       pi, 'counting the decimal point.'));
Using 10 places, pi has value 3.14159265,
counting the decimal point.
```

We see that the command is interpreted the same as if we had typed it all on one line.

A command that embeds `sprintf` inside a `disp` statement causes a warning that `fprintf('...')` can replace it. The former makes a string to then display to the user. The latter also makes a string, and prints it to a file, but that file happens to be the command window by default. MATLAB's editor provides information about this. The editor shows lines with `disp(sprintf('...'))` underlined in orange, and an orange bar appears on the right of the editor window. If you hover the cursor over either the line or the bar, it explains that `disp(sprintf('...'))` takes additional memory resources and time compared to `fprintf('...')`. However, the examples in this text use `disp(sprintf('...'))` since it has a clearer meaning.

1.9   DEBUGGING TECHNIQUES

A good way to figure out a program is to simulate the computer yourself. Take a deep breath, and try to clear your mind. Starting at the first line, go through the program line by line, performing each line as the computer would. Ignore the comments. Remember, the computer does not understand the comments, and the comments likely say what you want the commands to do, rather than what they actually do. For each variable, write down the value on paper, crossing out the previous value if there is one. Simulate what the computer does, substituting variables for their values. Think like a computer would.

Debug from the first error down, not from the last. When the computer encounters a problem, it generates an error message. Depending on the severity, it may not stop there, and continue to process the code. This can trigger "cascading errors," where one error causes another, only the description for the latter error might misdirect you. With some computer languages, a relatively minor error can set off a screen-full of error messages. Sometimes when a programmer fixes the very first error, the rest of them disappear.

If you are not sure where a program fails, use display statements to show the progress. You may want to add a `pause(0.5)` command after the display statements, to give the computer time to update the screen.

You can also set breakpoints, and use MATLAB's built-in debugging program. Chapter 11, *Getting Help and Debugging*, covers this in detail.

1.10 COMMON UNIX COMMANDS

Scientists use a variety of different computers. You may be surprised to learn that, in November 2017, it was announced that the all of the world's top 500 supercomputers run Linux [3, 4]. Linux is a popular, free, open-source operating system (OS), developed as a version of Unix for the IBM Personal Computer (PC), and PC compatible systems.

In the past few decades, the Unix OS dominated the high-performance computing market. Laboratories and businesses often have powerful and expensive computers to handle their work, called *servers*. People connect to these machines with less powerful (and much less expensive) computers called *clients*. Some clients are little more than a keyboard and monitor. You may be familiar with these terms already; when you use your laptop or phone to view web pages, your client device contacts a remote server for that content. In that sense, you already rely upon computers running Unix and Linux. Over the years, computing equipment has become more powerful, less expensive, smaller, and ubiquitous. However, there still remain classes of computers beyond the home computing market.

A *terminal* means a program that allows the user to interact with the operating system by issuing text-based commands. The Microsoft Windows®

equivalent is the command window, although the commands that it recognizes are a little different. Most users do not use a terminal window, since they can do what they need to do via the graphical user interface (GUI). Starting programs, editing files, renaming files, moving files, and deleting files can be done via the GUI, but these can also be done with the terminal. When we interact with the terminal window, such as in a classroom environment, we use Unix/ Linux commands. You do not need an in-depth knowledge of Unix, but the following list of commands include ones that you should know. Interestingly, Apple developed OS X based on a Unix variant. Thus, these commands are the same for many different devices, from a supercomputer running Linux, to a high-powered server running Unix, to a Macintosh running OS X[3], or a PC running Linux, and even down to small devices like the Raspberry Pi.

Unix workstations provided graphical user interfaces early on, with windowing standards such as X Window System from the 1980s. However, if your computer runs Unix/Linux, or if your data comes from such a machine, you might also need to know how to work from the terminal window. Here are some common commands.

- `cat` *file*
  This is short for con**cat**enate file(s), where you can specify multiple files. It prints the contents of all of the *file*(s) to the screen, one after another, without pausing. This command can also be used to create files. The MATLAB equivalent is `type` *file*.

- `cd`
  change **d**irectory. By itself, it will change to your home directory. The MATLAB equivalent is `cd ~`. For example, `cd /home/mweeks` says to change the directory to `/home/mweeks`, the home directory for user "mweeks". The MATLAB equivalent is `cd /home/mweeks`. Home directories vary from system to system, and your system could use something different. For example, on a Macintosh, the command might be `cd /Users/mweeks` instead. Two periods in a row signify the parent directory, so `cd ..` changes the directory to one level up. For example, from the directory `/home/myaccount`, this will change it to the `/home` directory. The command `cd ..` also works with MATLAB.

---

[3] At one time in the 2000s, your author regularly used Solaris Unix on a Sun SPARC server, BSD Unix on a Macintosh, RedHat Linux on a PC, and Familiar Linux on a hand-held device from Hewlett-Packard called an iPAQ PocketPC. While there are differences in Linux/Unix distributions, the vast majority of day-to-day interactions did not require awareness of the OS. In other words, switching from a terminal on one device to another was seamless.

- chmod

  change **mod**e. You probably will not need this. It allows you to set permissions on your files, for example, chmod 644 myfile sets read and write access for the owner of myfile, read access for everyone in your group, and read access for anyone else on the computer. To see how this works, consider that each digit represents an octal number (i.e., an integer from 0 to 7) corresponding to read, write, and execute bits, and the digit position means whether it applies to owner, group, or world. The octal number 6 has the binary pattern 110, so the owner can read or write the file, but cannot execute it. Next, the octal number 4 has the binary pattern 100, so the group members can read the file. After that, the world members (anyone on that computer) can read it, too. Octal, also called base 8, does not find much use outside of this. These file attributes allow you to control who on the computer has access to your files. The MATLAB equivalent is fileattrib.

- date

  gives a time-stamp including today's date. MATLAB has a date command, although it does not return the time. To get the date and time, MATLAB's clock command returns these as an array of six values. The following example shows the difference between date and clock in a MATLAB session.

  ```
  >> date
  ans =
  11-Dec-2017
  >> a = clock; sprintf('%d-%d-%d at %d:%d:%2.0f', a)
  ans =
  2017-12-11 at 18:22:37
  ```

  Meanwhile, this example shows the output of date in a terminal window.

  ```
  cascade:~> date
  Mon Dec 11 18:24:18 EST 2017
  ```

  As you can see, the terminal command was issued less than two minutes later.

- echo

  repeat back whatever follows. For example, echo hello results in the text "hello" being printed. MATLAB provides the disp statement for this purpose.

- `ls`
  list files in the current directory. You may use it with a filename, or a filename with a wildcard, like `ls *.m` to generate all files that have `.m` at the end of the name. You will often see this as `ls -l`: **l**ist files in the current directory in **l**ong format, which gives additional information. MATLAB also recognizes `ls` and `ls -l`.

- `man` *command*
  shows the **man**ual entry for the command. It provides information like `help` does in MATLAB.

- `matlab`
  starts the MATLAB program, assuming that it is installed. Of course, it may instead be invoked by clicking on the icon.

- `mkdir` *newdirectory*
  ma**k**e a new directory. MATLAB also can create a new directory with `mkdir`.

- `more` *file*
  shows the contents of *file* to the screen, one screen at a time, with a prompt showing that "more" content follows. Interestingly, many system include an improved version of it, called `less`. The MATLAB equivalent is `more on` followed by `type` *file*.

- `path`
  The "path" is more of a concept than a command, although the environmental variable `$PATH` contains important information. When looking for a file, the computer searches through the path, and reports the first file matching the name that it finds. If it cannot find the file, this may simply mean that it does not look at the correct location. The command `echo $PATH` reveals where the computer looks for matches, and in what order it does the search. In MATLAB, the `path` command returns the list of directories that it searches before it determines that something is an "undefined function or variable."

- `pwd`
  print **w**orking **d**irectory. It shows where you are currently located in the directory tree. MATLAB also supports `pwd`.

- `sftp` *account@computer*
  This runs the **s**ecure **f**ile **t**ransport **p**rotocol, allowing you to log in to a remote computer, and `get` files from it, or `put` files on it. There is no MATLAB equivalent.

- `ssh -Y -l` *account computer*
  This runs secure **sh**ell, allowing you to log in to a remote computer, and run commands as if you were in front of it. The `-l` indicates what account to use on the remote computer. Of course, it will prompt you for the password to that account. The `-Y` parameter specifies X Window forwarding. The *X Window System* is for graphical user interfaces, developed in the 1980s, and still widely used. On some systems, you might need to have the X Window System installed before you can run MATLAB. If you plan to run MATLAB remotely, and display the output locally, you will likely need to set up X Window forwarding. There is no MATLAB equivalent.

Table 1.1 Common Unix/Linux commands, and equivalents. Many of these commands expect additional information, such as the name of a file.

Unix/Linux	DOS	MATLAB	Meaning
`cat`	`type`	`type`	Concatenate/type a file
`cd`	`cd`	`cd`	Change directory
`chmod`	`attrib`	`fileattrib`	Change a file's mode (attributes)
`clear`	`cls`	`clc`	Clear the screen
`date`	`date`	`date, clock`	Show today's date, time
`echo`	`echo`	`disp`	Display something.
`exit`	`exit`	`exit`	Exit from the software
`ls` `ls -l`	`dir`	`ls, dir` `ls -l`	List files List files with more information
`man`	`help`	`help`	Show helpful documentation about a command
`matlab`	`matlab`		Run the MATLAB software
`mkdir`	`mkdir`	`mkdir`	Make a directory
`more`	`more`	`more on; type`	Show a file, one page at a time
`echo $PATH`	`path`	`path`	Display the path.

(continued)

Unix/Linux	DOS	MATLAB	Meaning
pwd		pwd	Print working directory
sftp	3rd party		Secure file transport
ssh	3rd party		Secure shell
vi	edit	edit	Visual editor

- vi *filename*
  Invokes the **vi**sual editor. It is good to know, since most computers running Unix/Linux support it. With ssh and vi, you can edit files on a remote computer. The closest MATLAB command is edit.

  Table 1.1 shows a summary of the commands. The column labelled "DOS" refers to Disk Operating System, originally PC-DOS or MS-DOS, and lists the commands supported by the *command* program (command.com or cmd.exe). The text "3rd party" indicates that third-party software exists to do this function.

1.11 THE MATLAB MOBILE APPLICATION

With a MathWorks account, you can download the MATLAB Mobile® application and access the computing enviroment from a phone or other mobile device. You must have Internet access available when you want to use it, since your mobile device does not carry out the computations. Instead, it communicates with another computer to perform the commands. Figures 1.2 and 1.3 show the application connecting, then executing a couple of example commands. Notice the keyboard includes some handy keys along the top, such as the up-arrow and down-arrow, parentheses, and single quote. Navigate to previous commands with the up-arrow.

FIGURE 1.2 MATLAB Mobile must have an Internet connection to work.

FIGURE 1.3 MATLAB Mobile can compute results and show figures, just like on a laptop/desktop computer.

The mobile environment uses "MATLAB Drive" that seamlessly links files stored on one computer to others, including mobile devices. Once set up, you can designate programs and other files to be available through it. Figure 1.4 shows the run of a program called `matches_example.m` that compares two strings. On the mobile phone, the user entered `matches_example`, the name of a program available on the MATLAB Drive. A computer ran the program, and reported the results back to the phone. Interestingly, this particular example calls the function `matches`, a command released in 2019. The phone does not do much with MATLAB unless it has an Internet connection. And the computer hosting the program has version R2016b, meaning that it gives an "undefined function" error when the user runs that program. This may seem nebulous; what computer ran the program? Where are the MATLAB Drive files stored? Remote servers take care of these details. This is "cloud" based computing.

Copying files on one computer to a specific sub-directory, makes those files available on other devices. For example, on a desktop computer, copying the file `mymagic5.mat` to the the `Published` folder under the `MATLAB-Drive` directory, allows it to sync with the MathWorks cloud, and then it becomes visible to the phone, as shown in Figure 1.5.

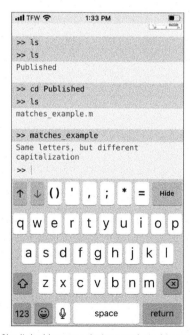

FIGURE 1.4 With files linked between devices, such as this `matches_example.m`, we can run a MATLAB program on a mobile phone.

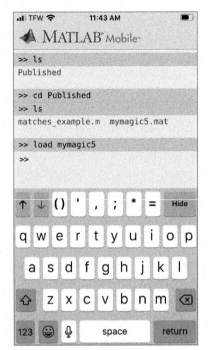

FIGURE 1.5 File `mymagic5.mat` became available on the mobile phone after being copied to the `MATLAB-Drive` directory.

1.12 SUMMARY

This chapter presents the environment, terminology, and concepts for computer programming in MATLAB. The following chapters use these terms repeatedly, and they should become clear with usage. The next chapter will add detail to the following concepts and include examples.

- An *algorithm*, informally, is a process, or set of steps, to solve a problem or achieve a goal.

- *Pseudo-code* is like English, broken into small steps that the computer can do.

- A *program* or *code* is a collection of commands for the computer. We also call this a *script*.

- A *function* is a special case of a program that can take parameters, and can return values.

- *Comments* are included in a program for people to understand the code. The computer ignores them.

- *Syntax* means how commands are specified, just like how grammar and punctuation affect human languages. The computer quickly points out a *syntax error*, where it does not understand the command.

- *Logic* means how commands fit together. A *logic error* occurs when the code makes sense to the computer, but does not solve the problem. As an analogy, consider driving directions that miss an important step, like "go forward one block, then turn right". The directions may be expressed in a way we understand, but they do not get us to the goal.

- How assignment statements differ from equations

- conditionals

- loops

- Command window, the command line interface (CLI)

- The MATLAB editor, invoked by the `edit` command

- interpreting versus compiling

- variables

- no declaration required

- floating point, integer, character, string, Boolean

- singular, array, matrix

- key shortcuts

- keywords

- basic MATLAB commands

- assignment

- `if .. else/elseif .. end`

- `for .. end`

- `while .. end`

- `switch .. case .. end`

- `try .. catch .. end`

- `length`

EXERCISES

1. Have the computer print "hello" plus your name.

2. What problem(s) does the following line have?
    ```
    end = 2;
    ```

3. What problem(s) does the following line have?
    ```
    disp('Hello);
    ```

4. What problem(s) does the following line have?
    ```
    DISP('One small step for man');
    ```

5. What problem(s) does the following line have?
    ```
    intrest = 5; sprintf('Rate is %d per year', interest);
    ```

6. What problem(s) does the following line have?
    ```
    sprintf('value = %d ,' 5)
    ```

7. How would you give a list of unique numbers from a long list of values? Forming an algorithm is not much more complex, if you can verbalize all the small steps you would take. Approach finding unique numbers (the test question) like how you would do it without a computer.

8. Remove non-numeric characters from a string, for example, making a phone number only numerals. For example, given (404) 555-5717 and it should output 4045555717. This makes the data conform to a common standard; it could be given as 404/555-5717 by one person and 404 5555717 by someone else. A simple comparison between the two would make the computer conclude that they are not equal.

9. See edu_jobs.m: recreate this problem. Given the government data, find what percentages of people have the education levels, e.g.: 9th – 11th grade is 6.3%.

10. Get help information for the strfind command, then use it to split a sentence into words, i.e., "one two three" becomes "one," "two," "three." Hint: try this interactively. Using the values returned by the function as an index, such as str(1:4) shows characters 1 through 4 of string variable str.

11. What is the difference between an algorithm and a program?

12. Why do we sometimes use `disp('...')` but other times use `disp(sprintf('...'))`? (Do not take ... to literally be part of the command.)

13. What is the difference between `disp` and `sprintf`?

14. What is the difference between the following pairs of similar-looking statements: `disp(a)` and `disp(sprintf('a'))`

15. The MATLAB session below shows an error. Briefly state how to fix it.

```
>> disp("hello")
??? disp("hello")
         |

Error: The input character is not valid in MATLAB statements
or expressions.
```

16. The MATLAB session below shows an error. Briefly state how to fix it.

```
>> sprintf('The variable has value %d, 6)
??? sprintf('The variable has value %d, 6)
           |
Error: A MATLAB string constant is not terminated properly.
```

17. The MATLAB session below shows an error. Briefly state how to fix it.

```
>> b=1;
>> b + 2 = b
??? b + 2 = b
          |

Error: The expression to the left of the equals sign is not
a valid target for an assignment.
```

18. What value do the variables have after executing the following code?

```
myAccountBalance = 478.35;
ATM_withdrawal = 100.00;
myAccountBalance = myAccountBalance - ATM_withdrawal;
service_charge = 2.50;
myAccountBalance = myAccountBalance - service_charge;
```

19. Someone wrote the code below, but left out the *most important* part of all, the comments. For each line, write a suitable comment. Be sure to indicate units and ranges for variables. For example, `timeSCount = 0` should have a comment like `% time in seconds, should be >= 0 and < 60`.

    ```
    hoursWorked = 60;
    payRate = 8.75;
    taxRate = 0.20;
    parking = 30;
    subtotal = hoursWorked * payRate - parking;
    taxes = subtotal * taxRate;
    pay = subtotal - taxes;
    ```

20. The formula

    $$s = sin(2 \times \pi \times frequency \times t + phase)$$

    describes a sine wave with an amplitude of 1. The value π is pre-defined in MATLAB as `pi`. The phase should be some value between $-\pi/2$ and $\pi/2$, including zero. You can use the following definition for `t`, which stands for time.

    ```
    t = 0:0.0001:0.03;
    ```

    Plot a couple of sine waves with 100 for the frequency, and different phase values.

21. To develop an algorithm, imagine that you are giving directions to someone over the phone. That person can see the input values, and has a large white-board for writing down values, and erasing. The instructions that you provide must be simple, such "copy the first value and write it next to the letter A." The person can do any arithmetic or logic function, like multiplication, subtraction, comparison, AND, and so forth. Conditionals, such as "if value 1 is less than value 2 then…" can be included, along with loops. Think about how you would describe the instructions so that they get arrive at the correct answer. How would you tell that person to order a list of numbers, e.g. 3, 7, 1, 4, 2, from largest to smallest?

PROJECTS

- **Documentation and Help**

  The first thing in your program should be documentation, such as the following. This should appear at the very top of your program.

  ```
  % (program_name).m
  %
  % Author: (Your Name)
  %
  % Date: (put the due date started)
  % Revision Date: (when you make changes later, put the date)
  %
  % Description:
  % (Give a brief description of what your program does.)
  %
  % Input:
  % (State what the program inputs are.)
  %
  % Output:
  % (State what the program outputs are.)
  %
  % Usage:
  % (Give an example of how to use your program.)
  % (For example: out = myabs(in); )
  %
  ```

  Create a file with an appropriate name, and enter the comments above. Verify that the command help followed by the program name shows this information.

- **Getting and Checking User Input**

  Your program will prompt the user for a few pieces of information, then print the information back to the command window.

  Your program should input the user's name, their age, and today's price for a gallon of gas. Make sure to prompt the user for information, such as "please enter your age: ."

Once the user has entered this information, print the following to the screen: Welcome age year old user name. Also print out the price of gas, and the price of gas squared. Include text to say what it is you are printing. If the price of gas squared is greater than the person's age, print "Congratulations on getting your driver's license." Otherwise, print "I bet you remember when gas was one dollar per gallon." Helpful hint: to print a single quote character, you need to use two in a row, as below.

```
disp('driver''s license');
```

Your program should work for all possible inputs. Make sure that you test it with several different cases. For example, what if the age is given as a floating-point number, like 21.4? What if the user enters 0, −10, or 1000? You can assume that the user will enter numbers for the age and price prompts.

## CHAPTER 2

MATLAB PROGRAMMING BASICS

This chapter aims to get you started writing your own code in MATLAB. First, we cover ranges, strings, and formatting. Then we move on to programming constructs. By the end of this chapter, you should be able to create a solution in MATLAB to a small programming problem.

2.1 RANGES

Often, we will want to generate a sequence of values, for example, the integers between 1 and 5. MATLAB provides an easy way to accomplish this, called a *range*. Here, we set the variable r to the values.

```
>> r = 1:5
r =
     1     2     3     4     5
```

The colon ("`:`") separates the starting value and the ending value. By default, the numbers increment by one. If we desire to count by another value, we specify it as starting value, colon, increment value, colon, and ending value. The next example creates a range of values between 5 and 13, consisting of only odd values.

```
>> 5:2:13
ans =
     5     7     9    11    13
```

The values do not have to be whole, as the next example shows.

```
>> 5.1:2.1:13.1
ans =
     5.1000      7.2000      9.3000     11.4000
```

Notice that the values incremented by 2.1 each time, and that the range does not include 13.1. That's because 11.4 + 2.1 = 13.5, which falls outside the specified range.

As you might expect, ranges work for values stored internally as integers, too. Some of the previous examples used whole values, but they had the default double type. The next example creates a range from 3 to 7, where the values have the uint8 type, which means unsigned integers of 8 bits.

```
>> a = uint8(3);
>> b = uint8(7);
>> c = a:b
c =
    3    4    5    6    7
```

Since a and b both are uint8, the resulting array held in c also has that type.

Range values are not limited to floating point numbers and integers, as the following example illustrates.

```
>> 'a':'f'
ans =
abcdef
```

Here, we generate an array of character values, starting with lower-case "a" and ending with lower-case "f." Note that the upper-case letters come before the lower-case letters in the encodings, so the following example generates the characters "Z," "a," and all the characters in between.

```
>> 'Z':'a'
ans =
Z[\]^_`a
```

However, the range 'z':'A' will generate an empty string, since you cannot start counting at lower-case "z" and reach the upper-case "A," unless you count backwards. The following example demonstrates this idea, with a smaller range.

```
>> 'z':-1:'v'
ans =
zyxwv
```

To count backwards, we simply specify a negative value for the increment. Can you list the alphabet, backwards, skipping every other letter? MATLAB can do it easily.

```
>> 'z':-2:'a'
ans =
zxvtrpnljhfdb
```

We simply put −2 as the increment.

Using a negative value for the increment also works for numbers. What if we want to count down from 75, to −75, skipping every 25 values? The next example shows this.

```
>> 75:-25:-75
ans =
    75    50    25    0    -25    -50    -75
```

While the ranges work with floating-point numbers, integers, and characters, they do not work with strings or complex values.

```
>> 1+5j:3+5j
Warning: Colon operands must be real scalars.
ans =
    1    2    3
```

The preceding example does generate a range, although it returns `double` values.

You may notice the similarity of a range and the syntax used with a `for` loop. In fact, you can use a range for the index of a loop, as the following example shows.

```
>> index = 1:5;
>> for i = index, disp(i);, end
    1
    2
    3
    4
    5
```

The commas separate the parts of the loop, allowing it to fit on one line. Typically, we would want to spread such a command out into multiple lines.

Ranges are especially useful when working with arrays and matrices. In the next example, we define a matrix called A, then access it using the range 2:3 for the rows and columns.

```
>> A = [23, 6, 11; 7, 3, 5; -4, 52, 0]
A =
      23       6    11
       7       3     5
      -4      52     0
>> A(2:3, 2:3)
ans =
       3       5
      52       0
```

As we see, the ranges allow us to isolate a subset of the matrix A, in this case, the bottom-right corner of values. The colon operation (ranges) allow us to specify a series of values in an easy, compact manner. You will likely see many MATLAB programs use ranges, so it is a good tool to master.

2.2 STRINGS AND FORMATTING OUTPUT

Strings are delimited by single quotes, meaning that we specify where the string begins and ends with single quotes. Recent changes to MATLAB allow the use of double quotes, too.

Notice the two single quotes in the following string.

```
disp('Don''t forget...');
```

Normally, we use a single quote to start a string, and another one to end it, but here we use two in a row to indicate a special case, where we want a single quote as part of the string itself.

The command sprintf creates a string, allowing the programmer to format the output. It has many similarities to the printf function in the C language, which prints formatted output. In either language, the format string contains a percent sign, followed by zero or more options, and ending with a type specifier. You may wonder why MATLAB uses the percent sign for formatting output when it also uses it for comments. The C language became well established in the 1970s, in fact, an early version of MATLAB was written in the C language shortly before the founding of The MathWorks in 1984 [5].

The format string can be as simple as `%d` for an integer number. For example, we can create a string with a number in it as follows:

```
n = 3;
str = sprintf('The value is %d for n.', n);
disp(str);
```

The computer prints "The value is 3 for n." in response. We can place the `%d` anywhere in the string, and the `sprintf` command replaces it with the first number in the parameter list.

We use type specifiers of `%f` for a floating-point value, `%c` for a character, and `%s` for a string. Table 2.1 shows a few of the possible type specifiers, with some examples. Those examples use dashes before and after the items printed, to show when the formatting has padding. In the next example, we create a string with another string embedded in it, along with a floating-point value, and a character.

```
c = '!';
s = 'float value';
f = 12.345;
str = sprintf('The %s is %f for f%c', ...
   s, f, c);
disp(str);
```

The computer responds with the following.

```
The float value is 12.345000 for f!
```

The `sprintf` command takes a variable number of parameters, although the first one should be the string that specifies the text and formatting. The parameters after that should correspond to the type specifiers in the string. In other words, mixing up the order of variables `s`, `f`, and `c` will produce odd results. In the following lines, we use floating-point value `f` with the integer value `n`. Internally, the computer stores `n` as a `double` value, although it does not have a fractional part in this example, and we want to show it as an integer.

```
>> sprintf('%d and %f', n, f)
ans =
3 and 12.345000
>> sprintf('%d and %f', f, n)
ans =
1.234500e+01 and 3.000000
```

In the first instance, we put a variable with a whole value as the first parameter, and a floating-point value in the second one. The second instance reverses the two parameters, so that the floating-point number appears where the integer was expected, and the integer appears where the floating-point number should be.

Earlier, we saw that two single quotes should be included with a string to make one appear in the output of `disp`. Similarly, if we want a percent sign to appear in the string, we use two of those in a row. The backslash also must be doubled up to appear, as the next example shows.

```
>> sprintf('Percents %% and backslashes \\ and '' quotes.')
ans =
Percents % and backslashes \ and ' quotes.
```

Actually, the `disp` command works with a single percent sign or a single backslash. The `sprintf` uses those characters as *escape* characters, special characters to indicate that the character after it means something. The next command illustrates this.

Table 2.1 Common type specifiers for the `sprintf` command.

Specifier	Meaning	Example	Result
`%d`	integer	`sprintf('-%d-', 3)`	`-3-`
		`sprintf('-%2d-', 3)`	`- 3-`
`%f`	floating point	`sprintf('-%f-', 3.12)`	`-3.120000-`
		`sprintf('-%5.2f-', 3.12)`	`- 3.12-`
`%c`	character	`sprintf('-%c-', 'M')`	`-M-`
`%s`	string	`sprintf('-%s-', 'Name')`	`-Name-`
		`sprintf('-%6s-', 'Name')`	`- Name-`
`%%`	percent sign	`sprintf('-99%%-')`	`-99%-`
`''`	single quote	`sprintf('-don''t forget-')`	`-don't forget-`
`\\`	backslash	`sprintf('-back \\ slash-')`	`-back \ slash-`
`\n`	new line	`sprintf('-one \n two-')`	`-one` `two-`
`\t`	tab	`sprintf('-one \t two-')`	`-one    two-`

```
>> sprintf('tab \t newline \n characters')
ans =
tab     newline
 characters
```

The output shows a tab character skips over several spaces like the "tab" key on a typewriter. The newline character advances to the next line. Since a space appears after the newline character and before the word "characters," it pushes that word one space to the right.

There are other possibilities for the type specifiers. The MATLAB documentation (i.e., `doc sprintf`) contains a good amount of detail. Incidentally, it refers to `%f` as fixed point; while the values to print are stored as floating-point (`double`) values, we specify the format as the digits in the whole part, along with the digits to use for the fractional part. For example, "`%5.2f`" says to format the number with 5 places in total, with 2 places after the decimal point. Let's revisit the example with the integer and the floating-point value.

```
>> sprintf('n=%4d and f=%5.2f', n, f)
ans =
n=   3 and f=12.35
```

Notice how there are blank spaces between the equal sign and the number 3. This comes from the `%4d` specifier, where we say to print an integer value, and the 4 says that that number should take up four spaces. Since the number only takes up one digit, the function pads it with spaces to its left. With the value f, the specifier `%5.2f` says to reserve five spaces total for the number, with two spaces appearing after the decimal point. Thus, we get two digits before the decimal point, and two digits after it.

What if we want to print the floating-point number with three digits after the decimal? The next example shows this.

```
>> sprintf('f=%7.3f', f)
ans =
f= 12.345
```

We changed the total number of spaces for the number to seven, which explains why a space appears after the equal sign. It would still work if we had left it at five, only because the `sprintf` function overrides that specification when the number does not fit.

MATLAB will print the entire whole part of the number, even if it exceeds the space. When it takes less space than the number of digits specified, the other positions are filled in with spaces. Consider the following example.

```
for k=-2:4
    disp(sprintf('%6.2f', pi*(10^k)));
end
```

When we run this code, we get the following results.

```
  0.03
  0.31
  3.14
 31.42
314.16
3141.59
31415.93
```

Observe that there are usually six places for the number, as we specified in the format. For the first three values, the output includes two spaces on the left. Then we have one space on the left. For the value 314.16, the output uses all the specified space. After this, the whole part contains more digits than are specified, that is, six minus two places after the decimal, minus one place for the decimal leaves us three spots for the whole part. The non-fractional part appears as a whole, even though it exceeds the room specified.

2.3   EXAMPLES OF MATLAB COMMANDS

This section provides a quick overview of the MATLAB commands that you will likely see in any MATLAB program.

2.3.1 Assignment

First, we have the assignment statement, where we associate a value to a label (variable name).

```
a = -2;
```

This statement creates a variable a, if it does not yet exist, and gives it the value –2. A computer "creates" a variable by reserving memory for it. If variable a already does exist, whatever value it has will be overwritten with –2.

```
b = abs(a);
```

Here we use a *function*, a set of directions that tell the computer what to do with the input a to turn it into the output b. This particular function returns the absolute value of the input. The function must be defined; some are built-in (like this one), while we will develop some of our own.

```
b = b + 1;
```

In this example, we perform an arithmetic function. The computer will take the value of b, whatever it happens to be, and add one to it. Then the computer stores the result in b. Let's suppose that b starts out with the value 2, as it would if we execute all of the above commands. The computer will take the value 2, add 1 to it, resulting in 3. Then the computer will put the value 3 in variable b's memory location, overwriting the previous value of 2. After this, any time we use b, the computer will remember the value 3.

2.3.2 Conditionals

The "if " statement

Now we have a more complicated example. Suppose we want to know if value a is negative. We will (re)define a, then use the if statement to see if it is less than zero. Note that we do not have to define a on the line directly before the if statement, but it should be defined somewhere before this if statement. If the condition (a < 0) evaluates to true, i.e., a has a value less than zero, then the computer will execute the block of code after the if. If this condition evaluates to false, then the computer will instead execute the code block after the else.

```
a = -2;
if (a < 0)
    disp('negative');
else
    disp('positive');
end
```

When we run the code above, the computer displays negative. Try it again, only replace the –2 with 2 in the first line. Now the computer should display positive.

Here we have a second example for the if command.

```
a = -2;
if (a < 0)
    disp('negative');
end
```

How will this example behave differently than the first example? The difference is that we have no `else` block here. Either the computer will display `negative`, or it will not display anything.

Now for a third example, consider the following code.

```
a = -2;
if (a >= 0)
    disp('positive');
else
    disp('negative');
end
```

This example does the same thing as the first `if` example. The main difference comes from the comparison; instead of checking to see if `a` is less than zero, we check to see if it is greater than or equal to zero. The `if` and `else` blocks are switched accordingly.

Here is another example, which prints "zero" in this case.

```
a = 0;
if (a > 0)
    disp('positive');
else if (a < 0)
        disp('negative');
    else
        disp('zero');
    end
end
```

We use an `if` statement inside the `else` block, and include them on the same line, even though they could appear on separate lines. Written in this fashion, they are two distinct keywords. The language also includes a special `elseif` statement, which acts like an `else` and an `if` statement combined together. With it, we can save an `end` statement, and avoid the need to indent additionally for this second `if`. The following code demonstrates this.

```
a = 0;
if (a > 0)
    disp('positive');
elseif (a < 0)
    disp('negative');
```

```
else
    disp('zero');
end
```

As in the example before it, the `if` statement checks the value of `a`, and prints "positive," "negative," or "zero," accordingly. While both accomplish the same goal, the latter version appears more orderly.

The "switch" statement

The `if` statement allows us to execute different code blocks based on a condition. But there are times when we need to evaluate the same variable, matching a behavior to a specific value, over and over again. For this situation, MATLAB provides the `switch` statement. We then specify a different code block depending on which `case` matches the variable.

For example, the code below demonstrates the `switch` statement as a way to print different responses based on the input. The `input` function displays a message, and waits for the user to type something on the keyboard. Once the user presses the return key (or enter, depending on the keyboard), the program continues. The first parameter to `input` specifies the message to show, so that the user knows what to do. The second parameter, `'s'` says that the response we expect will be a string.

```
% Get input from the user.
% Notice how the second parameter to "input" is 's',
% which specifies a string. Otherwise, input will not
% work for strings.
acronym = input('Enter an acronym: ', 's');
% Now print a response according to the input.
switch acronym
    case 'html'
    case 'HTML'
        disp('Hyper Text Markup Language');
    case {'MATLAB', 'matlab'}
        disp('MATrix LABoratory, by MathWorks');
    otherwise
        disp('I do not know that one.');
end
```

If you are familiar with other programming languages, you may have noticed that the keyword `break` does not appear here. MATLAB's cases are not fall-through, meaning that it only executes the code until the next `case` keyword. Also notice the `otherwise` keyword, which allows us to specify a default code block to run.

Below, we see several example runs of this code. The code responds differently according to what we type.

```
>> demonstrate_switch
Enter an acronym: html

>> demonstrate_switch
Enter an acronym: HTML
Hyper Text Markup Language

>> demonstrate_switch
Enter an acronym: MATLAB
MATrix LABoratory, by MathWorks

>> demonstrate_switch
Enter an acronym: matlab
MATrix LABoratory, by MathWorks

>> demonstrate_switch
Enter an acronym: CGI
I do not know that one.
```

Notice how it responds differently to HTML and html. There is nothing after the `case 'html'` except for the next `case` statement, so even though the program matches the text to the pattern, it literally does nothing because there is nothing specified before the next `case` statement. A few lines down from that shows how a block can be shared by multiple `case` patterns.

The "if " statement versus the "switch" statement

When it comes to selecting one of several courses of action to take, the `switch` statement comes in handy. But the `if` statement also achieves the same goal, so you can use your best judgment to determine when to use each.

Consider this example. We prompt the user for input, then based on their response, we do one of several possible things. To give this some context, suppose the application is a text-based minesweeper game. Instead of processing the input, we will simply show the user that we understand the what to do. An early version of a program may do this; this "scaffolding" provides structure and gives us immediate feedback.

First, we can do this with nested `if` statements.

```
userSays = input('Enter f, s, or q: ', 's');
if (userSays == 'f')
    disp(' flag');
else if (userSays == 's')
        disp(' step');
    else if (userSays == 'q')
            disp(' quit');
        else
            disp('not valid');
        end
    end
end
```

The indenting can be misleading, in that the display statements have the same importance. We choose the priority, that "flag" is processed first and thus its display statement appears with the least indentation. If we added more options, these would be indented further. We can redo this example with an `if` statement that uses multiple `elseif` extensions.

```
userSays = input('Enter f, s, or q: ', 's');
if (userSays == 'f')
    disp(' flag');
elseif (userSays == 's')
    disp(' step');
elseif (userSays == 'q')
    disp(' quit');
else
    disp('not valid');
end
```

The above example gives cleaner looking code, but we repeat the comparison over and over. Since we use the same variable every time, we can also have the option of expressing this with the `switch` statement.

```
userSays = input('Enter f, s, or q: ', 's');
switch userSays
    case ('f')
        disp(' flag');
```

```
case ('s')
    disp(' step');
case ('q')
    disp(' quit');
otherwise
    disp('not valid');
end
```

The `switch` statement provides a nice way to choose between several possible values of the same variable. When to use it versus when to use an `if` statement really depends on personal preference and how many possible choices there are.

2.3.3 Loops

The "for" statement

The `for` statement comes next. It allows us to repeat a block of commands a set number of times.

```
for k=1:10
    disp('This is repeated ten times.');
end
```

The code first sets up a variable k, and gives it the initial value 1. The the computer displays the line "`This is repeated ten times.`", and since the keyword `end` follows, the computer will turn its attention back to the start of the loop. Since k is the index for the loop, the computer adds 1 to k's value. Next, it compares k's value to the value 10. If k exceeds this value, then the computer will quit the loop, and execute whatever statement follows the `end`. If k's value is less than or equal to 10, then the code block is executed again, and the process is repeated.

Here is a second example.

```
for k=1:2:10
    disp('This is repeated five times.');
end
```

The main change between this example and the one before it is the `:2:` which appears in the first line. This tells the computer to increment k's value by 2 every time we go through the loop. Since k's value will go 1, 3, 5, 7, 9, (11), the loop will execute only five times.

Although we typically see a `for` loop for a range of numbers, MATLAB actually allows loops based on other ranges, like a range of characters, or even the characters that make up a string.

The "parfor" statement

A special version of the `for` loop exists for computers with parallel processing capabilities. The `parfor` statement runs a `for` loop in parallel, where different computing nodes handle parts of the job. These days, the computers do not have to be huge, specially built research platforms to take advantage of this. Multiple core processors have made their way into our desktop computers, laptops, and even phones.

Parallel processing greatly speeds up a task. Imagine if you, along with three other family members, take a long list of items-to-buy to a grocery store. Staying together will likely take as long as if one person were shopping alone. If you divide the shopping list into four smaller lists, each person can get the items from one. Working in parallel like this, you might finish in 1/4 the time. Parallel processing does not guarantee this speed-up, due to some complications. The grocery example works well because it does not contain dependencies, where one task depends on the result of another. Imagine if, in the grocery, your list contains a line that says "get the cheddar cheese slices if we get ham," while another person's list says to get ham only if the store has run out of salami. To proceed, you would need information that you do not yet have. In a programming example, we might have a line that calculates the value for variable `a`, and another command that uses `a` to find `b`. Obviously, we cannot find `b` until we know `a`. We call this a *dependency*.

The `parfor` command cannot always be used in place of a `for` loop. The "Parallel Computing Toolbox" supplies the parallel processing commands, meaning that your copy of MATLAB must include this toolbox to use them. The Mathworks sells MATLAB toolboxes as separate features, so your copy may or may not have it. Use the `ver` command to see what version of MATLAB you have, and what toolboxes it includes. Also, `parfor` places constraints on the loop index. It must be an integer, the range values must increase, and it cannot skip values in the sequence. The next few lines demonstrate the `parfor` command. Note that this example simply illustrates the usage, and does not represent a good case.

```
parfor k=1:10
    p(k) = k^2 + 3;
end
```

The first time we run this on the current MATLAB session, we get a message like the following.

```
Starting parallel pool (parpool) using the 'local' profile ...
connected to 4 workers.
```

It then splits up the tasks, sends them to the processors, they compute the calculations, and these results are combined. Notice that this includes overhead tasks of splitting up the work, communicating with the other processors, and combining the results. For a small example like this, this overhead can offset any speed-up.

The "while" loop

We could do the same thing as the previous for example, only with a while loop.

```
k=1;
while (k <= 10)
    disp('This is repeated five times.');
    k = k + 2;
end
```

We are responsible for giving k an initial value here, as well as updating its value (otherwise, the loop will never end!). The difference between the for and while loops is that the for loop repeats a set number of times; the computer updates a counter until the terminal value is reached. With the while loop, the computer executes the code block until a condition is reached. Consider the following example.

```
k=1;
while (k < 0)
    disp('This is never displayed.');
    k = k + 2;
end
```

Here, the condition for the while loop never is true. So the code block after the while never executes.

Now consider this example.

```
q=0;
while (q == 0)
    disp('This is displayed an unknown number of times.');
    q = input('Enter 0 to continue, or anything else to quit ');
end
```

The first statement sets variable q equal to zero. The while statement compares it to zero. Notice how two equal signs are used, to test for equality rather than set a value as in a for loop. The while loop will execute over and over again, until the user enters a non-zero value for q. Maybe this will happen the first time through the loop, or maybe the user will enter non-zero values for hours. We do not have any way of knowing in advance how many times this loop will execute.

Examples of "for" and "while" loops

Below is an example with a for loop.

```
m = 4;
for k = m:-1:1
    disp('hello there');
end
```

The computer initializes k's value with m, the value 4, and counts down by adding –1 to it every loop iteration, until it reaches 1.

Below is an example with a while loop.

```
m = 4;
my_index = 1;
while (my_index < m)
    disp('loop');
    my_index = my_index + 1;
end
```

Here we set my_index to 1, then start the loop. We check to see if it is less than m, we *increment* (add 1 to) my_index until it is greater than or equal to m.

When choosing between a loop structure, consider efficiency. For example, when looking for the first match in a sequence, using a while loop instead of a for loop makes sense. In other words, keep iterating the loop while the item has not been found, instead of looping through all possibilities. As an analogy, imagine trying to find bread at a grocery store: do you proceed to the checkout when you find it, or continue looking down every aisle?

2.3.4 Ways to Alter Flow Within a Loop

Sometimes we may need a loop to work a bit differently than imagined. For example, we might want to skip ahead to the next iteration. The continue keyword instructs the computer to do this. Another keyword to alter the flow of the loop is break, which stops the loop and goes on to the statements after it. If the loop is nested inside one or more other loops, it stops the inner-most loop. The `return` command provides a third possibility, and it stops the currently running function or program. While `continue` and `break` only work within a loop, `return` could be used outside of a loop, too. It gives us a useful tool to use when something goes wrong, for example, if the program attempts to read a file that does not exist, it can check for the file, print an error message, and return to whatever program called it.

2.3.5 Infinite Loops

We have seen how loops help us repeat the same steps over and over again, until the ending condition is met. But what if this condition never occurs? We call this an *infinite loop*, since the computer will continue the loop forever. Normally, we want to avoid this. (An exception is the operating system of an embedded system. For example, consider a computerized alarm system that monitors smoke detectors, opened doors, and motion sensors throughout a building. This control program will repeat indefinitely for the life of the product.) We can incorporate a *watchdog timer* within a program, to count down and stop the loop when it reaches zero. The idea is that it should never reach zero, unless there is a problem.

The key sequence CTRL-C can be used to interrupt a running MATLAB program. By CTRL-C, we mean hold down the control key, marked `ctrl` on the keyboard, then press the `c` key. Sometimes you may have a program that contains an infinite loop. Or perhaps you have a program that takes a long time to run, and you realize that you gave it the wrong parameters before you started it. In either case, interrupting the program with CTRL-C would be needed.

2.3.6 Error Handling

The "try" statement

Sometimes things do not go as planned. For example, we might want to write the results of our program to the hard drive. But what if the hard drive is full? We will not know until we try, and then our program will quit rather rudely. It would be better to anticipate a possible problem, and have our program handle it gracefully. The `try` and `catch` keywords allow us to do that. In the `try` section, we place code that might fail. Then the `catch` section will be executed if it does fail.

Normally, it is a good idea to use `try..catch` with commands for file input and output. Here we will use an even simpler test; we will call a function that does not exist.

```
% demonstrate the try..catch
try
    display('Trying an unknown function.');
    f = unknown(3);
    disp('The unknown function worked!');
catch
    disp('The function "unknown" must not exist.');
end
```

The computer will enter the `try` section, and execute each command. If there is a problem, it will skip the rest of that section and start executing the `catch` section. If the computer gets to the `catch` keyword without a problem, it will simply ignore the `catch` section. When we run the code, we get:

```
Trying an unknown function.
The function "unknown" must not exist.
```

If we had any code following the `try..catch` blocks, the computer would continue to run our program. This is much nicer than having our program suddenly stop at the error. It allows us to do any sort of "clean up" activities, as well as have our program attempt to continue the best it can.

Another example using "try," "catch," and "rethrow"

Below we have the `try` and `catch` statement. In the `try` section, we call `myfuncton`, an intentionally misspelled example. When MATLAB cannot locate a function by this name, it generates an exception and gives control to our `catch` section. Note that the programmer chooses the name that optionally appears after the `catch` keyword, such as `functionNotFoundException`. We could call it any valid variable name.

```
try
    disp('trying myfuncton');
    userSays = myfuncton(4);
    disp('OK, myfuncton worked.');
catch functionNotFoundException
    disp('Sorry, could not find "myfuncton".');
end
```

When the exception occurs, all that happens is what we specify in the `catch` portion. Any code after this block will continue to execute, as if nothing were wrong.

We could "rethrow" this exception, effectively halting the program with an error message.

```
try
    disp('trying myfuncton');
    userSays = myfuncton(4);
    disp('OK, myfuncton worked.');
catch functionNotFoundException
    disp('Sorry, could not find "myfuncton".');
    rethrow(functionNotFoundException);
end
```

Now when the exception occurs, we display the "sorry" message to the user, and let the system proceed with the exception the way it would if we did not have the `try` statement here. This gives us a degree of control over how the computer handles the exception. We could provide additional information to the user, or check another possibility before giving up.

The "error" command

The text that we show the user with the `disp` command appears in black. What if we really want to catch the user's attention? Using the `error` command in place of `disp` shows the message in red, with question marks preceding it, and it will make a sound. The following code shows an example.

```
>> error('You should not do that.');
??? You should not do that.
```

The error command will also alter the flow of execution. Consider the next example.

```
>> for n = 1:10
        error('You should not do this.');
        disp(n);
    end
??? You should not do this.
>>
```

Notice how it never printed the value of n, since it did not reach that line.

You can also make a window pop up with an error message of your choosing, with the `errordlg` command (i.e., "error dialog"). The example code below does this, encoding the n value in the message that it displays. If you run this, you will see that it pops up with three windows, with the text "Something went wrong, code 3." in the one on top, as in Figure 2.1.

```
for n = 1:3
    mystr = sprintf('Something went wrong, code %d.', n);
    errordlg(mystr, 'Pop-up window');
    disp(n);
end
```

The computer does not wait for the user to press the "OK" button, so you will see the three windows on top of each other. Notice that "Pop-up window" appears as the title of the window, and of course we could change it to something more meaningful.

2.3.7 Summary of MATLAB Program Structures

Here is a short summary of the program structures used in MATLAB. Words in italics show conditions, statement blocks, and variables. MATLAB does not require that conditions appear in parentheses, although this text shows conditions this way due to programming style. A block of statement(s) refers to one or more commands, including nested commands. For example, the block of statements inside an `if` statement can include more `if` statements.

FIGURE 2.1 A pop-up window generated by the "errordlg" command.

```
if (condition)
      block of statement(s)
end
if (condition)
      block of statement(s)
else
      block of statement(s)
end
if (condition)
      block of statement(s)
elseif (condition)
      block of statement(s)
end
if (condition)
      block of statement(s)
elseif (condition)
      block of statement(s)
else
      block of statement(s)
end
for variable = first index : last index
      block of statement(s)
end
for variable = first index : increment : last index
      block of statement(s)
end
```

By default, the increment is one. An increment can be positive or negative. Technically, we call a negative increment a decrement.

```
while (condition)
      block of statement(s)
end
```

A while loop should contain a way to update the condition in the body of the loop. A loop that never ends is called an *infinite loop*.

```
switch (variable)
      case value1
            block of statement(s)
      case value2
            block of statement(s)
      ...
```

```
        case valueN
                block of statement(s)
end
switch (variable)
        case value1
                block of statement(s)
        case value2
                block of statement(s)
        ...
        case valueN
                block of statement(s)
        otherwise
                block of statement(s)
end
switch (variable)
        case {value1, value2, ..., valueN}
                block of statement(s)
        case valueN+1
                block of statement(s)
        ...
        case valueM
                block of statement(s)
end
```

By *valueN+1* we simply mean some value following *valueN*. The *+1* is not meant literally.

```
try
        block of statement(s)
catch
        block of statement(s)
end
try
        block of statement(s)
catch exception
        block of statement(s)
end
try
        block of statement(s)
```

```
catch exception
    block of statement(s)
    rethrow(exception););
end
```

The *exception* specifies an object name for us to use in the block of catch statements.

2.4 EXAMPLES USING LOOPS AND CONDITIONALS

Often in computing, there are many ways to solve a problem. Each solution might have its own merits, such as speed, conservation of memory, ease of writing, etc. A singular, correct solution may not exist, and instead the programmer must choose between equally good alternatives. Other times there may be an optimal solution, or an optimal solution may emerge as the programmer grows and changes the program over time. Below, we have an example solution where we define an array, then find its sum. Chapter 4, Arrays and Matrices, covers arrays in more detail. For the moment, just think of an array as a list of numbers. You can refer to the first number on the list, or the second number on it, etc. The variables assigned in the following code store lists of numbers instead of just a single number.

```
A = [45, 21, 33, 9, 17];
mysum = 0;
k = 1;
while (k <= length(A))
    mysum = mysum + A(k);
    k = k + 1;
end
disp(mysum)
```

While the solution works, we know in advance of the `while` loop how many times to execute the loop's body. Why not use a `for` loop instead? The following code does that.

```
A = [45, 21, 33, 9, 17];
mysum = 0;
for k=1:length(A)
    mysum = mysum + A(k);
end
disp(mysum)
```

Using a `for` loop instead of a `while` loop allows us to express the solution in two fewer lines, an arguably better alternative.

MATLAB provides a `sum` function, so the loop could simply be replaced by a function call, as in the code below.

```
A = [45, 21, 33, 9, 17];
mysum = sum(A);
disp(mysum)
```

The solution involving `sum` is compact and clear, so without some other reason for finding the result in a loop, this solution is the best of the three. However, the purpose of this example is to show alternative ways to do a task. Given a `for` loop like the preceding one, you should be able to convert it to a `while` loop, and vice-versa.

Next, we start with an `if` statement.

```
b = input('enter a number ');
if (b==1)
    disp('one');
elseif (b==2)
    disp('two');
elseif (b==3)
    disp('three');
else
    disp('not one, two, or three');
end
```

This could have started simply with just printing "one," where an `if` statement would be the natural solution, with "two" and then "three" added later. Software does not remain the same over time, but instead changes and grows as programmers correct previous errors and implement new features. You probably have seen this, where your computer prompts you to download and install the latest version of software that you use. As the programmer adds more `elseif` conditions to the `if` statement, the solution reaches the point where a `switch` statement appears to be better suited. In the future, should the programmer forge ahead with adding a new `elseif`, or spend the time to re-write it? Sometimes the choice of how to invest your time may not be clear.

Converting the `if` statement to a `switch` statement will produce something like the following.

```
b = input('enter a number ');
switch b
    case 1
        disp('one');
    case 2
        disp('two');
    case 3
        disp('three');
    otherwise
        disp('not one, two, or three');
end
```

Try to convert an `if` statement to a `switch` statement, and then convert an example `switch` statement to an `if` statement.

2.5 EXAMPLE OF A WHILE LOOP, WITH USER INPUT

Sometimes we want our program to work with user inputs, and repeat a series of commands for each input. A `for` loop does not fit this model, since we do not know in advance how many times we will need to loop. The `while` loop works well, since we can continue to loop until a condition is met. Consider the following code.

```
done = 0;
while (~done)
    mykey = input('press q: ', 's');
    disp('you pressed a key');
    if ((mykey == 'q') | (mykey == 'Q'))
        done = 1;
    end
end
```

First, we set a Boolean variable `done` to 0 (`false`). Then we test for "not done," which will be 1 (`true`) the first time through. So we know that the loop will always execute at least once. Next, we get input from the user, and display a message. We then check to see if the input was a lower case q or an upper case Q. If one case or the other is true, then we set `done` to 1. When this happens, control will pass to the beginning of the `while` statement again. It will evaluate to `true`, and the computer will exit the loop.

If we were to type `qqqq` at the input, or `quit`, or some other such string, the computer will actually continue the loop! It checks the entire input to see if it is exactly one of the two possible characters. Any string longer than a character will automatically fail the test. As an exercise, consider how you would change the code to make it quit any time the letter `q` appears as the first character of the input.

2.6 COMMON MATLAB FUNCTIONS

MATLAB provides many functions, for a variety of tasks. Here we briefly discuss some of the more common ones. These commands convert data from one type to another, return information about the variable's size, or call a mathematical function.

If you have a floating-point number that you want to convert to an integer, you can use the `round` function to give back the closest integer to it. Other options include `ceil` to bring the value up to the next integer above it, or `floor` for the integer value below it. Each of these functions return a whole number, although it will have the `double` data type. You can also use the names of data types to convert, such as `uint8(x)` to return the 8-bit, unsigned integer version of `x`.

Functions `length` and `size` give the dimensions of an array or matrix, respectively. Both of these work with scalar values, too. The following variable definitions give us some data to use.

```
>> a = 10;
>> b = [9, 8, 7, 6];
>> c = [5, 4; 3, 2];
```

The next few commands use the "display" command (`disp`) to show the lengths of a, b, and c. We could also just type `length(a)`, although this way makes the output a little more compact.

```
>> disp(length(a));
    1
>> disp(length(b));
    4
>> disp(length(c));
    2
```

The first two lengths look like we might expect, although `length(c)` may seem odd. Variable `c` has the same number of values as `b`, so why does the computer report that it has a length of 2? The following examples shed some light on this question.

```
>> disp(size(a));
     1     1
>> disp(size(b));
     1     4
>> disp(size(c));
     2     2
```

Notice that scalar variable `a` has a 1 × 1 size. Variable `b` has a single row and 4 columns, like one would expect. When we examine the size of variable `c`, we see that it contains 2 × 2 elements, which explains the `length` command's output: it gives us the dimension of length. Since variable `c` has 2 columns, `length(c)` returns a value of 2. Before going further, let's explore the `length` and `size` commands a bit more. In the following lines, we define a new variable called `d` that contains a column vector. Like variable `b`, it has a list of numbers, but unlike `b`, we write them vertically instead of horizontally.

```
>> d = [1; 2; 3]
d =
     1
     2
     3
```

Next, we examine the dimensions of this new variable.

```
>> disp(length(d))
     3
>> disp(size(d))
     3     1
```

The `length` command gives us a value of 3, indicating that it returns the length of the dimension with the most values, not strictly the number of columns. Compare the size of variable `d` to what we saw for variable `b`; variable `d` has 3 rows and 1 column, while variable `b` has 1 row and 4 columns. The `size` command tells us the dimensions of the variable. Related to these size specifiers, the `numel` function gives us a third way to find out about a variable.

It stands for "number of elements," and returns how many values a variable holds. The following lines show examples of `numel`.

```
>> disp(numel(a));
     1
>> disp(numel(b));
     4
>> disp(numel(c));
     4
>> disp(numel(d));
     3
```

We see that variable a only has one value, while both b and c have a total of 4 values. Variable d holds 3 values. With `numel`, we could easily compare two the sizes of large matrices, if we needed to do so.

Mathematical functions include `cos` (cosine), `sin` (sine), `tan` (tangent), `acos` (arc-cosine), `asin` (arc-sine), `atan` (arc-tangent), `ode` (ordinary differential equation), `exp` (exponential of e), `log`, `log2`, `log10` (natural logarithm, logarithm with base 2, and logarithm with base 10). The trigonometric functions work in radians, so any angle in degrees should be converted. For example, to find the `sin` of 90 degrees, first multiply the angle by $\dfrac{2\pi}{360}$.

```
>> x = 90;
>> sin(x*2*pi/360)
ans =
     1
```

Of course, a conversion of $\dfrac{\pi}{180}$ gives the same result.

Notice that `pi` has a built-in value. Mathematical constant e does not, although we can easily generate it.

```
>> disp(exp(1))
     2.7183
```

Other built-in values include i and j, as in the following.

```
>> disp(i)
     0.0000 + 1.0000i
>> disp(j)
     0.0000 + 1.0000i
```

Both of these represent the "imaginary" value $\sqrt{-1}$. Some professions prefer one over the other. Many programmers use i and j as integer variables, and MATLAB allows this, too, as the following example shows.

```
>> i = 6;
>> disp(i)
     6
```

This can cause some ambiguity, as we see in the next few lines.

```
>> disp(3 + 4i)
   3.0000 + 4.0000i
>> disp(3 + 4*i)
   27
>> disp(3 + 4*j)
   3.0000 + 4.0000i
```

Parsing means to break something down in order to understand it. In the first line, the computer parses 3 + 4i to mean a complex number, with 3 for the real part, and 4 for the imaginary part. The second disp statement contains a similar-looking parameter, 3 + 4*i, which the computer understands as the addition of 3 to the result of 4 times variable i. After this, a disp statement prints the result of 3 + 4*j, resulting in a complex number, with 3 for the real part, and 4 for the imaginary part. In other words, if variable i had not been defined, all three of these statements would have produced the same result.

To convert a number from floating point to integer, options include round, fix, ceil, and floor. Note that these functions return values of type double, not an integer data type. The difference between these functions lie in the details. The round function returns the nearest integer value. To truncate the fractional part, use fix. For the ceil and floor functions, imagine a balloon floating in a level of a building. The ceiling function ceil causes it to rise to the next level, and the floor function causes to the fall to the bottom of the current level. Now imagine that the building has sub-basements, and picture the balloon as floating on level –3. The floor function brings it down to –3, while the ceil function would send it to –2.

Functions mod and rem return the modulus and remainder after division, respectively. The main difference comes down to how they respond when their two parameters have different signs. The rem function keeps the sign of the first parameter, the dividend. Also, rem returns NaN, short for "not a number", when the second parameter, the divisor, has a zero value. The mod function returns the dividend when the divisor is zero. The mod function sees a lot of uses in programming, where it can be used to keep a value from going beyond a limit. For example, if we want to have a variable with a value between 0 and 99, we can use the mod function to keep it within the desired range. Consider the following lines.

```
>> x = 98;
>> disp(mod(x+1, 100))
    99
>> disp(mod(x+2, 100))
    0
>> disp(mod(x-103, 100))
    95
```

With an initial value of 98, adding 1 to it gives us a result within the bounds. Adding 2 means that it wraps around to 0. If we subtract a large value from it, it wraps around the other way. Whatever value we add or subtract, we get a result with the whole part between the bounds 0 to 99. It does not guarantee that we get an integer value, however, since using a floating-point number such as mod(x+1.7, 100) results in the value 99.7. The floor function could take care of that for us.

2.7   PLOT

MATLAB provides several functions to graphically display data. One of the most useful is the plot function. To demonstrate it, we first need some data. The next few lines define some array variables, including y. The conv function computes the convolution of two arrays. Understanding convolution is not important for this example; it combines arrays together in an algorithm similar to the way we multiply large numbers on paper.

```
pascal3 = conv([1, 1], [1, 1]);
pascal5 = conv(pascal3, pascal3);
y = conv(pascal5, pascal5);
plot(y)
```

From the plot command, we see that MATLAB opens a new window, and shows a graph of the points in y, with lines connecting the points (by default). Figure 2.2 shows the resulting plot.

The code names two of the variables `pascal3` and `pascal5`, since these hold lines three and five of Pascal's Triangle, where line one holds the number one. The code that follows computes the lines of Pascal's Triangle in an alternate way, although if you inspect the value of `pascal3` and `pascal5`, you will find that they hold the same values as the variables by the same name in the preceding example.

```
pascal1 = 1;
pascal2 = conv(pascal1, [1, 1]);
pascal3 = conv(pascal2, [1, 1]);
pascal4 = conv(pascal3, [1, 1]);
```

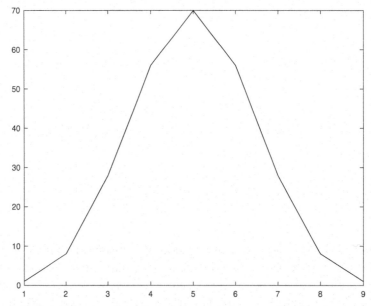

FIGURE 2.2 The plot of an example array. Array values come from Pascal's Triangle.

```
pascal5 = conv(pascal4, [1, 1]);
pascal6 = conv(pascal5, [1, 1]);
pascal7 = conv(pascal6, [1, 1]);
pascal8 = conv(pascal7, [1, 1]);
y = conv(pascal8, [1, 1]);
disp(pascal1);
disp(pascal2);
disp(pascal3);
```

```
disp(pascal4);
disp(pascal5);
disp(pascal6);
disp(pascal7);
disp(pascal8);
disp(y);
```

You might recognize Pascal's Triangle from the output. Note that the `plot` command above plots only `y`, which corresponds to the last line.

```
1

1   1

1   2   1

1   3   3   1

1   4   6   4   1

1   5   10  10  5   1

1   6   15  20  15  6   1

1   7   21  35  35  21  7   1

1   8   28  56  70  56  28  8   1
```

We could also generate this data from the built-in function `pascal`, however, it outputs a lot more data than just a line. See program `pascalPlot.m`, included in the supplementary material, for the commands shown here.

The `plot` command takes other arguments besides the values to graph. When we specify two arguments, it understands the first one to be the set of values along the *x*-axis, and the second set as the *y*-axis values. An optional third parameter provides information about how the points should appear: what kind of line, if any, should connect the points, what symbol to use for the points, and what color it should use to draw them. The lines between points appear solid, unless we specify dashed, dotted, dashed and dotted, or nothing, which does not connect the points. While the graphed values appear as very tiny dots by default, we can instead use other symbols, such as circles, triangles, squares, diamonds, etc. Not only does this allow us to make the points stand out, sometimes we may want to graph several arrays at once, and changing the symbol for each array helps the viewer follow the graph. Without specifying the third argument, the plot uses blue as the default color. Red, green, black, and cyan (a bright blue) can be selected instead, along with a few other options. See the built-in help information (i.e., type `help plot` in the command window) to see all of the options.

Figure 2.3 shows the stem plot of the `y` array used in Figure 2.2. As you can see, the `stem` command, `stem(y)`, generates a similar graph as `plot` does, only the values appear with stems under them. Sometimes this type of graph helps to communicate the data.

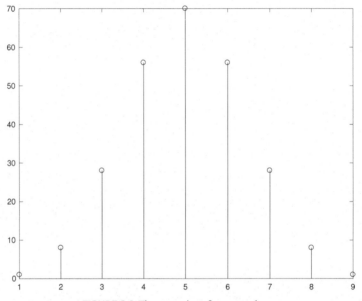

FIGURE 2.3 The stem plot of an example array.

To add text to a graph, we have several options. The `title` command places centered text above the graph. As you might expect from the names, `xlabel` places text under the x-axis, and `ylabel` places it to the left of the y-axis. A `zlabel` command also exists, for 3-D graphs. Another command, `text`, allows us to place a string of characters anywhere on the graph itself. If you use text that includes underscores, you might be surprised to see that the underscore does not appear, and the character after the underscore appears as a subscript. MATLAB follows some of the same conventions for formatting as "Latex" a powerful text-processing tool, one often used by scientists for academic papers.

Now let's demonstrate some of these options. First, we create a new array called x to serve as the *x*-axis coordinates. The range 1:length(y) may remind you of a for loop, since we often use expressions like this to define the loop index. Subtracting 5 from it makes it centered at zero, at least for this example, since y contains nine values. Next, we issue the figure(); command, which creates a new figure window. If a figure window already exists, it will not be overwritten when we use the plot command. After this, we graph the points specified by x and y, with the attributes r*: where r stands for red, * for the symbol to use at each point, and : to indicate a dotted line. With these commands, we will accomplish that.

```
x = (1:length(y)) - 5;
figure();
plot(x, y, 'r*:');
```

Suppose that we want to also show the square-root of each y value, which the sqrt function provides. Let's do that with the stem command, in green, with circles for the points, and dashed lines for the stems. Before calling the stem function, we invoke hold on, a command that changes the "hold" property of this figure to hold on to the plot that already appears. By default, a command like plot or stem will erase whatever the figure already shows before drawing the new graph.

```
y2 = sqrt(y);
hold on;
stem(x, y2, 'go--');
```

Now the figure should show both the original points, and the y2 points. Next, we give it a title, labels for the axes, and add some text. The string "maximum is here at y_0" will appear starting at point (0.5, 68) on this graph, close to the maximum value. Note that if we give it coordinates like (10, 10), we will not see it in this case, since that point would be so far to the right as to be off the graph. Notice that with the underscore, the zero displays as a subscript.

```
xlabel('centering at zero');
ylabel('triangle values');
title('Pascal''s Triangle');
text(0.5, 68, 'maximum is here at y_0');
```

Figure 2.4 shows a graph similar to what you will see, only in black and white.

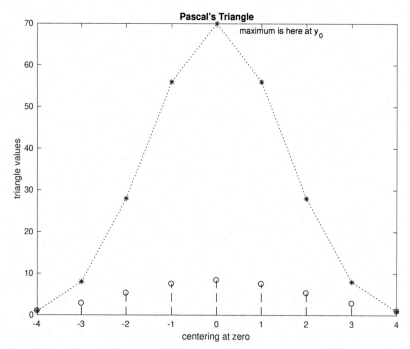

FIGURE 2.4 An example plot, stem plot, with text.

Now that we have seen the basics for plotting data, there are a few other commands to explore. First, assuming that your computer still shows the previous example's graph, we could use `clf` (i.e., "clear figure") to clear it. It will erase the contents of the current figure, although we could tell it which figure by passing the figure number as an argument. If you have multiple plots showing, many of the preceding commands apply to the current window, which the user might change simply by clicking on a different figure. The `figure` command itself returns a *handle*, a special value used to identify windows (and other objects). First, try the `clf` command by itself, just to see what it does to the figure.

```
clf;
```

You should observe the figure window change. The menu items and toolbar remain, although the area under these will appear blank. What if we want to get rid of all the figures? The `close` command does this, and we can invoke it with no arguments, where it will close the current figure, or we could specify the figure number as an argument, or we could tell it to close all of the figures. The following command closes all of them.

```
close all
```

Assuming that we have the x and y data from previous examples, we create a new figure, and save the figure's handle in a variable called myfigure. Besides plotting data on the same graph, we can break a figure up into sub-figures, called axes. The following subplot(2,1,1) command takes three arguments, and instructs the computer to split the figure into 2 × 1 smaller figures, i.e., 2 rows and 1 column. The third argument sets the current axis to 1, meaning the top sub-figure in this example. Then, show the plot in red as a bar graph with the bar function. Another subplot command sets the current axis to the second sub-figure. Finally, the stairs command shows the same data as a step graph, resembling a set of stairs.

```
myfigure = figure(); subplot(2,1,1);
bar(x, y, 'r');
subplot(2,1,2);
stairs(x, y, 'm');
```

The figure that you see should be just like that in Figure 2.5, except that it will appear in color on your screen.

Now try the saveas command, which uses the figure's handle. It tells the computer to save the figure as a JPEG file, in this case, naming the file "bar_and_stairs.jpg".

```
saveas(myfigure, 'bar_and_stairs.jpg', 'jpg');
```

Actually, the saveas command does not require the last argument in this example. It instructs the computer what format to use, and if left out, the saveas command looks to the filename to determine the format. However, specifying the format does add clarity to the command. If the filename does not include an extension, this should be included. Note that the image saved with saveas does not always match the figure saved using the menu options, so you might want to view the saved figure before closing your MATLAB session or clearing your variables. Program compareSaveAs.m, included in the supplementary material, gives a demonstration that compares the two ways to save an image. Using it revealed an image size of 900 rows by 1201 columns for the saveas command, versus 419 rows by 560 columns for the images created by menu options, on a laptop computer. Testing this on a desktop computer found a similar result, 900 × 1200 for saveas versus 864 × 1152 for the menu options. Your results may vary. A related command, savefig, saves the figure in MATLAB's "FIG" format, which you might prefer when actively editing it. That is, if you work on a figure, decide to stop, and think you may make further changes later, the savefig preserves the figure as an object, allowing you to alter details like the text font and size.

When finished viewing the resulting figure from the preceding example, try the following few commands.

```
figure();
plot(x, y, 'k');
grid on;
close(myfigure);
```

This creates a new figure window, then plots the data on it in black. As might be expected from the command name, `grid on` shows grid lines, a nice embellishment. Similarly, the command `grid off` gets rid of them. The `close` command passes variable `myfigure` as an argument, which means that the computer will close that figure, even though the new figure is the current one. This demonstrates that a program can control which window the commands apply to, as long as it has the figure's handle.

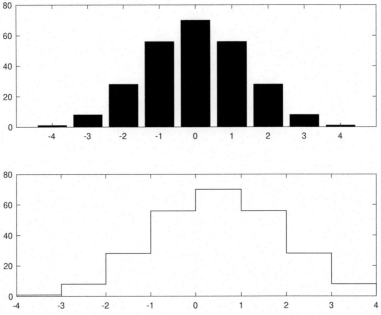

FIGURE 2.5 An example of the `subplot` command, along with the `bar` and `stairs` commands.

So far, we have seen 2-D plotting functions. MATLAB also provides 3-D plotting functions, such as `mesh`, `surf`, `waterfall`, and `contour`. The following example shows a surface plot. This does not rely on previous data, although we do use the `pascal` function to provide data.

```
x = -4:4;
y = 3:11;
z = pascal(9);
surf(x, y, z);
figure();
mesh(x, y, z);
figure();
contour(x, y, z);
figure();
plot3(x, y, z);
```

Here, we let x range from −4 to 4, just like previously. Variable y holds the integers from 3 to 11, which does not have any meaning for this example aside from the fact that it has 9 values, like x does. Setting y to be the same as x would also work. Variable z gets the 9 × 9 matrix of values that this particular pascal command returns. The code then shows the data with the surf, mesh, contour, and plot3 commands, as separate figures. Notice that x and y provide the axis numbers. These variables (x, y, and z) must be compatible in size. Figure 2.6 shows the mesh version of the plot.

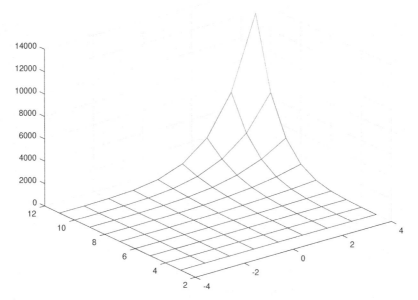

FIGURE 2.6 A 3-D plot made by the mesh command.

Figure 2.7 puts the surf, mesh, contour, and plot3 plots on the same figure. The following code does this.

```
x = -4:4;
y = 3:11;
z = pascal(9);
figure();
subplot(2,2,1);
surf(x, y, z);
subplot(2,2,2);
mesh(x, y, z);
subplot(2,2,3);
contour(x, y, z);
subplot(2,2,4);
plot3(x, y, z);
```

It uses the same data and plotting commands as the preceding code, but it invokes the subplot command to place each one in a different location.

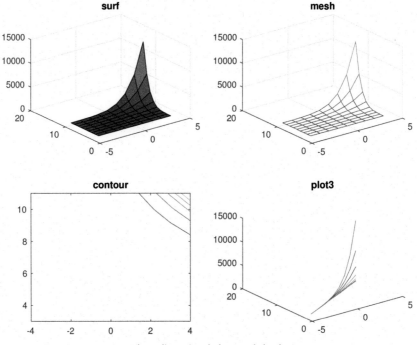

FIGURE 2.7 Three-dimensional plots made by the surf, mesh, contour, and plot3 commands.

2.8   CREATING OUR OWN FUNCTIONS

We have seen how to use functions that already are defined in MATLAB, such as the following abs function.

```
>> x = abs(-3)
x =
     3
```

Functions may return more than one value, which makes MATLAB a bit different from other programming languages. For example, the size function returns the number of rows and the number of columns in a matrix.

```
>> [rows, cols] = size(barray)
rows =
     1
cols =
     6
```

To define our own function, we use the keyword function. We might want to use our function over and over again, so we should store it in a file. But MATLAB needs a way to locate our new function, so whatever name we choose for it should also be used as the filename.

Let's create our own average function. First, create a new file called average.m. We will build it iteratively, but at the end of this example, we will have it working. Type the following into the MATLAB editor.

```
%
% Example function
% average
%
% usage:
%          avg = average(array);
%
function avg = average(x)
avg = x(1);
```

At this point, the function does not yet find the average, although we will fix this shortly. This function specifies a few things. First, we have the comments at the top that document our new function. Second, we use the function. keyword to specify that this is a function, and that avg will be what we call our output, while the function has the name `average`, and `x` will be what we call our input. This may seem backwards, but it makes sense to the user. In another program, we might use this function as `myavg = average(myarray);`.

When you click on "save," MATLAB will prompt you for the name. It will automatically call it `average.m`, unless you tell it otherwise. Save it under that name.

Now we can try the function. It does not do anything useful yet, but we can verify that MATLAB finds it.

```
>> help average
Example function
average
usage:
        avg = average(array);
```

When we use the `help` function, we find that it automatically finds our new function, and displays the initial comments as the help output. Note that any comments after the initial block will not appear in the help output.

Let's try to use our function.

```
>> average([1, 2, 3])
ans =
     1
```

The output is correct in the sense that it does what we told it to do; to return the first value. Now let's make it do averaging. We need to replace the last line of the function with `avg = sum(x)/length(x);`. The whole function will look like the following.

```
%
% Example function
% average
%
%   usage:
%           avg = average(array);
%
function avg = average(x)
avg = sum(x)/length(x);
```

Let's try the new version of the function. Be sure to save it before continuing. This is a common mistake; when we invoke a function from the command line, MATLAB will use whatever version of the function (or program) is saved as a file, not what version is in the editor. New versions of MATLAB anticipate this, and the editor may automatically save your changes when you switch to the command window. However, if you use another editor, you will not have this feature.

```
>> x = average([1, 2, 2])
x =
    1.6667
```

We see that our average function gives us a correct output. We can verify this with a calculator. It's always a good idea to verify our results!

This is a rather simple function, one that we can accomplish in a single line. Functions typically have many lines. If we ever need to leave a function early, we can use the `return` keyword. You can put the `end` keyword at the end of the function, although MATLAB does not require this.

We do not have to tell MATLAB what value to return, it will return the final value of `avg`. We can even use `avg` in the function multiple times, such as if we determine its final value over a series of steps.

All variables created during function execution are local to the function. When the function ends, these variables will be cleared automatically. Normally, this is nice because we do not have extra clutter in our variable space when the function completes. However, this can be frustrating when our function exits abnormally, but then all variables are gone.

Functions allow us to abstract a problem. For example, in the average function above, we do not really need to know its details once it works. We know the concept, and it does not matter to us if the function has one line or a thousand lines, as long as it does the job. Of course, if it were slow or had a bug, then we would be concerned.

2.8.1 Multiple Inputs and Multiple Outputs

In a function, we can have multiple inputs, and multiple outputs. The first line specifies this, with the format:

`function` [*output1, output2, ..., outputN*] = *name* (*input1, input2, ..., inputN*)

where *name* is the name of the function, *output1, output2, ..., outputN* specifies the outputs, and *input1, input2, ..., inputN* refers to the inputs. The following example illustrates this idea.

```
% ThreeIn3Out.m
function [a, b, c] = ThreeIn3Out(x, y, z)
a = (x + y + z)/3;    % average
b = (x + y + z);      % sum
c = sqrt(x^2 + y^2 + z^2);  % sqrt sum squared
```

An example run appears next.

```
>> [f, g, h] = ThreeIn3Out(2, 3, 4)
f =
    3
g =
    9
h =
    5.3852
```

Of course, we could suppress the printing of these values by adding a semi-colon to the end of the line when calling the function.

What if we call the function in a way that only assigns two outputs? The function call below demonstrates this.

```
>> [f, g] = ThreeIn3Out(8, 1, 5)
f =
    4.6667
g =
    14
```

In this example, the variables f and g receive the first two of the outputs. It ignores the third output. What if we take this further, and do not assign the outputs to variables at all?

```
>> ThreeIn3Out(4, 7, 0)
ans =
    3.6667
```

As we see, the default variable ans gets the first output. Let's try this one last time, passing the same inputs, with a semi-colon at the end. Before this, use clear to get rid of all variables.

```
>> clear
>> ThreeIn3Out(4, 7, 0);
>> disp(ans)
    3.6667
```

Here, MATLAB calls and runs the function, but suppresses printing all of the outputs. It does, however, assign `ans` just like in the example without the semi-colon.

Keywords `nargout` and `varargout` specify the number of argument outputs, and that we want a variable number of output arguments. Put `varargout` in the output list in the function declaration, then use `nargout` within the function to know how many outputs the function call specifies. This way, it can meet the demand.

The following program illustrates the idea of returning a variable number of arguments. Similar to `ThreeIn3Out.m`, it expects three inputs, and calculates the average, the sum, and the square-root of the sum of the squared values. Notice how the output variable list has been replaced with `varargout`.

```
% ThreeInVarOut.m
function varargout = ThreeInVarOut(x, y, z)
a = (x + y + z)/3;   % average
b = (x + y + z);     % sum
c = sqrt(x^2 + y^2 + z^2);   % sqrt sum squared
switch (nargout)
    case 1
        varargout{1} = a;
    case 2
        varargout{1} = b;
        varargout{2} = c;
    otherwise
        varargout{1} = a;
        varargout{2} = b;
        varargout{3} = c;
end
```

It gets interesting in the `switch` statement, where it determines what to do based on `nargout`, the number of output arguments that the user expects. With one output, it sets the sum as the return value. When the calling command specifies two outputs, it returns the sum and the square-root of the sum of the squared values. Three outputs means that it returns all three calculated values. Now, we can test it out. We expect it to behave just like `ThreeIn3Out` when we set the results to three variables, so the first example verifies this.

```
>> [rv1, rv2, rv3] = ThreeIn3Out(4, 6, 2)
rv1 =
     4
rv2 =
     12
rv3 =
     7.4833
>> [rv1, rv2, rv3] = ThreeInVarOut(4, 6, 2)
rv1 =
     4
rv2 =
     12
rv3 =
     7.4833
```

We see that, for the input values 4, 6, and 2, chosen at random, it gives us the same outputs. Now we can try it with only two return values.

```
>> [rv1, rv2] = ThreeInVarOut(4, 6, 2)
rv1 =
     12
rv2 =
     7.4833
```

As expected, it gives us the second and third outputs. The crucial difference between it and `ThreeIn3Out` is that the latter function would give us different values, i.e., the first and second, in this case.

```
>> [rv1] = ThreeInVarOut(4, 6, 2)
rv1 =
     4
```

Finally, we call it and store a single return value, which gives us the average. You may wonder, "why not have it return three values every time, and let the user discard the unwanted ones?" This is a valid point, and many functions do behave that way. The user might prefer to use a variable number of outputs, however.

With the flexibility in returning outputs, you might wonder about calling the function with fewer inputs, but that generates an error message. If the function should support a variable number of inputs, the `varargin` command provides a way to support this. The next example shows this.

2.8.2 Variable Argument Input

This program demonstrates `varargin`, a special variable in MATLAB that stores a **var**iable number of **arg**uments as **in**put as cells. A *cell* is a MATLAB construct similar to an array, although it introduces flexibility since cells allow storage of different data types. The function below demonstrates this by printing "hello" followed by a name, as zero or more strings. It uses another special variable called `nargin`, the **n**umber of **arg**uments **in**put.

```
% Variable argument input
function hello_varargin(varargin)
str = 'hello';
for k=1:nargin
    % Add a space, followed by next parameter.
    str = sprintf('%s %s', str, varargin{k});
end
disp(str);
```

Notice how our string variable `str` starts out with the text `hello`, then we add to it within the loop. The `sprintf` command creates a new string from the previous version of `str` followed by a space, and the `varargin` cell indexed by the current value of `k`. Let's call this function repeatedly to show how it works.

```
>> hello_varargin
hello
>> hello_varargin('John');
hello John
>> hello_varargin('John', 'Doe');
hello John Doe
>> hello_varargin('Mr.', 'John', 'Doe');
hello Mr. John Doe
```

Initially, we call it with no parameters, then one, then two, then three. It responds with "hello" followed by the parameters, in order. This allows us to write programs that conveniently provide default values, like how the MATLAB `plot` function works with one, two, or three (or more) parameters.

2.9   PASS BY VALUE OR REFERENCE

When a program calls a function, MATLAB passes the data by value. That is, it makes a copy of the data for the function to use, and if the function changes it, the calling function/program does not see the changes. Some computer languages use pass by reference, which means that there is only one copy of the data, so that if a function changes it, the data accessed by the calling function/program will also change. MATLAB does use pass by reference in special cases, notably the graphics objects such as figures and their sub-objects such as buttons and text boxes.

Pass by reference can save computer resources, like memory, especially when using large matrices, since it avoids the copy operation. The reference must be passed, although it occupies a small amount of memory. Think of web page as an analogy. If you see a web page that you like, and want to share it with another person via e-mail, you have a couple of options. You could highlight everything on the web page, select copy, click on the body of an e-mail you are composing, then select paste. All of the text on that page would then be part of the e-mail. (Yes, things like images and video would not copy into e-mail, so let's just assume that the text is all that you want to share.) Another way to share it would be to highlight the universal resource locator (URL), and paste that into the e-mail. The first way makes a copy of the text, possibly thousands of bytes or more, whereas the second way only sends the link, likely no more than a couple hundred bytes. If you were to alter the text pasted into the e-mail, only your recipient would see that change. If you send the URL, and the person maintaining the web page changes the content, your recipient would see that new version. If the server hosting the web page were to go down, your recipient would not be able to view the content if you only send the URL. In this analogy, copying and pasting the text is like pass by value, while sending just the URL is a pass by reference. In the latter case you do not send the content, but a pointer to where the content resides.

Pass by value can be inefficient, especially if the data are not changed. However, the programmers behind MATLAB understand this, and have taken steps to boost performance by not making unnecessary copies. There are a couple of points to take away from this. First, think of MATLAB as using pass by value for functions, meaning that a function should return any data that it changes. Second, if your code does not perform as well as you want, altering what you pass to functions may help.

2.10 FILE EXTENSIONS

We have seen that the ".m" extension is the convention used on files containing MATLAB programs. Other file extensions related to MATLAB include ".asv", ".m~", ".fig", ".mat", and ".mlx". The ".asv" extension comes from "auto save," that is, a file that the computer automatically saves for you. The ".m~" means the same thing as auto save. The difference comes down to what preferences you have set under the editor/debugger, along with how often the MATLAB editor will create a backup file for you.

MATLAB uses the ".fig" extension for a figure. If you plot some data, then select "save as," MATLAB defaults to this, its own figure format, unless you specify otherwise. For example, the following command plots the numbers from 1 to 100.

```
plot(1:100)
```

On the figure window, you can click on File, then Save As..., and it will open a small window allowing you to set the filename and choose the format. The default is likely to be "untitled.fig". You can then manipulate the figure in a future MATLAB session. However, if you want some other program to use the figure, you should choose another format. The "JPEG image" format saves the file with the familiar ".jpg" extension, allowing you to upload it to social media as you would a picture.

The ".mat" extension specifies a MATLAB data file. Consider the following MATLAB session. First, it defines variable a as an array of values, from 1 to 100. Then it defines b as another array, with values from 400 down to 301. Executing the whos command gives us a summary of these defined variables.

```
>> a = 1:100;
>> b = 400:-1:301;
>> whos
  Name        Size        Bytes      Class       Attributes
   a          1x100        800       double
   b          1x100        800       double
>> save mydata
>> clear
>> whos
>> load mydata
>> whos
```

Name	Size	Bytes	Class	Attributes
a	1x100	800	double	
b	1x100	800	double	

```
>> plot(a,b)
```

Next, the `save mydata` command creates a new file called "`mydata.mat`", that contains the variables that we have defined. The next command, `clear`, gets rid of all defined variables and frees up the memory that they used. The `whos` command has no output, showing that there are no variables defined at that point. Then, the `load mydata` instructs MATLAB to read the data file that we created, and restore those variables. Following that, the `whos` command returns the information about the variables a and b, just like before. Finally, the `plot(a,b)` command visually demonstrates that, as a increases from 1 to 100, b decreases from 400 down to 301. Thus, the data that we have now is the same as what we had before the `save` command. Normally, we would likely issue the `save` and `load` commands in different sessions. Suppose that you are working with MATLAB on a computer in a lab, and decide to stop for now. Next time you might not get the exact same computer, or perhaps will work in a different lab altogether. You can save your variables with the `save` command, take the file with you (i.e., on a USB-key), or upload it to a safe place, then pick up from this point later with the `load` command.

A fairly new feature is the "live script" format, which allows you to mix a program and output plots. Use the ".`mlx`" extension for these files. Note that the file produced might not be usable outside of MATLAB. While files ending in a ".`m`" extension can be viewed or modified by any text editor, this is not true of ".`mlx`" files. Instead, these have some text stored in the extensible mark-up language (XML) form, as several files that are then combined together and compressed (also called "zipped"). If you know how to "unzip" files that have a ".`zip`" extension, you could recover your code from a ".`mlx`" file, although the best way would be to use the MATLAB editor.

MATLAB can also read and write files for other programs, like ".`wav`", ".`jpg`", ".`csv`", and ".`xls`". The ".`wav`" extension stands for the wave-file format, a common way to store sound data. Images typically appear with an extension of ".`jpg`" (Joint Photographic Experts Group), ".`bmp`" (bit-mapped), ".`png`" (portable network graphics), and ".`tif`" (Tagged Image Format File), all of which (and more) are supported by MATLAB.

Another supported file type, ".`eps`" (encapsulated post script), has an interesting feature. It can store text as its individual characters, instead of as a pixelated image of the characters. In other words, if you include text like

"Example plot" in a file saved with an ".eps" extension, the words "Example plot" are actually stored in the file. A utility program that searches inside files will be able to find it. Here is an example. The following code generates a plot, and puts some text above it as a title.

```
a = 1:100;
b = 400:-1:301;
plot(a,b,'k')
title('Example plot.');
```

Suppose that we shrink it down to one inch wide and one inch tall, using the "Export Setup..." option under the figure's "File" tab. Perhaps at the moment, we need it to be that size, and do not foresee needing to have a larger version. After this, we use the "Save As..." options to store it in the ".jpg" format, and also as an ".eps" file. Later, we might use these two files in a document, where we specify the width as something larger than an inch. Figure 2.8 shows the results. This example illustrates an advantage of *vector graphics*, where the file specifies how to draw the image, over *bitmap graphics*, where the image only contains pixel colors. This advantage normally comes at the cost of file size, though. In this example, the EPS file takes up 2.7 times the size of the JPEG file.

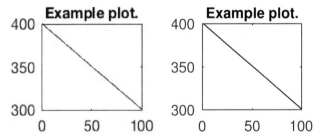

FIGURE 2.8 Saving a shrunken plot as a JPEG file looks blurry when we expand it, although one saved as an EPS file looks good.

The JPEG version shown in Figure 2.8 (left) looks blurry, while the EPS version shown in Figure 2.8 (right) appears sharp. As stated above, the JPEG file does not store the text; it stores everything as an image, where the computer reading the file cannot know if a black pixel is part of a line or part of the letter "E." The EPS file actually contains the text. To demonstrate this, consider the commands below. Note that this does not work with MATLAB. This comes from a Terminal window on an iMac, and uses a built-in command.

```
mweeks$ grep -n "Example plot" example_plot.jpg
mweeks$ grep -n "Example plot" example_plot.eps
618:(Example plot.) t
mweeks$
```

The `grep` command, on a Unix/Linux machine, looks for a pattern in a file. It's a handy utility to know. Here, the text `mweeks$` is the prompt in the Terminal window, similar to the `>>` prompt that MATLAB uses. The first line instructs the computer to look for the text "Example plot" in the file "example_plot.jpg," although it finds nothing. The second line says to look for the same text in the file "example_plot.eps," and the computer responds with the contents of line 618 of that file. It found the text.

Beware of file extensions that map to different things. A file with a ".`m`" extension could be MATLAB script/function, or it could be a program in the Objective-C language. Likewise, an extension of `.fig` could be a MATLAB figure, or it could be a figure used by the `xfig` drawing program. Most likely, the largest problem you will encounter is when you click on a file, and the computer opens up the wrong application. By starting the application and calling up the file through it, you can easily avoid this.

2.11 CHECKING IF A VARIABLE EXISTS

The `exist` command allows us to check to see if a variable already exists. While being a poor programming practice, a script could expect a variable to be defined before the user calls the program. A better approach is to turn the script into a function, then allow a variable number of arguments in the function call. Perhaps we are debugging some code, where a variable should be defined but it appears that it is not, maybe by an errant `clear` statement. This check would give us additional information. Another way it could be used it to learn more about a label, such as when we are not sure if a label refers to an array or a function. For whatever the reason, let's use this as the basis for a few examples. First, let's define a variable, then check to see if it exists.

```
A = 3:6;
if (~(exist('A', 'var')))
    A = 7:10;
end
disp(A);
```

Variable A receives a set of values in the first line. Then `exist('A', 'var')` determines if A has been defined as a variable. Note that we pass A to the `exist` function in single quotes. After function `exist` returns, we invert the value, because we want to know "if A does not exist ..." and in that case, we assign A a value. Running the code, we find the following output.

```
3     4     5     6
```

Since variable A already exists, the computer skips the body of the `if` statement. Now we try a counter-example. The first line makes sure to get rid of A, before we check to see if it exists.

```
clear A;
if (~(exist('A', 'var')))
    A = 7:10;
end
disp(A);
```

This time, the expression `exist('A', 'var')` returns a false value, inverting it turns it to true, and the computer executes the body of the `if` statement. The output confirms this.

```
7     8     9     10
```

Thus, we can check to see if a variable exists, and take appropriate action based on the result. The `exist` function does more than check variables. It can check for files, directories, and a few other things, too. The following lines of code checks to see if `disp` is a variable.

```
if (exist('disp', 'var'))
    disp('disp is a variable');
elseif (exist('disp', 'builtin'))
    disp('disp is a built-in function');
end
```

Running it revels the following.

```
disp is a built-in function
```

The first call to `exist` returns a false value, so we go on to check if it exists as a built-in function. Clearly, `disp` exists as a function. Finally, the `exist` function can be called with only one parameter, in which case it returns a code representing the type of definition it finds. Here are a few examples of that.

```
>> disp(exist('A'))
     1
>> disp(exist('disp'))
     5
>> disp(exist('notdefined'))
     0
>> disp(exist('disp', 'var'))
     0
```

We see that variables generate a code of 1, assuming that A has not been cleared. Functions return 5 when they are built-in, and 2 when defined by a .m file. Note that exist does not tell you if the .m file corresponds to a function or a script, since both instances uses 2 as the code. In the third example, we see that it returns 0 when the string passed to it does not correspond to anything that it can find. The final example shows how exist behaves depending on the second parameter; the expression exist('disp', 'var') specifically asks if disp exists as a variable.

2.12 PROGRAMMING TIPS

Although it may interfere with the readability of your program, you can put multiple commands on the same line using the semi-colon or comma to separate commands.

Remember to *document your code*. You should have relevant information in comments at the top of your program, including your name, the date, purpose of the code, usage information (describing the input parameters). You should also have comments throughout your code, describing what your code does. Also, if you have code from some other source, be sure to indicate where it came from, who wrote it, and where it starts and where it ends.

2.13 A VARIABLE NAMING EXAMPLE

This example comes from a program that processes input in a simple way. It should be flexible, so that it can work with standard input and standard output (called cin and cout in the C/C++ languages), or allow the user to specify an input file, or allow both an input and output file. It calls a function called

`Process`, however the details of that function are not important for this discussion. The code section looks like the following.

```
if (fnameCount == 0)
    Process(cin, cout);
elseif (fnameCount == 1)
    Process(inputfile, cout);
else
    Process(inputfile, outputfile);
end
```

As it counts the parameters passed to it, it assumes that the first one is the input filename, the second one is the output filename, and it ignores any others. It will give the user a warning if it ignores any parameters. Variable "fnameCount" is used to count the parameters, and can be used as above to determine how the user wants the I/O. But the code is not very clear.

Adding a couple of Boolean variables, "inputFileSpecified" and "outputFileSpecified" improve it, allowing the previous code to be expressed in a clearer way, as follows:

```
if (inputFileSpecified && outputFileSpecified)
    Process(inputfile, outputfile);
elseif (inputFileSpecified)
    Process(inputfile, cout);
else
    Process(cin, cout);
end
```

This way, the code appears somewhat more readable.

2.14 ALGORITHMIC THINKING

Algorithmic thinking means problem solving, and involves a systematic way of handling a problem, breaking it into steps. When you approach a large problem, it may overwhelm you. But if you can break it down into smaller tasks, then the whole problem becomes easier to handle. This *divide and conquer* approach is part of algorithmic thinking. Effective leaders will delegate responsibility among employees; effective computer programmers will delegate work to functions.

There are different ways to approach a problem. You may be able to solve it for a single instance, then iterate the solution. For example, consider writing a program to process paychecks for everyone in a large company. It does not really matter if there are 10 employees, or 10 million employees. Write a program to process the paycheck for one person, then repeat it again and again for all the others. Often, this means processing the first and / or last elements separately, with a loop for the ones in the middle.

We can design a program from the "top-down" (going from a global overview to a very specific one) or from the "bottom-up" (going from specific examples to a later view of the whole) depending on how you view the problem. Do you concentrate on the forest or the trees first?

2.15 FLUIDITY OF DATA

Internally, a computer stores every data value as a sequence of 0's and 1's, (**bi**nary **dig**its or *bits*). The *context* of the values means the interpretation that we give the sequence. Suppose we have the value 01000011. What does it mean? We could interpret this as the decimal number 67, since that is how 67 appears in base 2 (binary). How do we know? There are ways to convert the binary pattern, such as

$$0 \times 2^8 + 1 \times 2^7 + 0 \times 2^6 + 0 \times 2^5 + 0 \times 2^4 + 0 \times 2^3 + 0 \times 2^2 + 1 \times 2^1 + 1 \times 2^0$$
$$= 2^7 + 2^1 + 2^0$$
$$= 64 + 2 + 1 = 67.$$

Or you could make a table by writing down all possible combinations of 0's and 1's, in order. Assigning 00000000 the decimal value 0, and counting up from there, 01000011 corresponds to the value 67.

We might also consider the pattern 01000011 to be the letter "C." The American Standard Code for Information Interchange (ASCII) specifies encodings for numbers and letters (both capitals and lower-case). It also includes codes for punctuation, and most things that you find on an American keyboard. Under this standard, the letter "C" corresponds to the bit pattern 01000011.

Another way to interpret this binary pattern is as the binary-coded decimal value 43. Binary coded decimal breaks the pattern into groups of four, and each group of four stands for a number between 0 and 9. Technically, a pattern like 1010 has a decimal value of 10, but we ignore this (and anything higher) for binary coded decimal. The first four binary values, 0100, correspond to 4, while the second four binary values, 0011, correspond to 3.

Or 01000011 could be interpreted as an instruction for the CPU (called an *op-code*), in this case, it says to add 1 to the value stored in the BX register for an Intel-based CPU. Do not worry if this sounds confusing, because this discussion touches on a variety of topics. The point is that this same value can have several different interpretations, based on the context; it is interpreted according to how the computer is told to interpret it.

Notice that the binary number has 8 bits. We commonly express bits in groups of 8 (or multiples of 8). The name *byte* means 8 bits, while the name *word* (usually) means 16 bits. When talking about the computer's internal architecture, "word" has a different context. There it means the amount of bits that the computer works with. It would be inefficient for the central processing unit to work with a single bit at a time, and it would be impractical in terms of cost and size for it to operate on, maybe, 1024 bits at a time, at least by the standard of today's technology.

2.16 HEXADECIMAL AND BINARY

Besides decimal, programming often involves working with binary and hexadecimal values. Computers use binary values internally, although a single binary digit can only be one of two values. Computer designers allow for values beyond 0 and 1 by adding more digits, just as we do to represent a value greater than 9 in decimal. Thus, an unsigned integer like 5 has an internal representation of 101, in binary, as the following example shows.

```
>> disp(dec2bin(5))
101
```

As you might infer from the name, dec2bin converts a decimal value to a string of binary values. Consider the next example, where we create two variables, a and b, as unsigned integers of 8 bits (uint8). We start a with a zero value, and define b as a + 1. Then the body of a while loop adds one to each variable, and repeats as long as a does not equal b.

```
>> a = uint8(0);
>> b = a + 1;
>> while (a ~= b)
     a = a + 1;
     b = a + 1;
```

```
end
>> disp(a);
    255
>> disp(b);
    255
```

This sounds like an infinite loop, although it ends quickly. Inspecting the values, we see that both `a` and `b` become 255, the maximum possible value for the `uint8` data type. To someone unfamiliar with binary values, this does not make sense. However, looking at the value for `a` in binary, we observe that each of the 8 bits holds the value one.

```
>> disp(dec2bin(a))
11111111
```

In other words, an unsigned integer of 8 bits reaches its maximum value when all bits are ones.

What if we want to go the other way, and get a decimal value from a binary sequence?

```
>> disp(bin2dec('1111'))
    15
```

Just as `dec2bin` converts a decimal value to a binary string, we can use `bin2dec` to convert a string of binary digits to decimal. However, MATLAB now supports a new way to do this, allowing you to set value directly from binary, as the next line shows.

```
>> a = 0b0110
a =
    uint8
      6
```

In this case, it assigns `a` the value 6, which is the decimal equivalent of the binary sequence 0110. Specifying `0b` in front of the binary sequence lets MATLAB know to treat the value that way, instead of the decimal value 110.

In a similar fashion, we can use `0x` in front of a sequence of digits to indicate that we mean a hexadecimal value. Hexadecimal uses the digits 0 to 9, just like decimal, but it allows another six digits, `A` through `F`. Hexadecimal thus represents 16 possible values with a single digit. Each digit corresponds to a grouping of four bits. We use hexadecimal because it directly corresponds to binary, which the computer uses, and people find it much easier to use than binary. Next, we assign variable `b` the value `0x0f`, the hexadecimal equivalent of 15.

```
>> b = 0x0f
b =
  uint8
   15
>> b = 0x0123
b =
  uint16
   291
```

Notice that MATLAB assigns the data type fits the values. Since the second value does not fit in 8 bits, the computer uses a 16 bit unsigned integer instead. You might wonder how the hexadecimal value `0x0123` becomes the decimal value 291. Each hexadecimal digit corresponds to four bits, so the binary equivalent is `0000 0001 0010 0011`. The binary string can be written without spaces, although they help to see the groupings. To calculate the decimal equivalent, multiply each bit by 2^n from right to left, starting with $n = 0$, and add all of the results. The same idea holds for decimal numbers, such as $456 = 4 \times 10^2 + 5 \times 10^1 + 6 \times 10^0 = 400 + 50 + 6$. Thus, when we find the decimal equivalent of `0000 0001 0010 0011`, we get $1 \times 2^8 + 0 \times 2^7 + 0 \times 2^6 + 1 \times 2^5 + 0 \times 2^4 + 0 \times 2^3 + 0 \times 2^2 + 1 \times 2^1 + 1 \times 2^0$.

```
>> 1 * 2^8 ...
+ 0 * 2^7 + 0 * 2^6 + 1 * 2^5 + 0 * 2^4 ...
+ 0 * 2^3 + 0 * 2^2 + 1 * 2^1 + 1 * 2^0
ans =
   291
```

As the calculation shows, we get the same value as when we use the `0x` specification.

2.17 SUMMARY

This chapter presents the MATLAB specific commands needed to begin writing your own programs and functions. It covers variable assignment, ranges, formatting output, as well as the `plot` command and other common functions. This chapter explains MATLAB statements such as `if`, `while`, `for`, `try`, and `switch`, along with the associated keywords `else`, `elseif`, `end`, `catch`, and `case`. These statements provide the structure that allows us to define a program.

EXERCISES

1. Write a function to sort two numbers, and return them in sorted order.

2. Demonstrate `varargin`. Make a program to print "hello" followed by a name.

   The user specifies the name, as zero or more strings. Usage:

   ```
   hello_varargin2('Ms.', 'Rosie', 'the', 'Riveter');
   ```

3. Get the user input, and find statistics on it. The input should be within a loop, with some simple exit criterion (perhaps entering 0, or a complex number, or having a GUI with a "quit" button). Statistics to be performed should be simple, then progressively more complex. For example: print the sum, mean, median, and variance.

4. For the code below, what is the output? Also, what final values will all variables have? (Note: this is a variation of the project about making change for a dollar.)

   ```
   Q = 3;
   D = 3;
   N = 0;
   P = 2;
   amount = Q*25 + D*10 + N*5 + P;
   check_again = false;
   if (amount == 100)
       disp('Yes, we can make change');
   else if (amount > 100)
           disp('We might be able to make change');
           check_again = true;
       else
           disp('Cannot make change');
       end
   end
   ```

5. From *IEEE Potentials*: Suppose we have a square piece of metal, and we want to remove a small square from each corner, then fold the sides to form a pan to hold liquid. Assuming the metal has sides of 100 cm, what should x be to maximize the volume?

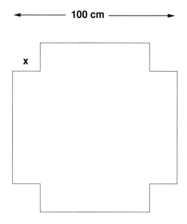

6. Write a program to display a menu of options to the user, then process each input. For example, the program could print `set value [A]`, `set value [B]`, `[S]um A and B` and `[Q]uit`. Set default values for `A` and `B`. Then display the menu, prompt the user, carry out the menu item, and repeat until the user enters "Q."

7. Give an example of each of the following types of commands.
loop (iteration)
conditional flow
error control

8. What problem(s) does the following line have?
```
if (x=3)
```

9. What problem(s) does the following line have?
```
name = input('What is your name?');
```

10. What problem(s) does the following line have?
```
for y = 10:-1:20,  x=y*2,  end
```

11. Is an infinite loop a logic error and a syntax error? Explain briefly.

12. Use a `for` loop to sum the numbers from 0 to 99. Next, find the same sum with a range. Which solution is more efficient?

13. Write a small program to get a day-of-the-month number from the user, until the number entered is acceptable. (An acceptable number in this case would be 1 or higher, but no more than 31.)

14. For the code below, what is the output? Also, what value will `correct_amount` have?

```
amount = 2.81;
target_value = 2.93; correct_amount = false;
if (amount > target_value)
    disp('Sorry, the amount is too much.');
elseif (amount < target_value)
    disp('Sorry, the amount is too little.');
else
    disp('You have the right amount!');
    correct_amount = true;
end
```

15. The MATLAB session below shows an error. Briefly state how to fix it.

```
>> myarray = 7:9;
>> myarray(7)
??? Index exceeds matrix dimensions.
```

16. What is the output from the following code? What are the final values for all variables?

```
k = 1;
maxV = 4;
for k = 1:maxV
    disp('hello');
end
```

17. The code below is an infinite loop. What is the problem? Show how it can be fixed.

```
count = 1;
maxV = 4;
while (count < maxV)
    disp('hello');
end
```

18. What is the difference between the following pair of similar-looking statements:

a = a + 1 and b = a + 1

19. What is the difference between the following pair of similar-looking statements:

a and b(a)

PROJECTS

- **Fortune Teller**

  The magic `fortune.m` program reads a question and randomly selects an answer. Modify the program to pick 5 lottery numbers, if the answer is positive (i.e., "Yes," "Possibly," "Probably so," etc.) The numbers should be in the range of 1 to 59. Do not worry about picking unique numbers, that is, the program can pick the same number multiple times.

  Additionally, expand the program to include "very unlikely" as a potential answer.

```
% fortune.m
%
% Simulate a fortune-teller with a switch statement.
%
question = input('What is your question? ','s');
% Give a random number between 0 and 5.
r = floor(6*rand(1));
disp('The answer to your question is:');
switch r
    case 0
        disp('Yes');
    case 1
        disp('No');
    case 2
        disp('Possibly');
    case 3
        disp('Probably so');
    case 4
        disp('Probably not');
    case 5:
        disp('90 percent likely');
end
```

• **A Game Show Problem**

Imagine a game-show where you are the contestant. There are several doors in front of you, and behind one there is a great prize. You can choose any door you like. After you select one, the game-show host will open one of the remaining doors that do not contain the prize. Now comes the tricky part: you have the option of changing your guess. Should you?

Your friend, a statistician, tells you your odds are better if you DO change your guess after one of the doors is eliminated.

The goal of this assignment is for you to verify the statistician's claim. You can measure this with a simulation. Write a program where the computer randomly picks one door for the prize. Then have the program randomly pick one of the doors as the initial guess. Next, have the computer pick one of the doors that is not the guess, and not the prize, to eliminate. Have the computer either switch the guess, or hold onto the original guess, depending on a parameter you provide. Count the results.

Also, keep a log of activity. Print messages to the screen, like "prize is behind door 3," "initial guess is door 2," "door 1 is eliminated," "guess is switched to door 3," and "player wins the prize."

Run this program for 3 door, 500 times, for not switching the guess. Then run it another 500 times with guess-switching enabled. What is your conclusion? Re-run the simulation for 4 doors. What is your conclusion this time?

Finally, what do you think the conclusion would be if there were 5 doors?

## CHAPTER 3

RELATIONAL OPERATORS, BOOLEAN VALUES, AND LOGICAL OPERATORS

MATLAB provides the arithmetic operators that you know well: addition, subtraction, multiplication, division, and exponentiation. These are specified with the symbols +, -, *, / and ^, respectively. The backslash character, \ also performs division, with the operands reversed. Additionally, MATLAB provides a few variations for arrays and matrices, namely .*, .\, ./ and .^. There are many other MATLAB functions for mathematical operations, although those are typically not done with symbols like these, but instead with function calls.

Here are a few examples.

```
>> disp(4 * 3)
    12
>> disp(4 ^ 3)
    64
```

First, we have multiplication and exponentiation. Next, we see division.

```
>> disp(4 / 3)
    1.3333
>> disp(4 \ 3)
    0.7500
```

Notice that the first computes $\frac{4}{3}$, while the second finds $\frac{3}{4}$. Next, we have a few examples of element-by-element operators. Variables A and B represent ranges 1:3 and 4:6, respectively. As we observe from the results, it performs the operations on each element individually.

```
>> A = 1:3;
>> B = 4:6;
>> disp(A .* B)
     4    10    18
>> disp(A ./ B)
    0.2500    0.4000    0.5000
>> disp(A .\ B)
    4.0000    2.5000    2.0000
>> disp(A .^ B)
     1    32    729
```

We must specify an element-by-element operation for variables like these, since matrix operations like multiplication and division have a different definition. Trying to find A * B results in an error, since matrix multiplication requires that the number of the first matrix's columns match the second matrix's number of rows.

3.1   RELATIONAL OPERATORS

In a conditional expression, such as with an `if` or `while` statement, we can test for the relation between two operands. These operands can be variables, function results, or hard-coded values. *Hard-coded* means that the value appears in the command itself, like the number 5 in the statement `if (a < 5)`. Of course it works; the problem comes about when updating or maintaining the code, where the programmer must ask himself what the value represents.

The relations can be equality, inequality, less than, less than or equal, greater than, or greater than or equal. Table 3.1 shows these relational operators.

Here are some examples using **MATLAB**. The three variables below do not change in these examples.

```
>> a = 4;
>> b = 78;
>> c = 5;
```

First, we will test for equality. We can add one to our a variable in the following code. Note that this does not change a's value, only the value to the left of the double equal signs. As we see, adding one to `a` produces a value that equals c's value.

Table 3.1 Relational operators.

Operator	Meaning
==	equal to
~=	not equal to
<	less than
>	greater than
<=	less than or equal to
>=	greater than or equal to

```
>> if (a+1 == c)
        disp('a+1 equals c');
    end
a+1 equals c
```

Next, we test for inequality. We have the value 78 hard-coded into this example, which is a poor programming practice. That is, we may want to change it later and would have to find every instance, and if we use the same value in a different context, this would really complicate things. Suppose we have an array that happens to have 78 elements, while elsewhere in the same program, we use 78 for a calculation involving principal and interest. (The loan industry uses an expression called "Rule of 78s".) How would we know which thing the number 78 represents? What if we have the computer do a find and replace operation on all instances of the number before we realize that it represents two different things?

As we see from the computer's response, the condition evaluates to false, and the computer executes the `else` block.

```
>> if (b ~= 78)
        disp('b does not equal 78');
    else
        disp('b must be equal to 78');
    end
b must be equal to 78
```

Here is an equivalent test, expressed in a different way. Instead of testing for inequality, we can test for equality, and negate the result.

```
>> if ~(b == 78)
        disp('b does not equal 78');
    else
        disp('b must be equal to 78');
    end
b must be equal to 78
```

The following code shows examples of other relational operators. The next example tests for the less than relation.

```
>> if (a < c)
        disp('a is less than c');
    end
a is less than c
```

The next example tests for the greater than relation.

```
>> if (a > b)
        disp('a is greater than b');
    else
        disp('a is not greater than b');
    end
a is not greater than b
```

We know from the earlier definition that c has the value five. The if statement below shows that it is at least five.

```
>> if (c >= 5)
        disp('c is at least 5');
    end
c is at least 5
```

We get a similar result if we test to see if c is greater than or equal to a smaller number.

```
>> if (c >= 1)
        disp('c is at least 1');
    end
c is at least 1
```

Finally, we have an example of the less than or equal to relation. This simply tells us if d (a character) is uppercase.

```
>> d = 'D';
>> if (d <= 'Z')
        if (d >= 'A')
            disp('variable d is upper case');
        end
    end
variable d is upper case
```

Notice how this last example used two ("nested") if statements to examine the value of variable d. Later on, we will see how these can be combined into a single if statement.

3.2 BOOLEAN VALUES

Boolean algebra is named for George Boole, a mathematician from the 1800s. It has two values: true and false. We can also express these two values as 1 and 0, or "on" and "off".

MATLAB supports Boolean values, and calls these logical values. For example, we can set variables to the results of conditions. Or we can use a Boolean variable as a condition.

As an example, consider the following code.

```
done = false;
while (~done)
    mykey = input('Press q to quit. ', 's');
    if (mykey == 'q')
        done = true;
    end
end
```

The while loop will continue until the user types "q". In the next example, we store the result of a condition into a variable, then use that variable in a conditional statement.

```
is_1_lt_2 = (1 < 2);
if (is_1_lt_2)
    disp('1 is less than 2');
end
```

When we run it, we get the output below.

```
1 is less than 2
```

We could instead print the value, as in

```
>> is_1_lt_2 = (1 < 2);
>> disp(is_1_lt_2)
      1
```

where the computer responds with 1, the logical value of "true."

3.3 LOGICAL OPERATORS: AND, OR, AND NOT

There may be times when we want to combine several conditions into one. The logical operators AND, OR, and NOT allow us to combine conditions much like we do in speech. Consider these statements: "any restaurant is fine as long as it is not fast-food," "but I want to get a burger and fries," "fine, I'll get a salad or yogurt." Actually, English usage varies slightly from the logical operator OR, which means one or the other or both. Your friend might say "salad or yogurt" order both of them, and be logically correct. When we speak as we normally do, when we say "or" we mean one thing, the other thing, but not both things. Computer logic has an equivalent of this, called the exclusive OR, or XOR for short. In MATLAB, the `xor` function performs the operation. It returns true when one or the other is true, but not both.

Table 3.2 shows the complement function, NOT. It is unary, meaning that it only takes one operand. Whatever binary value `a` has, `~a` will be the opposite value. In MATLAB, we express the NOT operation as `~a`, while more generally we will use `NOT a` or `NOT(a)`. Note that `NOT(a)` will generate an error message about being an undefined function, although the lower-case version of the command, i.e., `not(a)`, is a valid MATLAB command and will return a logical 0 or 1.

Table 3.2 The NOT operation.

a	NOT(a) ~a
0	1
1	0

Table 3.3 shows the AND function for single bits a and b. It is binary, meaning that it takes two operands. Like two phrases connected with the word "and" in English, both operands must be true for the result to be true. In MATLAB, you can use either a & b or and(a,b) to find the AND of the binary values a and b. You may also see a AND b in this text, meaning the more AND operation in a general sense, not as a MATLAB command.

Table 3.3 The AND operation.

a	b	a & b and(a,b)
0	0	0
0	1	0
1	0	0
1	1	1

Table 3.4 shows the OR function for single bits a and b. It is binary, meaning that it takes two operands. Like two phrases connected with the word "or" in English, the result is true when one of the operands is true. However, unlike how we use the word in speech, it also returns true (logic 1) when both operands are true. In a program, you can use a | b or or(a,b) to find the OR of two binary variables a and b. Although this does not work as a command in MATLAB, you might also see a OR b to describe this logical operation.

Table 3.4 The OR operation.

a	b	a | b or(a,b)
0	0	0
0	1	1
1	0	1
1	1	1

These logical functions have two implementations as conditional expressions. First, we have the "old" way, of specifying the function and or the function or, or even the function not. The "new" way uses double ampersands && or double vertical bars || for AND and OR, respectively. Earlier versions of MATLAB use the "old" way. They also support using a single ampersand, single vertical bar, or tilde: &, |, or ~. These special characters can be used in place of the functions and, or, and not, respectively.

To get started, let's revisit an earlier example.

```
>> d = 'D';
>> if (d <= 'Z')
       if (d >= 'A')
           disp('variable d is upper case');
       end
   end
variable d is upper case
```

We can combine the two `if` statements into one, using the AND operator. Here is that version.

```
>> d = 'D';
>> if (d <= 'Z') (d >= 'A')
       disp('variable d is upper case');
   end
variable d is upper case
```

A problem with this approach is that it is not verbose enough. MATLAB allows us to get away with a bit too much here; the AND operation is implied. It is better to add to this, for clarity, as the following example does. Also, since we look to see if d is in a range of values, switching the two conditions makes it appear naturally.

```
>> d = 'D';
>> if and(d >= 'A', d <= 'Z')
       disp('variable d is upper case');
   end
variable d is upper case
```

The author finds it a matter of good style to use parentheses around the condition, and anywhere else that makes the meaning explicit.

Suppose that we want to check a variable's value, and perform an operation only if it will work. We will use the function `isinteger` below, which returns true when the variable passed is an integer.

```
if (isinteger(a))
    disp(sprintf('12 / a = %5.2f',12/a));
end
```

But what if `a` is zero? To avoid a divide-by-zero warning, we can check for this.

```
if (isinteger(a) && (a ~= 0))
    disp(sprintf('12 / a = %5.2f',12/a));
end
```

We could also do this the "old" way.

```
if (and(isinteger(a), (a ~= 0)))
    disp(sprintf('12 / a = %5.2f',12/a));
end
```

The above examples only work when `a` is an integer. What if we want this to work when `a` is a double, too?

```
if ((isinteger(a) || isfloat(a)) && (a ~= 0))
    disp(sprintf('12 / a = %5.2f',12/a));
end
```

Again, we can use the "old" way of specifying this, too.

```
if (and( or(isinteger(a), isfloat(a)), (a ~= 0)))
    disp(sprintf('12 / a = %5.2f',12/a));
end
```

This is becoming cumbersome to work with, but it is just a matter of parsing the logic. Consider the code below.

```
a = int16(1);
if (and( or(isinteger(a), isdouble(a)), (a ~= 0)))
    disp(sprintf('12 / a = %5.2f',12/a));
end
```

We gave `a` a perfectly valid integer value. But the code does not work; we get an error message of `??? Undefined command/function 'isdouble'`. It's true, there is no function called `isdouble`, at least not yet. It is not needed, either, since the functions `isa` or `isfloat` can make this work.

The following shows the `isa` function.

```
>> f = 4;
>> isa(f, 'double')
ans =
    1
```

It tests the variable to see if it matches the class type. We did not explicitly define `a` as a double. And what is the difference between a float and a double, anyway? This comes down to capacity; a double uses twice as many bits to store a value as a float. The `isa` function gives the same result for our `f` variable.

```
>> isa(f, 'float')
ans =
    1
```

Here is a counter-example, showing the response when the variable and type do not match.

```
>> isa(f, 'logical')
ans =
      0
```

Going back to the example where we test the type of variable `a`, we did not really need to check to see if variable `a` is a double, since we already knew that it is an integer. Logically, it does not matter if the second argument to the `or` function evaluates to true or false when we know that the first argument is true. If it evaluates to false, then "true OR false" evaluates to true. If that second argument were true, then "true OR true" evaluates to true. Either way, the `or` function should return true. However, the code quit with an error.

Without defining variable `unknown`, the following code works.

```
hoursWorked = 45;
if ((hoursWorked > 40) || unknown)
    . . .
end
```

The computer reaches a conclusion just by looking at `(hoursWorked > 40)`, and stops evaluating the expression. In this case, two possibilities are connected by an OR operation. The first one evaluates to true, so why bother checking the second one? The result of *true OR x* will also be true, regardless of `x`.

The "new" way of specifying multiple conditions does what we call a "short-circuit" logical evaluation, where the evaluation quits as soon as it has an answer. The name comes from electronics. Electricity always takes the path of least resistance, so when a piece of metal connects two points with different charges, the electricity will travel across the metal, creating a "short-circuit." This can ruin equipment.

Suppose we specify this the "new" way.

```
a = int16(1);
if ((isinteger(a) || isdouble(a)) && (a ~= 0))
    disp(sprintf('12 / a = %5.2f',12/a));
end
```

When we run this code, the output is as follows:

```
12 / a = 12.00
```

Short-circuit evaluations help us avoid problems, especially in languages that are not as forgiving as MATLAB. Take the code below, for example.

```
a = 'my string';
if (isinteger(a) && (a+1 ~= 0))
    disp(sprintf('12 / a = %5.2f',12/(a+1)));
end
```

This does not cause a problem in MATLAB, although it could in other programming languages. Since a is a string in this example, adding one to it then comparing the result to zero does not make much sense. MATLAB just takes a as a group of values, so a+1 would just return each of the character's values, plus one.

Related functions include `bitand`, `bitor`, and `bitcmp`. They provide binary operations. For example, `bitand(5, 6)` returns 4, since the bit pattern 0101 (the binary equivalent of 5) ANDed with 0110 (the binary equivalent of 6) returns 0100 (the binary equivalent of 4). That is, taking a bit from each pattern and performing the AND operation (refer back to Table 3.3), we have 0 AND 0, 1 AND 1, 0 AND 1, and 1 AND 0 (going left to right). Table 3.5 shows this example. These logic operations can be performed left to right or right to left, unlike addition, since the result for any column only depends on the values in that column.

The `bitor` command works in a similar fashion, using OR operations instead of ANDs. Table 3.4 lists the possibilities for the two OR operands, so to find the bitwise result, take the two binary values in each column, locate the line on Table 3.4 with those two on the left, and write down the value at the end of the row (the a | b column). Table 3.6 shows this example with the example binary patterns 0101 with 0110, where we find 0111 as the answer.

The bitcmp command performs a complement of each bit, where the zeros become ones, and the ones become zeros. For example, bitcmp(5, 'uint8') complements each bit of the pattern 0101 (decimal 5), and returns a result for 8 bits (the second parameter). The result in this case would be the bit pattern 11111010. Table 3.7 shows an example of the bitwise complement.

We can demonstrate the previous examples with MATLAB code. Functions dec2bin and bin2dec convert a decimal value to a string of binary 1's and 0's, and a string of binary values to decimal, respectively. An example follows.

```
>> dec2bin(5)
ans =
101
>> bin2dec('0101')
ans =
     5
```

To find the AND of 0101 with 0110, we can do the following.

```
>> op1 = bin2dec('0101');
>> op2 = bin2dec('0110');
>> result = bitand(op1, op2);
>> dec2bin(result)
ans =
100
```

We see that the result is 100, or 0100 if we pad the left with a zero to keep the width consistent. Appending zeros to the left does not change the value, just as the decimal number 0123 represents the same value as 123.

We can also get the results for bitor, as follows:

```
>> result = bitor(op1, op2);
>> dec2bin(result)
ans =
111
```

Again, we can pad the left with zeros to make the width of the answer match the width of the operands. As expected, the result matches that of Table 3.6.

In the following example, we find the bitcmp of 0101, and pass a parameter of uint8 so that the results will be given in the form of an 8 bit, unsigned integer, which limits the resulting string to 8 characters.

```
>> result = bitcmp(op1, 'uint8');
>> dec2bin(result)
ans =
11111010
```

You should verify that the `bitcmp` result is correct, keeping in mind that an output of 8 binary digits implies that the input also has the same width.

As an exercise, what would happen if we change the commands by removing the `bit` letters, such as `result = and(op1, op2);`, and why?

Table 3.5 An example of a bitwise AND operation (`bitand`).

	0	1	0	1
AND	0	1	1	0
	0	1	0	0

Table 3.6 An example of a bitwise OR operation (`bitor`).

	0	1	0	1
OR	0	1	1	0
	0	1	1	1

Table 3.7 An example of a bitwise NOT operation (`bitcmp`).

NOT	0	1	0	1
	1	0	1	0

3.4   OPERATOR PRECEDENCE

Given an assignment statement involving several arithmetic operations, in what order will they occur? Obviously, 5 – 5 * 4 gives a different answer depending on whether the subtraction occurs before or after the multiplication. In MATLAB, multiplication has a higher precedence, meaning that it will be done first. So the answer will be –15. What if we want the subtraction to be carried out first? We can use parentheses to override the precedence, i.e., (5 – 5) * 4, which results in 0.

Raising to a power (exponentiation, the "^" operator) has the highest precedence, followed by multiplication "*" and division "/" sharing the next level of precedence, then the last level of arithmetic operations has addition "+" and subtraction "-". If you are not sure, or if you want to make the code explicit, you can always use parentheses. Logic operations also have precedence, with negation "~" having the highest precedence, followed by AND "&", also "&&", followed by OR "|", also "||". We can verify the order of logical operations with the following examples. Parentheses allow us to specify the order to evaluate the expression, if we do not want to use the default precedence. The precedence of operations are given in Table 3.8. When two operations have the same precedence, the computer performs them as they appear left to right.

Table 3.8 The precedence of operations, from highest to lowest.

parentheses	highest
exponentiation, inversion (NOT)	
multiplication, division	
addition, subtraction	
AND, OR	lowest

As an exercise, what is the result of the following expression according to MATLAB?

```
5*3-16/8+11
```

To check the answer, you can always type it into the MATLAB command window.

First, we see that parentheses change the order of operations.

```
>> disp(false & false | true)
    1
>> disp(false & (false | true))
    0
```

In the first instance, finding `false & false` results in `false`, then that result `| true` returns true. The second command finds `false | true` first, resulting in true, then it evaluates `false &` that result, giving an answer of false.

What will be the result of the following expression?

```
1 & 1 | 0
```

You should see that it results in 1. What if we use parentheses?

```
(1 & 1) | 0
1 & (1 | 0)
```

In these cases, changing the order of operations does not affect the result, since they both generate 1.

What if we mix operators? In practice, this is usually not a good idea. MATLAB allows it, however, and there can be cases where this provides a shortcut. Here are a few examples, combining different operators. We can AND the result of a subtraction.

```
>> 1 & (1 - 1)
ans =
     0
```

Next, we multiply the result of an OR operation with a number. Since the logical operation results in a true value, it acts as the number 1 for the multiplication.

```
>> (1 | 0 ) * 3
ans =
     3
```

Next, we OR two integers together. If this were a bitwise OR operation, it would find the OR of 011 with 101, which would result in 111, or the decimal value 7. Here, 3 | 5 are both considered true, in the sense that they are not false (0).

```
>> 3 | 5
ans =
     1
```

The following example finds that 5 > 3 results in true (1), then multiplies it by 100. As expected, this results in 100.

```
>> (5 > 3) * 100
ans =
   100
```

A similar example shows that 5 <= 3, which results in false (0), makes the multiplication result in 0, also.

```
>> (5 <= 3) * 100
ans =
     0
```

Next, we have an example where mixing operations makes a task short. Suppose that we have a set of test scores, and we want to find the average. First, we define the test scores, although realistically, we would read these from a spreadsheet with a command like `csvread`. Then we compute the sum, and divide by the length, as follows:

```
>> tests = [78, 0, 98, 93, 81];
>> sum(tests)/length(tests)
ans =
    70
```

An important step when making a program is to check the results. We see that the average score is 70, but this does not make sense: the lowest score is higher than that. Often, mismatches between what we get and what we expect come from an invalid assumption. Examining the scores, we see that student #2 does not have a valid test result. Perhaps that student dropped the class, had an excused absence, or simply did not show up on test day. Assuming that the student did not take the exam, 70 does not accurately describe the average. How can we revise the calculation to exclude any 0 scores? We can use the greater than relational operator, as follows:

```
>> tests > 0
ans =
    1    0    1    1    1
>> sum(tests > 0)
ans =
    4
```

We see that the greater than operator gives us a list of 1's for every score that is above 0. Summing them gives us the number of non-zero scores.

```
>> sum(tests)/sum(tests > 0)
ans =
    87.5000
```

We have a solution that finds the averages of all the non-zero test scores, and it matches our expectation of a score above 78 and less than 98. By the way, another approach is to create a set of scores that does not include any zero scores. The following code creates such an array.

```
>> nonzero_tests = tests(tests > 0)
nonzero_tests =
     78    98    93    81
```

The part that reads `tests > 0` generates an array of 1's and 0's. MATLAB will not treat that logical array as indices, but instead use it as a list of "yes" and "no" values to make a new array.

3.4.1 Establishing Precedence

How do we know that the AND operation has a higher precedence than the OR? Consider the following set of nested `for` loops, which mean that the `disp` command will receive all possible combinations of 0's and 1's for a, b, and c.

```
for a=0:1
    for b=0:1
        for c=0:1
            disp(sprintf('%d & %d | %d = %d', ...
                a, b, c, (a & b | c)));
        end
    end
end
```

The output appears next. With three binary variables, we have 2^3 or 8 possibilities. Most are not particularly interesting, in that they do not reveal anything about which operation happens first (i.e., the precedence). For lines 1, and 3 through 8, it does not matter if the AND or OR happens first, since either way we get the same answer. The second line, however shows an interesting case, `0 & 0 | 1`. If the computer performs the AND first, `0 & 0` results in `0`, then `0 | 1` results in `1`. If the computer instead performs the OR first, then `0 | 1` evaluates to `1`, and the next operation would find `0 & 1`, which equals `0`. Clearly, the computer finds the AND operation first.

```
0   &   0   |   0   =   0
0   &   0   |   1   =   1
0   &   1   |   0   =   0
0   &   1   |   1   =   1
1   &   0   |   0   =   0
```

```
1   &   0   |   1   =   1
1   &   1   |   0   =   1
1   &   1   |   1   =   1
```

Specifically, in line 2 of the output, the logic evaluates to 1. By itself, 0 | 1 results in 1, and 0 & 1 would result in 0. Thus, 0 & (0 | 1) results in 0, different from the answer on line 2. As we can see from the results, AND is done first, then the OR.

Thus, this establishes that, in an expression like a & b | c, the computer finds a & b first. Then again, the AND operation appears as the first logic operation as we scan the lines from left to right. The computer does evaluate lines like this from left to right, so a convincing case of AND having precedence over OR must show an exception. We repeat the nested for loops, with a slightly different order of logic functions.

```
for a=0:1
    for b=0:1
        for c=0:1
            disp(sprintf('%d | %d & %d = %d', ...
                a, b, c, (a | b & c)));
        end
    end
end
```

The output from the program appears below.

```
0   |   0   &   0   =   0
0   |   0   &   1   =   0
0   |   1   &   0   =   0
0   |   1   &   1   =   1
1   |   0   &   0   =   1
1   |   0   &   1   =   1
1   |   1   &   0   =   1
1   |   1   &   1   =   1
```

Notice how the second to last line reads 1 | 1 & 0 = 1. This only makes sense if AND (&) is done before OR (|). Therefore, in an expression like a | b & c, the computer finds b & c first. With these two tests, we can conclude that the AND operation has a higher precedence than the OR operation.

There will be times when you are not sure what to expect from the computer. When in doubt, test it. Eliminate as many unnecessary details (or program lines) as you can, yet include as many variations as needed to make a convincing case. The previous examples contain simplified expressions, ones with minimized content, yet the tests include all combinations of 0's and 1's. Of course, as the number of binary variables grow by one, the number of possibilities double. Thus, the tests aim to be as simple and complete at the same time, striking a balance between these two conflicting goals.

3.4.2 How One and Two Ampersands Differ

As mentioned previously, MATLAB employs short-circuit evaluation. It ignores the rest of a condition when it senses that it has all the information needed to make a decision. If you were to read directions that say "if it is raining and, ..." you might realize that it is not raining, and skip the rest of that statement. This illustrates short-circuit evaluation. In MATLAB, the double-ampersands are used to find a logical AND operation, with short-circuit evaluation. Consider the following code. Notice that it defines `condition1`, but it does not define `condition2`.

```
condition1 = false;
if (condition1 && condition2)
    disp('one and two are true');
else
    disp('one and two are not both true');
end
if (condition1 & condition2)
    disp('one and two are true');
else
    disp('one and two are not both true');
end
```

How do the operations `&` and `&&` differ?

```
>> a = [1,1,1,0];
>> b = [0,1,1,1];
>> a & b
ans =
     0     1     1     0
>> a && b
??? Operands to the || and && operators must be
convertible to logical scalar values.
```

We see that a & b is evaluated element-by-element, so the operands can be arrays of values. Meanwhile, a && b produces a scalar result, and require scalar operands. In other words, a && b would work if a and b were binary values, but not when they are arrays. Since the double-ampersands are used in logic expressions for conditional statements, generating an array of results does not make sense. Imagine trying to follow directions from someone who says "if the condition is true, do this." "OK," you might reply, "what is the condition?" With an answer like "the condition is an array of true and false values," what would you do? It makes sense to expect a single true or false value for the condition.

Incidentally, you can use an array as the condition in MATLAB, although the results might not turn out like you expect.

```
>> if [0,1]
      disp('yes');
else
      disp('no');
end
no
>> if [1,0]
      disp('yes');
else
      disp('no');
end
no
>> if [1,1]
      disp('yes');
else
      disp('no');
end
yes
```

In the previous lines, we used an array of [0,1] as a condition, which evaluates to false. Changing the array to [1,0] as the condition did not change the result. However, making the condition an array of all 1's did evaluate as true. Try it with the arrays [1,1,1,1,1,1,1,1] and [1,1,1,1,1,1,0,1] it appears to interpret an array of all 1's as true, and an array with one or more 0's as false. However, just because you can do something does not mean that you should. Using an array as a condition makes for an interesting side note, although it also makes the code hard to understand.

3.5 SUMMARY

This chapter covers operators, including arithmetic, relational, and logical. It also discusses the order of precedence.

Tables 3.9 and 3.10 show common symbols used in MATLAB. Table 3.11 contains predefined variables. Common keywords are listed in Table 3.12.

Table 3.9 Symbols.

Symbol	Meaning	Example	Result
...	continued	3 + ... 4	7
%	comment	% Usage:	ignored
%	used in `sprintf` for format	sprintf('A%d',5)	A5
%{	begin multi-line comment	%{	ignored
%}	end multi-line comment	%}	ignored
%%	comment, marks the start of a code cell	%%	recognized by editor
,	element separator	[3, -5]	3 -5
;	semi-colon	a=3;	suppresses output
;	row separator	[3; -5]	3 -5
:	colon (range)	5:2:9	5 7 9

Table 3.10 More symbols.

Symbol	Meaning	Example	Result
=	assignment	a = 9	a = 9
==	test for equality	9 == 8	0
~=	test for inequality	9 ~= 8	1
<	test for less than	9 < 8	0
<=	test for less than	9 <= 8	0

(continued)

Symbol	Meaning	Example	Result
>	test for greater than	9 > 8	1
>=	test for greater than	9 >= 8	1
&	bit-wise AND	[0,0,1,1] & [0,1,0,1]	0 0 0 1
|	bit-wise OR	[0,0,1,1] | [0,1,0,1]	0 1 1 1
~	bit-wise NOT	~[0,1]	1 0
&&	logical AND	(3 < 4) && (4 < 5)	1
||	logical OR	(3 < 4) || (4 < 3)	1
~	logical NOT	~(3 < 4)	0
()	parenthesis	4 * (0 + 2)	8
()	used with function calls	cos(pi)	-1
[]	array / matrix	a = [3, 4, 5]	a = 3 4 5
{}	cell array / matrix	a = {'red', 12}	a = 'red' [12]
+	addition	3+4	7
-	subtraction	3-4	-1
*	multiplication	3*4	12
/	division	3/4	0.7500
^	exponentiation	3^4	81
.*	element multiplication	[3,2].*[4,5]	12 10
./	element division	[3,2]./[4,5]	0.7500 0.4000
.^	element exponentiation	[3,2].^[4,5]	81 32
'	string delimiter	'string'	string
'	transpose conjugate	a = [3i, -5i]; a'	0.0000 - 3.0000i 0.0000 + 5.0000i
.'	transpose	a = [3i, -5i]; a.'	0.0000 + 3.0000i 0.0000 - 5.0000i

Table 3.11 Predefined variables.

Symbol	Meaning	Example	Result
i	predefined variable	2i	0.0000 + 2.0000i
1i	alternate version of i	2 + 1i i = 2; i + 1i	2.0000 + 1.0000i 2.0000 + 1.0000i
j	predefined variable	2j	0.0000 + 2.0000i
1j	alternate version of j	2 + 1j j = 3; j + 1j	2.0000 + 1.0000i 3.0000 + 1.0000i
pi	predefined variable	pi	3.1416
varargin	predefined variable	function myfn(varargin)	function takes arguments as cell array
nargin	predefined variable	if (nargin < 2) ...	number of variable arguments
varargout	variable with special meaning	varargout(1) = {1.2};	returns cell array from a function
nargout	predefined variable	if (nargout < 2) ...	number of outputs expected

Table 3.12 Keywords.

Keyword	Meaning	Example	See also
function	begins a function definition	function x = myfn(y)	
case	potential match for a switch	case 4	switch
otherwise	catch-all for a switch	otherwise	switch, case
switch	begins a multi-line conditional	switch	case
if	begins a conditional	if (a<3)	else, elseif, end

(continued)

Keyword	Meaning	Example	See also
`break`	quits loop	`break`	
`continue`	continues a loop	`continue`	
`return`	quits a function / script	`return`	
`try`	begins a block that may fail	`try`	`catch`
`catch`	begins a block to handle failure	`catch`	`try`
`exit`	quits MATLAB	`exit`	
`else`	continues a conditional	`else`	
`elseif`	continues a conditional	`elseif`	
`end`	ends a loop/ block	`end`	
`for`	begins a loop	`for k=1:5`	
`while`	begins a loop	`while (k<5)`	

Table 3.13 A short list of common commands.

Command	Meaning	Example	See also
`disp`	display	`disp('hello')`	`sprintf`
`fprintf`	file print function	`fprintf('%5.3f', pi)`	`disp`
`length`	length of array / matrix	`length(A)`	`size`
`pause`	pauses for a set time, or until user presses a key	`pause`	`plot`
`plot`	plot data	`plot(t, x, 'r')`	`stem`

(continued)

Command	Meaning	Example	See also
`size`	dimensions of array / matrix	`size(A)`	`length`
`sprintf`	string print function	`sprintf('%5.3f', pi)`	`disp`
`stem`	stem plot of data	`stem(t, x, 'r')`	`plot`

Table 3.14 A short list of common commands for the operating system, that MATLAB also understands.

Command	Meaning	Example	See also
`ls`	list files	`ls`	`dir`
`ls -l`	long list files (more information)	`ls -l`	`dir`
`dir`	directory (list files)	`dir`	`ls`
`cd`	change directory	`cd ..`	`pwd`
`pwd`	print working directory	`pwd`	`cd`

EXERCISES

1. What affect does the semi-colon (;) have when it appears at the end of a MATLAB command?

2. Suppose that we have 90 m of fencing to build a plant enclosure. How long should each rectangular side be to maximize the area?

3. What does `m(:,n).' .* b` do? What assumptions about the size of the variables `m` and `b` do you have?

4. What value(s) will be displayed?

```
A = [1, -3, 0, 2];
B = [0, 5, 0, 1];
disp(A >= B)
```

5. The MATLAB session below shows an error. Briefly state how to fix it.

```
>> x = ((12-15)/(4+(2-1))
??? x = ((12-15)/(4+(2-1))
    |
Error: Expression or statement is incorrect--
possibly unbalanced (, {, or [.
```

6. Suppose that a friend of yours enters the following line in MATAB.

```
a = 2 + 3 * 7 - 5 / 3
```

The computer responds with the value 21.3333, however, the person says he expects the result to be 10. How would you fix this?

7. The code below *always* prints "entry must be one or two," no matter what value `userEntry` has. Why? Explain step-by-step.

```
if ((userEntry ~= 1) || (userEntry ~= 2))
    disp('entry must be one or two');
end
```

8. Give an example of each of the following types of commands.
   assignment
   arithmetic
   calling a function
   logic operation

9. What is the difference between the following pairs of similar-looking statements: `a * b` and `a .* b`

10. What is the difference between the following pair of similar-looking statements: `a = b` and `a == b`

11. What problem(s) does the following line have?

```
mytime = * mytime;
```

12. What problem(s) does the following line have?

```
x = ((18-3)*(5+2.1);
```

PROJECT

- **Text Similarity Score**

  Spammers attempt to get around e-mail software filtering rules by using similarlooking characters in place of the original ones. For example, the Rolex company makes highly-valued watches, so a spammer selling counterfeit watches might use their name. An e-mail with the name in plain text could easily be filtered out, but what if the lower-case letter "L" is replaced with the digit "1"; would you spot the difference? Convert the string "Rolex" to an array of integers, `int('Rolex')`, then process these integer values with rules, such as adding spaces in between, or replacing characters with look-alikes ("r0||e><"). Ultimately, print a similarity score. Make an approximate comparison function, where similar-looking words map to a similar score, but dissimilar words do not.

## CHAPTER 4

ARRAYS AND MATRICES

We call a single number a scalar value, and a list of values an array (or vector). When the list of values has rows and columns, we call it a matrix. Matrices can be multidimensional, too. Think of this like an abstraction, where a scalar value is a special case of an array: it is a list with only one element. Likewise, an array is a matrix with only one row (or only one column). Arrays and matrices can contain other data types instead of numbers, although most of the discussion will focus on arrays or matrices with numeric values. As we will see shortly, working with a matrix can be as easy as working with scalar values.

4.1 WORKING WITH ARRAYS

To set a variable to an array, we use the assignment operator, just like we did before with scalar values. We use square brackets to specify the group of values in the array. The example below puts a group of test scores in a variable called testScores.

```
>> testScores = [71, 83, 71, 78, 74, 60, 80, ...
                 76, 80, 82, 71, 76, 68]
testScores =
  Columns 1 through 10
    71    83    71    78    74    60    80    76    80    82
  Columns 11 through 13
    71    76    68
```

Notice that when we refer to testScores now, we get not one value, but 13 of them.

Whenever we have test score information, we usually want to know a few things about it. What was the average? To find this, we need to know a bit about common array functions sum, length, and mean.

4.1.1 Some Array Functions: Finding the Average

The length function returns the number of elements in an array.

```
>> length(testScores)
ans =
    13
```

As we see, there were 13 values in the above array. Next, we can add all the elements together with the sum function.

```
>> sum(testScores)
ans =
    970
```

So, one way to calculate the average is to divide the sum by the number of elements.

```
>> sum(testScores)/length(testScores)
ans =
    74.6154
```

We see that the average for our test scores is 74.6. You might be surprised to find that MATLAB does not provide a function named "average" or "avg." We could always make our own, if we want, but MATLAB does provide an averaging function. We can find the average directly, using the mean function.

```
>> mean(testScores)
ans =
    74.6154
```

4.1.2 More Array Functions: Min, Max, and Median

Common questions include, "what is the minimum?" The min function provides the answer. As you might expect, a similar max function provides the maximum value of the array.

```
>> min(testScores)
ans =
    60
>> max(testScores)
ans =
    83
```

A related statistic to the mean is the median, the value in the middle. Since we know that we have an odd number of values, we find the median as the middle value. If there were an even number of elements, we would need to average the two values in the middle.

Before we can talk about finding the middle value, we need to talk about how we can access the elements of an array individually. Suppose that we want to get the very first value of the array, the value stored at position 1. Instead of just typing the variable's name, we specify the position in parentheses after the variable's name, much like we specify a parameter to a function. We call this position number the *index*, or *indices* if plural.

```
>> testScores(1)
ans =
    71
```

Note that while many languages use square brackets to index an array, MATLAB uses parentheses. As we see by reviewing the numbers we assigned to the array above, we have successfully selected the first value.

Arrays (and matrices) always start with position (index) 1 in MATLAB. This may cause dismay among computer scientists, since other languages allow you to index an array using an index of 0. This may sound strange, but once you become accustomed to indexing from zero, it comes naturally. Of course, we can always just add 1 to our index, in case it is 0. For example, we can address our array in the following manner.

```
>> a = 4;
>> testScores(a+1)
ans =
    74
```

Here's a neat trick. Suppose we want the very last value of the array. We know we can find the number of elements with the `length` function. We can use the results of that function as our index.

```
>> testScores(length(testScores))
ans =
     68
```

In a similar fashion, we can use the keyword `end` to specify this final index value.

```
>> testScores(end)
ans =
     68
```

Now that we have seen how to index our array, we will return to finding the median. Let's start by finding the array position of the number in the middle. The median is the middle value when there are an odd number of values, or the average of the two middle values when there are an even number. Since `length(testScores)` gives us the number of elements in the array, we just need to divide it by 2 to find the middle value's index.

```
>> length(testScores) /2
ans =
     6.5000
```

But there is a problem here; to find the value of an array's element, we must index the array with an integer (whole number). If we try to index an array with a number like this, MATLAB will return the error `??? Subscript indices must either be real positive integers or logicals`. To get around this problem, we use the `round` function.

```
>> round(length(testScores) /2)
ans =
     7
```

So we can find the value of the number in the middle by using the above statement as an index.

```
>> testScores(round(length(testScores) /2))
ans =
     80
```

Of course, we cannot simply grab the value in the middle of the array to find the median. If you look carefully at the original array, you will see that 80 is not the median value that we want. We have to sort the array values first! MATLAB provides such a function, called `sort`. Below, we will sort the test scores, and store the result in a new array called `sortedTests`.

```
>> sortedTests = sort(testScores)
sortedTests =
  Columns 1 through 10
    60    68    71    71    71    74    76    76    78    80
  Columns 11 through 13
    80    82    83
```

Now if we find the middle value, we can use it to index our sorted array.

```
>> middle_index = round(length(sortedTests) /2);
>> sortedTests(middle_index)
ans =
    76
```

As we see, the above code returns the value 76, the one in the middle. To verify this, point to the first value with your left hand and the last value with your right. Then move each hand closer together, one position at a time, until they meet in the middle.

Note that the code above only finds the median when there are an odd number of elements in the array. If there are an even number of values, we need to average the two middle values. It is left to the reader to figure out how to do this as an exercise. As with most problems, it is easier to see what to do by considering a simpler version of the problem. For example, think of finding the median of an array of two values. Then imagine how you would find the median of an array of four values. Then it should be clear how to generalize your answer to any number of even values.

Now that we have seen how we can find the median ourselves, we will do it the easy way. As you might expect, MATLAB provides a median function.

```
>> median(testScores)
ans =
    76
```

By the way, notice that we do not have to sort the array before calling median.

4.1.3 Arrays as Either a Row or a Column

An array may be a single row with multiple columns, or a single column with multiple rows. We can *transpose* an array (or a matrix) to change it from one to the other.

A related function to `length` is `size`, as seen below. It returns the dimensions of an array or matrix.

```
>> size(testScores)
ans =
     1    13
```

The `size` function indicates that we have 1 row and 13 columns.

Next, we use the `transpose` function to change our array from a single row to a single column.

```
>> transpose(testScores)
ans =
    71
    83
    71
    78
    74
    60
    80
    76
    80
    82
    71
    76
    68
```

If we pass the transpose to the `size` function, we see that the results are a bit different from before.

```
>> size(transpose(testScores))
ans =
    13     1
```

Now the `size` function tells us that the array has 13 rows and 1 column.

We can also use the short-hand notation of a period followed by a single quote to indicate the transpose, i.e., `testScores.'` as we see below.

```
>> testScores.'
ans =
    71
    83
```

```
71
78
74
60
80
76
80
82
71
76
68
```

Using a single quote without a preceding period, i.e., `testScores'` gives us the same results, as long as the numbers do not contain a complex part. Section 4.5 discusses this in more detail.

4.2 ADDING AND DELETING FROM ARRAYS

MATLAB allows us to specify arrays within other arrays. In the example below, we first make an array called `myarray`, which has elements

4, 5, 6.

Then, we include `myarray` as an element in a new array called `barray`.

```
>> myarray = [4, 5, 6];
>> barray = [1, 2, 3, myarray]
barray =
     1     2     3     4     5     6
```

As we see, `myarray`'s elements are included as the elements of `barray`. We could insert these values in the middle of an array, too.

```
>> [8, 9, myarray, 10, 3]
ans =
     8     9     4     5     6    10     3
```

As expected, the elements of `myarray` were included in the middle of the newly created array. Note that the elements of `myarray` are *copied* into these other arrays, meaning that we could change `myarray` later without affecting `barray`.

How do we delete an element from an array? One way to delete an array element is to set it to the *null matrix*, also called an *empty matrix*, denoted by [], an open and close square bracket.

```
>> myarray = [4, 5, 6];
>> myarray(2) = []
myarray =
      4       6
```

This example got rid of the element from column 2. Of course, this now means that myarray only has two elements. If we repeat the command, it will get rid of the element that now occupies column 2, as the following demonstrates.

```
>> myarray(2) = []
myarray =
      4
```

We can also delete from a matrix in a similar fashion, although it will remove an entire row or column. Now suppose that we set the entire array to the null matrix.

```
>> myarray = []
myarray =
      []
```

Interestingly, the variable still has a definition, as the whos command reveals.

```
>> whos myarray
   Name        Size      Bytes    Class     Attributes
   myarray     0x0           0    double
```

This means that setting a variable to the null matrix does not do the same thing as deleting it with the clear command.

An alternative to specifying the null matrix is to reassign the variable to the values that you desire to keep.

```
>> myarray = [4, 5, 6];
>> myarray = [myarray(1), myarray(3)]
myarray =
      4       6
```

We see that it gives the same result. Obviously, it would be a chore to have to individually specify each value that an array or matrix should keep. With ranges, discussed later in this chapter, we will see ways to easily specify a sub-array (or sub-matrix).

4.3   MATRICES

As the `size` function implies, an array is simply a one-dimensional matrix. Easy matrix manipulations are at the heart of MATLAB's success. We saw how data can be very fluid with MATLAB; we can assign a value or a group of values to a variable, then later re-assign something completely different to that variable.

We create matrices in a similar fashion as we create arrays. To separate rows, we use the semi-colon. (We can still use the semi-colon at the end of the line to suppress output, if we want.) Below, we create a simple matrix.

```
>> mymatrix = [ 1, 2, 3; 4, 6, 7]
mymatrix =
      1     2     3
      4     6     7
```

Let's find the length of this matrix.

```
>> length(mymatrix)
ans =
      3
```

We see that the length function returns 3, the number of columns that this matrix has, instead of the total number of elements. If we want the total number of elements, we can use the `numel` function.

```
>> numel(mymatrix)
ans =
      6
```

But suppose that we want to find the dimensions. We use the `size` function, as we did with arrays.

```
>> size(mymatrix)
ans =
      2     3
```

It tells us that we have 2 rows and 3 columns. We might want to use this information later. One possibility is to assign the result of `size` to a variable.

```
>> a = size(mymatrix)
a =
      2     3
```

Then we can access the array to get the number of rows and number of columns.

```
>> disp(a(1))
        2
>> disp(a(2))
        3
```

Another way to store the information returned by the `size` command uses two variables. Square brackets on the left side of the assignment statement specify what to do with the outputs. In the case below, we put the first output in `maxrow` and the second one in `maxcol`.

```
>> [maxrow, maxcol] = size(mymatrix);
>> disp(maxrow)
        2
>> disp(maxcol)
        3
```

The example above shows that the number of rows of `mymatrix` is stored in `maxrow` while the number of columns is stored in `maxcol`. We can access the value at this last position, much like we accessed values in an array. For a matrix, we specify the row and column in parenthesis. We separate the indices for row and column with a comma.

```
>> mymatrix(maxcol, maxrow)
??? Index exceeds matrix dimensions.
```

Well, we have to be careful to specify *rows first*, then columns. Also, we should be sure that our indices are within the bounds. There is no element at `mymatrix(3, 2)`; a row value of 3 exceeds the maximum row.

```
>> mymatrix(maxrow, maxcol)
ans =
        7
```

Above, we successfully find the element at `mymatrix(2, 3)`.

4.4   A FEW MATRIX CREATION FUNCTIONS

Sometimes a program needs to create a matrix, and MATLAB provides a few functions to do this quickly. Functions `zeros`, `ones`, and `eye` do what they sound like they do: create a matrix of all zero values, all one values, or the identity matrix, called `I` in mathematics. The following line demonstrates how to create a 3×3 matrix.

```
>> I = eye(3)
I =
     1     0     0
     0     1     0
     0     0     1
```

Variable `I` stores the resulting matrix, although of course it could be called something else beside `I`. Why do we call it the "identity" matrix? The following example shows why. First, we define a matrix `A` to be the numbers 1 through 9, split up into 3 rows.

```
>> A = [1, 2, 3; 4, 5, 6; 7, 8, 9];
>> A * I
ans =
     1     2     3
     4     5     6
     7     8     9
```

The result after multiplying by `I` equals the same matrix as the original. Thus, the name `I` represents the identity matrix.

The next two commands create 2×3 matrices, where the first has all zero values, and the second has all one values.

```
>> zeros(2, 3)
ans =
     0     0     0
     0     0     0
>> ones(2, 3)
ans =
     1     1     1
     1     1     1
```

These two functions allow us to quickly create matrices with as many rows, columns, and planes, as we desire. Multiplying the `ones` matrix with a constant gives us a matrix containing that value for each element. These functions define the data type when passing an argument like `'uint8'`, which comes up when working with images (see Chapter 8, *Images*). Creating a matrix in this way allocates the memory all at once. The following example creates a simple image.

```
x = zeros(500, 500, 3, 'uint8');
x(1:250, :, 1) = 255;
x(:, 1:250, 2) = 255;
imshow(x)
```

The first line makes a matrix, x, with $500 \times 500 \times 3$ elements, where each one holds an 8-bit, unsigned integer value, initially zero. Each plane represents a color: red, green, and blue. The second line sets the first half of the rows, and all columns, of the red plane to 255, the highest possible uint8 value. Each image pixel is a mixture of colors, and this is like turning the red value all the way up. Similarly, the third line sets all of the rows, and the first half of the columns, of the green plane to 255. The imshow command shows the matrix as an image, which appears as a yellow square in the upper left, a red square in the upper right, a green square in the bottom left, and a black square in the bottom right.

4.4.1 Repeating a "Tile"

Function repmat repeats a "tiling" to create a matrix. The terminology should be intuitive with the following example. We set up a 2×2 matrix called M, then pass it to repmat, to make 2×2 copies of it.

```
>> M = [11, 12; 13, 14];
>> repmat(M, 2, 2)
ans =
      11     12     11     12
      13     14     13     14
      11     12     11     12
      13     14     13     14
```

As you can see, if we think of M as a tile, like the backsplash above a sink, this function places 2 copies of it horizontally, and 2 copies vertically. Another way to use repmat copies a scalar value, along with its data type.

```
>> threes = repmat(double(3), 4, 5)
threes =
       3      3      3      3      3
       3      3      3      3      3
```

```
     3     3     3     3     3
     3     3     3     3     3
>> whos threes
  Name        Size      Bytes  Class      Attributes
  threes      4x5         160  double
```

Here, we see that it returned a 4 × 5 matrix, each with the value 3. Getting more information about the returned matrix shows that it does have the `double` data type.

Another command that redefines matrices is `reshape`. Suppose that we have a 2 × 8 matrix, and want to convert it to a 4 × 4 matrix. The `reshape` command does this, taking the values from the input matrix, going down the columns.

```
>> A = [6, 7, 8, 9, 10, 11, 12, 13;
    14, 15, 16, 17, 18, 19, 20, 21];
>> B = reshape(A, 4, 4)
B =
     6     8    10    12
    14    16    18    20
     7     9    11    13
    15    17    19    21
```

In this example, we see that the first column of B comes from the first column of A, followed by the second column of A. Other columns of B also come from two columns of A. Note that `reshape` needs the number of elements in the input matrix to equal the number of elements in the output matrix, specified by the two other arguments.

4.4.2 Building a Matrix and Memory Management

MATLAB allows us a lot of flexibility when making arrays and matrices, and we can even build an array one value at a time. Consider the following example.

```
tic
for k=1:1000000
    myarray(k) = k;
end
toc
```

Command `tic` sets up a timer, like pressing the button of a stop-watch to get it started. Then the `toc` command stops the timer, again like on a stop-watch. While `tic` does not output anything, `toc` tells us how much time elapsed since the `tic` command. Running this on an iMac from 2015, it reports:

```
Elapsed time is 0.071264 seconds.
```

Now consider this example that uses `zeros` to allocate the memory.

```
tic
myarray2 = zeros(1, 1000000);
for k=1:1000000
    myarray2(k) = k;
end
toc
```

Running on the same machine, with the same background processes, gives this answer:

```
Elapsed time is 0.023058 seconds.
```

This example also creates a large array of increasing values, although it runs faster than the preceding example, in about one-third of the time. It should be noted that the reported times have more precision than accuracy, in that the reported digits go beyond what we should believe. A second run of the example code with the `zeros` command produces the following result:

```
Elapsed time is 0.019185 seconds.
```

Memory management explains why we get the speedup. The operating system keeps track of the available memory, and assigns it to the programs as needed. With the first example, `myarray` grows. MATLAB requests some memory for it, and later needs to request more. Each request means that the operating system must find a large enough spot in memory, and likely moves the contents from the old place to the new place. This extra overhead takes time. As an analogy, suppose that you write down a list of items as they are spoken. With a notebook in hand, you flip to a blank space and begin writing in the available space, even if the page already has some writing on it. At some point, you might run out of space, so you find a larger one and copy the previous items to it, and continue to write. If you had known in advance how much space you would need, you could have saved some time and effort. Using the `zeros` function (or `ones`, `eye`, etc.) means that the operating system allocates the memory for `myarray2` only once. In effect, you are telling it how much space it will need.

4.5 SCALAR ADDITION AND MATRIX TRANSPOSE

We can perform arithmetic operations on matrices, just like we would with a scalar value. First, we define a matrix for the next few examples.

```
>> mymatrix = reshape(5:2:100, 8, 6)

mymatrix =
     5    21    37    53    69    85
     7    23    39    55    71    87
     9    25    41    57    73    89
    11    27    43    59    75    91
    13    29    45    61    77    93
    15    31    47    63    79    95
    17    33    49    65    81    97
    19    35    51    67    83    99
```

This generates the range from 5 to 100, skipping every other value. The `reshape` command takes the resulting array, and returns a matrix with 8 rows and 6 columns. The motivation here is simply to provide data to work with, and we could just as easily use a matrix with different values and dimensions.

Now, we add 1 to every element in `mymatrix`.

```
>> mymatrix + 1

ans =
     6    22    38    54    70    86
     8    24    40    56    72    88
    10    26    42    58    74    90
    12    28    44    60    76    92
    14    30    46    62    78    94
    16    32    48    64    80    96
    18    34    50    66    82    98
    20    36    52    68    84   100
```

Next, we have a slightly more complex example. We take `mymatrix`, divide every element by 10, then round the result and assign it to `newmatrix`.

```
>> newmatrix = round(mymatrix / 10)

newmatrix =
```

1	2	4	5	7	9
1	2	4	6	7	9
1	3	4	6	7	9
1	3	4	6	8	9
1	3	5	6	8	9
2	3	5	6	8	10
2	3	5	7	8	10
2	4	5	7	8	10

Did you notice how we passed a matrix to the round function, and it operated on the entire matrix? Flexibility such as this makes this language appealing and easy to program.

Just as we can find the transpose of an array, we can do so with a matrix.

```
>> newmatrix.'
ans =
```

1	1	1	1	1	2	2	2
2	2	3	3	3	3	3	4
4	4	4	4	5	5	5	5
5	6	6	6	6	6	7	7
7	7	7	8	8	8	8	8
9	9	9	9	9	10	10	10

We see that the transpose gives us a matrix of 6 rows and 8 columns. The operator ".'" (a period followed by a single quote) gives us the transpose of a matrix. However, a similar operator, "'" (a single quote) specifies a slightly different thing, at least when the matrix contains complex values. In the following line, we define a matrix a with complex values.

```
>> a = [2+3j, 4-5j; 6-7j, 8+9j]
a =
   2.0000 + 3.0000i   4.0000 - 5.0000i
   6.0000 - 7.0000i   8.0000 + 9.0000i
```

Next, display the transpose.

```
>> disp(a.')
   2.0000 + 3.0000i   6.0000 - 7.0000i
   4.0000 - 5.0000i   8.0000 + 9.0000i
```

As we should expect, this returns a matrix with the rows switched with the columns. By the way, a `transpose` function exists, and makes the code a little more verbose, and a little clearer, than using the `.'` operator.

```
>> disp(transpose(a))
   2.0000 + 3.0000i    6.0000 - 7.0000i
   4.0000 - 5.0000i    8.0000 + 9.0000i
```

The `transpose` function gives us the same results. Now let's see how the single quote operator behaves.

```
>> disp(a')
   2.0000 - 3.0000i    6.0000 + 7.0000i
   4.0000 + 5.0000i    8.0000 - 9.0000i
```

Notice that the signs in front of the complex parts change. Not only does this find the transpose, it finds the complex conjugate of each element, too.

4.6   ARITHMETIC WITH MATRICES

When multiplying two matrices, the computer follows the standard definition from mathematics. For example, if a and b are two 3×3 matrices, then the multiplication results c will also be a 3×3 matrix. The pattern follows:

$$
\begin{bmatrix} c_{1,1} & c_{1,2} & c_{1,3} \\ c_{2,1} & c_{2,2} & c_{2,3} \\ c_{3,1} & c_{3,2} & c_{3,3} \end{bmatrix} = \begin{bmatrix} a_{1,1} & a_{1,2} & a_{1,3} \\ a_{2,1} & a_{2,2} & a_{2,3} \\ a_{3,1} & a_{3,2} & a_{3,3} \end{bmatrix} \times \begin{bmatrix} b_{1,1} & b_{1,2} & b_{1,3} \\ b_{2,1} & b_{2,2} & b_{2,3} \\ b_{3,1} & b_{3,2} & b_{3,3} \end{bmatrix}
$$

where

$$
c_{i,j} = a_{i,1} \times b_{1,j} + a_{i,2} \times b_{2,j} + a_{i,3} \times b_{3,j} .
$$

This works for 3×3 matrices. Of course, if the dimensions of a or b change, we may need more or fewer terms in the expression for $c_{i,j}$.

The following shows a numerical example of matrix multiplication. Notice how the number of columns in the first matrix matches the number of rows of the second matrix. If these "inner" matrix dimensions do not match, then the matrix multiplication cannot be found.

```
>> [1, 2, 3; 4, 5, 6] * [1, 2; 0, 1; 1, 0]
ans =
       4       4
      10      13
```

As we see, the 2×3 matrix multiplied by the 3×2 matrix produces a 2×2 matrix. Generalizing this, multiplying an $M \times N$ matrix by an $N \times P$ matrix results in an $M \times P$ matrix. Here is a second example.

```
>> a = [1, 2; 3, 4; 5, 6]
a =
        1        2
        3        4
        5        6
>> b = [0, 1; 1, 0];
>> a*b
ans =
        2        1
        4        3
        6        5
```

Notice how the result has the same elements as matrix a, except that the columns are in a different order.

Next, we have another example of matrix multiplication. We define c and d as 2×2 matrices.

```
>> c = [5, 6; 4, 2];
>> d = [-1, 3; 7, 9];
>> disp(c * d)
       37       69
       10       30
```

We see that multiplying them together gives us a 2×2 result. If you are unfamiliar with this, look at some of the results and try to follow how they are computed. For example, $-1 \times 4 + 2 \times 7$ gives us the result of 10. Now let's see a slightly altered matrix operation.

```
>> disp(c .* d)
       -5       18
       28       18
```

Did you see the difference? Instead of "*" to specify matrix multiplication, we have ".*" which represents an element-by-element multiplication. In this case, the definition of the result becomes much simpler to follow. For element-by-element multiplication,

$$c_{i,j} = a_{i,j} \times b_{i,j},$$

so an output element for c only depends on the corresponding elements of a and b.

What if we want to add two matrices together? They must have the same dimensions, unless the dimension happens to be one. The operation happens on an element-by-element basis. Adding matrix c to matrix d returns the following.

```
>> disp(c + d)
    4     9
   11    11
```

Subtraction has a similar definition. As with addition, we can find the result as an element-by-element computation.

```
>> disp(c - d)
    6     3
   -3    -7
```

That is, to find the upper-left value of the result, subtract the upper-left value of d from c, $5 - (-1) = 6$.

What if we add a matrix with a dimension of 1, i.e., a row or column array? The next example shows the definition of f, a column array. Adding it to the previously defined c generates a matrix where each column has the sum of the corresponding c column and f.

```
>> f = [2; 8];
>> disp(c + f)
    7     8
   12    10
```

As shown earlier, we can find the addition (or subtraction) of a matrix and a scalar value. With two matrices, or a matrix and an array, the sizes of each must be compatible.

Using the same c and d matrices, we can find division of c by d.

```
>> disp(c / d)
   -0.1000    0.7000
   -0.7333    0.4667
```

As you can see, matrix division also has a mathematical definition. We can find the "inverse" of a matrix with the `inv` command, as the following example shows.

```
>> disp(inv(d))
   -0.3000    0.1000
    0.2333    0.0333
```

Not all matrices have an inverse, however. Here, you might notice that the result of the inverse of d reminds you of the division result. What if we multiply c with inv(d)?

```
>> disp(c * inv(d))
   -0.1000    0.7000
   -0.7333    0.4667
```

The result matches the output for c / d, and shows another way to get it. This comes from the mathematics; the matrix division definition typically makes use of the matrix inverse. Since some matrices do not have an inverse, not all matrices can be divided in this fashion. The following line shows a simple example where the matrix does not have an inverse.

```
>> disp(inv([1, 2]))
Error using inv
Matrix must be square.
```

MATLAB uses a different way to calculate matrix division; see the help entries of the commands mldivide and mldivide for more details.

Like multiplication, we can also explicitly compute division as an element-by-element operation. The next example shows the element-by-element division, using the . / operator.

```
>> disp(c ./ d)
   -5.0000    2.0000
    0.5714    0.2222
```

As with other element-by-element computations, we only need the corresponding elements from each matrix to find this. Finding the matrix division with a scalar value is inherently an element-by-element operation.

```
>> disp(c / 4)
    1.2500    1.5000
    1.0000    0.5000
```

Of course, would could have gotten the same results by multiplying c by 1/4.

Finally, exponentiation works with matrices with the ^ symbol, and can be performed as an element-by-element operation with . ^. First, we find the exponential of matrix c, to the power 2.

```
>> disp(c ^ 2)
    49    42
    28    28
```

Observe that this gives the same results as finding `c * c` does. The power does not have to be an integer, however. Now let's examine the element-by-element version of the exponential.

```
>> disp(c .^ 2)
    25    36
    16     4
```

Here, we see that result equals each element of the original, squared, in such a fashion that each result value depends only on the element at the same row and column of matrix `c`. Note that, for this example, we could get the same results with `disp(c .* c)`.

4.6.1 A Matrix of Random Values

We could use the `rand` function, which returns (pseudo-)random[1] values. Related functions include `randn` for a matrix of pseudo-random numbers with a normal distribution, and `randi` for integer values. Breaking it down, the `rand` function by itself returns values between 0 and 1, and `rand(8,6)` specifies that we want a matrix measuring 8 rows and 6 columns of such values. Multiplying by 100 and rounding the result gives us integer values between 0 and 100.

```
>>  mymatrix = round(100*rand(8,6))
ans =
     44    43    91    41    80    58
     90    87     2    21    93    64
     74    50    31    64    85    24
     70    83     6    74    38    56
     36    47    70    39    63    94
     18    47    66     2    74    35
     17    46    99    43    20    67
     20    42    56    76    91    40
```

---

[1] Pseudo-random numbers appear to us as random, although an algorithm generates them. Thus, the sequence can be repeated.

Expect a different matrix than what you see above, since by definition it should give unpredictable results.

Random number sequences must be repeatable, for testing and verification purposes. Thus, we use random number generators for this, which give us the same sequence when we specify the same "seed" value. We can use the rng command to specify the seed for the random number generator. By itself, rng will return the current state of the random number generator. Here, we give it a seed value to use. First, we set the seed value to an example value of 3.

```
>> rng(3)
>> disp(randi(10, 1, 4))
     6     8     3     6
>> disp(randi(10, 1, 4))
     9     9     2     3
>> disp(randi(10, 1, 4))
     1     5     1     5
```

This calls the randi function, which generates integer values, with a maximum of 10, forming a matrix of 1 row and 4 columns. Notice that every time we call the randi function, it gives us different results.

We repeat the preceding example, with one significant change: we call rng with the seed every time before the call to randi.

```
>> rng(3)
>> disp(randi(10, 1, 4))
     6     8     3     6
>> rng(3)
>> disp(randi(10, 1, 4))
     6     8     3     6
>> rng(3)
>> disp(randi(10, 1, 4))
     6     8     3     6
>> rng(3)
>> disp(randi(10, 1, 8))
     6     8     3     6     9     9     2     3
```

Notice how every time we get the same results. On the last call to randi, we request twice as many values, and the computer responds with the same 8 values that we saw previously. Thus, setting the seed value allows us to generate the same sequence of values.

4.6.2 Ranges as Indices

We can specify a submatrix by using a range of indices. First, let's start by making a larger matrix, to give us something to work with.

```
>> mymatrix = (1:8).' * (7:12)
mymatrix =
        7       8       9      10      11      12
       14      16      18      20      22      24
       21      24      27      30      33      36
       28      32      36      40      44      48
       35      40      45      50      55      60
       42      48      54      60      66      72
       49      56      63      70      77      84
       56      64      72      80      88      96
```

The assignment might look a little cryptic, so examine it in parts to see how they fit together. The (1:8) generates a range of values from 1 to 8, with an increment of 1. Next, the .' operation transposes it. Then (7:12) generates another range of values, from 7 to 12. If you have studied linear algebra, you may recognize that this instructs the computer to multiply an 8 × 1 array by a 1 × 6 array, which will result in an 8 × 6 matrix. An equivalent expression in mathematics is:

$$\begin{bmatrix} 1 \\ 2 \\ 3 \\ 4 \\ 5 \\ 6 \\ 7 \\ 8 \end{bmatrix} \times \begin{bmatrix} 7 & 8 & 9 & 10 & 11 & 12 \end{bmatrix}.$$

If this still seems cryptic, keep in mind that we simply need a command to make an example matrix, and that the details for how matrix multiplication works can be found in a good text on linear algebra.

To access a submatrix, we specify a range with two numbers separated with a colon, just like in earlier examples of the for loop. First, we will access the value in the top left corner.

```
>> mymatrix(1,1)
ans =
        7
```

Now let's try the same command, only with the range `1:2` in place of 1.

```
>> mymatrix(1:2,1:2)
ans =
        7        8
       14       16
```

As we see, the command returns the four values in the top left corner. What if we want to get the last last three rows and two columns? The following code does this.

```
>> [maxrow, maxcol] = size(mymatrix);
>> mymatrix(maxrow-2:maxrow, maxcol-1:maxcol)
ans =
       66       72
       77       84
       88       96
```

We specified these values in a relative fashion. We would get the same result if we had entered `mymatrix(6:8, 5:6)`.

```
>> mymatrix(6:8, 5:6)
ans =
       66       72
       77       84
       88       96
```

As we see, the results are the same. Explicitly including indices works well when you interact with the computer, however, the relative fashion works better in a program, especially when the matrix might have different dimensions. Also note that using `maxrow - 2` works here, but not on every possible matrix. If the matrix only has one or two rows, then the code would generate an error. We could check for this condition before using `maxrow - 2` as an index.

4.6.3 All Indices of a Row or Column

A short-hand way of specifying all rows or columns is to use a colon by itself. For example, let's get all rows for column 4. To do this, we use a colon to specify the rows.

```
>> mymatrix(:, 4)
ans =
    10
    20
    30
    40
    50
    60
    70
    80
```

By itself, MATLAB understands the colon as all of the elements of that dimension. Here is another way of specifying this, to return all columns of row 5. Remember that we already defined maxcol with the size function, previously.

```
>> mymatrix(5, 1:maxcol)
ans =
    35    40    45    50    55    60
```

We can also use end as a short-hand way of specifying the maximum row or column, as below.

```
>> mymatrix(5, 3:end)
ans =
    45    50    55    60
```

Thus, keyword end has different meanings depending on the context. With arrays and matrices, it means the extent of the elements along the respective dimension.

4.7   ARRAYS OF STRINGS

Strings have evolved in programming languages over the years. Most data types have a very uniform representation, even if they take multiple words of computer memory. For example, the integer value 100 takes the same amount of storage memory as the integer 1. Strings are inherently different, in that storing a string more closely resembles storing an array. In fact, MATLAB stores strings as an array of characters, and only recently introduced the string class as an alternative.

4.7.1 The Difference Between Character Arrays and Strings

We saw that we could have arrays of values. However, an array of characters presents some problems, especially when we want to have an array of character arrays. First, we must distinguish strings from character arrays. Older versions of MATLAB support character arrays. It provides functions like `strcat` and `sprintf` that return text, as an array of values, where each value maps to an ASCII/Unicode character. For example, the value 65 corresponds to capital "A," while lower case letters start with the code 97, so lower-case "b" corresponds to code 98. The code below illustrates this point.

```
>> g = 'Abc'
g =
Abc
>> h = g + 0
h =
     65    98    99
>> whos g h
  Name      Size       Bytes  Class      Attributes
  g         1x3            6  char
  h         1x3           24  double
```

Defining g, we see it is considered a group of characters. Setting h to the array g + 0 does not change the values, except that it changes their type. We see this in the `whos` information, that the first array (g) uses the character type, while the second array (h) stores the data as `double` values.

With the release of version 2016b, support for the `string` type appeared. The terms "character array" and "string" are sometimes used interchangeably, although for this discussion, we must differentiate between them. A string differs from a character array in the way that MATLAB stores them. In the following example, we create G as a string, with the same letters as g.

```
>> G = string(g)
G =
    string
        "Abc"
>> whos g G
  Name      Size       Bytes  Class      Attributes
  G         1x1          132  string
  g         1x3            6  char
```

While g has a size that reveals the number of characters, G does not. This means that we cannot use the length function with a string, since MATLAB considers a string as a singular entity. The function strlength finds the number of characters in either a character array or a string.

```
>> disp(length(g))
     3
>> disp(length(G))
     1
>> disp(strlength(g))
     3
>> disp(strlength(G))
     3
```

As we can see, using length works for character arrays, but indicates the number of strings that G holds, not the length of the string. Using strlength gives us the same results whether we pass a string or character array argument.

With other data types, we have built-in expectations, like what the "+" operations means. With strings, the common interpretation of the + operation is concatenation. The following example sets k as a character array, and K as a string.

```
>> k = 'hello';
>> K = string(k);
>> g + k
Matrix dimensions must agree.
>> G + K
ans =
  string
      "Abchello"
```

When we use the + operation on the character arrays, we get an error about how they have unequal length. If they were to have the same length, the result would be an array of double values. With the string versions, the + operation concatenates the two. We can still concatenate the character arrays, as follows:

```
>> disp(strcat(g, k))
Abcdehello
```

Since we can accomplish the same things with character arrays as we can with strings, what does a string really mean? A string type comes with its own methods, and can be thought of abstractly as an entity. If you ask someone what their name is, you expect the answer to be a sequence of characters. If you ask their age, you expect an integer. Adding 1 to the age makes sense; adding 1 to the name does not.

4.7.2 Arrays of Character Arrays

Now, we talk specifically about character arrays. Consider the two lines below.

```
strar1 = ['yes', 'no']
strar2 = ['yes'; 'no']
```

The first line results in a variable called `strar1`, which has a `yesno` as its value. It essentially concatenates the two character arrays `yes` and `no`.

The second line generates an error! It separates the two character arrays `yes` and `no` into two rows. But character arrays, by definition, are already arrays of characters, so the result is a matrix, with three character elements in the first row (`y`, `e`, and `s`), and two character elements in the second row. This is equivalent to specifying a matrix in the following form:

```
myarray = [1, 2, 3; 4, 5]
```

This generates the same error. MATLAB is pretty good at guessing, but it will not put a zero in the last column of the second row. Nor will it fill in the array of characters with spaces.

We can fix the matrix of numbers by adding a value for that last element, as seen below.

```
myarray = [1, 2, 3; 4, 5, -1]
```

This clearly states that each row has three elements. In a similar fashion, we can fix the matrix of characters:

```
strar = ['yes'; 'no ']
```

The above line does not cause an error, since we have the same number of elements in both rows.

4.7.3 Arrays of Strings

Let's revisit the previous example with strings, in place of character arrays.

```
>> strar1 = [string('yes'), string('no')]
strar1 =
  1×2 string array
    "yes"          "no"
```

```
>> strar2 = [string('yes'); string('no')]
strar2 =
  2×1 string array
   "yes"
   "no"
```

Here, we can see that the first command generates an array of strings, with a single row. The second command has no problem with the different string lengths, and stores them as an array of 2 rows. Since a matrix of strings stores each one as an entity, the lengths of the individual strings do not cause incompatibilities. The next example creates a 2 × 2 matrix of strings.

```
>> strar3 = [string('yes'), string('maybe'); ...
string('possibly'), string('no')]
strar3 =
  2×2 string array
   "yes"          "maybe"
   "possibly"     "no"
>> disp(strar3(2,1))
possibly
```

As we can see, we can store the strings in a matrix, and select a string like we might select a numeric value from another matrix. The examples above use the `string` function to convert character arrays to strings. The latest releases of MATLAB allow double quotes to define a string, such as `str4 = "yes"`.

4.8   USING A RANGE IN PLACE OF A LOOP

Often, a program will use a loop to go through an array. However, MATLAB excels at performing operations on matrices. Consider the following example.

```
tic
for x = 1:900
    g(x) = 2*x^2 + 5*x - 3;
end
toc
```

The `tic` and `toc` commands keep track of the time. You can think of `tic` as turning on a stop-watch, and `toc` as turning it off, then printing the results. The code could be better as the following.

```
tic
x = 1:900;
g = 2*x.^2 + 5*x - 3;
toc
```

We replace the exponential operator ("^") with the element-by-element exponential operator (".^") to accomplish this. Notice that the first use of x creates it as a scalar value that starts at 1 and increments during the loop until it reaches 900. In the second use of it, we set it to a range so that it becomes an array of 900 values, meaning that we use more memory to store variables in the second example.

Run times for these will vary. Since tic and toc use the system clock, the results do not necessarily tell us how busy the MATLAB code made the computer, it just tells us how busy the computer was. There could be other active programs making the response slow. Function cputime returns the amount of time that the CPU (Central Processing Unit) has spent running MATLAB. We could also use that, although then we would need to selectively clear variables and subtract the starting time from the stopping time. For the purpose of this demonstration, we will stick with tic and toc. We should not base any conclusions on one run. Instead, we can wrap the above code in a for loop, and clear the variables afterwards, since allocating memory for the variables takes a non-negligible amount of time. Revisiting the first set of commands, we get the following example.

```
for i=1:10
    tic
    for x = 1:900
        g(x) = 2*x^2 + 5*x - 3;
    end
    toc
    clear
end
```

Running this generates the following results on a Macintosh with an Intel® Core™ 2 Duo processor running at 2.16 GHz. Your results will vary.

```
Elapsed time is 0.000633 seconds.
Elapsed time is 0.000617 seconds.
Elapsed time is 0.000597 seconds.
Elapsed time is 0.000742 seconds.
Elapsed time is 0.000676 seconds.
```

```
Elapsed time is 0.000604 seconds.
Elapsed time is 0.000596 seconds.
Elapsed time is 0.000596 seconds.
Elapsed time is 0.000594 seconds.
Elapsed time is 0.000594 seconds.
```

Now we enclose the second code example in the same loop, as follows: The versions of these examples that generate timing measurements can be found as `loop1.m` and `loop2.m`.

```
for i=1:10
    % code goes here
    clear
end
```

Notice that the first line and the last two lines are the same as the previous example, to keep as much the same as possible. Running the second example in the loop, on the same machine, just seconds after the first code runs, generates the following.

```
Elapsed time is 0.000052 seconds.
Elapsed time is 0.000021 seconds.
Elapsed time is 0.000019 seconds.
Elapsed time is 0.000019 seconds.
Elapsed time is 0.000018 seconds.
Elapsed time is 0.000019 seconds.
Elapsed time is 0.000018 seconds.
Elapsed time is 0.000019 seconds.
Elapsed time is 0.000018 seconds.
Elapsed time is 0.000019 seconds.
```

The results show that the second example out-performs the first one. We should not jump to conclusions, however, we can say that the second example takes only a tenth as much time as the first one, at least on this computer.

Now let's suppose that we want to change the x values to –90 : 0.1 : 90. With the second set of commands, we implement this change easily. The altered code appears in the following lines.

```
x2 = -90:0.1:90;
g2 = 2*x2.^2 + 5*x2 - 3;
```

We use variables x2 and g2, mainly to re-enforce the idea that we have different code. Changing the code like this presents no problem.

But, if we did it the original way, using the `for` loop, how could we change the range? Perhaps we are simply trying to add the g(x) =... to an existing program, and cannot get rid of the `for` loop, such as if we help someone change their code. For whatever reason, suppose that we want code like the following.

```
for x = -90:0.1:90
    g(x) = ...
```

We cannot assign g(x) values, since x will be negative, non-integer, and zero, as well as positive. While MATLAB allows an array index to be double, as in g(1.0) = ..., it will not allow non-integers like g(1.1) = ... How could we handle this? A simple solution is as follows, where we use another variable as the index.

```
index = 1;
for x2 = -90:0.1:90
    g2(index) = 2*x2^2 + 5*x2 - 3;
    index = index + 1;
end
```

With the `index` variable in use, we always have integer values to access the array.

There are a couple of points to take away from this discussion. First, MATLAB works efficiently with arrays and matrices, so replace loop operations with arrays or matrices when possible. Second, testing your code with timing functions like `tic` and `toc` can help identify parts that take a long time. And finally, creating another variable to serve as the index to an array makes for a quick fix when the index you would like to use does not work.

4.9 SUMMARY

This chapter presents examples of arrays and matrices. We can use arrays and matrices as parameters to functions. Also, elements in arrays and matrices can be indexed by their row and column, and the colon (:) serves as a short-hand to specify all values in a row or column. Just as we can pass a matrix to a function, we can perform mathematical operations on a matrix, such as adding a constant to each element in a matrix.

EXERCISES

1. Make a program that sorts the numbers in row 1 of a 2 × N matrix, and swaps the columns. This means that the values in row 2 move along with any changes in row 1. At the end, we know the sorted order as well as the original order (since that's preserved in row 2).

    The idea here is that we have a list of responses to a survey, e.g., 3.32 2.91 2.55 2.55 2.95, etc. This is a survey where respondents ranked the importance of a list of 50 terms from unimportant (1) to very important (5). The position of each number corresponds to the question number, and ultimately, to the question itself. We want to sort this data, but knowing the maximum is useless unless we also know what question it goes with. Thus, we can put the position index in row 2 and use this sort routine. Here is an example.

    ```
    [ 3.32 2.91 2.55 2.55 2.95;
         1    2    3    4    5   ]
    ```

2. Let N=-100:100 for each N, find the sigmoid of N, and store the result in an array (sigmoid(-100:100) does not work) then plot the array.

    $$sigmoid(u) = \frac{1}{1+e^{-u}}$$

    ```
    sigmoid(u) = 1/(1+exp(-u))
    ```

3. Remove unique numbers from a list. For example, "2, 1, 7, 3, 1, 8, 2, 2, 7" should become "2, 1, 7, 1, 2, 2, 7," since values 3 and 8 only appear once in the original list.

4. Suppose you have a matrix with 5 rows, and 300 columns. How can you make a new array with 1 row and 300 columns, where each column is the sum of the 5 rows?

5. Given a matrix of image data, how can we make a mirror-image of it (along the right edge)?

6. Given a matrix of image data, how can we make a mirror-image of it (along the bottom edge)?

7. Given a matrix of image data, how can we make a mirror-image of it (along the diagonal)?

8. Given a matrix of image data, how can we rotate it by 90, 180, and 270 degrees?

9. Given a matrix of image data, how can we reverse it, making light colors dark and dark ones light?

10. Given a matrix of image data, how can we map certain colors to others? (That is, suppose any green color with >= 80% green, < 20% red and < 20% blue, is made 10% more blue.) (Or another way to approach this, set up a map where the specific color [10, 20, 30] maps to [90, 80, 70]. Add other colors to this map, too.)

11. Convert a sequence of values to run-length encoding. Count repeats in a sequence of numbers, then output count followed by number. For example, "2, 1, 1, 1, 1, 7, 3, 8, 2, 2, 7" should output "1 - 2, 4 - 1, 1 - 7, 1 - 3, 1 - 8, 2 - 2, 1 - 7." Also make this work for letters.

12. Remove repeated numbers from a list. For example, "2, 1, 1, 1, 1, 7, 3, 1, 8, 2, 2, 7" should become "2, 1, 7, 3, 1, 8, 2, 7."

13. Write an algorithm to remove duplicates from an array of numbers, keeping only the first instance, e.g., given the input "3, 8, 7, 3, 9, 7, 3, 3, 2" our algorithm should output "3, 8, 7, 9, 2." This is similar to, but a bit different from, an earlier problem that uses "2, 1, 1, 1, 1, 7, 3, 1, 8, 2, 2, 7" as an example list. It this version the result should be "2, 1, 7, 3, 8."

14. Suppose that we have an array of numbers, stored as the variable `myarray`. We want to calculate the following sum.

$$\sum_{n=1}^{N} n \times \text{myarray}(n)$$

Write MATLAB code to do this.

For example, suppose `myarray` has values {99.9, 17.6, 11.3}. The calculated sum would be as follows.

$$1 \times 99.9 + 2 \times 17.6 + 3 \times 11.3 = 99.9 + 35.2 + 33.9 = 169.0$$

15. The MATLAB session below shows an error. Briefly state how to fix it.

```
>> a = (1, 2, 3)
??? a = (1, 2, 3)
         |
Error: Expression or statement is incorrect--possibly unbala
nced (, {, or [.
```

16. The MATLAB session below shows an error. Briefly state how to fix it.

```
>> mymatrix = [7:9; 2:3]
??? Error using ==> vertcat
CAT arguments dimensions are not consistent.
```

PROJECT

- **Matrix-sweeper Game**

  This assignment is to implement a mine-sweeper game. Your program should create a grid with mines randomly placed in it. The user will either step on a square, or flag it. If the user steps on a square with a mine, then the game is over and the player loses. If the user steps on a square with one or mines in surrounding squares, your program should reveal the number of adjacent mines. The user can flag any square. If the user puts flags on all of the mines, then the game is over and the user wins. If the user flags a square twice, this should remove the flag.

  Your program will prompt the user whether to step or flag a square, then ask for which square (giving a row and column). Round the user's input to whole numbers. Do not let the user select a row or column out of bounds.

  Your program should display the minefield on the command window.

  Make sure to prompt the user for information. Your program should work for all possible inputs. Make sure that you test it with several different cases.

  To make the grid, you will need two matrices. The number of rows and columns should be specified that the top of your program, and your program should still work if we change these values. The first matrix should contain the mines, as well as the number of mines around each square. If there are no mines in an adjacent square, then mark it with 0. The second matrix should contain a record of where the user has stepped or flagged. Use a 0 if the user has not stepped there, 1 if the user has stepped there, and 2 if the user has a flag there.

  When printing the minefield, you will use both matrices. For each row and column, check to see if the user stepped there. If not, display a "." (or "@" if there is a flag). If there are no mines around, show an underscore "_". If there are mines around, show the number, e.g., "2". If there is a mine there, show a "*". You do not have to write this yourself; there is a function called ShowMineField.m available in the supplementary material.

GROUPING DATA

In MATLAB, we can store a value as a scalar, or a group of values as an array, or as a matrix. MATLAB also supports cells, structures, and classes; different ways to store related pieces of information together. For example, suppose that we run a business, and desire to work with employee data. An employee has several attributes that we would want to group together, such as a name (a string), an age (non-negative integer), an hourly pay rate (a floating-point number), a marital status (which could be a Boolean, or logical, true/false value), and a number of sick days left (which could be a positive or negative integer). While each one of these types of information is different, and each one would have a different storage and interpretation by the computer, it still makes sense to group them together.

5.1 GROUPING DATA TOGETHER

Here is a simple way to store this data, although it will be up to us to remember that these pieces of information are related. We will later see better ways to store data.

```
empName = 'John Doe';
empAge = 26;
empPayRate = 8.75;
empMarried = false;
empSickDaysLeft = 5;
```

We use the names of the variables themselves to indicate that they are all related attributes, but to MATLAB, these are just five different variables. It is simple, but how many attributes are there in total? That is, just because there is no `empPhoneNumber` above, how do we know that it does not exist? Yes, the `exist` function could check for that name and tell us if it currently has a definition, but it cannot tell us if it *should* be defined, or if another variable like `empCellNumber` holds that information. Also, working with multiple employees may be a problem.

Normal arrays or matrices hold all the same type of elements. This would not work for groups of data, like our employee example, except for cell arrays, which will be explained shortly. It is even tricky to have an array of strings, at least when the program defines them as character arrays. Now imagine that we have a second employee. How could we refer to that data? We might vary the names somewhat, like `empName2`, `empAge2`, etc., although this becomes a very cumbersome solution. Even creating arrays for each category presents problems—the data would be grouped by data, not by entity (employee).

5.1.1 Cells

A *cell* allows varied elements to be stored together. It can even contain another matrix as an element. We use it much like an array, except for the curly braces around the cell number. Below, we see an example of how we can store the employee data with cells.

```
employee{1} = 'John Doe';
employee{2} = 26;
employee{3} = 8.75;
employee{4} = false;
employee{5} = 5;
```

Let's verify that it stored these things.

```
employee =
    'John Doe'    [26]    [8.7500]    [0]    [5]
```

As we can see, the data are grouped together under the variable `employee`. We can also accomplish the entire example above with one line.

```
employee = {'John Doe', 26, 8.75, false, 5};
```

Cells store the data together, but we have no sense of what the values mean. We could easily mistake `{2}` as the number of sick-leave days, for example. We need to know what each element represents.

To get the data back, the `deal` command is useful. Think of it like a dealer in a card game, where everyone gets a card.

```
[name, age, pay, married, sick_days] = deal(employee{:});
```

The above command takes each of the five elements stored in `employee`, and places them in the variables listed on the left. As expected, `name` will be a string, `age` will be a double, `married` will be a Boolean value, etc.

How could we handle more employees? Just like we defined additional columns of data, we can add another row. Consider the following code.

```
employee{2,1} = 'Jane Public';
employee{2,2} = 32;
employee{2,3} = 11.12;
employee{2,4} = false;
employee{2,5} = 6;
```

When we check out the `employee` variable, we see the following response.

```
>> employee
employee =
    'John Doe'      [26]   [ 8.7500]   [0]   [5]
    'Jane Public'   [32]   [11.1200]   [0]   [6]
```

The cells easily allow us to store data of different types for multiple entries. Clearly, this provides a better solution than hard-coding the variable names. The main drawback is that we must rely upon documentation to know what each column represents, and if we accidentally switch two, say if we reverse `sick_days` and `age` in the list of `deal` command outputs, the error may be difficult to spot.

5.1.2 Structures

Structures allow various data to be grouped together, and accessed by *field names*. This brings another level of documentation to programs. For example, we could have a field named "age," and access it with commands like `employee.age = 25`. This makes a lot more sense to a human reading the code, as opposed to storing the age in cell 2. The programmer may later forget that they chose the second cell to store the employee's age but can easily remember the field name "age". If you have been trying these examples in a MATLAB session, use the `clear all` instruction to get rid of all declared variables before going further.

```
employee.name = 'John Doe';
employee.age = 26;
employee.payRate = 8.75;
employee.married = false;
employee.sickDays = 5;
```

We next verify that this was stored correctly.

```
>> employee
employee =
    struct with fields:
         name : 'John Doe'
          age : 26
      payRate : 8.7500
      married : 0
     sickDays : 5
```

As with cells, we are able to store many different data types together in the same variable. Field names offer the advantage of labeling our data. Now we have names describing each element, and it is clear that these things belong together. We could define functions to use this data, but the data and the functions would not necessarily be linked, i.e., we have to read the function's comments to know this.

5.1.3 Tables

MATLAB includes commands to create and use *tables*, meaning data arranged in rows and columns, like in the everyday usage of the word. In computing literature, a table may refer to databases or spreadsheets. To demonstrate a MATLAB table, let's return to the cell array for a moment.

```
employee{1} = 'John Doe';
employee{2} = 26;
employee{3} = 8.75;
employee{4} = false;
employee{5} = 5;
employee{2,1} = 'Jane Public';
employee{2,2} = 32;
employee{2,3} = 11.12;
employee{2,4} = false;
employee{2,5} = 6;
```

As we saw previously, this creates a 2 × 5 cell array, mixing several data types. We could certainly keep the data like this, although storing it as a table gives us a bit more self-documentation. Consider the following code.

```
names = {'John Doe'; 'Jane Public'};
ages = [26; 32];
payrate = [8.75; 11.12];
married = [false; false];
sick_days = [5; 6];
mytable = table(names, ages, payrate, married, sick_days);
```

Everything should look familiar, except the last line. We see that the code creates several column arrays, then the last line passes them all to a function. We store the result in a variable called `mytable`, which we compare to the `employee` cell array.

```
>> whos employee mytable
Name         Size          Bytes   Class      Attributes
employee     2x5            1208   cell
mytable      2x5            2127   table
```

Besides the difference of the size for the internal representation, these two may seem the same. Let's examine the contents.

```
>> employee
employee =
  2x5 cell array
    {'John Doe'}     {[26]}   {[ 8.7500]}  {[0]}   {[5]}
    {'Jane Public'} {[32]}   {[11.1200]}  {[0]}   {[6]}
>> mytable
mytable =
  2x5 table
        names         ages   payrate   married   sick_days
    ------------------ ------ --------- --------- -------------
    'John Doe'     26     8.75      false     5
    'Jane Public' 32     11.12     false     6
```

The contents have the same values, as we expect, but the table form has additional information: the names of the columns. These come from the names of the variables used in the table creation step. The obvious advantage is that we do not have to remember what each column means. The column names appear with the data, even when we only display one value. As shown in the following lines, we do not get the extra information with the cell array.

```
>> disp(employee{2,3})
   11.1200
>> disp(mytable(2,3))
    payrate
    ----------------
    11.12
```

How does the table retain its column headings when we write it to a file? It simply puts the names for each column as the first row. The following command writes the table to a file.

```
>> writetable(mytable, 'example_table.csv');
```

We can check this by examining the file's contents with the `type` command, since the computer stores plain text in a comma separated value (.csv) file.

```
>> type example_table.csv
names,ages,payrate,married,sick_days
John Doe,26,8.75,0,5
Jane Public,32,11.12,0,6
>>
```

Note that a similarly named function exists called `tblwrite`, which creates a file that stores a table from a matrix of data. We can read the table data with `readtable`, although `tblread` or `tdfread` (to read a tab-delimited file) also could be used.

MATLAB supports the table data type with some specialized functions, like `cell2table` and `table2cell`. Other specialized functions exist, such as `summary`, which gives minimum, median, and maximum values for each column. Here, we convert a cell array to a table.

```
>> mytable_from_cell = cell2table(employee);
>> mytable_from_cell
mytable_from_cell =
    employee1      employee2   employee3   employee4   employee5
    ----------------   ----------------   ----------------   ----------------   ----------------
    'John Doe'     26          8.75        false       5
    'Jane Public'  32          11.12       false       6
```

As you can see, it uses generic column names since we have not specified anything better. Shortly, we will rename the columns.

In the following lines, we read the table from a file, and make sure that it looks like we expect.

```
>> employee_table = readtable('example_table.csv');
>> employee_table
employee_table =
            names        ages    payrate   married   sick_days
        ------------------  ------  ----------  ---------  -------------
        'John Doe'      26        8.75    0         5
        'Jane Public'   32       11.12    0         6
```

Next, we copy the table into a cell array.

```
>> employee_from_table = table2cell(employee_table);
>> employee_from_table
employee_from_table =
  2x5 cell array
  {'John Doe'}        {[26]}   {[ 8.7500]}   {[0]}   {[5]}
  {'Jane Public'}     {[32]}   {[11.1200]}   {[0]}   {[6]}
```

We can access information about the column names via the `Properties` method.

```
>> employee_table.Properties
ans =
struct with fields:
            Description: ''
               UserData: []
         DimensionNames: {'Row'  'Variables'}
          VariableNames: {'names'  'ages'  'payrate'
          'married'  'sick_days'}
   VariableDescriptions: {}
          VariableUnits: {}
               RowNames: {}
```

Specifically, if we want to know the column name of column number 2, we can display it as follows:

```
>> employee_table.Properties.VariableNames{2}
ans =
ages
```

Not only do we have column names, we can define names for the rows, too. The next line sets these.

```
>> employee_table.Properties.RowNames = {'marketing', 'sales'};
>> employee_table
employee_table =

                    names        ages    payrate    married    sick_days
              ------------------  ------  ----------  ----------  ------------

   marketing  'John Doe'          26         8.75    0           5

   sales      'Jane Public'       32        11.12    0           6
```

Since we converted `mytable_from_cell`, we do not have names for the columns. We can correct this with the following line. Notice that `sickdays` varies slightly from what we had before. The space presents a problem, and we can remove it, or replace it with an underscore.

```
>> mytable_from_cell.Properties.VariableNames = ...
{'name', 'age', 'pay', 'married', 'sickdays'}
```

Next, include descriptions for each column, too.

```
>> mytable_from_cell.Properties.VariableDescriptions = ...
{'person''s name', 'employee age', 'pay rate', 'marital
status', ... 'sick days'};
```

What does the table look like now?

```
>> mytable_from_cell
mytable_from_cell =

     2x5 table

        name          age    pay       married      sickdays
   ------------------  -----  -------  -----------  ------------

   'John Doe'          26      8.75    false        5

   'Jane Public'       32     11.12    false        6
```

This might seem strange; we manipulated properties of the table, however it looks the same as before. The property values are not normally displayed. To see the differences, we can examine the table properties directly.

```
>> mytable_from_cell.Properties
ans =

  struct with fields:

            Description: ''
               UserData: []
         DimensionNames: {'Row'  'Variables'}
```

```
       VariableNames:{'name' 'age' 'pay' 'married' 'sickdays'}
    VariableDescriptions:{'person's name' 'employee age' 'pay rate'
'marital status' 'sick days'}
        VariableUnits:{}
   VariableContinuity:[]
             RowNames:{}
```

Now let's examine the tables as they are stored.

```
>> writetable(mytable_from_cell, 'example_table2.csv');
>> type example_table.csv
names,ages,payrate,married,sick_days
John Doe,26,8.75,0,5
Jane Public,32,11.12,0,6
>> type example_table2.csv
name,age,pay,married,sickdays
John Doe,26,8.75,0,5
Jane Public,32,11.12,0,6
```

Notice that the files are almost identical, except for the underscore in `sick_days` in the first. The extra table properties are not preserved in the `.csv` file.

In the following example, we read a comma separated value file as a table. Suppose that the table contains grades for a class of 35 students for several quizzes, each one out of 20 points.

```
>> x = readtable('grades.csv');
>> summary(x)
Variables:
    NAME: 35x1 cell array of character vectors
    Quiz1: 35x1 double
        Values:
            min      7
            median  17
            max     20
    Quiz2: 35x1 double
        Values:
            min      0
            median  14
            max     20
```

```
Quiz3: 35x1 double
    Values:
            min        8
            median    13
            max       17
Quiz4: 35x1 double
    Values:
            min       10
            median    15
            max       20
```

From the information presented by the summary command, we might determine that Quiz3 is the most difficult. Note that the median function, used to find this information, considers 0 to be a valid score, whereas we might expect that it means a missing value. Without the zero score, Quiz2 has a median value of 14.5.

By the way, we have to be a bit cautious in how we get data from a table. Consider the following example.

```
>> q2 = x(:, 3);
>> plot(q2)
Error using tabular/plot (line 133)
There is no plot method for the 'table' class. Plot the
variables in a table using dot or brace subscripting.
```

Examining the workspace information reveals that q2 has the class table, just like the table x. How do we just get the values? As with many programming questions, this one has multiple answers. We could convert the q2 table into an array with the table2array command, as follows:

```
q2a = table2array(q2);
```

As you probably have guessed, MATLAB also includes an array2table command to do the opposite.

Another way to get the Quiz2 values is to use the curly braces when accessing them from the x table.

```
q2b = x{:, 3};
```

This returns a column array of type double, which we can plot. Several other variations exist, and the following command presents the documentation page.

```
docsearch access data in a table
```

Whatever way you choose, remember that many functions need their input data in a form other than the `table` container.

5.1.4 Classes

Finally, MATLAB provides support for classes. Object-oriented programming is a well established trend, and classes are the way to implement it. A *class* is the definition of a new data type, made from existing data types, as well as functions. We label an *object* the version of the class, called an *instance* of the class, that the program uses. There may be many objects of the same class type. To use an old cliché, the class is the cookie-cutter, while the object is the cookie.

Think of a class and objects in the context of strings. We can talk about strings abstractly, defining terms for them like length. While you may have many different strings within a program, and each may have a different length, the idea of what length means does not change. The abstract definition, including methods like length, forms the class, and the any string variables are the objects. Note that programs often store strings as arrays of characters, although MATLAB, along with some other computer languages, do define a "string" class. An array of characters does not have the built-in methods that a string class has. For example, in the programming language C, a special character with the value zero marks the end of an array of characters. Functions made to support strings in that language rely on that value; if it does not appear within the array, some function will continue to look through memory regardless of the array's size. With a string class, the length can be stored together with the character data.

Classes grew out of the idea of structures, but it goes a few steps further. It allows *inheritance*, which means that a class may be derived from another class. If you were to represent employee data as an object, the object could be of a class called worker, which could be derived from a class American, which could be derived from another class called person. This object could have an attribute of salaried, but you could just as easily have an hourly employee. All people (i.e., members of the person class) have an age, American workers have social security numbers, and all workers have a pay rate. But not all people are American, and not all Americans have jobs, therefore a member of the person class might not have a social security number or a pay rate. Such an employee object would have the age attribute that it inherited from the person class, and perhaps a social security number inherited from the American class, and a pay rate since it is an instance of the worker class.

Classes also allow the programmer to group functions and data together. Some data should have certain things done to it, but not others. An employee object should have functions like `CalculatePay`, or `DeductHealthInsurancePremium`. A car object may have associated functions like `CalculateDepreciation` or `NotifyTimeForOilChange`. It would not make sense for either object to use one of the other one's functions. We call a function associated with a class a *method*.

5.2 DEFINING CLASSES THE OLD WAY

MATLAB has evolved over the years, and defining classes has changed significantly. This section presents the "old way" of defining and using classes, since you might run across code that does this. Section 5.3 covers the newer, improved way to define classes, with the `classdef` keyword. The two ways of defining classes differ in that the "old way" requires a subdirectory with an at-sign ("@") as the first character in the name, and the methods related to that class go under that subdirectory.

The "old way" of creating a class in MATLAB is a little complicated. To make an `employee` class, we must create a directory called `@employee` with a command like `mkdir @employee`:

```
mkdir @employee
```

Note that if you have changed your directory with the `cd` command, you should make sure that the current directory is the correct one. If you use the command-line of a terminal shell in Linux, Unix (including Macintosh), or MS-DOS/Windows, you may recognize this command. It works under MATLAB's command window, too. Also, the operating system of your computer probably allows you to create a subdirectory using the graphical user interface.

Now that we have the subdirectory, we need to store a file called `employee.m` there. Here is an example, much like the structure example above. We assume that the employee's name, age, and marital status will be given when a program makes an object. For simplicity, we use the same pay rate and sick days for everyone, as default values.

```
% @employee/employee.m
% An example class
%
```

```
function emp = employee(name, age, married)
tempStructure.name = name;
tempStructure.age = age;
tempStructure.payRate = 8.75;
tempStructure.married = married;
tempStructure.sickDays = 5;
emp = class(tempStructure,'employee');
```

Notice the last line, which is very important for this to work. We return an object via the temporary variable `emp`, which we define as being an instance of the `employee` class.

There are two methods to support this example. Below, we see the `Get-Name` method, which simply returns the name as a string. It must be in the `@employee` directory.

```
% @employee/GetName.m
% Example method for employee class
%
function mystr = GetName(emp)
% return the name
mystr = emp.name;
```

Methods like this allow access to data that are normally hidden. We will have a second method momentarily, but let's see how well this works so far.

First, we create a new variable called `my_emp`.

```
>> my_emp = employee('John Doe', 26, false)
my_emp =
     employee object: 1-by-1
```

Notice that we did not see the contents of `my_emp`. We can find the name with the `GetName`, as seen below.

```
>> GetName(my_emp)
ans =
John Doe
```

If we do not know the available methods, we can find them by using the `methods` command.

```
>> methods(my_emp)
Methods for class employee:
Birthday    GetName    employee
```

We also could have used `methods('employee')`. Another possibility is to get a list of files in the `@employee` directory, with `ls @employee`.

You may have noticed the `Birthday` method listed above. Here is what it looks like:

```
% @employee/Birthday.m
% Example method for employee class
%
function Birthday(emp)
% Print a nice message
disp(sprintf('Happy Birthday, %s!',emp.name))
% Update the age info
disp(sprintf('You were %d',emp.age));
emp.age = emp.age + 1;
disp(sprintf('You are now %d',emp.age));
```

Next, we try to invoke the `Birthday` method, just like we would in a language like Java or C++.

```
>> my_emp.Birthday()
??? Access to an object's fields is only permitted
within its methods.
```

And we see that it does not work! Instead, we use the method name like a normal function, except that we pass the object to it.

Let's run `Birthday` twice, to test it.

```
>> Birthday(my_emp)
Happy Birthday, John Doe!
You were 26
You are now 27
>> Birthday(my_emp)
Happy Birthday, John Doe!
You were 26
You are now 27
```

Something is wrong—the value was changed in the method, but the change was not (permanently) applied to the object. We will revise the birthday function, where we return the updated object. Notice that only the `function` line has been changed.

```
% @employee/Birthday.m
% Example method for employee class
%
function emp = Birthday(emp)
% Print a nice message
disp(sprintf('Happy Birthday, %s!',emp.name))
% Update the age info
disp(sprintf('You were %d',emp.age));
emp.age = emp.age + 1;
disp(sprintf('You are now %d',emp.age));
```

Now let's try it again. Notice that the line calling `Birthday` is a little different: we use

```
my_emp = Birthday(my_emp);
```

instead of

```
Birthday(my_emp)
```

as we did in the preceding example.

```
>> clear
>> my_emp = employee('John Doe', 26, false);
>> my_emp = Birthday(my_emp);
Happy Birthday, John Doe!
You were 27
You are now 28
>> my_emp = Birthday(my_emp);
Happy Birthday, John Doe!
You were 28
You are now 29
```

As we see from the above run, the `Birthday` method now works as intended.

Once we define a class, it should be something that we can reuse. Also, classes allow us a level of abstraction. The class presents a complex data type to the user, with methods already defined. The user can ignore details like how the data are stored and how the methods accomplish their tasks, as long as they work. MATLAB's support for classes is relatively new, and will certainly be expanded in the future.

5.3 THE "CLASSDEF" KEYWORD

We know that structures allow you to group varied types of data into a logical set. But what about the functions that operate on these structures? Someone using your structure would need to know several key pieces of information: how to create a compatible structure, how to initialize it, and what functions can be used with it. In MATLAB, classes provide the ability to group the data like structures, with the added benefits of grouping the functions that work with it, including one for creating and initializing it.

In 2008, The MathWorks introduced the `classdef` keyword into MAT-LAB. If you are familiar with an object oriented programming language like C++, you will appreciate how this keyword allows you to specify the class in a familiar way. Under the `properties` we have the class-specific variables. Likewise, we define the class methods under the `methods` keyword. Each of these keywords (`classdef`, `properties`, and `methods`) has a corresponding `end`. See [6] for more details.

We define the class, then the user creates objects based on that class. Think of this like other data types that we have seen. MATLAB can create an integer value, a floating-point value, a character, or a string. There must be one definition for each of these, but you can use as many integers, strings, etc., as you need. In a similar way, a programmer creates only one class definition, although the user may create many instances of that class, called objects.

The `classdef` keyword allows us to define the class. The `properties` section allows us to define variables used in the class. And the `methods` section allows us to specify functions that are used with this class. A special method, called a "constructor," should be included in the methods. It has the same name as the class, and can take parameters. It has duty of initializing the variables or any other set-up work required for the class.

Here is a skeleton layout of a class. Note that "classname" is not to be taken literally; you should replace both instances of it with whatever name you wish to call your class. Also, "parameters" should also be replaced with whatever parameters to pass to the constructor.

```
classdef classname
    properties
        % Variables go here
    end
    methods
        % Constructor function
        function obj = classname(parameters)
```

```
        % ...
    end
    % Other functions go here
  end
end
```

The terms `classdef`, `properties`, `methods`, `function`, and `end` are all keywords and should appear as they are. Also, `obj` is a specially defined word that refers to the object. We use it whenever we have a class-defined function that returns our object, or whenever we want to refer to a class-specific variable from the `properties` section.

5.3.1 Building a Simple Class

Let's start with a simple example. Suppose that we want a class to represent body-mass index (BMI). This is a rough indicator of health, given by the ratio of a person's weight to their height. To calculate BMI, all we need are the two values: height (in inches) and weight (in pounds). We define the first class as given in the following code.

```
classdef BMI_class1
    properties
        height; weight;
        methods
        end
    end
end
```

For the moment, we have not defined any methods (functions that work with the class). All we have are two variables, `height` and `weight`, as well as the class name `BMI_class1`. For this example, the class is similar to a structure.

First, we create an object called `bmi_object1`, as an object of the `BMI_class1` class.

```
>> bmi_object1 = BMI_class1
bmi_object1 =
    BMI_class1
    Properties:
        height: []
        weight: []
    Methods
```

Both `BMI_class1` and `Methods` appear in the command window as links, that we can click on to reveal more information. We see that the two properties do not have values. We can assign them as follows:

```
>> bmi_object1.height = 70;
>> bmi_object1.weight = 175;
>> bmi_object1
bmi_object1 =
  BMI_class1
  Properties:
    height: 70
    weight: 175
  Methods
>>
```

That is all that we do with this example: store a couple of values. Next, we make a simple function to calculate the body-mass index.

5.3.2 An Example Method

After the `methods` keyword and before its corresponding `end`, add the following code. Also update the class name (from `BMI_class1` to `BMI_class2`), after the `classdef` keyword. Whenever adding new code and functionality to working code, always make a back-up copy first.

```
function bmi = getBMI(obj)
    % Calculate Body Mass Index, and return it
    % For the formula, see http://www.cdc.gov/healthyweight/
    % assessing/bmi/adult_bmi/index.html
    bmi = obj.weight * 703 / (obj.height * obj.height);
end
```

Then save this new version as `BMI_class2.m`.

As you can see, this calculates the body-mass index based on a formula documented by a website hosted by the Center for Disease Control. Now let's test it. First, we create an object, just like before.

```
>> bmi_object2 = BMI_class2
bmi_object2 =
  BMI_class2
```

```
Properties:
   height: []
   weight: []
Methods
```

Also like before, we specify the two values.

```
>> bmi_object2.height = 70;
>> bmi_object2.weight = 175;
```

Now we can test the getBMI function that we defined.

```
>> disp(bmi_object2.getBMI);
   25.1071
```

The function returns the BMI value, which is then displayed.

We have now seen the basic utility of a class. It allows us to group data together, and also group functions with the data that specify how to operate on that data.

5.3.3 Constructor

The next example uses a constructor, a special function that the computer executes when it creates an object from the class. Add this to the line after the methods keyword. It should be the first function listed in this section. As before, change the example name from BMI_class2 to BMI_class3.

```
function obj = BMI_class3(height, weight)
   obj.height = height;
   obj.weight = weight;
end
```

Notice the name obj that we use to specify the object itself. Using height in the function below refers to the first parameter. Using obj.height refers to the data value called height defined in the properties section.

Now we use this class, invoking the constructor function.

```
>> bmi_object3 = BMI_class3(70, 175)
bmi_object3 =
  BMI_class3
  Properties:
    height: 70
    weight: 175
  Methods
```

We see that it populated the two variables, as we expected. Now we call the getBMI function to find the body-mass index.

```
>> disp(bmi_object3.getBMI);
   25.1071
```

This may seem repetitive, since it has only a few changes from the previous example. Mainly, this example sets the two properties when the computer creates the object, instead of setting them individually as separate instructions.

5.3.4 Variable Argument List

Finally, we consider one more example. In other programming languages, we can specify different functions (and different constructors) by using a function with the same name, but different parameter lists. In other words, there can be several constructors, each with their own unique list of variables to pass. We call this "function overloading," and it is clear from the context what function to call, based on the arguments. We might have someone create an object (possibly from the BMI_class) where they specify none of the parameters, or perhaps one parameter but not the other. In MATLAB, we do this with the varargin keyword, which the next example shows. The keyword nargin holds the number of arguments to the method, and MATLAB defines it for us.

Suppose that we replace the constructor function with the one below. Then change the class name to BMI_class4.

```
function obj = BMI_class4(varargin)
    if (nargin > 0)
        obj.height = varargin{1};
    end
    if (nargin > 1)
        obj.weight = varargin{2};
    end
end
```

Now we can invoke the class in one of several ways. First, we can pass no parameters, much like the very first example.

```
>> bmi_object4 = BMI_class4()
bmi_object4 =
  BMI_class4
  Properties:
```

```
     height: []
     weight: []
  Methods
>> bmi_object4.height = 70;
>> bmi_object4.weight = 175;
>> disp(bmi_object4.getBMI);
   25.1071
```

Or, we can specify the first parameter, which our constructor assumes to be the height. We then must specify the weight before we can continue.

```
>> bmi_object4 = BMI_class4(70)
bmi_object4 =
  BMI_class4
  Properties:
     height: 70
     weight: []
  Methods
>> bmi_object4.weight = 175;
>> disp(bmi_object4.getBMI);
   25.1071
```

Another possibility is to specify both the height and weight when computer creates the object.

```
>> bmi_object4 = BMI_class4(70, 175)
bmi_object4 =
  BMI_class4
  Properties:
     height: 70
     weight: 175
  Methods
>> disp(bmi_object4.getBMI);
   25.1071
```

The supplementary material includes another version, BMI_class5, with minor changes. It includes bmi as a property, and sets it with the following method.

```
function obj = getBMI(obj)
    bmi = obj.weight * 703 / (obj.height * obj.height);
    disp(bmi);
    obj.bmi = bmi;
end
```

Notice that instead of returning the calculated value, it displays it, and returns the object instead.

A final version, BMI_class6, inherits from the handle class. With a figure handle, we can make a change to a figure without having to store the results of the function that makes the change.

```
classdef BMI_class6 < handle
```

To see how this works, first consider the following example. We create an instance of the BMI_class5 class.

```
>> bmi_object5 = BMI_class5(70, 175)
bmi_object5 =
    BMI_class5 with properties:
        height: 70
        weight: 175
           bmi: []
```

Now, we use the getBMI method.

```
>> bmi_object5.getBMI
    25.1071
ans =
    BMI_class5 with properties:
        height: 70
        weight: 175
           bmi: 25.1071
```

It displayed the calculated value, and returned a copy of the object with the calculated value included. Let's inspect the object.

```
>> bmi_object5
bmi_object5 =
    BMI_class5 with properties:
        height: 70
        weight: 175
```

```
    bmi: []
```

Notice how the `bmi` property has an empty matrix for the value? We might expect it to be 25.1071, since the call to the method calculated this. However, if you examine the output carefully, you will observe that the new object with the calculated `bmi` property was returned to the variable `ans`; the original `bmi_object5` variable did not change.

Keeping in mind the only real difference between `BMI_class5` and `BMI_class6` is the `classdef` line, we repeat this example with `BMI_class6`. Like before, we create an instance of the `BMI_class6` class.

```
>> bmi_object6 = BMI_class6(70, 175)
bmi_object6 =
    BMI_class6 with properties:
      height: 70
      weight: 175
         bmi: []
```

Also like before, we call the `getBMI` method.

```
>> bmi_object6.getBMI
    25.1071
ans =
    BMI_class6 with properties:
      height: 70
      weight: 175
         bmi: 25.1071
```

Since the method call does not end in a semi-colon, it returns a copy of the object in `ans`, like it did previously. Now inspecting the object reveals a difference.

```
>> bmi_object6
bmi_object6 =
    BMI_class6 with properties:
      height: 70
      weight: 175
         bmi: 25.1071
```

This time, the computer remembers the `bmi` value that it calculates. For completeness, here is the last class definition in its entirety.

```matlab
classdef BMI_class6 < handle
    properties
        height;
        weight;
        bmi;
    end
    methods
        % constructor
        function obj = BMI_class6(varargin)
            if (nargin > 0)
                obj.height = varargin{1};
            end
            if (nargin > 1)
                obj.weight = varargin{2};
            end
        end
        function obj = getBMI(obj)
            % Calculate Body Mass Index, and return it
            % For the formula, see http://www.cdc.gov/healthyweight/
            % assessing/bmi/adult_bmi/index.html
            bmi = obj.weight * 703 / (obj.height * obj.height);
            disp(bmi);
            obj.bmi = bmi;
        end
    end
end
```

In summary, we have used the `classdef` keyword to create a class in MATLAB. We saw how, at its simplest, a class allows us to group together data. But it also allows us to group the data with functions specific to the data. We saw an example of such a function, and we used a special function called a constructor. By using the `varargin` keyword, we can create a flexible constructor that processes a variable number of arguments.

5.3.5 Applying a Class to the Previous Employee Example

Below is a class definition, providing the same functionality as the previous employee example. This class definition should be stored in an appropriately named file, such as employee2.m.

```
classdef employee2
    properties
        name;
        age;
        payRate = 8.75;
        married;
        sickDays = 5;
    end
    methods
        % constructor
        function obj = employee2(name, age, married)
            obj.name = name;
            obj.age = age;
            obj.married = married;
        end
        function obj = Birthday(obj)
            % Print a nice message
            disp(sprintf('Happy Birthday, %s!',obj.name))
            % Update the age info
            disp(sprintf('You were %d',obj.age));
            obj.age = obj.age + 1;
            disp(sprintf('You are now %d',obj.age));
        end
        function mystr = GetName(obj)
            % return the name
            mystr = obj.name;
        end
    end
end
```

Notice how the keyword obj specifies the current object. For example, to specify the name property, we reference obj.name.

The first method is of particular interest. Called a "constructor," the computer executes this function whenever it creates an object of this class. The constructor expects exactly three parameters for this example, although it is possible, as in the previous section, to have a variable number using `varargin`. Below, we make an object of this class.

```
>> my_emp = employee2('John Doe', 26, false)
my_emp =
employee2
properties:
        name: 'John Doe'
         age: 26
     payRate: 8.7500
     married: 0
    sickDays: 5
list of methods
```

As with previous examples, it does not list the methods, but the word "methods" is a link. We can find the methods by entering `methods(my_emp)` at the command line.

```
>> methods(my_emp)
Methods for class employee2:
Birthday    GetName    employee2
```

A similar command, `properties(my_emp)` will reveal the variables that the object uses (`name`, `age`, etc.).

Now let's try a few of the methods. First, we use `GetName` to return the name stored by the object.

```
>> my_emp.GetName()
ans =
John Doe
```

We can also access the name directly, by specifying the property as if it were a structure.

```
>> my_emp.name
ans =
John Doe
```

We can do this because the `name` property is public. Public means that any other code (such as a command given by the user) can read or overwrite the property's value directly. It is possible to have private properties, as well as private methods, just like in other object-oriented programming languages. Private means that you, the programmer, can restrict access to the object's variables (or methods). Often, a variable will be private but allow indirect reading and writing of the value through public "get" and "set" methods. MATLAB evens recognizes `get` and `set` as keywords, used with graphical objects like figures. See Chapter 9 on graphical user interfaces for more information.

Now let's try the `Birthday` method.

```
>> my_emp.Birthday()
Happy Birthday, John Doe!
You were 26
You are now 27
ans = employee2
properties:
          name: 'John Doe'
           age: 27
       payRate: 8.7500
       married: 0
      sickDays: 5
list of methods
```

This returned a little more information than we might expect. Although the call looks like what you would expect in other object oriented languages, the methods will *not* actually change the values in a permanent way. That is, although we updated the age in the `Birthday` method, the computer changed a copy of that value within that function. Once the function ends, the changed value is lost. The original value is not changed unless we store the object again.

This is why we see so much information from the function call; since we do not suppress the output with a semi-colon, MATLAB returns the object to the default `ans` variable.

Next, we call the `Birthday` function, and store the returned object back into `my_emp`. Notice that we include the semi-colon, so we only see what the function prints. Also, this example confirms that the stored age was not changed within the object by the previous example.

```
>> my_emp = my_emp.Birthday();
Happy Birthday, John Doe!
You were 26
You are now 27
```

Next, we call the `Birthday` method again, to show that the age property was changed by the previous example. A second call to this method appears below that, with a slightly different syntax.

```
>> my_emp = my_emp.Birthday();
Happy Birthday, John Doe!
You were 27
You are now 28
>> my_emp = Birthday(my_emp);
Happy Birthday, John Doe!
You were 28
You are now 29
```

We still have to set the object to the returned values, to make the changes stick. Both `my_emp = my_emp.Birthday();` and `my_emp = Birthday(my_emp);` are equivalent. MATLAB knows where to find method `Birthday`, even when specified like a normal function.

What if we want to have a variable number of parameters with the constructor? The following code uses the `varargin` and `nargin` keywords, along with a `switch` statement, to select from a variety of possibilities.

```
% employee2b
%
% Show that you can use varargin with the constructor function.
%
% Usage:
%   my_emp = employee2b;
%   my_emp.ShowName;
%
%   my_emp = employee2b('John Doe');
%   my_emp.ShowName;
%
%   my_emp = employee2b('John Doe', 25);
```

```
%    my_emp.ShowName;
%
%    my_emp = employee2b('John Doe', 25, 9.25);
%    my_emp.ShowName;
%
%    my_emp = employee2b('John Doe', 25, 9.25, true);
%    my_emp.ShowName;
%
%    my_emp = employee2b('John Doe', 25, 9.25, true, 7);
%    my_emp.ShowName;
%
%
classdef employee2b
    properties
        name;
        age;
        payRate = 8.75;
        married;
        sickDays = 5;
    end
    methods
        % constructor
        function obj = employee2b(varargin)
            % We expect up to 5 parameters
            % examples:
            %    employee2b()
            %    employee2b(name)
            %    employee2b(name, age)
            %    employee2b(name, age, pay)
            %    employee2b(name, age, pay, married)
            %    employee2b(name, age, pay, married, sickdays)
            switch nargin
                case 1
                    obj.name = varargin{1};
```

```matlab
        case 2
            obj.name = varargin{1};
            obj.age  = varargin{2};
        case 3
            obj.name    = varargin{1};
            obj.age     = varargin{2};
            obj.payRate = varargin{3};
        case 4
            obj.name    = varargin{1};
            obj.age     = varargin{2};
            obj.payRate = varargin{3};
            obj.married = varargin{4};
        case 5
            obj.name    = varargin{1};
            obj.age     = varargin{2};
            obj.payRate = varargin{3};
            obj.married = varargin{4};
            obj.sickDays = varargin{5};
        %otherwise
    end
end
function obj = Birthday(obj)
    % Print a nice message
    disp(sprintf('Happy Birthday, %s!',obj.name))
    % Update the age info
    disp(sprintf('You were %d',obj.age));
    obj.age = obj.age + 1;
    disp(sprintf('You are now %d',obj.age));
end
function mystr = GetName(obj)
    % return the name
    mystr = obj.name;
end
function mystr = ShowName(obj)
    disp(sprintf('name = %s',obj.name))
```

```
        disp(sprintf('age = %d',obj.age))
        disp(sprintf('pay rate = %6.2f',obj.payRate))
        if (obj.married)
            disp('married');
        else
            disp('single');
        end
        disp(sprintf('number of sick days = %d',obj.sickDays))
        % return the name
        mystr = obj.name;
    end
  end
end
```

Running the `employee2b` constructor with different parameters shows that it populates the object and overwrite defaults as needed.

5.4 INHERITING THE "GET" AND "SET" METHODS

Next, we see an example that uses inheritance, the idea of defining one class as a refinement of an existing one, allowing reuse of the good parts. For example, a new class called "cashier" could inherit from the "employee" class.

File "exClass.m" contains a simple example of a class, used to represent colored squares. Each square has properties of a row, a column, a color, and a size. It has a constructor method, to set the row, column, and color when the user creates an object. Other methods allow the user to set the row, column, or color individually. A final method, called `draw`, uses the `plot` function to show the square on a figure. The class defined in "exClass.m" appears in the following listing.

```
classdef exClass
    properties
        myRow = 0;
        myCol = 0;
        color = 'red';
        mySize = 20;
    end
```

```
methods
    % Constructor
    function obj = exClass(r, c, colorStr)
        obj.myRow = r;
        obj.myCol = c;
        obj.color = colorStr;
    end
    function obj1 = setCol(obj1, c)
        obj1.myCol = c;
    end
    function obj1 = setRow(obj1, r)
        obj1.myRow = r;
    end
    function obj1 = setColor(obj1, colorStr)
        obj1.color = colorStr;
    end
    function draw(obj1)
        hold on
        % Put a square at this location.
        plot(obj1.myCol, obj1.myRow, ...
        strcat('s', obj1.color(1)), ...
         'MarkerFaceColor', obj1.color(1), ...
         'MarkerSize', obj1.mySize);
    end
    end
end
```

To demonstrate the class, we can create an object from this class, then draw it. (See the "use_exClass.m" program.) First, we create a figure window, and set the axis to 0 through 10 for both the x-axis and y-axis. We could skip the axis command, although this example looks better with it.

```
>> figure();
>> axis([0 10 0 10]);
>> myobject = exClass(1, 2, 'blue');
>> myobject.draw();
```

The `exClass` command calls the constructor method and returns an object. Then a call to the `draw` method shows the square on the figure. Next, we change the color and row, and draw the square again.

```
>> myobject = myobject.setColor('green');
>> myobject = myobject.setRow(2);
>> myobject.draw();
```

At this point, you should see a small blue square, with a small green square above it.

So far, we have only one object. What if we want a variety of objects of this class? The next example shows the creation of a small array of such objects. Creating an array makes drawing all of the squares easy.

```
myobjects(1) = exClass(1, 2, 'blue');
myobjects(2) = exClass(2, 2, 'green');
myobjects(3) = exClass(1, 3, 'red');
myobjects(4) = exClass(2, 3, 'yellow');
for k=1:length(myobjects)
    myobjects(k).draw();
end
```

As the preceding code shows, we can draw each square in turn with a simple `for` loop. Running this code, you should see the same blue and green squares as before, with a red square to the right of the blue one, and a yellow square above the red one.

Next, we modify the example to inherit the `set` and `get` methods like the figure handles use. To do this, change the `classdef` line accordingly. Since the class should have the same name as the file, the file "exHandleClass.m" will contain a copy of the "exClass.m" example, with some modifications.

```
classdef exHandleClass < matlab.mixin.SetGet
```

This defines `exHandleClass` as a subclass of `matlab.mixin.SetGet`, allowing it to use the methods of that class. (MATLAB also allows `hgsetget`, although it will be phased out in favor of `matlab.mixin.SetGet`.) Besides the altered `classdef` line, and renaming from `exClass` to `exHandleClass`, we can remove the `setCol`, `setRow`, and `setColor` methods. This makes the new example smaller.

The following code sets up the figure, creates an object, and draws it, just like before. (File "use_exHandleClass.m" contains the following code.)

```
figure();
axis([0 10 0 10]);
myobject = exHandleClass(1, 2, 'blue');
myobject.draw();
```

We can, however, still change the attributes.

```
set(myobject, 'color', 'green');
set(myobject, 'myRow', 2);
myobject.draw();
disp(get(myobject, 'color'));
```

Here, the code uses the `set` method to alter the `color` and `myRow` properties of the object. Drawing the object shows a green square, again above the blue one. In response to the `disp` command, the computer prints "green," showing that the `get` worked as expected.

Now we try one more example. It changes the color to yellow, gets the current value of `myCol`, adds one to that, then sets `myCol` to the new value.

Table 5.1 Data grouping comparison.

	Mix of datatypes?	Sub-part names?	Special functions?
array/matrix	no	no	no
cell array	yes	no	no
structure	yes	yes	no
class	yes	yes	yes

```
myobject.set('color', 'yellow');
newColumn = myobject.get('myCol') + 1;
myobject.set('myCol', newColumn);
myobject.draw();
```

The resulting figure shows the yellow square to the right of the green one, that is, one column over.

Inheritance is a good object-oriented programming concept to know. Other languages, such as Java, use it extensively. Using the inheritance mechanism to allow `get` and `set` methods makes programming with objects more uniform, and keeps us from having to implement our own set and get methods.

5.5   COMPARING DIFFERENT WAYS TO COMBINE DATA

We have seen several ways to group data. Table 5.1 shows a comparison of the different data grouping ways, from the least complicated (array/matrix) at the top, getting progressively more abstract down the list. Classes allow for the most features, yet are the most complex grouping. Proponents of object-oriented programming argue that well-defined classes are re-usable. One person can develop the class, then many others can utilize it without having to understand how it works. Of course, the same could be said about functions. Given the options, how should you group your data? Without further considerations, use the least complicated way among the options.

5.6   ENUMERATION AND CATEGORIES

Some computer languages, such as C, support enumeration. The word *enumerate* comes from Latin, meaning to count or recount, so an enumeration just means a list of possible values. In a computing language, an enumeration assigns numbers to different categories, where the numbers do not really matter, as long as they are consistent.

For example, data records with people might include their marital status. It could be as simple as married or unmarried, or something more complex that includes separated, divorced, and widowed. Whatever the case, there will be a rather small number of discrete possibilities, where a person falls into one and only one group. One possibility is to encode each possible status with a string, although this can be cumbersome as strings take more memory to store than integers, and comparing to strings takes more comparisons than comparing two numbers. That is, if two strings start with the same character, we must also compare the second characters, and we do not know that they match exactly until we have examined all of the characters. Thus, a status could use enumeration instead, where each possible status has an integer associated with it: a code like 1 for unmarried and 2 for married, but the numbers have no obvious relation to the category. In the program, we do not normally care what the value a status has, since we work with it symbolically, i.e., with the label. The following examples demonstrate ways to work with categories, using survey responses as the categories.

5.6.1 Enumeration with a Structure and Numbers

With MATLAB, we can do enumeration in a natural way, using a structure and fields. In the following example, we set up a structure called RESPONSE, and give it fields called STRONG_DISAGREE, DISAGREE, NEITHER, AGREE, and STRONG_AGREE. This example uses all capital letters in the structure and field names, since these values would be set at the beginning of the program, and not altered. We use his convention for constants. While they could be re-assigned, using all capital letters indicates to programmers that these should not be changed.

```
RESPONSE.STRONG_DISAGREE = 0;
RESPONSE.DISAGREE = 1;
RESPONSE.NEITHER = 2;
RESPONSE.AGREE = 3;
RESPONSE.STRONG_AGREE = 4;
```

Once the structure has been defined, we use it as in the following code.

```
b = RESPONSE.NEITHER;
% many lines later..
switch (b)
    case RESPONSE.STRONG_DISAGREE
        disp('very unhappy');
    case RESPONSE.DISAGREE
        disp('unhappy');
    case RESPONSE.NEITHER
        disp('in the middle');
    case RESPONSE.AGREE
        disp('happy');
    case RESPONSE.STRONG_AGREE
        disp('very happy');
    otherwise
        disp('unknown value');
end
```

It outputs the following.

```
in the middle
```

Using a numeric value means that it takes a relatively low amount of memory. Also, comparing two numbers happens much faster and more efficiently than comparing two strings, since we make a single comparison instead of comparing the first character of each string, then the second characters if the first characters matched, then the third characters if the second ones matched, etc. Using `RESPONSE.NEITHER` to encode the "neither agree nor disagree" response makes it clear to the people writing or maintaining the program.

5.6.2 Enumeration with a Structure and Strings

What if we desire to encode the values as strings rather than numbers? The following code defines the structure with strings.

```
RESPONSE.STRONG_DISAGREE = 'strongly disagree';
RESPONSE.DISAGREE = 'disagree';
RESPONSE.NEITHER = 'neither agree nor disagree';
RESPONSE.AGREE = 'agree';
RESPONSE.STRONG_AGREE = 'strongly agree';
```

Now we assign a variable, and later use it.

```
b = RESPONSE.NEITHER;
% many lines later..
switch (b)
    case RESPONSE.STRONG_DISAGREE
        disp('very unhappy');
    case RESPONSE.DISAGREE
        disp('unhappy');
    case RESPONSE.NEITHER
        disp('in the middle');
    case RESPONSE.AGREE
        disp('happy');
    case RESPONSE.STRONG_AGREE
        disp('very happy');
    otherwise
        disp('unknown value');
end
```

From our point of view, the code looks almost identical to the earlier example using numbers. There are a couple of differences, however. First, we store strings, so a variable like b in the preceding code takes more memory space than a value of type double. Another difference becomes apparent when comparing two items.

```
>> RESPONSE.NEITHER < RESPONSE.AGREE
Matrix dimensions must agree.
```

This generates an error because it attempts to compare two strings of different lengths. Even if the strings have the same lengths, the results are not quite what we want. Suppose that we add another possibility, with an extra space so that it matches the length of the "disagree" string.

```
>> RESPONSE.NEUTRAL = 'neutral ';
>> RESPONSE.DISAGREE < RESPONSE.NEUTRAL
ans =
  1x8 logical array
   1  0  1  1  1  0  1  0
```

The logical array only indicates that some letters meet the condition. For example, the character in the first position, "d" in "disagree," is less than the "n" in "neutral." Given that the responses may not have an inherent order, using strings certainly does work.

5.6.3 Enumeration with a Class Definition

Using the enumeration keyword inside a class definition provides another way to accomplish an enumeration. The following class definition comes from a file called RESPONSE_Enum.m. The text "Enum" simply reminds us what this class accomplishes.

```
classdef RESPONSE_Enum
    enumeration
        STRONG_DISAGREE
        DISAGREE
        NEITHER
        AGREE
        STRONG_AGREE
    end
end
```

With the class defined, we can have MATLAB tell us about it through the enumeration command.

```
>> enumeration RESPONSE_Enum
Enumeration members for class 'RESPONSE_Enum':
    STRONG_DISAGREE
    DISAGREE
    NEITHER
    AGREE
    STRONG_AGREE
>> a = RESPONSE_Enum.NEITHER;
>> b = RESPONSE_Enum.AGREE;
```

Can we compare them?

```
>> disp(a < b)
Undefined operator '<' for input arguments of type
'RESPONSE_Enum'.
```

Aside from the order that the set members appear, we do not specify how the different responses relate to each other. We could list them in any order that we like. To allow for relative comparisons, we must give the set members additional information. In the next example, we have the class RESPONSE_Enum_v2 inherit from the uint8 class. This means that the new class gets the properties and methods from the uint8 class, including comparison operations. In the following, each element of the enumeration now gets a number associated with it.

```
classdef RESPONSE_Enum_v2 < uint8
    enumeration
        STRONG_DISAGREE (-2)
        DISAGREE (-1)
        NEITHER (0)
        AGREE (1)
        STRONG_AGREE (2)
    end
end
```

If we define two variables according to this class, can we compare them now?

```
>> a = RESPONSE_Enum_v2.NEITHER;
>> b = RESPONSE_Enum_v2.AGREE;
>> disp(a < b)
    1
```

Defining `a` and `b` with this class means that we can compare them relatively. The values used here could be simply 1, 2, 3, and so forth, or they could have a more logical meaning. In this example, the numbers represent how positive or negative the survey response is, i.e., a negative value indicates a negative opinion. What if we desire to get the value directly? We can try using `disp`, although it returns the set member. Converting it to `uint8` first will give the internal number.

```
>> disp(b)
   AGREE
>> disp(uint8(b))
   1
>> disp(double(b))
    1
```

As the last example shows, converting the set value to `double` also gives us the number.

5.6.4 Categorical Sets

Categories are a way to deal with data that fall into one of several possibilities. As mentioned previously, we might use a string to store a status, however, strings can take up a lot of memory space. MATLAB supports a "categorical" array, which works like storing strings, but with efficient memory usage. In other words, if we have thousands of data points to store, and each one can only be one of a few possibilities, it makes sense to store simply which possibility it is. MATLAB gives us a way to do this, a way that hides some of the details. We create a "categorical" array using the `categorical` constructor, a method for the class, called when the computer creates a new variable from the class type. Let variable `RESPONSE_ValueSet` comprise the example set of values.

```
RESPONSE.STRONG_DISAGREE = 'strongly disagree';
RESPONSE.DISAGREE = 'disagree';
RESPONSE.NEITHER = 'neither agree nor disagree';
RESPONSE.AGREE = 'agree';
RESPONSE.STRONG_AGREE = 'strongly agree';
RESPONSE_ValueSet = {RESPONSE.STRONG_DISAGREE, RESPONSE.DISAGREE, ...
    RESPONSE.NEITHER, RESPONSE.AGREE, ...
    RESPONSE.STRONG_AGREE};
```

A value-set contains only unique values; i.e. the set of possible values that a categorical array can have. Notice how the RESPONSE_ValueSet stores a cell array; if we use square brackets to define it instead, it would run all of the strings together. Now imagine that variable survey holds the results of a survey administered to one person, for brevity, as in the following.

```
survey = {RESPONSE.NEITHER, RESPONSE.STRONG_DISAGREE, RESPONSE.AGREE, ...
    RESPONSE.NEITHER, RESPONSE.DISAGREE, RESPONSE.AGREE, ...
    RESPONSE.AGREE, RESPONSE.AGREE, RESPONSE.NEITHER, ...
    RESPONSE.DISAGREE};
```

Next, we store the survey as a categorical array, in a variable called survey_cat. The next line of code shows an example of the categorical constructor.

```
>> survey_cat = categorical(survey, RESPONSE_ValueSet)
survey_cat =
  1x10 categorical array
  Columns 1 through 3
    neither agree nor...    strongly disagree    agree
  Columns 4 through 7
    neither agree nor...    disagree    agree    agree
  Columns 8 through 10
    agree    neither agree nor...    disagree
```

How does the variable survey_cat differ from the variable survey? They both appear to store the same information, but a closer look with the whos command reveals that categorical variable, survey_cat, takes up about half as many bytes of memory.

```
>> whos
  Name                Size    Bytes    Class         Attributes
  RESPONSE            1x1      1020    struct
  RESPONSE_ValueSet   1x5       700    cell
  survey              1x10     1376    cell
  survey_cat          1x10      712    categorical
```

This shows that making a category can take less space than using strings. Using the categorical array comes with some "overhead" of the value-set, although that quickly becomes negligible when the data (i.e., survey_cat) grows large.

We can use the ordinal categorical array like an enumerated type. The word *ordinal* means ordered, or position within a list. The categories in these arrays have an order, so that we can compare them relatively.

```
survey_cat_ordinal = categorical(survey, ...
    RESPONSE_ValueSet, 'Ordinal', true);
```

Examining the variable `survey_cat_ordinal`, we see that it appears to be a categorical array like `survey_cat`. The comparison between two entries of each shows the difference.

```
>> disp(survey_cat(1) < survey_cat(2))
Error using  <  (line 26)
Relational comparisons are not allowed for categorical
arrays that are not ordinal.
>> disp(survey_cat_ordinal(1) < survey_cat_ordinal(2))
    0
```

As the code shows, the first array `survey_cat` does not have the less than operation defined. However, the ordinal version of it, `survey_cat_ordinal`, does allow such a comparison. A categorical array does not necessarily have an order; for example, a survey question might ask if a visitor is there for business, vacation, or both. MATLAB supports categorical arrays with a variety of methods, such as `hist` for a histogram and `sort` to group the same responses together. For example, the `sort` method gives the following response.

```
>> sort(survey_cat)
ans =
  1x10 categorical array
  Columns 1 through 3
    strongly disagree    disagree    disagree
  Columns 4 through 5
    neither agree nor...    neither agree nor...
  Columns 6 through 9
    neither agree nor...    agree    agree    agree
  Column 10
    agree
```

Figure 5.1 shows the result of the command `hist(survey_cat)`, which makes a bar chart of the responses. The documentation under `categorical` lists many more supporting methods.

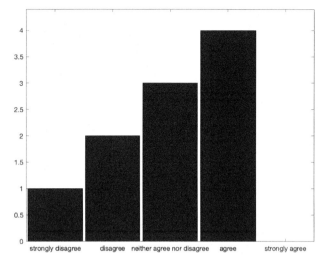

FIGURE 5.1 An example output from the `hist` command on a categorical array.

5.7 SUMMARY

This chapter presents a few advanced ways to group data together. When writing a program, we may start with data stored as individual variables. As the program develops, and we add more data, the need to group the data together becomes apparent. We can store homogenous data (i.e., values all of the same type) in an array or matrix. However, heterogeneous data (i.e., data of different types like strings and integers) presents a challenge, and MATLAB gives us several options. Cell arrays allow us to mix types of data and refer to it by the same variable name, indexing with curly braces. Structures provide a way to store data with named fields, so that a variable plus the field name provides a description of what the data represents, at least when the programmer chooses the names thoughtfully. Classes take this a step further by allowing special functions, called methods, to be defined and associated with the data.

EXERCISES

1. Create a structure to store an array of run-length encoded values. It should store the value, and the number of repetitions as two fields. Then make an array of this structure for the sequence "1 - 2, 4 - 1, 1 - 7, 1 - 3, 1 - 8, 2 - 2, 1 - 7." With a simple loop to access and print each element of the structure array, verify that it gives the expected output.

2. Convert a sequence of character values to run-length encoding, using a class. The class should have variables to store the original sequence of characters, as well as the run-length encoding information, and methods to convert back and forth between the two ways of representing the values. Count repeats in a sequence of numbers, then output count followed by the character. For example, "baaaagchbbg" should output "1 - b, 4 - a, 1 - g, 1 - c, 1 - h, 2 - b, 1 - g."

3. Using an example table in .csv format (e.g. `example_table.csv`), read it in, change a data value (such as adding 1 to John Doe's age), and write it back to a .csv file.

4. Using the example employee class definition, change a data value (such as adding 1 to John Doe's age). Verify that the object has the updated value.

5. Using the last example BMI class definition, add a Boolean property called `active`, and create a new method to calculate BMI using that information. An active person such as a jogger or weight-lifter is likely to have more muscle mass than an inactive person, and the new method can produce a lower BMI as a result. This is non-standard, so make the active adjustment whatever you want it to be.

PROJECT

• **A Structure for Lines and Points**
Create a structure to store line segments and points. Each line has a starting X and Y, an ending X and Y, a color, and an optional symbol. Each point has a starting X and Y, a color, and a symbol. Make a function to plot all of the line segments and points in an array of structure elements. The colors and symbols should be compatible with MATLAB's plot function, such as b for blue.
The following code may be helpful as a template.

```
plot(10, 20, 'r*');
hold on
plot([1, 10], [1, 20], 'g');
```

This plots a red asterisk at (10, 20), then draws a green line from (1, 1) to (10, 20).

## CHAPTER 6

FILE INPUT AND OUTPUT

To work with a file, programming languages provide commands to open a file, read from it, write to it, and close it. A program can have several files open at the same time. For example, it might open one file to read, and another to write. Typically, a program will open a file for either reading or writing, although it is possible to do both. Opening a file informs the computer's operating system what name to use for the file, and how the program will interact with it. The operating system assigns a *handle* to the file: an integer allowing the program to refer to the file, even with several other open files.

The following command opens a file named "exampledata.z" for writing, indicated by the second parameter (`'w'`). MATLAB's help calls this the permission, although it should not be confused with the Unix-style file permissions. Note that opening the file with `'w'` will overwrite the file if it already exists. Also note that the extension ".z" does not mean anything, and was chosen in an attempt to give the file a unique name. Command `fopen` attempts to open the file, and assigns the handle to variable `myfile`. Normally, you are encouraged to try out the commands as we come across them. However, the following example creates a new file, so you might want to wait until Section 6.1, before trying this.

```
fname = 'exampledata.z';
myfile = fopen(fname, 'w');
fclose(myfile);
```

Notice that it "attempts to" open the file. A lot of things can go wrong: maybe the file system is full, maybe the user does not have permission to write to the current directory, or maybe the filename is already being used and cannot be overwritten. If the computer could not open the file, it will return a value of -1. We should check for this, as detailed in the next section.

If we want to open a file to read, we also use `fopen`. The parameter (`'r'`) tells the computer to open this file for reading.

```
fname = 'exampledata.z';
myfile = fopen(fname, 'r');
fclose(myfile);
```

If you are following along with a MATLAB session and trying these commands, you should either change the filename above, or try this after the first file has been closed.

Besides opening a file for reading or writing, another possibility is to open the file using `'a'`, for append. This also allows a program to write to the file, except that it does not erase the file's contents. Instead, everything written will be added to the end of the file.

All of these ways to open a file can be mixed with the addition of the plus sign, e.g., `'r+'` opens it for reading and writing. So does `'w+'`, except that the former does not create the file if it does not already exist, while the latter does create the file in that case, and destroys the previous contents. Opening a file with `'a+'` allows both reading and writing, where writing to it adds to the end. There are a couple of other, more advanced, permissions; see the MATLAB help if you are curious.

6.1   CHECKING IF THE FILE OPENED SUCCESSFULLY

A lot of things can go wrong, so we must examine variable `myfile` to see if the attempt failed. An incorrect filename is the most likely problem when a file fails to open. Other potential problems include a lack of permission, and trying to read from the wrong directory. That is, the filename could be correct, and the file may exist, but if the computer cannot locate it, it will fail. A way to fix this is to specify the complete path with the file. The following shows what it might look like, for several different operating systems.

```
myfile = '/Users/myaccount/matlab_work/exampledata.z'; % Mac
myfile = '/home/myaccount/matlab_work/exampledata.z'; % Linux
myfile = 'C:\myaccount\matlab_work\exampledata.z'; % Microsoft
```

In any of these, the text "myaccount" needs to be replaced with whatever your computer uses. Depending on how your computer is configured, you may need to alter other parts of the preceding text, too. The "matlab_work" directory will not exist unless you create it, although there might be a suitable directory already in place, such as "Documents/MATLAB." Also, you could simply use `cd` to change to the correct directory.

The code below checks to see if the file opened successfully.

```
if (myfile == -1)
    error(sprintf('File "%s" open did not work.', fname));
    return
end
```

If it worked, variable `myfile` will have a positive, numeric value that MATLAB uses to refer to that file. The `error` command allows the program to gracefully display a message, and the `return` command stops this program from running. It is a good idea to tell the user the name of the file that could not be opened, especially if the user specified the filename. Perhaps they mistyped it.

The `fopen` command can also provide a second return value of a string, indicating the problem. For example, let's attempt to open a file that does not exist. See program `readWriteEx1.m` in the accompanying files.

```
fname = 'Idonotexist';
[myfile, myerror] = fopen(fname, 'r');
if (myfile == -1)
    disp(myerror);
end
```

Suppose that we run the above commands. It should print the following message.

```
No such file or directory
```

Of course we can combine this with the preceding `error` command, to provide as much information as possible to the user.

Whenever we open a file, we must close it later, unless the operating system returns an error with `fopen`. In this example, we attempt to open a file that does not exist, and then close it.

```
>> fname = 'Idonotexist';
>> myfile = fopen(fname, 'r');
>> fclose(myfile);
Error using fclose
Invalid file identifier. Use fopen to generate a valid file
identifier.
```

The file did not open, although the computer did not explicitly tell us that at the time. Only when we try to use `myfile` again do we get an error. Notice that this example fails because it cannot close a file that did not open. Normally, whenever we have an `fopen` command, we also have a matching `fclose` command. To avoid an error message like this, we should check the file identifier (`myfile`) and quit. Often, you will see code like the following.

```
if (myfile == -1)
    error(sprintf('File "%s" open did not work.', fname));
    return
end
```

Not only does it print an error message, the `return` command stops the program and "returns" control to whatever called it. In these examples, control returns back to the command window, although you could have a program call another program, and it could call another program, and so forth. The computer skips any remaining commands in a program after it reaches a `return` statement. Many programs assume that the file open will be successful, and when it fails, they simply quit. Other commands also quit a program, such as the `exit` and `quit` commands, although you should avoid these unless you have a good reason to use one of them. Not only do they quit the program, they also close the MATLAB session as if the user types `exit` at the command prompt.

Since the `fopen` command does not stop the program when the file does not open, we have the flexibility to handle this the way that we choose. For example, we might try to open a file just to see if it already exists. Suppose that we have the user specify the name of a file that our program will overwrite. If the file already exists, we might want to prompt the user to ask if another filename should be used instead. Thus, we can use `fopen` to open the specified file for reading, and if it succeeds, we close it and ask the user if it is OK to overwrite it. If the file open command fails, the program can quietly go on to the next part, such as opening the file again, but this time for writing.

6.2 MACHINE FORMATS AND ENCODINGS

MATLAB also supports various machine formats and encodings for files. To illustrate the machine format, `'b'` stands for a "big-endian" format, meaning the big, or more significant part, is stored at the end. At any one time, a computer works with a limited amount of data, called its word size. Most likely, you do the same thing. If you have to add two numbers with ten digits each, most people cannot look at the numbers and figure out the answer in their head. Instead, they write down the two numbers, add the two digits in the right-most column, write down the resulting sum and carry digits, then add the two digits in the next column, along with the previous carry. In this way, a person works from right to left one column at a time, and only has to add at most three digits. With the aid of writing on the paper, anyone can add numbers together, no matter how many digits they contain. Think of working with digits like this as a one-digit word size. What if someone employs this same algorithm, but writes the numbers from left to right, and adds them one column at a time from left to right? It would still work, but we would need to know that the result should be read in the opposite order of what we expect. This is analogous to the big-endian versus little-endian format. Perhaps a better analogy is the date code. People in the US write the date as month-day-year, while people in Europe write it as day-month-year. Either way works, but when examining a date like 02-11-18, we need to know if this means February 11th or November 2nd. When your computer stores a value larger than its word size, it must store it either with the big part first, or the small part first. Either way could work; and both have been used.

An example encoding is `'US-ASCII'`. ASCII stands for American Standard Code for Information Interchange, a character set that specifies numbers for letters A to Z, lower-case letters, punctuation, numerals 0 to 9, and some other codes to control output. Some codes are useful, like the code for a space, a tab, and end of line. It also contains codes for things like the bell and vertical tab, that are not as useful for modern computers as they were for the early days of typewriter keyboards and paper displays. Many of the symbols on your keyboard have a definition in ASCII. ASCII is still widely used, however, other encodings like UTF-8 (short for Unicode Transformation Format, 8 bit) are also commonly used.

6.3   COMMANDS TO READ FROM, AND WRITE TO, A FILE

Once the file has been opened, we can write to it, or read from it. You can also have multiple open files, for example, to read from one and write to another. MATLAB provides several functions to read from a file, and several other functions to write to a file. The main differences between these commands comes down to the data format: should the data be treated as text, numbers, or a combination? Commands `fgetl` and `fgets` both get the sequence of characters from the file until the next new-line character, and differ with the inclusion of the new-line character (`fgetl` does not include it). Thus, `fgetl` gets the next line from the file, while `fgets` gets the next string from the file, with an optional argument to specify the number of characters to get. A new-line character is a special one that indicates that the current line ends, and a new one will begin. It may be coded as a carriage-return, a line-feed, or both, depending on your computer's operating system. (Yes, the new-line "character" may in fact be two characters to your computer.) The commands `fread` and `fwrite` are duals of each other, meaning that they are equivalent in the opposite sense, as are `fscanf` and `fprintf`. That is, if one program uses `fwrite` (or `fprintf`) to write to a file, another program would likely use `fread` (or `fscanf`) to read that file's contents.

When reading from a file, the computer must internally keep track of a file pointer, so that it knows what to read next. Imagine that you are reading a book and are interrupted; you might place a finger on the last line that you read, literally pointing to keep track of it. Going back to the book, especially if you are asked to read the next line, you might move your finger along the text to make sure you do not lose the place. In a similar way, the computer keeps track of what to read next. Just as you could skip ahead by a certain amount, or skip backwards by a number of pages, the computer could skip forward or backward in the file. The command `ftell` returns the location of the file's pointer (called a "file position indicator" in the MATLAB help text). To skip to a different location, the command `fseek` moves the pointer to the given place. Also related, the command `feof` lets the program know if the computer has reached the end of file. When reading a file a little at a time, a program typically uses `feof` as part of a `while` loop condition, in effect saying "while we have not reached the end of the file ...".

Just as a `fopen` prepares the computer to use a file, a good program will call `fclose` when finished with the file. Keep in mind that the computer's operating system governs the use of files, and carries out the commands we give it as efficiently as possible. This means that it might not physically write to a file as soon as we tell it; instead it will "buffer" the data. Closing the file lets the computer know that there will be no more updates to the file, at least until we open it again. The computer can therefore finish up anything left to do, such as writing out the last part, and freeing resources like buffer memory. Whether reading, writing, or both, always instruct the computer to close the file when done using it.

Table 6.1 summarizes the file commands. A program that uses one of the commands shown in the table would also use other commands. For example, a program would open a file, check the file identifier for success, read from the file, and close it. If it does multiple reads, it should check to see if the end-of-file has been reached before trying to read more. Another program might open a file, check the file identifier for success, write to the file, and close it.

6.4   A FEW COMPLETE EXAMPLES OF FILE I/O

Now that we have an idea about that file input/output process, let's try a few complete examples. First, we create a file. The name "exampledata.z" should not correspond to anything that you already have. Before experimenting, always make back-up copies of any important files. Note that if the file already exists, the following code overwrites it. See program `readWriteEx2.m`.

Table 6.1 File input and output commands.

Command	Description	Type of activity
fopen	Open a file, the first thing to do.	set up
ferror	Get the error message.	error
fgetl	Get a line of input until new-line character. The new-line character is not part of the string.	file input
fgets	Get a string of input until new-line character. The new-line character is part of the string.	file input
fprintf	Write to a file according to a specified format.	file output
fread	Get some (or all) of a file at once.	file input
fscanf	Get some of a file, according to a specified format.	file input
fseek	Move the file pointer that determines where to read/write next.	set up
ftell	Report the file pointer that determines where to read/write next.	set up
feof	Determine if we have reached the end-of-file.	set up
frewind	Move the file pointer to the file's start.	set up
fwrite	Write to a file.	file output
fclose	Close a file, the last thing to do.	set up

```
fname = 'exampledata.z';
myfile = fopen(fname, 'w');
if (myfile == -1)
    error(sprintf('File "%s" open did not work.', fname));
    return
end
fprintf(myfile, '%d', 100:-1:0);
fclose(myfile);
```

This example opens the file "exampledata.z" for writing. Then it checks to make sure the file opened without error. Next, it prints integer values to the file, from 100 down to 0. Finally, it closes the file. After this runs, how do we know if it worked? We use the `type` command, which simply echoes the file contents to the command window. The `type` command does not work with variables. Even though we have the name of the file stored in variable `fname`, we must still repeat the name with the `type` command.

```
>> type exampledata.z
10099989796959493929190898887868584838281807978777675747373727
17069686766656646362616059585756555453525150494847464544443424
14039383736353433323130292827262524232221201918171615141312121
1109876543210
```

Note that the preceding output has only one line, and was formatted to fit the page's width. From this, we observe that it worked. Somewhat. It certainly did create the file and write the numbers 100 down to 0. How do we make sense of it now? If we want to read these values, how do we know how many digits to expect per value? We need a better solution.

The following code repeats what we had previously, with one crucial difference. The `fprintf` command now contains a space in the format specifier. In other words, this prints a number to the file, followed by a space. See program `readWriteEx3.m`.

```
fname = 'exampledata.z';
myfile = fopen(fname, 'w');
if (myfile == -1)
    error(sprintf('File "%s" open did not work.', fname));
    return
end
fprintf(myfile, '%d ', 100:-1:0);
fclose(myfile);
```

Let's examine the output.

```
>> type exampledata.z
100 99 98 97 96 95 94 93 92 91 90 89 88 87 86 85 84 83 82 81
80 79 78 77 76 75 74 73 72 71 70 69 68 67 66 65 64 63 62 61
60 59 58 57 56 55 54 53 52 51 50 49 48 47 46 45 44 43 42 41
40 39 38 37 36 35 34 33 32 31 30 29 28 27 26 25 24 23 22 21
20 19 18 17 16 15 14 13 12 11 10 9 8 7 6 5 4 3 2 1 0
```

Again, the output shown has been reformatted to fit this page. With the spaces, we can easily see that this file contains a list of integer values. It clearly shows where each value ends. If another program reads this file, it should also be able to parse the numbers.

Now we attempt to read the file. You might want to use `clear` to get rid of the currently defined variables, and `clc` to clear the command window. Notice that the following code looks a lot like what we had in the last example. We define the filename, open this file for reading, and check to see if the computer had a problem. Next, the `fscanf` command reads the file, expecting an integer number followed by a space, or in this case, a list of integer numbers with a space following each one. Finally, we close the file. See program `readWriteEx4.m`.

```
fname = 'exampledata.z';
myfile = fopen(fname, 'r');
if (myfile == -1)
    error(sprintf('File "%s" open did not work.', fname));
    return
end
mydata = fscanf(myfile, '%d ');
fclose(myfile);
```

If this works, variable `mydata` will contain the numbers from 100 down to 0. To confirm this, we simply display the array on the command window.

```
>> disp(mydata)
   100
    99
    98
    97
   ...
```

```
3
2
1
0
```

The output here shows an ellipsis ("...") in the interest of space. Trying this yourself should result in all 101 values.

Now that we have an example of writing a file, and an example of reading it, we can try appending to it. In the example below, we open the same file as before, only with the append mode. We check to make sure it opened, then use `fprintf` to write more data to it, in this case the numbers –1 down to –10. Last, we close the file. See program `readWriteEx5.m`.

```
fname = 'exampledata.z';
myfile = fopen(fname, 'a');
if (myfile == -1)
    error(sprintf('File "%s" open did not work.', fname));
    return
end
fprintf(myfile, '%d ', -1:-1:-10);
fclose(myfile);
```

Did it work? We check the file contents with the `type` command.

```
>> type exampledata.z
100 99 98 97 96 95 94 93 92 91 90 89 88 87 86 85 84 83 82 81
80 79 78 77 76 75 74 73 72 71 70 69 68 67 66 65 64 63 62 61
60 59 58 57 56 55 54 53 52 51 50 49 48 47 46 45 44 43 42 41
40 39 38 37 36 35 34 33 32 31 30 29 28 27 26 25 24 23 22 21
20 19 18 17 16 15 14 13 12 11 10 9 8 7 6 5 4 3 2 1 0 -1 -2
-3 -4 -5 -6 -7 -8 -9 -10
```

As we can see, the new version of the file includes the negative integers –1 through –10.

As mentioned previously, the command `fwrite` also writes data to a file, and command `fread` reads data from a file. The following code presents an example using these. First, we set the filename, although this one has an extra character in it ("exampledata.z2"). We open it for writing, and check to make sure that it worked, just like earlier examples. Next, the `fwrite` command writes the integers 100 down to 48 to the file. (Why we stop at 48 instead of 0 will be clear in a minute.) The `fwrite` command returns an integer, the number of values written, although this example simply ignores it. Finally, this example ends with a call to the `fclose` function. See program `readWriteEx6.m`.

```
fname = 'exampledata.z2';
myfile = fopen(fname, 'w');
if (myfile == -1)
    error(sprintf('File "%s" open did not work.', fname));
    return
end
fwrite(myfile, 100:-1:48);
fclose(myfile);
```

So far, this looks just like a previous example. There is a catch, however, which shows up when we examine the file.

```
>> type exampledata.z2
dcba'_^]\[ZYXWVUTSRQPONMLKJIHGFEDCBA@?>=<;:9876543210
```

What happened? Instead of the numbers appearing as integer values, we instead see character codes. A look at the file sizes gives us a clue: the "exampledata.z" file created in previous examples has a file size of 326. This makes sense, since it contains 111 integer values, most with two digits and a space separator. The "exampledata.z2" file only has 53 bytes, and 53 happens to be the number of values written. The following output shows these file sizes.

```
>> ls -l exampledata.z*
-rw-r--r--  1 mweeks  staff  326 Oct 24 21:27 exampledata.z
-rw-r--r--  1 mweeks  staff   53 Oct 24 21:45 exampledata.z2
```

Recall the `ls` generates a list of files, where `-l` specifies a long format listing. While MATLAB supports `ls` on all platforms, the `-l` modifier might not be universally supported.

The preceding output tells us several things about these files. The first set of characters encode the access control list (file permissions), in the format `drwxrwxrwx`, where `d` stands for directory, `r` stands for read permission, `w` for write permission, and `x` for execute, with a - indicating a lack of permission. The `rwx` repeats three times, once for the file's owner, next for the group, and the third time for the world. Therefore, reading `-rw-r--r--` from right to left means that the file is not a directory, the owner can read it, write it, but not execute it, someone in the group can only read it, and someone who has access to the computer can only read it. It makes sense to disallow execution for a data file, however, MATLAB scripts also do not have execute permission since the operating system cannot run them directly. The next column, 1, indicates the number of links to the file, a topic outside the scope of this discussion. Next comes the owner, mweeks in this case, then the group name, staff in this case. Only one person would use the owner's account, but many people could be part of the group. After that, we have the file size, e.g., 326 bytes for the first file. The file's time-stamp indicates the most recent October 24 at 21:27 (9:27 p.m.). Finally, we have the name of the file.

The fwrite command wrote each value as an 8-bit quantity. This explains why the file contents have lower-case "d" down to the numeral "0"; looking at an ASCII table, lower-case "d" has the code 100, while the digit "0" has a code of 48. By the way, although the example stopped at 48, it could have gone down to 32 without a problem. ASCII code 32 means a space, and codes 33 to 47 represent punctuation. What if the example went all the way down to 0? That would include control codes, that do things like mark a new line, along with the bell, back space, tabs, etc. These include many "non-printable" characters, and the results of printing them may be different for different computers. It is a good idea not to print files, including using the type command on them, unless you know that they are text files.

Here, we use fread to get the file contents. We open the file for reading and check to make sure that worked, like before. Then, we read the file. How much should we read at once? We could read the entire file, or we could read a part of it. This example reads a little at a time, asking for 10 values each time. After reading them, it displays them as integers, with a space after each one. Finally, it closes the file. See program readWriteEx7.m.

```
fname = 'exampledata.z2';
myfile = fopen(fname, 'r');
if (myfile == -1)
    error(sprintf('File "%s" open did not work.', fname));
    return
end
while (~feof(myfile))
    dataFromFile = fread(myfile, 10);
    disp(sprintf('%d ', dataFromFile));
end
fclose(myfile);
```

The `feof` condition lets us know if we have reached the end of the file. If not, there must still be data in it to read, so we read it. Note that there might not be 10 values left to read, and the `fread` command returns a second, optional value indicating the number read, as in the following line.

```
[dataFromFile, count] = fread(myfile, 10);
```

We can examine variable `count` to see if it matches the number that we attempted to read.

The number of values to read, 10, illustrates the idea of reading part of a file at a time. However, a larger number might give better performance. Underneath this example, and underneath the MATLAB software itself, lies the operating system that handles file commands. It might do a wonderful job of efficiently doing everything we ask it, or it might simply do what we ask it. If your program run slowly, you might be able to optimize it, and file input/output serves as a good place to look. In other words, reading a larger amount with `fread` might make a noticeable difference in your program's speed.

6.5 SUMMARY

MATLAB provides some built-in functions to import and export data, such as those appearing in Table 6.2. As the table shows, a MATLAB user can read and write a variety of formats for files, depending on the data. For example, the `dlmread` command reads the numbers from a "delimited" file, meaning one that uses certain characters to separate entries. The "delimiter" can be specified, such as a tab or space, although the computer may get it correct without specifying it. For example, if you created the "exampledata.z" file from the preceding example code (readWriteEx3.m), the following command reads it.

```
mydata = dlmread('exampledata.z');
```

If a built-in command will complete the task, it should be used. Aside from being easy, a built-in solution will be simpler for a programmer to follow, and the code will be portable. Sometimes, the problem includes a format that cannot be used with an existing command. In those situations, a good programmer will use the flexible file input/output commands to open the file, check for error, read, write, or append the contents as needed, and close the file.

Table 6.2 Built-in functions to read and write data.

Commands	Description	Format (extension)
`audioread/` `audiowrite`	Audio files	`.wav`, `.mp3`, etc.
`wavread`/`wavwrite` (no longer supported)	Audio files	`.wav`
`csvread`/`csvwrite`	Spreadsheets	`.csv`
`xlsread`/`xlswrite`	Spreadsheets	`.xls`
`dlmread`/`dlmwrite`	Delimited numeric data	user specified
`load`/`save`	MATLAB variables	`.mat`
`imread`/`imwrite`	Image files	`.jpg`, `.jpeg`, `.png`, etc.
`genbankread/` `getgenbank`	Genetic sequence data	`.gbk`

EXERCISES

1. Given a set of e-mail messages in a file, sort them by subject. (This is not a good application of MATLAB, but it is enlightening.)

2. Make a fold/shuffle program: open file `a` and `b`, write out line `a1` with `b1`, then `a2` with `b2`, etc. Thus, each line of file `a` has the corresponding line from file `b` appended to it.

3. Write a program to do base64 encoding/decoding, where a 6 bit value maps to/from a character. The original values should be in a file, and the output values should be written to a new file.

PROJECT

- **Searching Through Data**
  This assignment is to implement a search utility. Given a pattern, your program should look through data until it finds the next occurrence. It should also show that occurrence.

Your program should present the user with an interface that includes the pattern to search for, a "next" button to find the next occurrence of the pattern, and a "quit" button. Also show the data where there is a match, i.e., show a bit before and a bit beyond the search pattern, too.

Use the data in the array "data." This was "save[d]" and available under the file `example_data.mat`. Use the load command to access it. This is example data; be sure that your program works with data besides this single example. If you need it, you can convert from text to integer with a command like: `int8(data(40))`.

To solve your problem, write a program that reads the necessary information to compute and output the indicated values, as efficiently as possible. Design your program by specifying its behavior, identifying the variables and operations it needs to solve the problem, and then organizing the variables and operations into an algorithm. Then code your design in MATLAB using stepwise translation. Finally, test your program thoroughly.

Your program should work for all possible inputs. Make sure that you test it with several different cases.

For an additional challenge: include a "previous" button to allow the user to find the last occurrence. Also, show on the interface the total number of matches found.

RECURSION

Recursion is a programming technique, where we solve a problem by looking at progressively simpler cases of the problem, until we reach a stopping point. To illustrate this, we will use the example of computing a factorial. Suppose we want to find 3!. The answer is $3 \times 2 \times 1$, or 6. If we wanted to then find 4!, we get $4 \times 3 \times 2 \times 1$. Notice how the answer for 4! is $4 \times (3!)$, so if we know 3!, we can do a simple multiplication to find 4!. In general, we can say that $N! = N \times (N - 1)!$. Here is a single-step algorithm to find $N!$, based on the above analysis.

```
1. Find (N-1)!, and multiply the result by N.
```

OK, so how do we find $(N - 1)!$? We can reuse the algorithm above, except for one thing: the algorithm must come to an end. We will revise it, looking for the case when $N = 1$, since 1! = 1.

```
1. If N == 1, return 1
   else Find (N-1)!, and multiply the result by N.
```

Now consider the following function. It computes the factorial using recursion, with an algorithm very similar to the one above.

```
% myfact.m
% Recursion example: factorial
%
function result = myfact(N)
if (N < 2)
    result = 1;
else
    result = N*myfact(N-1);
end
```

To start the program off, we will call it from MATLAB.

```
>> myfact(4)
ans =
    24
```

It gives us the right answer, but to trace through what the computer does, we must know a bit more about how it works.

A *stack* is a common data structure, and the operating system has one. Imagine a set of cafeteria plates, on a spring mechanism. When we remove a plate, another one pops up to take its place. If a cafeteria worker puts some clean plates on the stack, then the next one removed from this stack will be the last one put on it. The data structure that we call a stack works in the same fashion: we *push* new numbers onto the stack, and *pull* (also called *pop*) numbers off the top. We call this a last-in-first-out (LIFO) system. Like a stack of plates, we will have a problem if we go to get a value and the stack is empty, called *underflow*. We also have a problem if we try to put more on the stack after it has reached its capacity, an *overflow* condition. For our purposes here, we will ignore the latter problem. For the former one, we will always push something onto the stack before we pull it off.

Internally, and typically invisible to the user, the computer uses a stack to keep track of a program's execution. When we call a function, the computer will remember its current state. For an analogy, imagine if you are reading a book when someone calls you on the phone. You mark your place, answer the phone, and turn your attention to the conversation. While on the phone, you may hear a knock at the door, in which case you tell the caller to hold on for a minute, while you answer the door. After, say, signing for a package, you close the door and turn your attention back to the caller. Once you end the conversation, you go back to the book. The point of this analogy is that you are able to put one context on hold (e.g., the book), turn your attention to something else, then return to the original context. You do not confuse them, and can pick up where you left off. A computer uses a stack in much the same way; it stores its current context on the stack, does something else such as calling a function, then pulls the context back off the stack when it returns. For the computer, the context includes the location of the next instruction, as well as anything else it must remember, such as the values of registers in the CPU.

7.1 FUNCTION CALLS AND THE STACK

Before we look at how the concept of the stack applies to recursion, let's start with a simple example. Consider the function `sub1mult2`, which subtracts one from the parameter, then multiplies that result by two, then returns it.

```
function x = sub1mult2(y)
x = 2 * (y-1);
```

Calling this function gives us output like the following.

```
>> sub1mult2(5)
ans =
      8
```

We can confirm that this produces the desired function, i.e., $2 \times (5 - 1)$ does equal 8. What if we call it twice from the same line?

```
>> sub1mult2(5) + sub1mult2(7)
ans =
      20
```

The computer obviously finds the result for `sub1mult2(5)` like it did earlier, then finds the result for `sub1mult2(7)`, then adds the two results together. The two function calls are handled much like a person might perform this calculation: read the first part, process it, write down the answer, read the second part, process it, write down the answer, then add the two answers to find the final result. Now what if we use the result from one call as the input to another?

```
>> first = sub1mult2(5);
>> sub1mult2(first)
ans =
      14
```

This case does not present much of a problem; we can see that the first line returns a value to the variable `first`, which we then pass as the parameter to the function on the second line. We can even remove the variable `first`, as in the following code.

```
>> sub1mult2(sub1mult2(5))
ans =
      14
```

This example calls the function twice, once with a parameter of 5, and again with the parameter 8, the result of the first function call. If we were to write out the steps involved in the evaluation, it would look like this.

```
Start function sub1mult2, y = 5
x = 2 * (5 - 1)
```

```
End function sub1mult2, return x (8)
Start function sub1mult2, y = 8
x = 2 * (8 - 1)
End function sub1mult2, return x (14)
```

Now we move to something more complex, even though it does the same thing. The following function subtracts one from the parameter.

```
function x = sub1(y)
x = y - 1;
```

Next, we have a function that multiplies the parameter by two.

```
function x = mult2(y)
x = 2 * y;
```

And finally, we have a function that uses the previous two functions, called `sub1mult2b` since we already use the name `sub1mult2`.

```
function x = sub1mult2b(y)
x = mult2(sub1(y));
```

Keeping track of these takes a bit more effort, especially since each one uses the variables x and y, and each one of those variables has a different meaning. Let's again suppose that we are tracing the execution of the command `sub1mult2b(sub1mult2b(5))`.

```
Start function sub1mult2b, y = 5
Start function sub1, y = 5
x = 5 - 1
End function sub1, return x (4)
Start function mult2, y = 4
x = 2 * 4
End function mult2, return x (8)
x = 8
End function sub1mult2b, return x (8)
Start function sub1mult2b, y = 8
Start function sub1, y = 8
x = 8 - 1
End function sub1, return x (7)
Start function mult2, y = 7
```

```
x = 2 * 7
End function mult2, return x (14)
x = 14
End function sub1mult2b, return x (14)
```

As we can see, the variables change values frequently. What may not be so obvious, is that there are different versions of the variables that exist at the same time. Consider the line x = 2 * 4. According to mult2, x has the value 8 when that line executes. But function sub1mult2b has not yet defined the variable it calls x, meanwhile, function sub1 had a variable called x with a value of 4. If we could talk to the computer, a question like "what is the value of x?" would be met with the reply "which one?".

Now consider the following function.

```
function x = recursiveSub1(y)
disp(sprintf('starting recursiveSub1: y is %d', y));
if (y > 0)
    x = recursiveSub1(y-1);
else
    x = 1;
end
disp(sprintf(' ending recursiveSub1: y is %d', y));
```

Notice that it calls itself, a defining trait of recursion. It prints the y value, then potentially calls itself with y-1, then prints the y value a second time. When called, we get output like the following.

```
>> recursiveSub1(2);
starting recursiveSub1: y is 2
starting recursiveSub1: y is 1
starting recursiveSub1: y is 0
  ending recursiveSub1: y is 0
  ending recursiveSub1: y is 1
  ending recursiveSub1: y is 2
```

During the lines where "starting" prints, we see that the value for y changes, decreasing each time. Then as the "ending" lines print, the value increases. The decreasing part makes sense because of the y-1 in the x = recursiveSub1(y-1) command, but why does the value increase? The key is to realize that the value does not increase; that there is no one value of y.

Instead, there are several y values at once, and after printing the "ending" message, the function ends and the computer resumes the function with the previous value of y.

Table 7.1 shows a chart that keeps track of this function. Each row represents time moving forward, while each column shows the depth of the stack. As the computer does a recursive call, it keeps the old value of y, shown as a move to the column on the right. As a function call ends, the computer will restore the old value of y, represented by a move to the column on the left.

Variable x does not have a value assigned until the call where y has the value zero. Then the function sets it to one, and the computer returns that value to the calling function, which in turn returns it.

Notice that the function includes a clear case where the recursion stops. Also, each recursive call brings us closer to the terminating case. What if you cannot be sure that the algorithm will converge to a solution? Such cases are like infinite loops. Each recursive call uses some of the computer's resources, mainly space on the stack. If the stack runs out of space, the process will crash. In fact, in the early days of computing, a malicious person could crash the (shared) computer by doing this, bringing the computer down for everyone who was using it at the time. Modern operating systems are much better at preventing such problems.

7.2 COMPUTING A FACTORIAL WITH RECURSION

Table 7.2 shows the states of the processor as it recursively computes the myfact function. Each time we call the myfact function, it performs the following pseudocode steps, even though some of them are implied.

```
N = (whatever_value_was_passed)
if N < 2
    rval = 1
else
    find myfact(N-1)
    rval = N * (value_returned_in_above_line)
end
return rval
```

Table 7.1 A simple recursion example. Time flows from top to bottom, while stack depth goes from left to right.

start recursiveSub1(2) y = 2 print y (2) call recursiveSub1(1)		
	start recursiveSub1(1) y = 1 print y (1) call recursiveSub1(0)	
		start recursiveSub1(0) y = 0 print y (0) x = 1 print y (0) end recursiveSub1(0)
	x = 1 print y (1) end recursiveSub1(1)	
x = 1 print y (2) end recursiveSub1(2)		

Table 7.2 How recursion works with the "myfact" function. Time flows from top to bottom, while stack depth goes from left to right.

N = 4 if (N<2) *false* find myfact(N-1)			
	N = 3 if (N<2) *false* find myfact(N-1)		
		N = 2 if (N<2) *false* find myfact(N-1)	

(continued)

(*continued*)

			N = 1 if (N<2) *true* rval = 1 return 1
		rval = 2*(1) return 2	
	rval = 3*(2) return 6		
rval = 4*(6) return 24			

Notice that the right-most column shows the complete run of one iteration of the pseudo-code, done without a recursive call breaking the line.

Could this be done in a more efficient manner? Yes, using a loop should be more efficient. But the point here is to demonstrate how recursion works, and the factorial problem is a simple example of it. Not all recursion problems work easily as loops. Sometimes recursion provides a simple, elegant solution.

7.3   SOLVING A MAZE

Finding the way around a maze poses another example where recursion works well. Here we are presented with a series of choices to go forward, most of which lead to a dead end. With a recursive solution, we advance until we come to a dead end, then work our way backwards until we can try a new route.

First, we define the maze. We will keep things as simple as possible, using a matrix of characters to represent our walls. A blank space represents a spot that we can occupy, the number-sign (#) signifies a wall, and we use the at-sign (@) for the goal.

```
maze = [ ...
'#########################################'; ...
'#            # #                        #'; ...
'####### ##### # #################### #'; ...
'#            # #                   # #'; ...
'# ############ #### ############## ###'; ...
'#               # #         #        #'; ...
'#### ############### # ##### ### #######'; ...
```

```
'#                      #     #        #'; ...
'# ################################### #'; ...
'#     #      #                        #'; ...
'##### ##### ###### ####################'; ...
'#          #       #      #           #'; ...
'############### ###### ### ######### #'; ...
'#       #                             #'; ...
'###### ###### #####################  #'; ...
'#                             @ #    #'; ...
'######################################'];
```

Next, we initialize the current position to the starting row and column. After that, we call the `maze_solver` function (defined below) to find a path to the goal.

```
row = 2;
col = 2;
maze_solver(maze, row, col);
```

See `mymaze.m` for the code defining these variables and calling the maze-solving function.

7.3.1 The Maze Solver Function

How should the maze-solving function work? It is possible for the function call to provide an invalid row and column, so we will first check this. Next, we will check to see if we are at the goal, and print the maze solution if so. Assuming otherwise, we check to make sure that we can occupy the given location. Then we mark this position as visited, and try to move right, then up, then left, then down. The order does not matter, as long as we consistently try the four possibilities in turn.

Now for the code. To know if we have a valid row and column, we do the following.

```
function [valid] = maze_solver(maze, row, col)
valid = false;
[MAXROW, MAXCOL] = size(maze);
% check the row and col
if ((row >= 1) && (row <= MAXROW) && ...
    (col >= 1) && (col <= MAXCOL))
    % continued below
```

We will use Boolean variable `valid` later. For the moment, we assume that the move is invalid until we see otherwise. Next, we find the size of the maze, and check to see if the `row` and `col` variables can be used as indices for our maze matrix.

Now we check to see if we are at the goal.

```
if (maze(row,col) == '@')
    disp('Solved!');
    disp(maze);
end
```

Simply enough, we print the maze to the command window when we find a solution.

Next, we check to make sure that we can occupy the location specified by the `row` and `col` variables by comparing the matrix value to a space.

```
if (maze(row,col) == ' ')
    maze(row, col) = '.';
    valid = true;
end
end % checking the row and col
```

The last `end` statement goes with the first `if` of this function. If the maze has a blank stored at (`row, col`), we then mark it with a period and set `valid` to true. What if the maze has a period stored here? The `valid` flag will not be set to true, and the program treats it the same as a wall character. Think of what this means: any location marked with a period has already been tried, and if we were to try it again, the program could go in cycles indefinitely. At best, re-trying an already-visited spot means that a more efficient solution could exist. Keep in mind that the recursive program naturally "back-tracks" through the data, meaning that markers along a dead-end path are imperma-nent, so a solution could try one of the visited locations again. For example, at an intersection, the program will try one of the directions first, follow it to a dead-end, then back up to that intersection and try the next direction. If it were to come to that intersection again, without backing up, it means that it could not find a solution with the previous direction choice.

Notice that we do not set variable `valid` to true if we arrive at our goal, since the goal character differs from the space. This makes sense logically; we do not keep looking for the goal when we arrive at it. However, this function will actually keep searching after finding a solution. The way it is written, it will find all possible solutions, not just the first one.

Finally, if we are at a spot that we can occupy, we try to move closer to the goal from here. But we perform a blind search; we do not know the goal's location. Instead, we try moving different directions hoping that it will take us one step closer to the goal.

```
if (valid)
    maze_solver(maze, row, col+1);    % Try moving right
    maze_solver(maze, row+1, col);    % Try moving down
    maze_solver(maze, row, col-1);    % Try moving left
    maze_solver(maze, row-1, col);    % Try moving up
end
```

That is all that there is to the maze solver function. If we run it for the maze given above, we get the following output.

```
Solved!
########################################
#.......    # #                        #
#######.##### # #################### #
#.......      # #   ................# #
#.############ ####.##############.###
#.....         #.#          #..... #
#####.##############.# ##### ###.#######
#    ...............     #     #.......#
# #################################.#
#     #       #   ..................#
##### ##### #######.##################
#         #   ....#     #         #
###############.####### ### ######### #
#         #....                     #
###### ######.######################## #
#         ...................@ #   #
########################################
```

We see that the computer found the one (and only) path from the upper left corner to the goal near the bottom right corner. See `maze_solver.m` for the code.

7.3.2 Tracing Through a Small Maze Example

To understand how it works, consider a very simple case, where we can move three spots to the right, and then two spots down to the goal. Assume that all other locations are walls. The code below demonstrates this.

```
maze2 = [ ...
    '######'; ...
    '#    #'; ...
    '#### #'; ...
    '####@#'; ...
    '######'];
row = 2;
col = 2;
maze_solver(maze2, row, col);
```

At the start, we verify that location (2, 2) contains a blank, then try location (2, 3), also a blank, then successfully try location (2, 4), then try location (2, 5). This also contains a blank, so we try one more square to the right, location (2, 6). Since that contains a wall, we do not occupy it. Still at location (2, 5), we try moving down to location (3, 5), which we can occupy. Next, we try location (3, 6), which is also a wall. Still at location (3, 5), we try moving down to location (4, 5). It contains the goal, so we print the maze, as below.

```
Solved!
######
#....#
####.#
####@#
######
```

But we are not yet done. We do not occupy location (4, 5). Instead, from location (3, 5) we try going left (where there is a wall), then up where there is a period marking the fact that we have already been there. With no other possible movements, the function ends for this call. This means that we exhausted all moves from location (3, 5). When the function call returns, the computer will pop the previous state of our variables from the stack.

We will continue on with the function where we left it when the location was (2, 5). Since we have already tried moving right and moving down, we next try moving left. However, that location contains a mark signifying that we were already there, so we cannot move to it. Next, we try moving up, but are blocked by a wall. After exhausting all possibilities from location (2, 5), we return.

Popping the previous variable values from the stack, we now look at moving from location (2, 4) again. Here we have a similar situation: we already explored moving right from here (previously), now we try moving down, moving left, and moving up. None of those are blank squares, so the function call terminates for this location.

Next, we revisit location (2, 3), and meet the same situation as above. Then we try location (2, 2) again, and try going down, then left, then up. Since we have exhausted all possibilities, this function call ends. The call to the function was the first one to `maze_solver`. There is no command after it, so the computer returns the prompt to us in the command window.

For even a small example like this, we see that there is a lot of processing that occurs after we find the goal. A good exercise would be to modify it to quit immediately after discovering a solution.

Given the maze below, what do you think will happen?

```
>> maze3 = [ ...
    '######'; ...
    '#    #'; ...
    '# ## #'; ...
    '#   @#'; ...
    '######'];
>> maze_solver(maze3, 2, 2);
```

There are two possible solutions. Will the program find one solution, the other solution, or both? What should the program do? Which solution do you expect it will find first? If you are not sure, try running it.

Also note that we return the `valid` variable, although we do not actually use it. If desired, the calling function could check its value. Although MATLAB returns it, the program simply ignores it.

7.4   THE KNIGHT'S TOUR

Another problem that lends itself well to recursion is the "knight's tour," using the chess piece. Suppose that the knight is alone on the chess board. Is it possible to move the knight so that it lands on each square once, and only once?

We need to keep track of which squares the knight has visited, and in what order. We do not want a simple "yes" or "no" answer to this problem; we need a solution that we can verify ourselves. Therefore, we will keep a board with the knight's moves on it, for example, a 1 in a square means that the knight started at this square, whereas a 2 in a square means the knight moved to that square next. We need to keep track of squares that have not been visited yet, and initialize all squares on the board to that value. Obviously, we cannot use integers like 1, 2, and 3, since we plan to use those to mean when the knight visits the square. And we cannot use an arbitrarily large value like 100, since the solution will be flexible enough to allow different board sizes. While the standard chess board has 64 squares, the user could want a larger board. We could have another matrix, to represent if a square has been visited or not, then keep the other matrix only for move numbers. However, having a second matrix means using more memory, so we will keep all information on a single matrix. We could use a negative value like –1 to indicate a non-visited square, or we could use 0. Using zero actually saves some time, since the `zeros` function populates a matrix with these values. Therefore, this program represents an unvisited square with a zero.

Now we need to start the knight's tour function. Similarly to the maze solving example, we must give a starting row and column. Also, we initialize the board to a matrix of zeros, and the program looks to the matrix dimensions to know the extent of the board. A typical board has eight rows and eight columns, as a standard chess board, however, this program works with both smaller and larger boards. In the example below, we use a 5×5 board. As you will soon see, a solution exists for a board of that size.

```
row = 1;
col = 1;
board = zeros(5,5);   % A 5x5 board
[solved, solution] = knightstour(row, col, 1, board);
```

We refer to these lines as `run_knightstour` below.

Actually, we can put all of that together into a single line:

```
[solved, solution] = knightstour(1, 1, 1, zeros(5,5))
```

Either way, it is nice to have a small program available to start this function. While we may remember everything about the program now, we are likely to forget. Taking a little time now to document our code can save us much frustration later. The following shows the output for the program.

```
>> run_knightstour
>> solved
solved =
  logical
    1
>> solution
solution =
     1    20    17    12     3
    16    11     2     7    18
    21    24    19     4    13
    10    15     6    23     8
    25    22     9    14     5
```

Above, we run the knight's tour function. Next, we want to know if it worked, so we get the value for `solved`, and see it is 1, corresponding to a solution.

The code for `knightstour` appears below. Notice that it starts with comments, indicating how to use it. Then it checks the `row` and `col`, to make sure that they have valid values. Since these are used to index the `board` matrix, bad values for these indices mean that the program would halt with an error message. A good program should avoid this. The program then checks to see if we have a solution. If not, it attempts to place the knight with one of the eight possible moves. If you are unfamiliar with the game of chess, the knight can jump to a square that is one column and two rows away, or one that is two columns and one row away, resulting in eight possibilities. Each move means a recursive call to this same function. If the function call returns without success, we try the next possible move. For our own convenience, we check that the row and column are valid at the start of the function, rather than having to check each row and column before calling the function.

```
%
% Recursive function to solve the knight's tour.
% This function finds the FIRST solution only.
%
% [solved, solution] = knightstour(row, col, piece, board)
% inputs:
%    row, col specify the starting square
%    piece is the current step; it should be 1 the first time
%      sure, you could make it something else, like 100.
```

```
%     But if it is ever zero, then the function will not work.
%   board is the current state of the board
% outputs:
%   solved tells us if the puzzle have been solved yet.
%     There may be times when there is no solution,
%     such as with a 3x3 board.
%   solution is the final board, with all squares filled.
%     The solution may not be valid, unless solved is true.
%
% example usage:
%     [solved, solution] = knightstour(1, 1, 1, zeros(5,5))
%
function [solved, solution] = knightstour(row, col, piece, board)
% if (cputime > 800)
%     disp('hold on;');
% end

solved = false;    % unless we find it true later.
solution = board;  % give an initial value to the solution
                   % This won't be correct, but at least we
                   % will have something to return.
% Check are the row, col coords OK?
[MaxR, MaxC] = size(board);
if ((row > 0) & (row <= MaxR))
    % No Problem with row
    if ((col > 0) & (col <= MaxC))
        % No problem with col
        if (board(row, col) == 0)
            % board is clear here,
            % so put the piece here,
            board(row, col) = piece;
            % check: is board full? yes -> show it
        solved = true;  % assume it is solved
            done = false;   % assume we are not done
            r = 1;          % start with row 1
            % continue for all rows
```

```
while ((r <= MaxR) && (~done))
    for c=1:MaxC   % do this for all columns
        if (board(r,c) == 0)  % clear square?
            done = true;     % yes, so quit
            solved = false;
        end
    end
    r = r + 1;
end
% and try to move it again
if (solved)
    solution = board;
end
% If we have not yet found a solution, then
% try the possibilities in this order
% 1: r-2, c+1
if (~solved)
    [solved, solution] = knightstour(row-2, ...
    col+1, piece+1, board);
end
% 2: r-1, c+2
if (~solved)
    [solved, solution] = knightstour(row-1, ...
    col+2, piece+1, board);
end
% 3: r+1, c+2
if (~solved)
    [solved, solution] = knightstour(row+1, ...
    col+2, piece+1, board);
end
% 4: r+2, c+1
if (~solved)
    [solved, solution] = knightstour(row+2, ...
    col+1, piece+1, board);
end
```

```
% 5: r+2, c-1
if (~solved)
    [solved, solution] = knightstour(row+2, ...
    col-1, piece+1, board);
end
% 6: r+1, c-2
if (~solved)
    [solved, solution] = knightstour(row+1, ...
    col-2, piece+1, board);
end
% 7: r-1, c-2
if (~solved)
    [solved, solution] = knightstour(row-1, ...
    col-2, piece+1, board);
end
% 8: r-2, c-1
if (~solved)
    [solved, solution] = knightstour(row-2, ...
    col-1, piece+1, board);
end
            end
        end
    end
```

If the board has more rows than columns, would this program still work? How would the code need to be changed with a different piece? The rook might seem trivially easy, since it can move along rows and columns, so one can easily imagine how it visits every square. The bishop also presents an easy case, since that piece can only move along the diagonals, it can only visit half the squares, except for a 1 × 1 board. People have invented other, non-standard pieces, some going back hundreds of years. For example, the squirrel cannot move to an adjacent square, although it can jump to any square on the other side of the adjacent squares. What would the "squirrel tour" look like?

7.5   SUMMARY

This chapter provides an overview of recursion, a programming technique that uses the computer's ability to remember the context. A recursive function is one that calls itself, although it should have a terminating condition, and the algorithm should be one that converges to a solution. Recursion can provide a simple, elegant solution to complex problems. This chapter included a few examples of recursive functions, such as factorial calculation, finding a path through a maze, and solving the knight's tour.

EXERCISES

1. The summation from 1 to n can be expressed as n plus the summation from 1 to $n - 1$.

$$\sum_{i=1}^{n} i = n + \sum_{i=1}^{n-1} i$$

    For example, the sum of 1 to 4 is $1 + 2 + 3 + 4$, which equals $4 + (1 + 2 + 3)$, or 4 plus the sum of 1 to 3. With this in mind, write a recursive function to compute the summation from 1 to a given value.

2. Apply recursion to sorting. Given a list of values, create a function to sort them. It should take an array of values, return the value if it's the only one in the array, return the smallest and largest values if they are the only two, otherwise call itself with the array except for the first value, then return the resulting array with the first value put into its place.

PROJECT

*   **Traversing a Fixed Cost Maze**
    Based on the code to recursively solve a maze, create a set of programs that finds all paths from A to B through a maze, like the following one.

```
###############################
# A 3      3        5     2    #
# ###### ###### ###### ###### #
#1#     #2#     #1#     #3#    #9#
# ###### ###### ###### ###### #
```

```
#    3       7       2       8      #
# ##### ##### ##### ##### #
#1#    #3#    #6#    #5#    #1#
# ##### ##### ##### ##### #
#   6       4       B       2      #
##############################
```

There are many ways to get from A to B, but the numbers represent a cost, such as the amount of time that it takes to traverse that path. If the maze represents a set of city streets, the numbers could mean the amount of travel time in minutes due to traffic. What is the minimum travel time, and what route does that take?

## CHAPTER 8

IMAGES

MATLAB provides powerful functions to work with images. In this chapter, we will see how to access the color values that make up individual color squares (pixels), which in turn make up an image. We will load, manipulate, and save images, as well as make our own images. We will even make a simple animation.

8.1   WORKING WITH AN IMAGE

Some advanced computer science classes, such as image processing, use MATLAB as the language for assignments. Students, who are already proficient in other languages, sometimes ask why. The following three lines demonstrate a motivating answer.

```
x = imread('stRing.JPG');
imshow(x)
imwrite(x, 'stRing.tiff');
```

The first line reads in an image stored as a JPEG file, making the data available under the variable x. Yes, the filename is case sensitive. The oddly capitalized filename comes from the words "string" and "ring" put together. The second line shows the image to the screen. The third line makes a copy of the image, writing it out as a new file and converting it to the TIFF format (with an extension of .tif or .tiff). These three lines show the power of this platform; in another computer language, writing a program to do these things could take all semester!

The code for this example, as well as the following examples, appears in the file image_demo.m. It uses the pause function between the examples, so that you can step through them as desired. The `pause` function, without a parameter, waits for the user to press a key before continuing. You may also want to try changing the `pause` commands to `pause(5)`, indicating that the computer should wait for 5 seconds before automatically continuing. If you make a long program with calls to `imshow`, you may want to include a brief pause if you notice that the display lags. A small amount, such as `pause(0.1)`, i.e., to pause for a tenth of a second, gives the system a chance to show the image. The examples in this chapter are short enough that this should not be a problem. Also, be aware that on some systems, clicking on the main MATLAB window may cause the image in the figure window to be re-displayed behind it. If the figure seems to disappear, try moving the other windows.

By the way, MATLAB allows you to pass a filename to the `imshow` function. This way, it directly shows the image without the need to store it as a matrix first. The following command demonstrates this.

```
imshow('stRing.JPG');
```

However, while this technique works well for some tasks, like verifying that the image filename is the correct one, you might find that storing the data to a variable to be preferable, since it allows for a great deal of flexibility.

While this chapter uses `imshow`, MATLAB provides another function called `image` that also shows image data as a figure. The `image` command includes axes along the left and bottom edges. Depending on your goal, you might prefer one command over the other.

8.2 CONVERTING AN IMAGE TO BLACK AND WHITE

Sometimes we have too much information, where we might desire a simpler representation. For example, edge detection is a common image processing task. Developing an edge tracing program can be challenging with a color image, so could we get the data in black and white instead? MATLAB provides the `im2bw` function to do this. Consider the following code.

```
x1 = imread('stRing.JPG');
imshow(x1)
b = im2bw(x1);
figure(2);
imshow(b)
```

First, we read an example image to the variable `x1`. Then we use `im2bw` to map that color image data to a logical matrix. The command `figure(2);` specifies that we want to have another figure up, although we can also use that command to bring the figure in focus, if it is already up. The second `imshow` command shows the `b` matrix, containing the result of the `im2bw` command. Figure 8.1 shows what the `b` matrix looks like as an image.

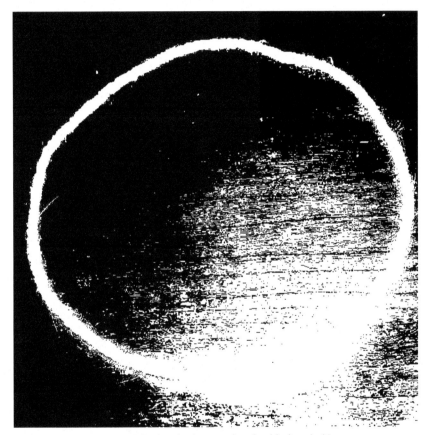

FIGURE 8.1 A color image reduced to black and white.

The version of the image in Figure 8.1 does not work well for edge detection. It defines the upper-left corner clearly, but the lower-right corner has too much saturation to see the edges. While the algorithm might be just what we need, the default threshold should be adjusted. Fortunately, the `im2bw` function allows us to override the default threshold value. We might need to experiment to get this right. The following code uses a threshold of 0.8.

```
b2 = im2bw(x1, 0.8);
imshow(b2)
```

This new data, held in variable b2, can be seen in Figure 8.2. Most of the details have been removed by the im2bw function, although it does a good job of separating the string from the table. The edges appear clearly, all the way around, so an edge-detection program could easily follow the edges.

As already mentioned, the figure command can open a new figure, as follows:

```
figure(2);
```

The number specifies the figure to either open or to get focus. Without a number in the parenthesis, it will open a new figure. We can close an individual figure with the close command, such as the following.

```
close(2);
```

8.3   MAKING A SIMPLE IMAGE

The word *pixel* comes from the words "picture element," and it means a color value at a particular location. An image is nothing more than a matrix of pixels. If you find this idea strange, consider the pointillism art movement, where paintings, viewed up close, are little points of color, densely packed together, yet form vivid scenes when viewed from a distance. (For reference, see the famous painting "A Sunday Afternoon on the Island of La Grande Jatte" by Georges Seurat.)

We will start making an image simply, with the following example.

```
x = zeros(128,128,'uint8');
x(10:118, 10:20) = 255;
imshow(x)
```

It creates the matrix x with the zeros function, one that returns a matrix of zero values, in this case, 128 × 128. The 'uint8' parameter specifies that the values in that matrix will be unsigned integers, with 8 bits of precision per value. For a uint8 data type, the value must be between 0 and 255. In the second line, we change a subset of x values to 255, where this subset has dimensions of 108 rows and 10 columns. The third line calls imshow which, as the name suggests, shows x as an image. Figure 8.3 shows the resulting black and white image.

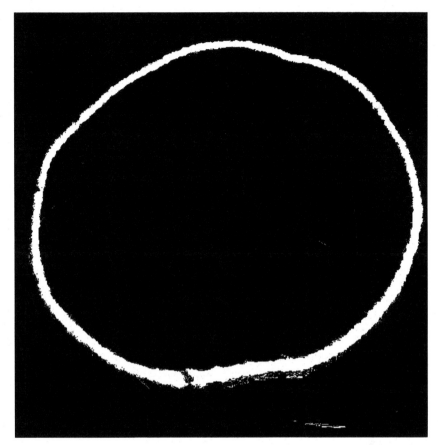

FIGURE 8.2 A color image reduced to black and white, with a higher threshold.

FIGURE 8.3 An image made from a couple lines of code.

We can add to the image with the following lines.

```
x(10:118, 20:30) = 128;
imshow(x)
```

Here we draw a second tall, thin rectangle in grey. The resulting image can be seen in Figure 8.4. We can use any value from 0 to 255 in matrix x, and it will make the image appear to be darker or lighter in that spot when we next display it with the `imshow` command. Note that any changes to x after we call `imshow(x)` will not be shown until we call `imshow(x)` again. These grey-scale values range from 0 (dark black) to 255 (bright white), with 128 about halfway in the middle. Greyscale images are quite useful in research, since anything that can be done to a greyscale image can be done to a color one.

The next example shows a gradual change from dark to light, with a grey-scale image. The first line sets array t to the range 0 to 127. Then the `sin` function returns a smoothly oscillating array of values, between –1 and +1, so adding one keeps the y array positive. At this point, t and y both have 128 values, so when we transpose y to become a column vector (128 × 1), then multiply by the row vector t (1 × 128), we generate a matrix with 128 × 128 elements.

```
t = 0:127;
y = sin(t/100*2*pi) + 1;
x2 = y.' * t;
imshow(uint8(x2))
```

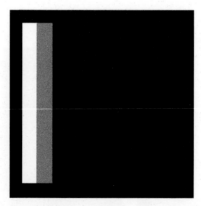

FIGURE 8.4 An image made from a couple lines of code with a second rectangle.

The `imshow` command receives the `uint8` version of the `x2` values. Figure 8.5 shows the resulting image.

FIGURE 8.5 An image made from a sine wave and a matrix multiplication.

The next example uses the same idea, where we generate a couple of arrays based on sinusoids, then transpose one and multiply them together. Adding one changes the values to be 0 to 2, and multiplying them by 127 means the result will range from 0 to 254.

```
s = sin((0:127)/100*2*pi);
c = cos((0:127)/100*2*pi);
x3 = c.' * s;
x3 = uint8((x3+1)*127);
imshow(x3)
```

As can be see in Figure 8.6, it forms a diagonal pattern of greyscale values.

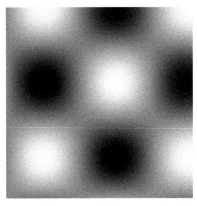

FIGURE 8.6 An image made from a couple of sinusoids.

8.4 COLOR IMAGES

Of course, your computer can display colors. How do we make a color image in MATLAB? One way is to add depth to the matrix, to give it a third dimension. Instead of a single 2-D matrix for greyscale values, we will have three 2-D matrices, one for each color depth: red, green, and blue.

We can start simply. In the following code, we define x4 as a 128 × 128 × 3 matrix of 8-bit, unsigned integers. The second line sets a large subset of values, for rows 10 to 118, columns 10 to 118, and color depth 1, to 255. Earlier, we saw that zero values appeared dark, and values of 255 appeared light. Note that all other color depth values remain 0.

```
x4 = zeros(128,128,3,'uint8');
x4(10:118, 10:118, 1) = 255;
imshow(x4)
```

The result for this code? As Figure 8.7 shows, we get a large square in the center. On the computer screen, it appears red. Color depth 1 corresponds to the red component.

FIGURE 8.7 An image where color depth 1 has values of 255.

We mix the intensities of each color depth to produce a wide range of colors. Mixing an equal amount of blue paint and red paint gives us a purple color, while mixing a little blue paint with a lot of red paint makes a purple color closer to red. Similarly, we can mix the red and blue color components to make a purple color, or make it closer to blue, or closer to red. In the next lines, we alter x4 to change the third color depth, corresponding to blue, up to 255.

```
x4(10:118, 10:118, 3) = 255;
imshow(x4)
```

Figure 8.8 shows the result. In color, it looks like a bright purple square, as we might expect.

FIGURE 8.8 An image where color depths 1 and 3 have values of 255.

In the following example, we create a new image, x5, then make a red rectangle. Then we make a green rectangle, and finally a blue one, arranging them so that they overlap. The end result can be seen in Figure 8.9.

```
x5 = zeros(128,128,3,'uint8');
maxR1 = 64+20;
maxC1 = 64;
x5(10:maxR1, 10:maxC1+15, 1) = 255;
x5(10:maxR1, maxC1-15:118, 2) = 255;
x5(maxR1-40:118, 20:108, 3) = 255;
imshow(x5)
```

Variables maxR1 and maxC1 define the extents of the rectangles. As Figure 8.9 shows, on a color monitor, red appears in the upper-left, green appears in the upper-right, and blue appears in the lower part. The overlapped areas appear as yellow, purple, white, and cyan. Any places where all three color components have a zero value appear black, while the places where all three color components have 255 values appear white. Wherever the three color components share the same value, we will see grey.

FIGURE 8.9 An image where color depths 1, 2, and 3 have values of 255 in overlapping rectangles.

8.5 SEEING DIFFERENT COLOR COMBINATIONS

Now we set up values to define the extents of three squares, to show how the colors overlap to make other colors. We choose the value 20 for variable `overlap`, with 10 for the variable `border`. Everything else derives from these two. The red and green squares overlap each other by the `overlap` value. So the image must be wide enough to have a border, some pixels with only red values, then some with red mixed with blue, then some red, green, and blue mixed together, then green mixed with blue, then green only, then another border. This defines variable `square_size`.

```
overlap = 20;
border = 10;
square_size = border * 2 + overlap * 5;
x6 = zeros(square_size, square_size, 3, 'uint8');
minRedRow = border;
minRedCol = border;
maxRedRow = minRedRow + overlap * 3;
maxRedCol = minRedCol + overlap * 3;
minGreenCol = maxRedCol - overlap;
maxGreenCol = minGreenCol + overlap * 3;
minBlueRow = maxRedRow - overlap*2;
minBlueCol = minGreenCol - overlap;
```

```
maxBlueRow = minBlueRow + overlap * 3;
maxBlueCol = minBlueCol + overlap * 3;
```

We also have variables like `minRedRow` and `minRedCol` to define the upper-left corner of the red square, then `maxRedRow` and `maxRedCol` for the lower-right corner. Since the green square uses the same rows as the red one, we only define the `minGreenCol` and `maxGreenCol`. You may find that the coordinates for images are different from what you expect. Normally, when we graph a mathematical function, we have an origin of (0, 0) at the lower-left corner, and count up and/or to the right from there. With MATLAB images, the "origin" is the upper-left corner since an image's (1, 1) pixel is located there. When using the `image` command in place of `imshow`, you can see the coordinates.

With the squares defined, we next more to varying the color values of each square. Earlier, we discussed how mixing an equal part red and blue produces purple, and we have seen what the mix of the two looks like. But what if we use unequal amounts? With paints, we expect that mixing twice as much red paint as blue paint makes a reddish purple color. The following code shows how we can see this with color intensities, too. It defines `red` to be the index of a `for` loop, going from 127 to 255. Next, it defines a `green` and a `blue` variable in a similar fashion. It sets the image `x6` to use these intensity values for the colors, displays the resulting image and waits.

```
for red = 127:128:255
    for green = 127:128:255
        for blue = 127:128:255
            % Red
            x6(minRedRow:maxRedRow, border:maxRedCol, 1) = red;
            % Green
            x6(minRedRow:maxRedRow, ...
            minGreenCol:maxGreenCol, 2) = green;
            % Blue
            x6(minBlueRow:maxBlueRow, ...
            minBlueCol:maxBlueCol, 3) = blue;
            imshow(x6)
            % pause
            pause(1);
        end
    end
end
```

You may want to comment out the `pause(1)` command and un-comment the `pause` command instead. There should be a pause here, otherwise the images will not be displayed correctly. The parameter of 1 indicates that it should pause for 1 second, and no parameter means that the computer waits for the user to press a key. When you run the program, you will see an image like the one shown in Figure 8.9, in fact the final image shows the same color intensities as that image. It forms a simple animation, where the color values vary, and the code shows each for a short time. You might want to alter the pause amount to a higher or lower value, if you want it to slow down or speed up, respectively.

Another experiment with the code is to change the ranges of the `for` loops, such as using `31:32:255` instead of `127:128:255`. Be forewarned that changing all three `for` loops at once means that each one will have 8 iterations, for a total of $8^3 = 512$ iterations, and pausing for one second for each iteration means that it runs for 512 seconds, i.e., over eight and a half minutes. Changing the time parameter for the `pause` function to something like 0.1 will make this much more tolerable.

8.6 COLOR SHIFTING

The next example provides an interesting effect. We start with an image, one that we used previously. Next, we store the color components as separate matrices, in this case, `redValues`, `greenValues`, and `blueValues`. Then, we copy these back to the image, only into the other color components.

```
x7 = imread('stRing.JPG');
redValues = x7(:,:,1);
greenValues = x7(:,:,2);
blueValues = x7(:,:,3);
x7(:,:,1) = greenValues;
x7(:,:,2) = blueValues;
x7(:,:,3) = redValues; imshow(x7)
```

Figure 8.10 shows the result. We replaced the red intensities with the green ones, the green ones with the blue ones, and the blue ones with the red ones. Of course, there are several other possible ways to mix the intensities for different effects. Besides switching them around, try copying the intensities to two of the image's color components at once, such as in the following.

```
x7(:,:,1) = greenValues;
x7(:,:,2) = redValues;
x7(:,:,3) = redValues;
imshow(x7)
```

Also, altering the values changes the image in interesting ways, too, such as the following code.

```
x7(:,:,1) = greenValues;
x7(:,:,2) = redValues;
x7(:,:,3) = blueValues / 4;
imshow(x7)
```

Finally, the next example uses the transpose of the blue intensities, to create a ghostly effect on the image. Figure 8.11 shows the result. On a color monitor, a faint blueish string appears over a yellow one, on a surface that looks like lime-green wood.

```
x7(:,:,1) = greenValues;
x7(:,:,2) = redValues;
x7(:,:,3) = blueValues.';
imshow(x7)
```

Having the image data to manipulate, we can create a variety of different effects.

8.7 CROPPING AN IMAGE MANUALLY

When we work with pictures, we often crop them to improve them. We might want to remove something from the picture, such as unsightly garbage at the edge of a vacation photo. Or perhaps we want to center the image, or focus the viewer's attention on one part of the image. Cropping even has research application, where we give a program less information to work on, so that it improves its speed or accuracy. For example, imagine a program that automatically detects an abnormality, such as arthritis, from X-rays. The X-ray data might include areas outside the patient's body, which we do not need to analyze. Cropping that out could speed up the process and increase accuracy. Whatever the reason, cropping an image is a common task.

 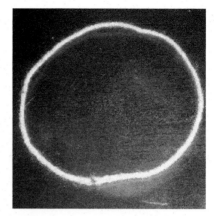

FIGURE 8.10 The original image (left) and the result after switching color depths (right).

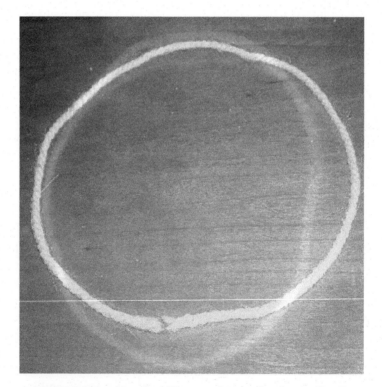

FIGURE 8.11 Another color shifting example, using the transpose function.

The following code reads in an image with `imread`, then gets its dimensions with the `size` function. It uses `image` to show it, so that we can see the coordinates along the edges. After this, the `title` command places the text "Select two points" above the image, so that the user knows what to do. Next, we call the `ginput` command, short for graphical input. That command places cross-hairs over the image, to allow the user to select a point. We actually want two points, so we use `ginput(2)` to specify that.

```
x0 = imread('stRing.JPG');
[MAXR, MAXC, MAXD] = size(x0);
image(x0);
title('Select two points');
[xpts, ypts] = ginput(2);
```

The `ginput` function returns the selected points in two arrays, thus, even if we only want one point, we still need to specify two variables in the return list (`[xpts, ypts]` in this case). The two points define a rectangle, although they may not be integers, so we next round the values to work as matrix indices. However, the user might not have had the pointer over the actual image, and if the user clicked within the figure but outside the image boundary, we cannot use the points. Therefore, we set a Boolean variable `outOfBounds` to false, i.e., we initially assume that the user did not click outside of the image's bounds, then we check the points, and set `outOfBounds` to true when we find an out-of-bounds point.

```
rows = round(ypts);
cols = round(xpts);
outOfBounds = false;
% Check the rows and cols
if ((min(rows) < 1) || (max(rows) > MAXR))
    outOfBounds = true;
end
if ((min(cols) < 1) || (max(cols) > MAXC))
    outOfBounds = true;
end
```

Notice that the `ginput` command returns (X, Y) pairs of points (called `xpts`, `ypts` here), and that we need to map them to (`row`, `column`) matrix indices. We check all of the `rows` at once, then all of the `cols` at once. Now, if there are no out-of-bounds points, we copy a submatrix of image x0 from the least row and least column to the maximum ones, then display the resulting image. Otherwise, we print a message to the user about why the cropping failed. Copying it to the title overwrites the "Select two points" message, to avoid confusion.

```
if (~outOfBounds)
    % these are OK
    x8 = x0(min(rows):max(rows), min(cols):max(cols), :);
    imshow(x8);
else
    title('Out of bounds of the image');
    disp('Out of bounds of the image');
end
```

Using the min and max functions allows us to overlook the details of the selection order. That is, the user may select an upper-left point, then a lower-right point, or perhaps the user will select the lower-right point first. Or maybe the user will select a lower-left point and an upper-right point. We do not need to figure this out when we use min and max to specify the boundaries. If you want to make the code more "user-friendly," you might want to get the points via ginput one at a time, perhaps also changing the title to reflect the progress. However, this means making the code a bit more complex, and you may have to examine the point information in more detail.

8.8 MAKING AN IMAGE OF A BEE

In a recent computer science class, students had an assignment for a game where the user would move a bee around a maze to a flower. The programming assignment used a different language, Objective-C, since the iPhone/iTouch served as the target platform. But making a solution required creating a bee image. While there are software packages that allow you to create an new image, this can be done fairly easily in MATLAB. This section documents such a solution.

The make_bee_png.m program creates a .png image of a 16 × 16 bee. Here is how it works. First, we define a matrix of colors, called bee, that define what the image will look like. To keep it simple, we use the numbers 0,

1, 2, and 3. So a simple matrix of 1, 0, 0; 0, 1, 0; 0, 0, 1 would correspond to a 3x3 image with a diagonal line from the top left to bottom right. Realistically, an image would be larger, but the same idea of a two-dimensional matrix defining the colors of the image applies. The original version of the program used 16 × 16 as the matrix/image size. This version uses 32 × 32. One advantage of using a 2-D matrix to specify where each color will go is that we can visualize, to some extent, what the final image will look like from the matrix. It is relatively easy to change.

Next, we create a second matrix called z. It will be three dimensional, specifying the colors (red, green and blue) used to mix to produce the final color. Every color has a mix of these three primary colors; even a color we describe as red likely has some green and blue in it. The colors we use here are yellow (defined by your author for this application as 240, 170, 35), black (0, 0, 0) and white (255, 255, 255). The program looks at every value of the bee matrix and copies the corresponding set of three values to the z matrix. Thus, we create a 3-D matrix of colors from the initial 2-D matrix.

If we were making an image in another format, like a Joint Photographic Experts Group format (.jpg), we could skip the next step. But Portable Network Graphics (.png) images allow for an opaqueness value, called alpha. This allows you to "see through" an image, and is great for animation.

Figure 8.12 shows an example .png image. The command to show it follows.

```
imshow('stripes.png');
```

Notice how it fades in from the left, which comes from the alpha values gradually becoming larger from the left to the right.

FIGURE 8.12 An image of stripes with alpha (transparency) values increasing to the right.

The alpha component allows the background to appear behind our bee, even although the bee image is defined as a square. For our purposes, we only care about two alpha values: 0, where we completely see through to the background, or 255, where we only see the bee in the foreground. The following line allows this. It makes a new matrix from the `bee` matrix, with values of 0 where there are zeroes, and 255 where there is another color.

```
alpha = uint8((bee>0)*255);
```

Notice that this allows us to distinguish between black and transparent. Finally, we show the image to the screen and write it to a file. The following two lines accomplish this.

```
imshow(z);
imwrite(z, ,bee.png,, ,PNG,, ,Alpha,, alpha);
```

Here is the entire program.

```
% make_bee_png.m
BEE_LENGTH = 16;
BEE_WIDTH = 16;
% pattern to use
% Each number stands for a color,
% (transparent / yellow / black / white)
bee = [ ...
        0, 0, 0, 0, 0, 0, 0, 0,    0, 0, 0, 0, 0, 0, 0, 0;
        0, 0, 0, 0, 0, 0, 0, 0,    0, 0, 0, 0, 0, 0, 0, 0;
        0, 0, 0, 0, 0, 3, 3, 3,    3, 0, 0, 0, 0, 0, 0, 0;
        0, 0, 0, 0, 3, 3, 3, 3,    3, 3, 0, 0, 0, 0, 0, 0;
        0, 0, 0, 0, 3, 3, 3, 3,    3, 3, 3, 0, 0, 0, 0, 0;
        0, 0, 0, 1, 2, 3, 3, 3,    3, 3, 1, 1, 1, 0, 0, 0;
        0, 0, 0, 1, 2, 2, 1, 1,    2, 2, 1, 2, 2, 1, 0, 0;
        1, 1, 1, 1, 2, 2, 1, 1,    2, 2, 1, 2, 1, 1, 0, 0;

        0, 0, 1, 1, 2, 2, 1, 1,    2, 2, 1, 1, 1, 1, 0, 0;
        0, 0, 0, 1, 2, 2, 1, 1,    2, 2, 1, 1, 1, 0, 0, 0;
        0, 0, 0, 1, 2, 2, 1, 1,    2, 2, 1, 1, 1, 0, 0, 0;
        0, 0, 0, 0, 1, 2, 1, 1,    2, 2, 1, 0, 0, 0, 0, 0;
        0, 0, 0, 0, 1, 0, 0, 0,    0, 0, 1, 0, 0, 0, 0, 0;
        0, 0, 0, 0, 1, 0, 0, 0,    0, 0, 1, 0, 0, 0, 0, 0;
        0, 0, 0, 0, 0, 0, 0, 0,    0, 0, 0, 0, 0, 0, 0, 0;
        0, 0, 0, 0, 0, 0, 0, 0,    0, 0, 0, 0, 0, 0, 0, 0];
```

```
% Make it all black by default
z = uint8(zeros(BEE_LENGTH, BEE_WIDTH, 3));
% Now color in the pixels
[R, C] = size(bee);
for r = 1:R
    for c=1:C
        % Examine each bee(r,c) value, and color z.
        if (bee(r,c) == 1)
            % color this pixel yellow
            z(r, c, 1) = 240;
            z(r, c, 2) = 170;
            z(r, c, 3) = 35;
        elseif (bee(r,c) == 2)
            % color this pixel black
            z(r, c, 1) = 0;
            z(r, c, 2) = 0;
            z(r, c, 3) = 0;
        elseif (bee(r,c) == 3)
            % color this pixel white
            z(r, c, 1) = 255;
            z(r, c, 2) = 255;
            z(r, c, 3) = 255;
        else
            % color this pixel black
            % If the bee value is 0, this
            % pixel will be transparent.
            z(r, c, 1) = 0;
            z(r, c, 2) = 0;
            z(r, c, 3) = 0;
        end
    end
end
% Try to use alpha values to make the bee appear
% without a black background (i.e., in case we want to
```

```
% show it with a different background, or over top of
% another object).
alpha = uint8((bee>0)*255);
imshow(z);
imwrite(z, ,bee.png,, ,PNG,, ,Alpha,, alpha);
```

The bee image worked well on the simulator. The user could easily click on the bee and drag it around as imagined. But when the code was ported to the actual iPhone/iTouch, we quickly discovered that it was too small to easily "grab" with a finger. To make a larger bee, we could change the MATLAB program to use a 32 × 32 pixel image instead of a 16 × 16 one. How would you change the matrix bee to accomplish this? How could you use MATLAB to help changing it?

8.9 CENTERING AN IMAGE

In this section, we create an image as a backdrop, one that we could use as the background on a computer screen. First, we start with an image from a scanner. The file redBottleCap1.jpeg comes from a scan of a bottle cap, with most of the background cropped out. Then plan is to center it, then add more of the color around the edges, to make it larger. How do we center the design on a solid background? The included program centerImage.m contains the code discussed in this section.

First, we read in the scanned image, show it, and get its dimensions. There are example images to go along with this example. File redBottleCap1.jpeg is the original, scanned image, redBottleCap2.jpeg is a cropped version, redBottleCap2.png is a copy of the cropped version that has been converted to a .png file, and some of the pixels have been removed by setting the alpha components to zero. We use this property later to allow the background to show through those places.

```
[x, m, xa] = imread('redBottleCap2.png');
imshow(x)
[MAXR, MAXC, MAXD] = size(x);
```

Then, select a point to use for the solid background. If you copy and paste this code, remember that the ginput command will cause the computer to wait until you select a point on the image, i.e., use the mouse to click on the image.

```
[c,r] = ginput(1);
c = round(c);
r = round(r);
```

The round command allows these to be used as matrix indices. Variable r is short for row, c is short for column.

Now create a new matrix, y, to be used as an image. The following code makes it 512×512, and there are 3 color depths (red, green, and blue). Next, copy those colors to every location of y, that is, x(r,c,1) specifies the red value for the pixel shown at (r, c), while x(r,c,2) and x(r,c,3) specify the green and blue components. Setting y(:,:,1) to a value means that every pixel in y's image will have the red component assigned.

```
y = zeros(512,512,3, 'uint8');
y(:,:,1) = x(r,c,1);
y(:,:,2) = x(r,c,2);
y(:,:,3) = x(r,c,3);
figure(); imshow(y)
```

The line figure(); imshow(y) calls up a new figure and shows the image. The image looks good, so we go on with the next step. We reuse the r and c variables as indices. Looking at each pixel value, we copy it from x (the scanned image) to y (the image we are creating) whenever the alpha component is 255. Image x has dimensions MAXR×MAXC, in this case, x is smaller than y in both height and width. The code assumes this. If this were not the case, the following code would need to be adjusted to avoid an error.

```
for r=1:MAXR
    for c=1:MAXC
        if (xa(r,c) == 0)
            x(r,c,1) = y(r,c,1);
            x(r,c,2) = y(r,c,2);
            x(r,c,3) = y(r,c,3);
            xa(r,c) = 255;
        end
    end
end
imshow(x)
```

Breaking it down, the `for` loops generate all possible indices r and c for the x matrix. Then it examines xa, the alpha component for the x image. Many of the alpha values are zero, meaning that the pixel at those indices would be completely clear. To make a solid image, we change those places to an alpha component of 255, not transparent at all. At the same time, the code copies in the red, green, and blue color components from the y image, meaning the x image will get the background color at that location.

Now you should see the image with a red background, assuming that you clicked on a red pixel in the image.

Copy the new image to z, in case we make a mistake. We could figure out exactly where the center is, and copy it there, or we can take a guess and correct it as needed. We'll start with a guess.

```
z = y;
ROW = 100;
COL = 100;
z(1+ROW:MAXR+ROW, 1+COL:MAXC+COL,:) = x;
imshow(z)
```

It looks pretty good, but shifting it down and just a bit to the left should make it look better.

```
ROW = 120;
COL = 95;
z = y;
z(1+ROW:MAXR+ROW, 1+COL:MAXC+COL,:) = x;
imshow(z)
imwrite(z, 'redBottleCap3.jpg', 'JPG');
```

It looks good, so the last command writes it to a new file.

8.10 MAKING A RECTANGULAR IMAGE SQUARE

Suppose that we have an image that we want to make square. The file `berryTree.png` is an example, a drawing of a tree on a white background. The image has 480 rows and 640 columns. Looking at the image, we can see that is not centered, so while we could just take the first 480 columns, the results will not be satisfactory. Instead, we add an offset to the column to make the result look centered. The code below does this.

```
[x, m, xa] = imread('graphics/berryTree.png');
y = x(1:480,100+1:100+480,:);
imshow(y)
```

We could even do this in an iterated way, as follows:

```
[x, m, xa] = imread('graphics/berryTree.png');
y = x(1:480,100+1:100+480,:);
imshow(y)
pause()
y = x(1:480,75+1:75+480,:);
imshow(y)
pause()
y = x(1:480,60+1:60+480,:);
imshow(y)
```

Even better, although more complex, is to have a menu and update the image as many times as we desire. The following code does this. The central idea is that it shows the image, and we specify to pan left, right, or quit. There are some features added to enhance the user experience, such as accepting lower-case and upper-case input, along with checking to make sure the offset is a value that will not cause a problem. Additionally, the dimensions of the image are used instead of expecting them to be 480 by 640.

The following code can be found in the file berryTree.m. It is an example of a *utility* program, one made to accomplish a specific task. It might be used only once, or it could be helpful enough to run again and again. Briefly, it shows a square image from a rectangular one, and allows the user to specify commands like left and right to change the part of the image shown. First, the code reads in an image, and sets some variables to its dimensions.

```
[x, m, xa] = imread('graphics/berryTree.png');
[MAXR, MAXC, MAXD] = size(x);
```

Next, we set up an initial guess for the offset, and start a while loop. Since this program has interactions with the user, we do not know in advance how many times this loop will iterate.

```
done = false;
offset = 100;
while (~done)
    % continued
```

Now we make a new image, y, from the one that we read earlier. It uses MAXR in both the rows and columns, to get a square subset of x. Note that this makes assumptions about the dimensions of the input image. While the berryTree.png image has many more columns than it has rows, another image may not. If we later expand this program, we would need to revisit this assumption.

```
y = x(1:MAXR,offset+1:offset+MAXR,:);
imshow(y)
```

At this point, we created a square image from the rectangular one, based on a guess for the offset variable. Maybe the image looks great to the user, or perhaps it needs to be adjusted to the left or to the right. We ask the user what to do.

```
response = input('(l)eft (r)ight or (q)uit: ', 's');
if ((response == 'q') || (response == 'Q'))
      done = true;
      % continued
```

The code presents three options: left, right, or quit, then reads a string. Another unstated assumption is that the user will respond with a single character, like the prompt indicates. If they type the entire word, the program will not process it correctly; in fact, a comparison like (response == 'q') generates an array of results when response has multiple characters. Instead of a scalar, logical value, the condition becomes an array, resulting in an error. We could add code to check for that, and handle it well, although this prompts the question: will we keep and reuse this program?

Notice that the program does check for both upper-case as well as lower-case. If the user decides to quit, we set the Boolean variable done to true, meaning that the program will exit the loop when it gets to the end of the loop body.

We check for left or right, and adjust the offset. The new offset might be too small or too large, so we examine it and change it when needed. We adjust the offset by 10, a value hard-coded into the program. A better approach is to set it to a variable at the top of the program, in case we later want to make the change finer or coarser. The value 10 works fairly well here, discovered through "trial and error." An adjustment too small means that it takes many iterations to get the offset where the user wants it. Too large of an adjustment means that the user might not be able to get it just right, and have to accept the better of two poor choices. Setting such a parameter often takes thought and experimentation.

```
elseif ((response == 'l') || (response == 'L'))
    offset = offset - 10;
    % Make sure we did not go too far left.
    if (offset < 1)
        offset = 1;
    end
elseif ((response == 'r') || (response == 'R'))
    offset = offset + 10;
    % Make sure we did not go too far right.
    if (offset + MAXR > MAXC)
        offset = offset - 10;
    end
end
% Anything else input will be ignored.
end
```

Since the code includes no further checks, it ignores any other input. Finally, we end the loop. The loop will iterate again and again, until the variable done becomes true.

Up to this point, we have shown the user the image, and have not been concerned about the alpha component. Now we make a new variable, ya, by copying the corresponding alpha values from the original image. Next, we write the new image to a file.

```
ya = xa(1:MAXR,offset+1:offset+MAXR);
imwrite(y, 'graphics/newBerryTree.png', 'PNG', 'alpha', ya);
```

Be careful not to overwrite the original image, in case the user changes his mind later. Notice that the imwrite command uses a different filename for the new version.

There are more enhancements that we could add. The code writes the result by default; perhaps it should ask the user first. Variable offset is given an initial guess of 100, although that could be too large for some images. Speaking of which, should the filename be easy to change? Should it come from the uigetfile function, which allows a nice interface for the user? Is the left or right movement intuitive, or would it make more sense to switch them? In other words, should "left" mean moving the tree to the left, or moving the view to the left? Should the offset changes use a finer grain, like +/ – 5 instead of +/ – 10? Should the program be more verbose, like telling the user if it ignores input? What happens if the user types `LL` in response instead of just `L`? Maybe it should say something if it corrects the `offset` due to the value being too large or small? What if the `imread` or `imwrite` commands fail? Could the image be more tall than wide, and how should we deal with that? There are a lot of potential improvements that could be added. How much effort we put into this depends on what we want to get out of it. If we plan to use this once, finding the offset should be done with the simplest method available. If we are developing a tool to be used many times, or to be used by others, we should make it as robust as possible.

8.11 SELECTING A FILE WITH THE GRAPHICAL USER INTERFACE

The `uigetfile` function calls a window to pop up, allowing the user to select a file to use. In the example below, we specify that the user should select only files that end with the `.png` extension. Also, the text in the second parameter appears as the window's title.

```
>> [f, p] = uigetfile('*.png', 'Please choose an image file.');
>> disp(f)
berryTree.png
>> disp(p)
/Users/mweeks/matlab_work/graphics/
```

The function gives the filename in the first value returned. The second value returned specifies the path. To get the complete filename, we need to put the path and filename together. The `strcat` function concatenates the two strings p, the path specifying where the file exists, and f, the name of the file. The line below completes name of the file.

```
>> strcat(p, f)
ans =
/Users/mweeks/matlab_work/graphics/berryTree.png
```

Note that `uigetfile` does not read the file, it simply returns the name. To read the file, we use a line like the following.

```
>> [x, m, xa] = imread(strcat(p, f));
>> figure(); imshow(x)
```

Program `uigetfile_example.m` contains this `uigetfile` example. It assumes that the user selects a file. If the user instead closes the selection window, it will not have a valid path and filename. MATLAB provides several ways to check for this; view the `help uigetfile` output for details. See Chapter 9 for more information about the graphical user interface.

8.12 BOUNCING BOX: A SIMPLE ANIMATION

Suppose that we want to show a simple animation, one where a square bounces around a window. Animation can be achieved easily: we show an image, wait a small amount of time, then show another image in its place. See the program `bouncing_box1.m` which contains the code explained here, if you prefer to copy and paste relevant lines, rather than typing them. The first thing that we need is to define the background. This can be a simple black square, as the following command provides.

```
background = zeros(400,400,3,'uint8');
imshow(background)
```

If you enter this at the command prompt, you should see a black square appear that is 400 pixels tall by 400 pixels wide. A *pixel* is a portmanteau of picture element, a tiny square of color. The `zeros` command creates a matrix of 0 values, in this case, one with 400 rows, 400 columns, and 3 planes. The planes correspond to RGB colors, i.e., red, green, and blue. The string `uint8` specifies the data type, unsigned integers of 8 bits. Whenever the red, green, and blue values are the same for a pixel, it appears gray, somewhere between black and white.

Next, we need a much smaller square for the box that will move around. The next command reserves memory for it with the `zeros` command, then sets the first two planes to 255, which is the maximum that an 8 bit value can store.

```
box = zeros(20,20,3,'uint8');
box(:,:,1) = 255;
box(:,:,2) = 255;
imshow(box)
```

The `box` variable has 20 rows, 20 columns, and 3 planes. Since the first two planes have the value 255 for all locations, the pixels appear as bright yellow. Assuming that `imshow` drew this on the same figure as before, you should see a small, yellow square. Now we combine the two squares onto one image.

```
myimage = background;
% show the box on myimage, too
myimage(1:20,1:20,:) = box;
imshow(myimage)
```

First, it makes a copy of the `background` variable to a new variable called `myimage`. Then it overwrites some of `myimage` with the contents of variable `box`. Notice that the command `myimage(1:20,1:20,:) = box;` copies all of the contents of `box` to the first 20 rows, first 20 columns, and all 3 color planes of `myimage`. This assumes that `box` has exactly these dimensions. If you want to use a larger or smaller yellow square, these values would have to be altered. "Hard-coding" these values is not good programming practice, however in this case, we use it to get started and will replace these numbers with something better soon. With the `imshow` command, you should now see the yellow square in the upper-left corner of a larger, black square.

Next, we define a few new variables to allow us to repeat what we have done previously, only in a more flexible way. Defining the rows and columns of the `box` variable, as in the following code, makes sense if we put it before the definition of `box`. If variable `box` already exists, we could instead use the `size` function to report what they are.

```
box_ROWS = 20;
box_COLS = 20;
row_offset = 200;
col_offset = 200;
```

Variables `row_offset` and `col_offset` will be used to locate the yellow square. Next, we show the square in a new location, starting at the defined `row_offset`, `col_offset`.

```
myimage(row_offset+1:row_offset + box_ROWS, ...
    col_offset+1:col_offset + box_COLS, :) = box;
imshow(myimage)
```

The command above that copies `box` to `myimage` may look complicated, although it is very similar to the one from before. Take the command

```
myimage(1:20,1:20,:) = box;
```

and replace the hard-coded values of 20 with `box_ROWS` and `box_COLS` respectively, then add `row_offset` to the rows and `col_offset` to the columns, and you should have the same expression as shown here.

You may have noticed that the new images has two yellow squares on it. We did not reset `myimage` from earlier, so the upper-left corner still has a yellow square. We can fix this easily enough. The following command copies the background over the upper-left corner. Reshowing the `myimage` matrix reveals that the upper-left corner now appears black.

```
myimage(1:20,1:20,:) = background(1:20,1:20,:);
imshow(myimage)
```

Ones of the ideas behind this walk-through of the code is to specify what we want to happen. After trying out the code, and getting the results we want, we will combine all of it together into a program. This develops the program a little at a time, called an iterative process.

So far, we have drawn a small square onto a larger one, and showed it in a couple of locations. In the next step, we overwrite the previously shown square, then redraw the square. The code changes `row_offset` each time through the `for` loop. It also waits for one second with the `pause` command to allow us to see the results.

```
for row_offset=200:2:300
    % get rid of the box we previously showed
    myimage(row_offset+1:row_offset + box_ROWS, ...
        col_offset+1:col_offset + box_COLS, :) = background( ...
        row_offset+1:row_offset + box_ROWS, ...
        col_offset+1:col_offset + box_COLS, :);
    % now show the box in this location
    myimage(row_ offset+1:row_offset + box_ROWS, ...
        col_offset+1:col_offset + box_COLS, :) = box;
    imshow(myimage)
    % wait a bit, say 1 second
    pause(1);
end
```

Did this work as planned? Not quite. You probably observed that the yellow square appeared in the middle of the black background, and slowly moved down, but it did not cover up the previously shown square. The problem is that we don't really erase the old box. We instruct the computer to overwrite the pixels with the background, although this comes after `row_offset` updates. In other words, we overwrite `myimage` with the background before we display the yellow square, but we overwrite the exact same locations that the square will appear, not where it did appear a moment ago. We could move the command used to get rid of the previously shown box to after the pause command. While this works, it has the unfortunate side-effect of making the yellow square disappear at the end of the program.

Now, let's take care of the overwrite problem by remembering more information, namely, the previously used row and columns, `old_row_offset` and `old_col_offset`. We will initialize these to the starting row and column.

```
% initialize myimage
myimage = background;
old_row_offset = 200;
old_col_offset = 200;
for row_offset=200:2:300
    % get rid of the box we previously showed
    myimage(old_row_offset+1:old_row_offset + box_ROWS, ...
        old_col_offset+1:old_col_offset + box_COLS, :) = ...
        background(old_row_offset+1:old_row_offset + ...
        box_ROWS, old_col_offset+1:old_col_offset + box_COLS, :);
    % now show the box in this location
    myimage(row_offset+1:row_offset + box_ROWS, ...
        col_offset+1:col_offset + box_COLS, :) = box;
    imshow(myimage)
    % update the old information so we remember it next time
    old_row_offset = row_offset;
    old_col_offset = col_offset;
    % wait a bit, say 1 second
    pause(1);
end
```

While this does not address the speed, you should see that it does erase the previously drawn yellow square, so that it does not leave a trail. Also, this solution keeps the yellow square on the image, so when the loop ends, we still see it. Program `bouncing_box1.m` contains the code up to this point.

To make the animation faster, we can have a bigger step size for the `for` loop, like using 4 instead of 2. Every time the code redraws the square, it appears a certain number of rows down (governed by the step size). Making the step size larger makes the yellow square cover the distance faster, although it can make it appear choppy instead of smooth if we make the step size too large. We could also use a fraction of a second for the pause. In similar manner to the step size, the pause amount should be set with care. With a long pause, the animation appears slow. With a short pause, the system may lag, causing poor response. We can improve the speed by changing the wait time from one second to a hundredth of a second, as in the following command.

```
pause(0.01);
```

In the code so far, we have allowed `row_offset` to vary between set values. However, at some point we will want the yellow square to "bounce," to move up to an edge, then reverse direction. How will the computer know that the square reaches an edge? We need to store the dimensions of the background as well. Then we can compare the location of the yellow square to the boundary of the background. The following line assigns variables `backgr_ROWS`, `backgr_COLS`, and `backgr_DEPTH` to the dimensions of the background.

```
[backgr_ROWS, backgr_COLS, backgr_DEPTH] = size(background);
```

Since the `background` variable stores image data, we know that `backgr_DEPTH` will have a value of 3. We could also set the `backgr_ROWS` and `backgr_COLS` variables at the top of the program, before defining the `background` data. That would work equally as well.

The program should still control the yellow square for a set number of iterations, even though `row_offset` will not be used as the index. Instead, we will use a new variable, called `iteration` to control the loop.

```
for iteration = 1:300
    ...
end
```

The ellipsis (three periods in a row) is used here only as a place-holder for the other code in the loop.

Within the body of the loop, we update the `row_offset` and `col_offset`, initially, just by incrementing each. The code below updates the coordinates of the yellow square.

```
row_offset = row_offset + 1;
col_offset = col_offset + 1;
```

Once the coordinates have a new value, we must check to see if the new coordinates work. Is the yellow square still completely on screen, or would part of it be off screen? We could handle this in a couple of different ways; we could not allow it to be partly off screen, or we could only show the on-screen part. The code below does not allow the square to be off-screen, and resets the `row_offset` if needed.

```
if (row_offset + box_ROWS > backgr_ROWS)
    row_offset = 1;
end
```

We use a similar `if` statement for the `col_offset`. Note that this works for this example, only because the coordinates increase every time. In a general case, we must check the other boundaries, too.

Program `bouncing_box2.m` shows the progress so far. It is not the final version, but it is a step closer. When you run it, you should see the yellow box starting in the middle of the black background, then move down and to the right. It moves down since the image shown is based on rows and columns, such that the upper left corner corresponds to row 1 and column 1. Note the difference between this and a coordinate system like one used with the `plot` command, where the origin (the point at location 0,0) appears to the bottom and left (assuming that it shows only positive data).

While the `bouncing_box2.m` program moves the square, it does not have it bounce. To do that, we need to instruct the computer to reverse direction of the square when it reaches a boundary. We create new variables `delta_row` and `delta_col` for the change in the square's row and column, respectively. We can start these off with values of 4, then change them when the square reaches an edge of the background. That is, we start the square at the location specified by `row_offset` and `col_offset`, and add the delta values in every iteration of the loop.

Let's examine the code for that defines and updates the `row_offset`. Remember that the three periods here indicate that other things are skipped.

```
row_offset = 100;
delta_row = 4;
for iteration = 1:300
    ...
    new_row_offset = row_offset + delta_row;
    if (new_row_offset + box_ROWS > backgr_ROWS)
        new_row_offset = row_offset;
        delta_row = -delta_row;
    elseif (new_row_offset < 1)
        new_row_offset = row_offset;
        delta_row = -delta_row;
    end
```

```
    row_offset = new_row_offset;
    ...
end
```

Outside of the loop, we define the `row_offset` and `delta_row` variables. Inside the loop, we set a variable called `new_row_offset` as the location where we expect the square to go next. But before we use it, we must check that it is within bounds. Since `new_row_offset` specifies the upper row of the square, we must check the lower row: `new_row_offset` plus the number of rows in the square, `box_ROWS`. The `if` shown in the preceding code compares the last row of the square to the maximum row of the background. If the square's last row goes beyond the background, we change the new row to the old one.

Note that this is an unstated assumption, that the previous `row_offset` will always be a valid location. If we were to reduce the size of the background or enlarge the size of the square, then this initial value may need to change accordingly. In an extreme case, one could define the square and background in a way such that there is no valid `row_offset`. That would violate another assumption, i.e., that the yellow square is smaller than the background.

By the way, we also assume that the variables for the row have positive, non-zero, integer values. The `elseif` part of the preceding code checks to make sure that the `new_row_offset` is at least 1, ensuring that it is positive and non-zero. We do not check that it has integer values, although the initial value and delta value are integers, so no way exists for it to become a non-integer without changing the code to do so. It could become negative or zero, as discussed in the next paragraph.

Whenever the `new_row_offset` has a value out of bounds, the code resets it to `row_offset`, then changes the sign on the delta value with the following command.

```
    delta_row = -delta_row;
```

If `delta_row` has the value of 4 before this command, it will have the value −4 afterward. Likewise, if it starts with a −4 value, it will get a value of 4 afterward. This has the effect of changing the vertical direction. With a positive `delta_row` value, the next iteration of the loop will attempt to place the square further down on the background. If the `delta_row` value is negative, the code will attempt to place the square further up on the background. The `delta_row` value could be zero, meaning that the square will not move vertically.

While the preceding code details how the yellow square's row will change, we have similar code to change its column. With code to update both row and column, we can summarize the program. See the program `bouncing_box3.m`, for the version incorporating the code discussed here. In it, we define the background, the square, and the current image to show, which combines the background and square. Next, it defines some variables related to the row and column. A loop starts, first overwriting the square's current location. Then the loop updates the location, checking to make sure that the new location keeps the square within bounds. Next, the loop shows the square in the new location, and finally, it pauses briefly.

When is software finished? You have probably seen software products change over time, as the software makers fix bugs, add features, or improve the look and feel of their product. When writing software, people often start with a set of functionality and features in mind, and may think of new features to add during development. A professional project should adhere to deadlines and satisfy the specifications. For a personal project, you may desire to keep adding to it, and there always seems to be something to make it better. A good strategy is to keep clearly labeled backup copies, and make changes gradually. Code versioning software, such as "git," can fill this role and provide extra features.

With this example, the different versions are numbered. Encoding the last change date is another way to keep track of different versions, for example, you could call something "`myprogram_010219.m`" to indicate that this version of "`myprogram`" was last changed on January 2, 2019. Your computer keeps the last change date on files already, as the MATLAB command `ls -l` demonstrates, but there can be problems with this. If you copy a file to your computer, perhaps from an e-mail or USB storage device, the computer will assign the current date to it. If you have a newer version on the computer under a different directory, you might think it is the older version, since its time-stamp is the older of the two. If you encode the date in the filename, you would know for sure which one is older. While outside the scope of this book, there are online code repositories like "Github" and "Bitbucket" that store program files. Previously mentioned "git" can be set up independently from "Github," allowing an organization to use their own server as a code repository. Chapter 14, *Other Useful Computing Tools*, includes an example of how `git` could be used with a MATLAB project.

These help with more than just keeping track of backups and the latest version. They also employ mechanisms to allow multiple people to work on the same files, without overwriting each other's changes.

Why call this program a variant of "`bouncing_box`"? It shows a square, after all, and the primary definition of a box is a three-dimensional container. Whenever beginning a new project, we choose a name for it, even if the first name only holds the place for a better one. In this case, the name "`bouncing_box`" stuck, perhaps because it sounds more evocative than "`moving_square`" does. With this in mind, this book includes a final version called `bouncing_box4.m`. It includes a bit more code to make the square look three dimensional.

What about other improvements? Here are a few ideas.

- start from a random spot (use the `rand` function to provide the initial row and column)

- make the yellow square a smiley-face

- use a different background, such as a picture

- apply "physics"-like forces, i.e., bounce along the bottom

- allow the fore-image to use an "alpha" matrix from a PNG file

- add a way for the user to start and stop the movement (a button)

- color the sides of the box in `bouncing_box4.m`, then show it "turn" as it reflects off of a wall

The list orders these improvements from easy to difficult. Some things require knowledge from other chapters. For example, the chapter on graphical user interfaces (Chapter 9) covers how to add a button to a figure.

8.13 SUMMARY

Images are important to many projects, and MATLAB provides many image processing commands, including an optional image processing toolkit. This chapter discusses some practical image manipulations that should work with most MATLAB licenses. It covered making completely new images, as well as altering images from another source, such as a scan. Examples worked with greyscale and colors, showing and manipulating existing images as well as creating images. Finally, by showing an image, pausing, changing it, and showing it again, we are able to create a simple animation.

EXERCISES

1. Using the `rgb2gray` function, convert a color image as a grayscale one. Show the two in different figures.

2. Use the function `imbinarize` (or `im2bw`) to convert an image to a black and white representation.

3. Use the `edge` function on an image, with four of the different methods to find edges. Show all four results on one figure, using the `subplot` command. Hint: use the command `subplot(2, 2, n);` right before each `imshow` command, where n should have the value 1, 2, 3, or 4.

4. Create a function to show an image, such as `plant.jpg`. The function should have two parameters, the image name, and an integer for rotation. If the rotation value is 0, show the image normally. If the rotation value is 1, 2, or 3, show the image rotated clockwise by 90, 180, or 270 degrees, respectively. Before attempting a solution, think about how you would handle a small example, like a matrix with values `[1, 2; 3, 4]`. Also, you might want to try this with a grayscale image first.

5. Given a grayscale image, use `ginput` to get a set of coordinates. Turn the pixel at that location blue. Also turn any neighbor pixel with the same (original) value as that one blue, and any of its neighbors, etc. The color should spread throughout the image, as long as the pixels are connected. A good addition to this is to make "same" relative, where two values within a given tolerance are considered equal (and thus changed).

PROJECTS

• **Image Thumbnail View**
This assignment is to implement a "thumbnail view" utility for images. Given the filename of an image, your program should create a "thumbnail view" of the image, and write it out under a second filename.

People use MATLAB to quickly implement their ideas. Sometimes the program takes a long time to run, possibly overnight, or even several days. A way to deal with this is called batch programming, where you set the computer to run and leave it alone (i.e. overnight), then check its output the next day. We will approach the project like this.

Your program should not present the user with an interface. Instead, create at least three files:

- a function to receive image data as a matrix, and return an average matrix as one-fourth the size

- a function with two filenames as the input, an image file to read and an image file to create. It should call the matrix-shrinking function.

- a script to create (and later close) a diary file, and call the read/create image function repeatedly.

Calling the second function once will produce a thumbnail view image from a larger one. The idea behind the script is to make thumbnails for many images, e.g., a group of vacation photos from a digital camera.

Use the diary command for the log.

Your program should work for all possible inputs. Make sure that you test it with several different cases.

Your solution should work with grayscale images. You can make it work for color images if you want. Decide on a reasonable cut-off for what makes a "thumbnail" sized image. Document your cut-off value, including a rationale for why you chose it. Your function should create an image with fewer rows than the cut-off.

For an additional challenge: make your solution work with color images. Also, allow a variable number of arguments to your second function. It should have at least 2 inputs: the filename of the image to read, and the filename of the thumbnail sized image to create. Allow the user to pass a cut-off value for the number of rows in the thumbnail image. Your function should create an image with fewer rows than the cut-off.

- **Automatic Measurement**
  This assignment is to implement a measurement utility. This project is inspired by a research problem of measuring filopodia: long, thin, extensions from a brain cell. It is of interest to biologists to see how they grow or shrink over time (i.e., multiple images).

  Your program should load an image and display it, and allow the user to select two points: a start and an end point. Your program should mark the first point, then, once the second point is selected, it should draw a line to the second point. It will then indicate how long the line is, by displaying the following information to the screen: first point's coordinates, second point's coordinates, and the distance between them.

The distance should include units. To calibrate your program, you will need to experiment. There is a measuring tape shown on the available test image (`hmwk3_image.jpg`) that indicates length. Use this to figure out lengths in real units.

Use the `ginput` command, and left and right buttons to indicate start and end points, respectively. If the user presses the left button, your program should visibly mark that spot (use a 3x3 solid color around the point). On the Macs, the right button should correspond to a button click while the Control-key is pressed. If the user presses the left button again, your program should undo the marking of the first spot, and then mark the new spot. The second spot should also be 3x3, but the line between them only has to be 1 pixel wide.

There may be many filopodia to measure. The user needs an easy way to quit. When they left click outside the image, prompt them if they want to quit, then read their input. If they want to quit, write the image that they created to a file.

To solve your problem, write a program that reads the necessary information to compute and output the indicated values, as efficiently as possible. Design your program by specifying its behavior, identifying the variables and operations it needs to solve the problem, and then organizing the variables and operations into an algorithm. Then code your design in MATLAB using stepwise translation. Finally, test your program thoroughly.

Your program should work for all possible inputs. Make sure that you test it with several different cases.

Your program should call at least one function that you wrote.

For an additional challenge: First, allow the user to save the image under any (reasonable) filename that they choose. Second, put the measurements on the image itself near the filopodia. Investigate the text command for this.

- **Augmenting an Image**
  Television broadcasts of football games add lines to the image to convey information to the viewers, such as where the offense needs to move the ball to get a first-down. To the viewer, the lines look natural, and appear to be beneath the players. This problem has much more complexity to it than it sounds. As a project, take a digital picture of a sports game, then make a program to draw a first-down line as if it were painted on the field.

## CHAPTER 9

WORKING WITH A GRAPHICAL USER INTERFACE

We can do a lot of work interacting with the command-line window. When you know what you are doing, you get to work quickly and efficiently. However, it is easy to forget what to do. And having someone else use your software presents them with a learning curve. Simply put, working with the command window can intimidate novice users.

To make using your program user-friendly, add graphical user interface (GUI) components. These components will be familiar to the user, and allow you to present a simplified window where the user can interact. Perhaps even more important than presenting what the user can do is the fact that you support a small range of functionality. That is, you effectively *limit* what the user can do with your program.

Programming with a GUI is different than making a "normal" program. Often with a GUI, you set up the display, and the programs finishes. As long as the screen (figure) is in place, the user can interact with it. The computer waits until the user does something (called an *event*), then responds. You can make your interface respond, too, by specifying that it call other functions based on the event.

It is also possible to have your program keep running while the interface is up, but we will explore the first case now. The example code, given in the following sections, also appears in the script GUI_example1.m, with each example set up as a code cell.

9.1 A SIMPLE PUSHBUTTON EXAMPLE

Just as we can plot data to a new figure, we can display a push button. The code below does this with the `uicontrol` command. The name `uicontrol` is short for "user interface control," a function that allows us to set up the interface as we desire. It returns a *handle*, a small amount of data that refers to the interface, which we will need later. When we make a graphical interface, this function does most of the work. Related functions include `get`, `set`, `uimenu`, and `uicontextmenu`.

```
handle1 = uicontrol('Style', 'pushbutton', ...
    'String', 'Say Hi', ...
    'Position', [250 200 50 50], ...
    'Callback', 'disp(''hello!'')');
```

This command specifies several things. Each pair of parameters informs MATLAB about this interface item. First, it has a `Style` of `pushbutton`, a button that flashes when you click on it, much like how a key on a keyboard changes appearance as you press on it. This is a standard interface element, like you would expect on the window of an application or on a web page. The next pair of parameters specifies that the text written on the button should be `Say Hi`. Then we specify the position with the number of pixels from the bottom-left (250 right, 200 up), and the extent of the button from this point (50 right, 50 up). Finally, the command specifies a "callback," a function to execute when the user interacts with this interface element. In this case, we call the `disp` function with the parameter `'hello!'` whenever the user clicks on this button. (Remember that two single quotes in a row specifies a single quote within a string.)

In summary, the command above provides a button with the text "Say Hi" in approximately the middle of the figure, and displays the text "hello!" whenever the user clicks on it. This displayed text appears in the MATLAB command window.

9.2 MESSAGE BOX

Commonly, we show the user a status message and wait for an "OK." We can do this in MATLAB with a simple GUI. First, we create a new figure.

```
figure_handle = figure;
```

Next, we show a message to the user. The text `Click OK` can be replaced with whatever message fits.

```
text_handle1 = uicontrol('Parent', figure_handle, ...
    'Style', 'text', ...
    'String', 'Click OK', ...
    'Position', [30 100 100 100]);
```

The default text size can be changed, to make the text larger.

```
set(text_handle1, 'FontSize', 50);
```

Now we add an "OK" button. When the user clicks on this, it calls the `close` function. Since this figure must be the one in focus when the user presses the button, it will close this figure.

```
quitButton_handle = uicontrol('Parent', figure_handle, ...
    'Style', 'pushbutton', ...
    'String', 'OK', ...
    'BackgroundColor', [0.9, 0.8, 0.8], ...
    'Position', [475 50 80 60], 'Callback', 'close();');
```

The complete text of this example is available as the program `messageBox.m`.
There are times when we may want to do a few additional things after the user decides to quit working with our interface. For example, we may want to make sure the data are saved before exiting. We explore this idea in Section 9.15.

9.3 CREATING A GUI

The main commands for creating and using a graphical user interface are `figure`, `uicontrol`, `get`, and `set`. First, `figure` opens a new window or brings focus to one already open. It returns a handle, and when making a GUI, it is a good idea to store it in a variable. Then `uicontrol` places elements on the figure, such as text, buttons, drop-down menus, etc. A figure has a list of items associated with it, like a structure. The `get` command allows you to single out one of the items, and find information about it. Similarly, the `set` command allows you to change the value of one of the items. The system automatically updates the interface.

The `set` and `get` commands are a type of pass by reference, as opposed to pass by value. MATLAB passes parameters to functions by value (i.e., pass by value), meaning that the variable contents are copied, and the function receives the copy. This is why changing a variable within a function does not change the original. The changes only happen to the copy, and the computer deletes the copy when the function ends. To get around this, we pass the data back to the calling function through an output variable.

Working with handles is a much different experience. Computer languages such as C, C++, and Java, allow pass by reference, where a function receives a "pointer" to data. There is only one copy of that data, so if the function changes it, the calling function will also see the changes. A benefit of this approach is that very little data needs to be passed from one function to another. Think of how efficient this is when, for example, passing image data to a function. A pointer may only be 8 bytes wide, while a typical image has millions of bytes of data.

So the `get` and `set` commands provide an exception to normal MATLAB function calls, when the parameters are handles. With the handle information, we can access (`get`) and change (`set`) the data used by the interface.

Commands related to figures are also useful, such as `clf`, to clear a figure. This removes the interface elements currently shown on the figure. The `close` command removes the figure window.

The following example creates a new figure with the `figure()` command. Then it displays text on the figure via `uicontrol`. Next, it pauses for 5 seconds. The `clf` command instructs it to clear the figure, removing the displayed text. The code pauses for another 5 seconds, then closes the figure.

```
fig_handle = figure();
text_handle1 = uicontrol('Parent', fig_handle, ...
    'Style', 'text', ...
    'String', 'Wait 5 seconds', ...
    'Position', [30 100 100 100]);
pause(5);
clf(fig_handle)
pause(5);
close(fig_handle)
```

You can find this code under the name `clf_vs_close.m` with the other programs from this book. As you can see when running the code, a cleared figure appears as a blank window, and `close` gets rid of the window.

When you present a set of controls to the user through a graphical user interface, your program may need to change or update the interface as the user makes changes. For example, you may have a drop-down list of items for the user to choose from, then a secondary set of options that are affected by the first choice. To respond when the user makes a change, we implement a "callback" function. A *callback function* is a special purpose function designed to react when the user makes a selection on the user interface.

The callback function can be specified in the `uicontrol` command. Callback functions can be specified as a handle, a string, or a cell array. Two expected callback parameters are `source` and `eventdata`, where `source` can be used to get or set data in the interface. It provides us with the handle to the interface element. The other parameter, `eventdata`, appears to be reserved for a future use.

Next is a simple example where the system presents a checkbox that the user must choose before proceeding. For example, this could be part of a form where the user must agree to the terms before being allowed to continue. Here, we simply close the window when the user clicks to "proceed." We call this program "proceed.m."

```
figHandle = figure;
buttonHandle = uicontrol(figHandle, 'Style', 'pushbutton', ...
    'String', 'Proceed', ...
    'Position', [40 40 50 20], ...
    'Visible', 'off', ...
    'Callback', 'close(figHandle);');
checkHandle = uicontrol(figHandle, 'Style', 'checkbox', 'Value', 0, ...
    'String', 'You must check this before you can proceed', ...
    'Position', [40 80 250 20], ...
    'Callback', 'proceedCB(checkHandle, 0, buttonHandle);');
```

Here is the callback function, called `proceedCB.m`. We can name it anything that we want, so we will include the name "proceed" with "CB" short for callback.

Whenever the checkbox value changes, it displays the status and shows or hides the "proceed" button.

```
function proceedCB(myHandle, eventInfo, buttonHandle)
if (get(myHandle, 'Value') == true)
    disp('Checkbox value is true');
    set(buttonHandle, 'Visible', 'on');
else
    disp('Checkbox value is false');
    set(buttonHandle, 'Visible', 'off');
end
```

When run, the program shows the checkbox, with the text "You must check this before you can proceed" next to it. If the user checks the checkbox, the button labelled "Proceed" appears. When the user clicks on that button, the system closes the figure. A more realistic usage would go on to whatever the next step would be.

One issue that you will run into with callback functions is their limited variable scope. *Scope* means the part of the code where a variable has a definition. For example, a program with the commands

```
a = 3;
...
a = a + 1;
```

works without a problem. But if we rearrange the lines to be

```
a = a + 1;
...
a = 3;
```

then MATLAB generates an error: it cannot use variable a unless we assign a value to it first. Now suppose that we move the a = a + 1; line to a function, as shown in the following function definition.

```
function scope_test(x)
y = 2;
whos
a = a + 1;    % This causes an error
```

Reading the comment, we might expect the function to generate an error because a has not been defined. However, see what happens when we call that function after assigning a to a value.

```
>> a = 3;
>> scope_test(1)
  Name       Size           Bytes   Class      Attributes
   x         1x1                8   double
   y         1x1                8   double
Undefined function or variable 'a'.
Error in scope_test (line 12)
a = a + 1;    % This causes an error
```

We still get an error. Functions have their own workspace, so variable a is out of scope to it, unless we pass it to the function as an argument. Similarly, variables x and y are out of scope outside of the function, unless we pass them back from the function. Variable a has a definition in the "base" workspace, while x and y have definitions in the function's workspace. Thus, the scope of a variable depends on where it has a definition.

You will likely have variables that your main program sets up, then want to access those variables in the callback functions. Callback functions do take parameters, but they do not allow you to return multiple values. That is, you may be able to read data with the callback function if you pass it as a parameter, but you cannot overwrite the data without resorting to a trick. The global declaration allows you to access a variable from one function when it is normally only defined in another. Similarly, the evalin and assignin commands allow you to access and overwrite variables, respectively, from the base workspace. That is, if you use a variable at the command line, then call a function, that function could see the variable's value with evalin and give it a new value with assignin. Finally, sub-functions do work as callbacks, but you have to use a handle for this instead of a string, e.g., use @myCallback instead of 'myCallback'.

9.4 CHANGING THE BUTTON'S STATE

When we go from one example to the next, we should start with a blank figure. Otherwise, the interface elements will be drawn on top of each other. If you click on the "exit" button on the top left corner of the figure, it will close. (This may appear as an X. On a Macintosh, it looks like a small red circle with an X in it.) Alternatively, we can type close at the command line to get rid of the current figure. Another possibility is the clf command, which clears the figure but leaves it as an open window. If you are following these examples with your computer, try entering clf now.

The next example calls our own function. The main change is the callback function, changeText. We will define this function shortly. First, notice that the function name appears as a string within a cell. MATLAB treats this as a function call, and passes parameters to it automatically.

```
handle1 = uicontrol('Style', 'pushbutton', ...
    'String', 'Say Hi', ...
    'Position', [250 200 50 50], ...
    'Callback', {'changeText'});
```

The following shows an equivalent call, using the at-sign instead.

```
handle1 = uicontrol('Style', 'pushbutton', ...
    'String', 'Say Hi', ...
    'Position', [250 200 50 50], ...
    'Callback', @changeText);
```

Either way, this code places a pushbutton on the current figure, and MATLAB runs the callback function every time the user clicks on the button.

Now let's examine the changeText function, which we define next. Remember that this function does not come with MATLAB. You need to either copy it to your working directory or type it and save it under the filename changeText.m.

```
% changeText.m
function changeText(uihandle, future)
current_greeting = get(uihandle, 'String');
if (strcmp(current_greeting, 'hello'))
    set(uihandle, 'String', 'HELLO');
else
    set(uihandle, 'String', 'hello');
end
```

This function returns nothing. The two inputs are passed by MATLAB automatically. The first one, called uihandle in this example, gives us the handle for the pushbutton that the user pressed. There could be multiple pushbuttons, or even multiple windows with pushbuttons.

The second input parameter, future, is something that MATLAB will implement in the future. For now, we will simply ignore it. But we have to include it as an input, although we could call it something else. If we had more inputs, i.e., inputs passed to this function through the callback that we established, these would appear after future in the input parameter list.

Next, we use the handle to obtain information about the user interface. Specifically, get(uihandle, 'String') returns the current value for String. You may recall that we assigned it the text Say Hi above. Although we will soon change it, the first time that the user presses this button, the text Say Hi will be assigned to variable current_greeting.

The if statement checks current_greeting to see if it matches the text hello. The strcmp command compares the two strings. While the test-for-equality == could be used, it also generates an error when the strings made form character arrays do not match in length. Therefore, strcmp is better. The next example demonstrates this idea. First, we assign several strings to variables: str1 and str2 have a character array definition, while str3 and str4 are objects of the string class.

```
str1 = 'green';
str2 = 'blue';
str3 = string('green');
str4 = string('blue');
```

Checking the variables with the whos function gives us a bit more information.

```
>> whos
    Name        Size            Bytes    Class      Attributes
    str1        1x5                10    char
    str2        1x4                 8    char
    str3        1x1               132    string
    str4        1x1               132    string
```

We see that MATLAB considers str1 and str2 as arrays with multiple elements. Meanwhile, str3 and str4 each have only one element. Next, we check for equality.

```
>> if (str1 == str2)
disp('equal')
end
Matrix dimensions must agree.
>> if (str3 == str4)
disp('equal')
end
>> if (str1 == str4)
disp('equal')
end
```

Using the test-for-equality (==) operation generates an error when the character arrays have different lengths. Even though the two string objects store data of different lengths, the test-for-equality operation works without a problem. When we try the test-for-equality with a character array (str1) and a string object (str4), it also works.

```
>> if (strcmp(str1, str2))
disp('equal')
end
>> if (strcmp(str3, str4))
disp('equal')
end
>> if (strcmp(str1, str3))
disp('equal')
end
equal
```

Finally, we use `strcmp` to compare the strings. When comparing two character arrays, `strcmp` does not give us an error when they have different lengths. It also works well for string objects. As the last `if` statement shows, it allows a comparison between a character array and a string object.

The `matches` function could also be used here. It allows some powerful extensions, such as the ability to ignore the case. For example, consider the following code.

```
str1 = 'One';
str2 = 'one';
if (strcmp(str1, str2))
    disp('Equal');
elseif (matches(str1, str2, 'IgnoreCase', true))
    disp('Same letters, but different capitalization');
else
    disp('Not equal');
end
```

The `strcmp` command returns a `false` value, indicating that the two strings differ. Repeating the comparison with `matches`, and passing to it that we want it to treat upper and lower case as the same, returns a `true` value, and the computer displays "Same letters, but different capitalization." Thus, we can treat two strings as equal even if they do not match exactly.

We will next execute a call to the `set` function to change the text of `String`. Whether the condition is met or not only determines which text we will use. Assuming the availability of the `changeText` function, the preceding `uicontrol` command sets up a pushbutton on the current figure.

This button will initially have the text "Say Hi" on it. When the user presses this button, the callback function `changeText` will check the button's text, then change it to "hello." A second click on this button will change its text to "HELLO." Any further clicks on it will alternate the text between "hello" and "HELLO."

9.5   KEEPING DATA IN GLOBAL VARIABLES

What if we want to have our callback function change data besides what the handle stores? We could try a script, one that expects variables to already be defined. Here is an example of that.

```
myvalue = 1;
handle1 = uicontrol('Style', 'pushbutton', ...
    'String', 'Inc myvalue', ...
    'Position', [225 200 100 50], ...
    'Callback', 'changeData');
```

First, we assign the variable `myvalue` the value one. We create a pushbutton similar to the previous examples, although you may notice a slightly different size and position, with new text. The `changeData` script appears below.

```
% changeData.m
myvalue = myvalue + 1;
disp(sprintf('myvalue is %d', myvalue));
```

This script simply increments variable `myvalue`, and displays the new value to the command window.

The script has no way of knowing what action (event) triggered its call. It would have access to the handle, since `handle1` would be defined. But if there were multiple interfaces, it would not be able to determine which one called it. Some applications may be fine with this.

As a side note, if the user enters the `clear` command, it will remove the variable `myvalue`. If the figure is still present, the user could press the pushbutton, and this would result in an error. Interestingly, this was not a problem before. Even if the user clears all variables with the previous "Say Hi" example, MATLAB retains the function handle on some level until the user closes the figure.

Suppose that we want to make the callback function an actual function, one that would receive the handle and perhaps other parameters. We could try to make changeData a function, but variable myvalue would not be known to the function. Even if we passed its value as a parameter, the updated value would be lost once MATLAB exits the function.

Global variables provide a way to make this work. Declaring a variable global means that all other functions and scripts can access or alter it. But they must also indicate that this is a global variable.

Now we create a new function called changeData2.m that uses myvalue as a global variable. This function does not define it, but we expect that some other code gives it an initial value before this function runs.

```
% changeData2.m
function changeData2(uihandle, future)
global myvalue;
myvalue = myvalue + 1;
disp(sprintf('myvalue is %d', myvalue));
```

We modify the pushbutton below to incorporate myvalue as a global variable. Also, we change the name of the callback function and the way that we refer to it, so that it will receive the handle information.

```
global myvalue;
myvalue=1;
handle1 = uicontrol('Style', 'pushbutton', ...
    'String', 'Inc myvalue', ...
    'Position', [225 200 100 50], ...
    'Callback', @changeData2);
```

If the last two parameters were 'Callback', and 'changeData2', the function would appear to work, but any modifications in changeData2.m to access uihandle would fail. With the at-sign (@), the changeData2 function will receive the handle as a parameter. Note that you can also put curly braces around the callback function, as the next lines show.

```
% Another way to set up the callback
global myvalue;
myvalue=1;
handle1 = uicontrol('Style', 'pushbutton', ...
```

```
'String', 'Inc myvalue', ...
'Position', [225 200 100 50], ...
'Callback', {'changeData2'});
```

With the global variable in place, `myvalue` increments any time that the user clicks on the button.

9.6   AN EXIT BUTTON

The next example keeps running until the user clicks on the button. We set up the button like before, and make its text say "Quit." Then we start a loop that does nothing but waits for half a second at a time. Of course, a better example would have the program doing something interesting here, perhaps processing user input from other interface elements. When the user clicks the button, the callback function changes the variable that controls the loop. It also executes the `close` command, to close the current window. So the window disappears right after the user clicks the button.

```
finished = false;
handle1 = uicontrol('Style', 'pushbutton', ...
    'String', 'Quit', ...
    'Position', [225 200 100 50], ...
    'Callback', 'finished=true; close');
while (~finished)
    pause(0.5);
end
```

It looks like an infinite loop, and would be except for the button. What would happen if we removed `finished=true` from the callback, and left the `close` command? If you try that, control-C stops it.

There are other ways to do this. We could change the pushbutton to a toggle button, and monitor the `Value` it has directly. The code below does this. Notice that we do not use a callback function, and that we set the `Value` to zero initially.

```
finished = false;
handle1 = uicontrol('Style', 'togglebutton', ...
    'String', 'Quit', ...
    'Value', 0, ...
    'Position', [225 200 100 50]);
```

```
pause(0.1);
while (~finished)
    pause(0.1);
    if (get(handle1, 'Value') ~= 0)
        finished = true;
        disp('Button clicked. Exiting.');
    end
end
close
```

Including the pause is good practice. We need to give the computer some time to do the things that we tell it to do. That is, without the pause, the program will not run as expected. First, the figure may not be visible to the user while the program runs. Second, the user's interaction with the interface may be delayed.

Both pauses above are not necessary, since the one inside the `while` loop will allow MATLAB time to display the button. To demonstrate the need for the `pause` command, try running the code with the second `pause` command commented out. Then comment out the first one as well. You should observe that the first pause allows the computer to display the button, and the second pause allows it to process the user's input.

We see that we can have our code remain active until the user decides to quit. Upon quitting, we exit our loop and close the window with the button. This ensures that the user will not continue to try to use it.

9.7   USING THE "SET" COMMAND

Like the `get` command retrieves values for us, we can change values with the `set` command. This example puts up a user interface control, then waits three seconds, then changes the value associated with it. To make this change stand out, we use a checkbox.

```
handle1 = uicontrol('Style', 'checkbox', ...
    'String', '3 seconds elapsed', ...
    'Value', 0, ...
    'Position', [225 200 150 50]);
pause(3);
set(handle1, 'Value', 1);
```

Executing this example, we see a checkbox on a figure, with the check initially cleared. After three seconds, the `set` command executes, and a check appears in the checkbox.

Here we have a second example, where we change the text associated with the checkbox.

```
handle1 = uicontrol('Style', 'checkbox', ...
    'String', '10 seconds', ...
    'Value', 0, ...
    'Position', [225 200 150 50]);
pause(5);
set(handle1, 'String', '5 seconds');
pause(4);
set(handle1, 'String', '1 second');
pause(1);
set(handle1, 'String', 'checked');
set(handle1, 'Value', 1);
```

We start with "10 seconds" displayed next to the checkbox. After five seconds, the text becomes "5 seconds." Four seconds later, we change it to "1 second." After a final pause of one second, we change the text to "checked" and check this box. The `set` command allows us to change the properties of the user interface elements as we choose.

9.8   HOW DO WE KNOW WHAT TO GET?

In the preceding examples, we `get` and `set` various attributes of the user interface. It may seem like magic, leading to the question "how do we know what attributes exist?" Documentation provides an answer, although we will soon see another way. To get started, consider the following example.

```
fig_handle = figure();
count_handle1 = uicontrol('Parent', fig_handle, ...
    'Style', 'text', ...
    'String', 'X', ...
    'FontSize', 50, ...
    'Position', [100 200 100 100]);
```

```
for count = 10:-1:1
    set(count_handle1, 'String', sprintf('%d', count));
    pause(1);
end
set(count_handle1, 'String', '0');
set(fig_handle, 'Color', [0.5 0.1 0.1]);
```

It creates a new figure, then places a text element on it, starting with an "X." Then the code starts a count down loop using count as the index. Immediately, it changes the string in the text element to whatever value count has, then it waits a second. In this way, it displays the numbers 10, 9, 8, .. 1. After the loop finishes, it sets the text to "0," then changes the background of the figure to a crimson color.

How did we know that fig_handle has an attribute called "Color"? The get command tells us, if we pass it the handle only.

```
>> get(fig_handle)
                  Alphamap: [1x64 double]
             BeingDeleted: 'off'
               BusyAction: 'queue'
            ButtonDownFcn: ''
                 Children: [1x1 UIControl]
                 Clipping: 'on'
          CloseRequestFcn: 'closereq'
                    Color: [0.5000 0.1000 0.1000]
                 Colormap: [64x3 double]
                CreateFcn: ''
              CurrentAxes: [0x0 GraphicsPlaceholder]
         CurrentCharacter: ''
            CurrentObject: [1x1 Figure]
             CurrentPoint: [50 152]
                DeleteFcn: ''
             DockControls: 'on'
                 FileName: ''
       GraphicsSmoothing: 'on'
         HandleVisibility: 'on'
            InnerPosition: [118 908 560 420]
```

```
       IntegerHandle: 'on'
       Interruptible: 'on'
       InvertHardcopy: 'on'
          KeyPressFcn: ''
        KeyReleaseFcn: ''
              MenuBar: 'figure'
                 Name: ''
             NextPlot: 'add'
               Number: 1
          NumberTitle: 'on'
        OuterPosition: [118 908 560 493]
     PaperOrientation: 'portrait'
        PaperPosition: [0.3611 2.5833 7.7778 5.8333]
    PaperPositionMode: 'auto'
            PaperSize: [8.5000 11]
            PaperType: 'usletter'
           PaperUnits: 'inches'
               Parent: [1x1 Root]
              Pointer: 'arrow'
     PointerShapeCData: [16x16 double]
  PointerShapeHotSpot: [1 1]
             Position: [118 908 560 420]
             Renderer: 'opengl'
         RendererMode: 'auto'
               Resize: 'on'
        SelectionType: 'normal'
        SizeChangedFcn: ''
                  Tag: ''
              ToolBar: 'auto'
                 Type: 'figure'
        UIContextMenu: [0x0 GraphicsPlaceholder]
                Units: 'pixels'
             UserData: []
              Visible: 'on'
```

```
    WindowButtonDownFcn:  ''
  WindowButtonMotionFcn:  ''
      WindowButtonUpFcn:  ''
      WindowKeyPressFcn:  ''
    WindowKeyReleaseFcn:  ''
    WindowScrollWheelFcn:  ''
            WindowStyle:  'normal'
               XDisplay:  'Quartz'
```

As you can see, the figure has many attributes. If you prefer to alter the figure using a graphical tool, try the `inspect(fig_handle)` command. Figure 9.1 shows the window that the `inspect` command opens.

9.9 READING KEY PRESSES

Can we read a key-press in MATLAB? We can, if we have a figure up and in focus. MATLAB provides a "CurrentCharacter" attribute of a figure handle, so we examine that to know what keys the user presses. Better yet, we can set the "KeyPressFcn" to handle key presses. The following function reads the "CurrentCharacter" attribute and displays it.

```
function keypress_call(obj1, obj2)
a = get(gcf, 'CurrentCharacter');
disp(sprintf('keypress: %c', a));
```

We will call that `keypress_call.m`. To utilize it, we set the "KeyPressFcn," as in the following code.

```
fig_handle = figure;
set(fig_handle, 'KeyPressFcn', 'keypress_call');
```

This creates a new figure, and informs the computer to call function `keypress_call` for each key press event. You may notice a "KeyReleaseFcn" attribute as well, that is, we can look for a key press or a key release, or both. A "keypress" event happens when the user's finger presses the key, while a "keyrelease" event occurs when the user's finger lifts up from the key. To a human, these seem instantaneous, but the computer works much faster than the user. A similar function to `keypress_call.m`, called `keyrelease_call.m`, can be set with a similar command, as follows:

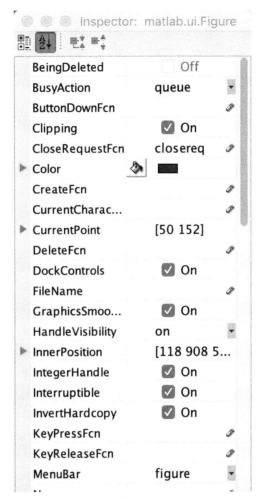

FIGURE 9.1 An example of moving text with arrow keys.

```
set(fig_handle, 'KeyReleaseFcn', 'keyrelease_call');
```

With these settings in place, we can select the figure window and type. The output looks something like this.

```
keypress: q
keyrelease: q
keypress: w
keyrelease: w
keypress: e
```

```
keyrelease: e
keypress: r
keypress: r
keyrelease: r
```

Here, the keys "q," "w," "e," and "r" were each pressed in turn. Notice that the text "keypress: r" appears twice, due to that key being held down long enough to call the `keypress_call` function again.

By reading the keypresses, we can allow the user to interact with our programs. For example, the following is the `moving_text.m` script along with the related function `keypress_cursors.m`.

```
fig_handle = figure;
set(fig_handle, 'KeyPressFcn', 'keypress_cursors');
global x y hndl
x = 135;
y = 380;
hndl = uicontrol(fig_handle, ...
    'Style', 'text', ...
    'String', 'Moving with Arrow Keys', ...
    'FontSize', 20, ...
    'Position', [x, y, 300, 24]);
```

This script sets up the figure, much like before. It displays some text on it, at offsets x and y. The numbers 300 and 24 specify the extents of the text box. The variables have global scope, so that the following function can change them.

```
function keypress_cursors(obj1, obj2)
global x y hndl
a = get(gcf, 'CurrentCharacter');
switch (a)
    case 28
        % left
        x = x - 10;
        if (x < 1)
          x = 1;
        end
```

```
case 29
    % right
    x = x + 10;
    if (x > 260)
      x = 260;
    end
    % ... some code omitted
end
set(hndl, 'Position', [x, y, 300, 24]);
```

The `keypress_cursors` function uses these global variables, too. Building on the idea of the `keypress_call` function, it gets the current character whenever a key press occurs. Key codes 28, 29, 30, and 31 go with the left, right, up, and down arrows, respectively. Based on the key code, this callback function changes the x or y variable accordingly. We must also check to make sure that these coordinates do not go out of bounds. At the end of the callback function, it sets the position of the text to the new values. Figure 9.2 shows the figure as it initially appears. As the user types the arrow keys, the text moves about the figure.

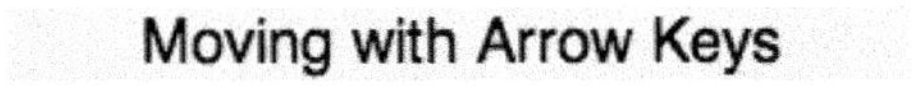

Moving with Arrow Keys

FIGURE 9.2 An example of moving text with arrow keys.

9.10 CALLBACK FUNCTIONS AND GLOBAL VARIABLES

This section contains some examples of a drop-down menu, along with a discussion about callback functions. It uses a simple menu consisting of three options: red, green, and blue. It does not actually change the color of anything, although it could.

The following example shows a drop-down menu, working with a callback function. The callback function, which follows, takes the argument "`myparam`." For the moment, we simply display `myparam` without using it for anything further. Next, it accesses the currently selected value with the `get` command. That line does not end with a semi-colon, intentionally, so that the result appears in the command window. After that, the code copies the value stored in "`current_choice`" to a new variable called "`old_choice`". You might wonder, correctly, where these variables come from, since they have not yet been defined. This problem stands out since we examine the callback function first.

```
% GUI_dropdown_CB1.m
function GUI_dropdown_CB1(obj1, obj2, myparam)
disp(myparam);
% Get the newly selected value
Value = get(obj1, 'Value')
% Remember what the choice was last time.
old_choice = current_choice;
% Find out what the choice is now.
if (Value == 1)
    current_choice = 'red';
elseif (Value == 2)
    current_choice = 'green';
else
    current_choice = 'blue';
end
disp(sprintf('Switching from %s to %s', old_choice, current_choice));
```

The calling function appears next. It defines the variable `current_choice`, but that does not fix the problem. The variable remains outside the scope of the callback function.

```
% GUI_dropdown_example1.m
disp('This example does NOT work.');
fig_handle = figure();
current_choice = 'red';
handle1 = uicontrol('Style', 'popup', ...
    'String', 'red|green|blue', ...
    'Position', [250 200 100 50], ...
    'Callback', {'GUI_dropdown_CB1', 'hello'});
```

It does not work, since the callback attempts to change a variable that is out of its scope. When run, it displays the text "This example does NOT work.", although it does open a figure and display a drop-down menu. If we were to run the program and close the figure window, we might not know that an error exists.

FIGURE 9.3 An example of a drop-down menu.

The drop-down menu shows the current choice of "red," and selecting an option causes it to use the callback function, Figure 9.3. This generates the following output.

```
hello
Value =
    2
Undefined function or variable 'current_choice'.
Error in GUI_dropdown_CB1 (line 17)
old_choice = current_choice;
Error while evaluating UIControl Callback
```

We see the text "hello" displays, revealing that the callback did receive the argument as expected. That is, the function call to GUI_dropdown_CB1 assigns myparam as the string "hello," where the callback function displays it. Also, the new assignment for Value works, and the number 2 means that the user selected "green" from the list in this example. Now we get to the part that uses variable current_choice, and see that it generates an error. This can be tricky. Suppose that we think that it *should* work, since the code defines that variable, we might try to check the value, as follows:

```
>> current_choice
current_choice =
red
```

The computer complains that variable current_choice has no definition, then it tells us that it has the value "red". This only makes sense when we realize that the error comes from the callback function, which does not have a definition for current_choice, even though the MATLAB session does.

9.10.1 Using a Global Variable

We can get around this problem by introducing current_choice as a global variable. The program "GUI_dropdown_example2.m" repeats most of the same code as "GUI_dropdown_example1.m", except for the addition of a global declaration, and a couple of minor differences.

```
% GUI_dropdown_example2.m
global current_choice
disp('This example does work.');
fig_handle = figure();
```

```
current_choice = 'red';
handle1 = uicontrol('Style', 'popup', ...
    'String', 'red|green|blue', ...
    'Position', [250 200 100 50], ...
    'Callback', {'GUI_dropdown_CB2', 'hello'});
```

In the callback function, "GUI_dropdown_CB2.m," we must also include the global declaration, before using the current_choice variable.

```
global current_choice
```

When running the program, and selecting "green" from the menu, the code gives the following output.

```
This example does work.
hello
Value =
    2
Switching from red to green
```

Examining the variable, we see that it has changed.

```
>> disp(current_choice)
green
```

Summarizing up to this point, we have seen a non-working example and a working example. To fix the non-working example, we declared the variable to be global. The next example presents another solution.

9.10.2 Commands "evalin" and "assignin"

The program "GUI_dropdown_example3.m" has almost identical content as "GUI_dropdown_example1.m". The only notable difference sets "GUI_dropdown_CB3.m" as the callback function. The following code shows this callback function.

```
% GUI_dropdown_CB3.m
function GUI_dropdown_CB3(obj1, obj2, myparam)
disp(myparam);
% Get the newly selected value
Value = get(obj1, 'Value')
% Remember what the choice was last time.
```

```
old_choice = evalin('base', 'current_choice');
% Find out what the choice is now.
if (Value == 1)
    current_choice = 'red';
elseif (Value == 2)
    current_choice = 'green';
else
    current_choice = 'blue';
end
disp(sprintf('Switching from %s to %s', old_choice, current_choice));
% Update the variable that the main script/workspace accesses.
assignin('base', 'current_choice', current_choice);
```

Two lines stand out: one with `evalin` and the other with `assignin`. Instead of setting variable `old_choice` to `current_choice` with a simple assignment like we did previously, we use `evalin` to "evaluate" `current_choice` "in" the workspace "base". While this example only shows a variable access, we could have asked it to do more, like `evalin('base', 'current_choice + 1')` to add 1. The "base" workspace is the one you see labelled as "Workspace" if you have your MATLAB session configured to show it. It includes the variables currently defined through the command window, or as a result of scripts that you invoke from the command window. In other words, it refers to the same variables that you see listed in the output of `who` or `whos`. When a function executes, it will have its own workspace. MATLAB also recognizes "caller" as a workspace name. Additionally, the MATLAB commands `eval`, `feval`, and `evalc` provide ways to evaluate an expression given as a string. As you might expect from the name, `evalin` is a variation on `eval`.

The `evalin` command can provide a variable's value. Likewise, the `assignin` command provides a way to set a variable in another workspace to a new value. The parameters include the workspace where the variable has a definition, the variable's name as a string, and the new value for it. Thus, `evalin` and `assignin` allow the callback function to get around the problem of the variable's limited scope.

Typically, when we write a MATLAB function, we put it in a separate file. We must do this when we want to call it from a script. If the function is well written and flexible, we might want to reuse it again and again, calling it from many different scripts or functions. However, if we have a very specific need, we can define a sub-function in the same file as the function that calls it.

If we define the code that makes a GUI as a function, why not put the callback function(s) in the same file? A couple of other, non-working, examples are provided in the supplementary material, that attempt to do this. Function "GUI_dropdown_example4" includes the callback "GUI_dropdown_CB4", however, it generates the following error message when the user attempts to change the drop-down selection.

```
Undefined function 'GUI_dropdown_CB4' for input arguments of type
'matlab.ui.control.UIControl'.

Error while evaluating UIControl Callback
```

That function tries to pass the variable to the callback function, and fails, since it cannot find the callback function. If we instead make the variable global, would that work? Function "GUI_dropdown_example5" does this, although it generates an error right away. It also changes the callback function set-up to use @GUI_dropdown_CB5 instead of putting the name in single quotes. Using @GUI_dropdown_CB5 to specify the callback function works.

```
>> GUI_dropdown_example5
Error: File: GUI_dropdown_example5.m Line: 37 Column: 16
The GLOBAL or PERSISTENT declaration of "current_choice" appears
in a nested function, but should be in the
outermost function where it is used.
```

This counter-example declares the variable as global, but does not quite get it right. MATLAB informs us that the problem lies in the current_choice variable, where the computer takes exception to the sub-function's definition of it.

Function "GUI_dropdown_example6" provides a working example, with the callback as a sub-function.

```
% GUI_dropdown_example6.m
function GUI_dropdown_example6
disp('This example does work.');
fig_handle = figure();
current_choice = 'red';
mystr = 'hello';
handle1 = uicontrol('Style', 'popup', ...
    'String', 'red|green|blue', ...
    'Position', [250 200 100 50], ...
    'Callback', {@GUI_dropdown_CB6, mystr});
```

```
%
% GUI_dropdown_CB6.m
% This is the callback function for GUI_dropdown_example6.m.
%
function GUI_dropdown_CB6(obj1, obj2, myparam)
disp('hello from GUI_dropdown_CB6');
disp(myparam);
Value = get(obj1, 'Value')
% Remember what the choice was last time.
old_choice = current_choice;
% Find out what the choice is now.
if (Value == 1)
    current_choice = 'red';
elseif (Value == 2)
    current_choice = 'green';
else
    current_choice = 'blue';
end
disp(sprintf('Switching from %s to %s', ...
    old_choice, current_choice));
    end % GUI_dropdown_CB6
end % GUI_dropdown_example6
```

Running this example, and selecting "green" from the menu, produces the following output.

```
>> GUI_dropdown_example6
This example does work.
hello from GUI_dropdown_CB6
hello
Value =
    2
Switching from red to green
```

It tells us "hello from GUI_dropdown_CB6" as soon as the user selects a value from the menu, along with the other output messages.

9.10.3 Operating System Utilities "diff" and "patch", and MATLAB's "diff" and "patch"

When given two similar programs, where one works and the other does not, you may wonder what the significant differences are. A diff utility provides a good way to discover this. The diff command exists on all major operating systems. The git program even has a built-in diff function, which can show the changes in the current file compared to the one in the repository. This is not to be confused with the diff command in MATLAB, which works with matrices, and returns the differences. The operating system command diff compares two files, and points out where they differ.

The differences between GUI_dropdown_example5.m and GUI_drop-down_example6.m include minor things like comments, and name changes from 5 to 6. Both programs use a sub-function as the callback. The only crucial difference is that the non-working GUI_dropdown_example5.m defines current_choice as a global variable, while the working GUI_dropdown_example6.m does not.

The following shows the output of the diff command, with many of the non-crucial lines removed. The text file GUI_dropdown_examples5_6_diff, included with the programs, shows all of the differences. The output from diff shows the differences, along with information about where the changes appear.

```
$ diff GUI_dropdown_example5.m GUI_dropdown_example6.m
12,14c12
< global current_choice
<
< disp('This example does NOT work.');
---
> disp('This example does work.');
24c22
<     'Callback', {@GUI_dropdown_CB5, mystr});
---
>     'Callback', {@GUI_dropdown_CB6, mystr});
35,37c33,34
<     function GUI_dropdown_CB5(obj1, obj2, myparam)
<
<         global current_choice
```

```
---
>       function GUI_dropdown_CB6(obj1, obj2, myparam)
>
```

For example, 12,14c12 says to change line 12 to 14 of the first file to line 12 of the second file. The less than sign indicates lines from the first file, while the greater-than sign specifies that the line come from the second file. The three dashes separate the lines from the two files.

Another handy utility to know about, called patch, uses the output from diff to change a file. For example, if we just want to change the lines shown above, the patch utility allows us to do so. The following commands do this. First, make a copy of the GUI_dropdown_example5.m file with the cp command. Of course, you could do this in other ways, such as using your operating system's user interface. Next, find the differences between the newly copied file and GUI_dropdown_example6.m, where the output goes to a file called changes. Then, edit the changes file to only the lines that we want. For this example, this step does not matter, however, editing the diff output to change only part of the file is a powerful ability to know about.

```
$ cp GUI_dropdown_example5.m GUI_dropdown_example5_test.m
$ diff GUI_dropdown_example5_test.m GUI_dropdown_example6.m > changes
$ vi changes
$ patch GUI_dropdown_example5_test.m changes
patching file GUI_dropdown_example5_test.m
```

Doing this alters the GUI_dropdown_example5_test.m program, changing it just enough to make it work. At this stage, it is no longer a copy of GUI_dropdown_example5.m, nor is it exactly the same as GUI_dropdown_example6.m. Instead, it mixes the two files enough to form a working version.

Remember that diff and patch are not MATLAB commands in the preceding context, but utilities at the operating system level. However, MATLAB does have commands named diff and patch, for finding differences between matrices and drawing filled polygons. This example shows MATLAB's diff command.

```
>> diff([12, 20, 17, 4])
ans =
     8    -3    -13
```

It generates an array where each value is the difference between value n and value $n + 1$. In other words, $20 - 12 = 8$, $17 - 20 = -3$, etc. We could also find the difference in the following way.

```
>> myarray = [12, 20, 17, 4];
>> N = length(myarray);
>> myarray(2:N) - myarray(1:N-1)
ans =
       8    -3    -13
```

However, MATLAB's `diff` command has other functionality, too. Next, we examine MATLAB's `patch` command.

```
figure();
patch([50, 30, 70], [70, 40, 40], 'g');
```

Using the coordinates (50, 70), (30, 40), and (70, 40), this command draws a polygon on the figure, with the color specified by `'g'`, which appears as a green triangle.

Finally, example "GUI_dropdown_example7" does a couple of new things. Most visibly, it sets the background color of the figure, then changes it when the user selects a different option from the drop-down list. The line below demonstrates the color change.

```
set(fig_handle, 'Color', [0.6 0.0 0.0]);
```

The three values in the array specify the red, green, and blue amounts from 0 to 1. Since this line contains 0.6 for the first value, the color will have red at a 6/10 intensity. Values for green and blue have 0 intensity, so the resulting color appears as red. The callback function contains similar lines to adjust the color according to the other color selections.

9.10.4 The "persistent" Keyword

This code changes the way it uses variable `old_choice`. First, it uses the `persistent` keyword. Like `global`, the `persistent` keyword changes the way MATLAB treats a variable. In this case, a `persistent` variable remains after a function stops executing. With it, a function could define a variable, then access the previously defined value in a future call. The first time we use the variable `old_choice`, however, it will have an empty-set value. In other words, MATLAB creates the variable, and sets it to a default value. It will not be any of the valid color names when the callback function runs for the first time. Thus, we can check to see if `isempty(old_choice)` returns true before trying to use it.

```
persistent old_choice;
```

```
if (isempty(old_choice))
    disp(sprintf('Switching to %s', current_choice));
else
    disp(sprintf('Switching from %s to %s', ...
        old_choice, current_choice));
end
old_choice = current_choice;
```

If the `old_choice` variable holds an empty array, the function reports only what the new value will be. Otherwise, it uses the `old_choice` value along with the new value. Finally, we set the `old_choice` value at the end.

9.11 A CALLBACK PROBLEM

Suppose that we have a MATLAB program that sets a variable when a button is pressed on the GUI. The program is complicated and has a lot of functions (especially callback functions) that must communicate with each other. It employs global variables to do this. Pressing the button sets the variable, but then the function that uses this value does not see the update. What is going on? (See the file `callback_bug.m` for a scaled-down version.) Figure 9.4 shows the interface used in the demonstration of this bug. It only has two buttons, one to set variable `Bval`, and one to use it.

The callback line looks like the following.

```
'Callback', 'Bval=true;' ...
```

Then another callback function checks the value, and resets it to false.

```
'Callback', 'useBval' ...
```

This should work, since other programs use a similar assignment as the callback. However, the second callback reports the value as 0 (the default).

Strange bugs sometimes occur in MATLAB programs that use global variables, so we should check this suspicion. A normal callback function, one written as a separate function, must declare the variable as global before it can use it. Otherwise, it cannot access the variable and generates an error, or it creates a new variable by the same name, without generating an error. Could this be the case here? We can try the following in place of the callback command that sets the value to true. (See the file `callback_good.m`.)

```
'Callback', 'global Bval;Bval=true' ...
```

After this, the `useBval` callback reports the value correctly. Why does this problem exist? The program is a function itself, rather than a script, and has a different variable context. Therefore, it cannot access the global variable the way it would from a script, defined in the base context.

To see this for yourself, try `callback_bug`. When finished, close the figure and clear the variables, to get rid of the locally defined `Bval` variable. Then run `callback_good` to see what the response should be. The following results appear when clicking the "Use Bval" button, then clicking the "set Bval to true" button, then clicking "Use Bval" again.

```
>> callback_bug
Variable Bval is false.
Variable Bval is false.
>> close
>> clear
>> callback_good
Variable Bval is false.
Variable Bval is true. Resetting it to false.
```

Notice that we got a different response the second time, where it actually set the correct `Bval` variable. Informing MATLAB that variable `Bval`, used in the callback, should be a global variable fixes this problem.

When it comes to setting up a GUI, we must include callback functions to process user selections. This causes a problem when code in a script or function must communicate with a callback function. How do we use variables across different workspaces? Making the variables global solves this problem. Alternatively, we can use `evalin` and `assignin` to access and change variables across a workspace boundary. As in the `GUI_dropdown_example6` code, we can bundle the callback function with the function that creates the GUI, effectively allowing the sub-function to access the same workspace. Also, the `persistent` keyword provides a useful way to keep a variable around after a function completes execution.

9.12 A NOTE ABOUT FIGURE HANDLES

Up to this point, we have always associated a button with a single window. We could have multiple windows open at the same time. In the code below, we combine a couple of earlier examples and put a different button in two figures. Notice how we use the parameters `'Parent'` and `figure_handle1` for the first button to indicate that the first button should be put on the first figure.

FIGURE 9.4 A GUI example that shows a bug with a global variable.

```
figure_handle1 = figure(1);
handle1 = uicontrol('Parent', figure_handle1, ...
    'String', 'Say Hi', ...
    'Position', [250 200 50 50], ...
    'Callback', {'changeText'});
figure_handle2 = figure(2);
handle2 = uicontrol('Parent', figure_handle2, ...
    'Style', 'togglebutton', ...
    'String', 'Quit', ...
    'Value', 0, ...
    'Position', [225 200 100 50], ...
    'Callback', 'close all');
```

This opens two figures, and puts the buttons in them. Like the example in Section 9.6, the button labeled "Quit" will end the example, this time by closing all open figures.

The second figure may be drawn over top of the first figure. The user can simply move this window with the mouse. Or we can find the figure's placement with the `get` command, and change it with the `set` command, like the code below.

```
location = get(figure_handle1, 'Position');
location(1) = 100;
set(figure_handle1, 'Position', location);
```

The `get` command gives us the current location of the window. Next, we set the location's first value to be 100, corresponding to the horizontal offset on the user's screen. This only changes the value in our array called `location`. To apply this to the window, we use the `set` command, as in the third line above. The net result, assuming that the first figure was placed at a horizontal offset of much more than 100, is that the computer repositions the first figure to the left.

We see here how to use the `'Parent'` parameter to associate an interface element with one of several possible user interfaces. Also, the figure properties can be retrieved with the `get` command, changed, and updated with the `set` command. Keep in mind that `get` and `set` will generate an error if called on a closed figure.

9.13 A SLIDER INPUT FROM A TO Z

In the following example, we make a simple GUI with a "slider" input to select a character from "A" to "Z." A callback function will show a character of the alphabet, and change it according to a slider input. To facilitate communication between the program that creates the GUI and the callback function, we use global variables `letter` for the currently selected alphabetic character, and `tx` for a text element. Whenever the user moves the slider, the callback function should update the text element, letting the user know which letter corresponds to the current slider position.

First, we set up a new figure window, remembering the handle in variable `fh`, because we need that information to set up the features of the interface. Next, inform the computer that we have some global variables, and set their values. Since `tx` will be an element of the GUI, use `uicontrol` to create it.

```
fh = figure();
global letter
global tx
letter = 'A';
tx = uicontrol('Parent', fh, ...
    'Style', 'text', 'String', letter);
set(tx, 'Position', [250, 100, 100, 50]);
```

After creating `tx`, we use the `set` command to change its position attributes. Yes, this could have been included with the call to `uicontrol` instead.

Next, we set up the slider. Use the `uicontrol` for that, and keep the handle for it in variable `sl`. Using the `set` command, we change some attributes of the slider to specify its location, connect the callback function, and establish the slider's maximum and step size. The callback function will be called `AZslider_callback.m`, which follows shortly. For this program, see the file called `AZslider.m`.

```
sl = uicontrol('Parent', fh, ...
    'Style', 'slider');
set(sl, 'Position', [150, 100, 100, 50]);
set(sl, 'Callback', {'AZslider_callback'});
set(sl, 'MAX', 25);
set(sl, 'SliderStep', [1/25 0.1]);
```

We set the slider's maximum value to 25. The slider's minimum has the default value of 0, which can work for this example. The slider's value will thus give a value from 0 to 25, telling us how many characters from "A" it is. Finally, the `SliderStep` gets two settings. The first of these says that the value should change by 1 when the user clicks the arrow buttons. The second value adjusts the amount the slider indicator moves when clicked, i.e., 10% in this example. A `docsearch` on "uicontrol" gives further information on the slider's `SliderStep`, `Min`, and `Max`.

The callback function should show the alphabetic character on the figure, starting with "A." As the user moves the slider from left to right, show another character, in increasing order, up to "Z." Of course, it should also work when the user moves the slider to the left, and show the character in decreasing order in that case. The callback function appears next. It should be in a file called `AZslider_callback.m`. Note that it does not need to know the slider's handle, since it has this supplied to it through the `object` argument.

```
function AZslider_callback(object, ignore)
global letter
global tx
V = round(get(object, 'Value'));
letter = 'A' + V;
s = sprintf('%c',letter);
disp(s);
set(tx, 'String', s);
```

Like the `AZslider` program that sets up the figure, we must declare variables `letter` and `tx` as globals before we use them. The `get` command requests the current "`Value`" of the slider. Actually, this code could be used for a variety of GUI elements that use "`Value`." We use `round` on the value, `V`, since we must insure that it has an integer value when using it in the line assigning `letter` as a character. The line with `'A' + V` might look a bit odd, although the computer interprets it as the code for the letter "A" plus an offset. If the offset has a zero value, we just have "A". With an offset of 1, we generate character "B," and so forth. Next, the code echoes the currently selected letter on the command window. Finally, it sets the `String` attribute of the `tx` variable (the text handle) to the current letter. Now, running `AZslider` shows the starting letter, and allows the user to change it with the slider.

9.14 A "KITCHEN SINK" EXAMPLE

The idiom "everything but the kitchen sink" means to include everything that you can think of, except perhaps plumbing fixtures. Supposedly, that expression comes from advertisements for pre-manufactured houses, although most people know it from cartoons like the Warner Bros. *Bugs Bunny*. Here we mean that the following example contains just about everything you would want in a graphical user interface. It presents several different types of elements on a single window. You may notice that each has a unique `Position`. You are encouraged to change the positions to see the results in the element placement.

This example includes the push button, toggle button, and check box that we have already seen. It also includes text and a text field that the user can edit, an `axes` for displaying an image, a radio button, a pop-up (drop-down) menu, a list box, and a slider. The radio button is much like the checkbox, but radio buttons are often used to select one option from several. The listbox and drop-down menus are similar, except in appearance.

Interface elements can be grouped together into subgroups called frames or panels. Sometimes interface elements have rules associated with them. For example, a form with a question like "have you shopped here before?" might have a checkbox, with a follow-up question of "how long since your last visit?" If the user selects "no," then the follow-up question should not be answered. A button group allows you to implement such rules. This is beyond the scope here, but you can explore with a command like `docsearch uicontrol`. The MATLAB `help` function and `docsearch` command provide many good, focused examples of the user interface elements incorporated here.

There are several callback functions used, so we briefly describe them here. The `hello.m` script is very simple; it consists of a single line: `disp('hello!');`. A `hello2.m` function displays similar text, only it includes a greeting string to personalize the message.

```
function hello2(one, two, greeting)
disp(sprintf(' hello %s!', greeting));
```

We ignore parameters `one` and `two` for this example.

The final callback function ignores parameters, and simply increments a count variable. It must be defined as global for this function to alter it.

```
function GUI_incCount()
global count
count =  count + 1;
disp(sprintf('count now is %d', count));
```

As you can see from the code, it also reports the current value of `count` whenever it changes.

Now for the "kitchen sink" example. Figure 9.5 shows the interface generated by this program. You are encouraged to try it out (`GUI_example2.m`) before or while reading the rest of this section. First, we set up our variables and open a figure. The variable `count` will be available globally, that is, any other functions/scripts can access and change it. We give it an initial value of 23. Next, we open the figure and get its handle. The `set` command changes one of the figure's attributes, its background color. The color values correspond to red, green, and blue components, on a scale from 0 to 1. Since green has a value of 0.2 and the others have 0, the color produced is a dark green.

```
global count;
count = 23;
disp(sprintf('count is initially set to %d', count));
figure_handle = figure(1);
set(figure_handle, 'Color', [0.0 0.2 0.0]);
```

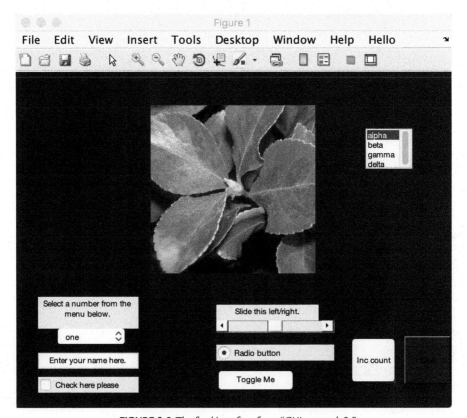

FIGURE 9.5 The final interface from "GUI_example2."

To see what other figure properties can be changed, use the `get(figure_handle)` command.

Now we add two buttons, one to increment our `count` variable, and one to quit. We specify which figure gets these buttons by passing the `figure_handle` variable. We do not have to specify 'Parent', but this helps readability. We keep the handles to these interface controls, in case we want to access them later.

```
incButton_handle = uicontrol('Parent', figure_handle, ...
    'Style', 'pushbutton', ...
    'String', 'Inc count', ...
    'Position', [430 30 60 60], 'Callback', 'GUI_incCount');
quitButton_handle = uicontrol('Parent', figure_handle, ...
```

```
    'Style', 'pushbutton', ...
    'String', 'Quit', ...
    'Position', [500 30 60 60], 'Callback', 'close');
set(quitButton_handle, 'BackgroundColor', [0.5 0 0]);
```

The `set` command again changes the background color, this time for the button. It will show up as red. Other button properties can be changed, and the `get(quitButton_handle)` command will show the changes.

Next, we show an image in the figure. First, we get the image from the disk, storing it in the matrix x. Second, we create an `axes` interface element, which defines a box for us to place the image. Position values are relative, such as 25% and 40%, in the next example. The `imshow` command puts the image in the box created by `axes`.

```
x = imread('graphics/plant.jpg');
image_handle = axes('Parent', figure_handle, ...
    'Position', [.25 .4 .5 .5]);
imshow(x);
```

The `axes` function specifies not only where the image will go, but how big it will be. The position gives the location of the axes with the first two parameters, measured from the left-bottom corner, and the last two numbers define the extent of the image. Here, they are both the same value (0.5). Since our image is square, they really should be the same value. If they are not, MATLAB will stretch our image to make it fit within the box.

The drop-down menu (called a pop-up menu here) will be added next. The main difference between this and other interface elements is that the `String` has several possibilities. We start the example with the first string selected. Notice that the `Position` array specifies integer values, corresponding to pixel offsets. This is a different command than the `axes` command of the last example.

```
dropDownMenu_handle = uicontrol('Parent', figure_handle, ...
    'Style', 'popupmenu', ...
    'String', {'one','two','three','four'}, ...
    'Value', 1, 'Position', [50 80 100 20], ...
    'Callback', {'hello2', 'drop-down menu'});
```

The callback function, `hello2`, has the string "drop-down menu" passed to it as the third parameter. With this parameter, the function can tell which interface element called it. It ignores the first two parameters that MATLAB automatically passes. Incidentally, the first parameter that MATLAB automatically passes is the interface element's handle, so the function could tell who called it from that information, too.

Next, we have an initially unchecked checkbox (`Value` has the initial value of 0).

```
checkbox_handle = uicontrol('Parent', figure_handle, ...
    'Style', 'checkbox', ...
    'String', 'Check here please',...
    'Value', 0, 'Position', [30 20 130 20], ...
    'Callback', {'hello2', 'checkbox'});
```

It also uses `hello2` as the callback function. The next example creates changeable text, with the default value "Enter your name here."

```
editText_handle = uicontrol('Parent', figure_handle, ...
    'Style', 'edit', ...
    'String', 'Enter your name here.', ...
    'Position', [30 50 130 20], ...
    'Callback', {'hello2', 'editable text'});
```

Like the changeable text, we can place non-changeable text on our interface. In this case, it gives directions for the interface element below it.

```
text_handle1 = uicontrol('Parent', figure_handle, ...
    'Style', 'text', ...
    'String', 'Select a number from the menu below.', ...
    'Position', [30 100 130 40]);
```

The way to tell what will appear below it lies in the position information. See if you can figure out which interface element will be below it, knowing that it should be approximately 30 pixels from the left border and less than 100 pixels from the bottom.

A toggle button appears below. The `Value` tells whether the user has clicked on it or not. Actually, it tells us whether the user has clicked on it an *odd number* of times, since two clicks changes its value back to its initial one.

```
togglebutton_handle = uicontrol('Parent', figure_handle, ...
    'Style', 'togglebutton', ...
    'String', 'Toggle Me', ...
    'Value', 0, 'Position', [260 20 100 30], ...
    'Callback', {'hello2', 'toggle button'});
```

The next example shows a radio button. Like other buttons, the `Value` allows it to be initialized selected or deselected.

```
radiobutton_handle = uicontrol('Parent', figure_handle, ...
    'Style', 'radiobutton', ...
    'String', 'Radio button', ...
    'Value', 1, 'Position', [260 60 150 20], ...
    'Callback', {'hello2', 'radio button'});
```

Now we add a slider, which allows the user to change a value gradually with the mouse.

```
slider_handle = uicontrol('Parent', figure_handle, ...
    'Style', 'slider', ...
    'Max', 100, 'Min', 0, 'Value', 50, ...
    'SliderStep', [0.05 0.2], ...
    'Position', [260 80 150 30], ...
    'Callback', {'hello2', 'slider'});
text_handle2 = uicontrol('Parent', figure_handle, ...
    'Style', 'text', ...
    'String', 'Slide this left/right.', ...
    'Position', [260 110 130 20]);
```

We also add text above the slider, to inform the user about it.

Like a drop-down menu, we can have several items to choose from with a listbox. The code below gives an example.

```
listbox_handle = uicontrol('Parent', figure_handle, ...
    'Style', 'listbox', ...
    'String', {'alpha','beta','gamma','delta'}, ...
    'Value', 1, 'Position', [450 300 60 50], ...
    'Callback', {'hello2', 'list box'});
```

It allows the user to select between "alpha," "beta," etc. Notice that the `String` parameter allows us to set the different selection items.

The final interface element below does not show up in the window like the others (and we do not specify the `Position`). It adds an option on the menu bar at the top of the figure, one that calls `hello.m` when selected.

```
uimenu('Label', 'Hello', 'Callback', 'hello');
```

Now that have set up our interface, we instruct the user to select one through four (from our drop-down menu), and wait three seconds to give the user time to respond.

```
disp('Select one through four');
pause(3);
v = get(dropDownMenu_handle, 'Value');
disp(sprintf('The drop-down menu has current value of %d.', v));
disp('This script is terminating.');
```

After the three seconds elapse, we read the `Value` for that drop-down menu and report it. Finally, we indicate that our script terminated. After this, the menu we created will still be available for the user, but it relies on callback functions to do the work. This will last until the user closes the figure, such as with the "Quit" button, as can be seen on Figure 9.5. See the script `GUI_example2.m` for this complete example.

By the way, we can choose `File` and then `Save` on the figure's menu items, to save the figure to the hard-drive/permanent storage. MATLAB uses a `.fig` extension by default. Later, we can open it up with the command `openfig('filename.fig')`, where `filename` is whatever you called it upon saving. Or, if you prefer using the mouse, you can select `File` and `Open` on MATLAB's menu bar, then select the figure file.

9.15 CLOSING A FIGURE IN DIFFERENT WAYS

What do we do when the user does not follow our directions? This example, `ex_close.m` shows a window with a button marked "Close."

```
figHandle = figure;
buttonHandle = uicontrol(figHandle, 'Style', 'pushbutton', ...
    'String', 'Close', ...
    'Position', [40 40 50 20], ...
    'Callback', 'ex_closeCB');
```

It has a callback function, `ex_closeCB.m`, to handle the close function. It displays a message and pauses for a second, to simulate doing clean-up tasks, such as saving data.

```
function ex_closeCB(obj1, obj2)
disp('Doing some clean-up tasks before closing...');
```

```
pause(1);
close();
```

Finally, the callback function closes the window. Now suppose that we run this program several times.

```
>> ex_close
Doing some clean-up tasks before closing...
>> ex_close
>> ex_close
>> close
```

The first time, the user clicks the button, which invokes the callback function, as we might expect. The second time, the user clicks the red "x" on the window itself. This dismisses the window, although it did not invoke the callback function, so the user might be dismayed to realize that any changes are not saved. In the third run, the user types close, which closes the window, again without allowing the callback function a chance to run. How can we protect the user from himself?

Just as we can control many aspects of the interface with get and set, we can specify that our own function be called when the user attempts to quit, i.e., in place of close(); in the preceding example. The following program, called ex_closereq.m, calls a special function to close the window, regardless of how the user attempts to dismiss it.

```
figHandle = figure;
disp('The default close function is:');
disp(get(figHandle, 'CloseRequestFcn'));
buttonHandle = uicontrol(figHandle, ...
    'Style', 'pushbutton', ...
    'String', 'Close', ...
    'Position', [40 40 50 20], ...
    'Callback', 'close');
set(figHandle, 'CloseRequestFcn', @ex_closereqCB)
```

Now ex_closereqCB will be called when the user quits the interface. This can happen in several different ways; the user can click the "x" button on the window itself, he or she can type "close" or "exit" at the command line. In any of these situations, MATLAB will invoke the ex_closereqCB function.

Notice how the callback function is `close` for the button. After we set the `CloseRequestFcn`, it does not matter how the user closes the window, as the following session illustrates.

```
>> ex_closereq
The default close function is:
closereq
Closing the window in 1 sec.
>> ex_closereq
The default close function is:
closereq
Closing the window in 1 sec.
>> ex_closereq
The default close function is:
closereq
>> close
Closing the window in 1 sec.
>>
```

Like the earlier example, the first time, the user clicks the button. The second time, the user clicks the red "x" at the top left corner. The third time, the user types `close` at the prompt. In each instance, we see that the callback function displays a message, pauses, and closes the window. The example uses the `pause` command to simulate time taken to do other tasks; if you implement a similar callback function, you can leave that out.

9.16 SUMMARY

Most people interact with computers via graphical user interfaces. MATLAB supports these, and this chapter demonstrated how these graphical elements can be added to your figures and programs. Other relevant commands include: `guihandles`, which returns the handles for objects within a figure, `guidata`, a command to get or store data related to your program with the figure handle, and `gcf`, short for get current figure handle. While this chapter focusses on making GUI components through programming examples, MATLAB includes a GUI Design Environment (GUIDE) that you may find useful. To get started with it, try the following command.

```
guide('GUI_example_two.fig')
```

It calls up the GUIDE program, with a previous example, `GUI_example2.m`, stored as a MATLAB `.fig` file.

You may find GUIDE useful for designing a user interface. It allows you to drag control elements around, so that they look like what you envision. GUIDE also generates code. However, you must have knowledge about how the code works to fully control it. You might be able to accomplish your entire task with GUIDE, or you might use it as a starting point, then tailor the generated code to suit your needs. The computer can save us time and effort, although ultimately, we as programmers must take ownership of the code. We are responsible for it.

This chapter covers commands related to graphical user interfaces, such as `uicontrol`, and the components of the interface, like text, a pushbutton, a checkbox, a toggle-button, a pop-up (also called a drop-down) menu, a slider, `axes` (for editable text), a radiobutton, a listbox, and `uimenu` (to change the window's menu bar). A program needs a way to reference the GUI components which we achieve via handles. With handles, functions `get` and `set` allow a program to probe current values for interface elements, and change them to something else. The computer reacts to the user's input with callback functions, and sometimes this means accessing `global` variables, or examining and changing variables in another workspace through the `evalin` and `assignin` commands. We also saw how the program can call its own `CloseRequestFcn` instead of the default one, to do any clean-up work before closing the interface. For example, the program could prompt the user to save their changes before exiting.

EXERCISES

1. Start with a sufficiently large image, at least 400 × 400. Create a simple GUI to display a 200 × 200 section of the image, with a slider on the right side and another under the image. As the user moves one slider or the other, the part of the image shown should change as a result.

2. After finding a solution to the previous problem of an image with two sliders, add a "crop" button to the GUI, and allow the visible portion of the image to be saved under a different filename when the user presses the button.

3. Make a GUI element to specify a filename of a data set, along with a button to load it. If the file is present, load the data in it, and set the background of the GUI to green. It should show a stem plot of the data. If the file is not found or cannot be read, set the background to red. To get started, create an array with random values, then use the `save` function. The program can then use `load` to read the array. Note that this approach can be problematic, i.e. if the variables stored in the file do not match what your program expects.

PROJECT

• **Matrix-sweeper Part 2**

Redo the Matrix-sweeper game (project in Chapter 4) using a GUI.

SOUND

Sound travels by pressure changes in a medium, such as air. You can think of this as molecules moving, and hitting others, causing them to move and hit others in a wave motion. Visualize this by watching the surface of water as it is disturbed, perhaps by a pebble falling into it: the water moves in ripples away from that point. Most modern computers, including laptops, tablets, and phones, come with microphones and speakers built-in. These devices can sense sound, and record the sound data through the microphone. They can send sound data to the speakers, allowing you to hear it. In this chapter, we talk about using MATLAB to read, play, create, store, and record sound data.

10.1 PLAYING A SOUND FILE

The companion files contain some example sound files. In this first example, we read in the data from a file called "piano1.wav". Command `audioread` loads the file. We expect two pieces of information; the sound data (`x`), and the sampling frequency (`fs`). We have to know the correct sampling frequency, or the playback will not sound right.

```
>> [x, fs] = audioread('piano1.wav');
>> sound(x, fs);
```

Once the data has been read, we use the `sound` command to play it. For fun, try this example.

```
>> sound(x, fs*2);
```

You should hear the same sound, except with a higher frequency. For another variation, divide all sound data by 2.

```
>> sound(x/2, fs);
```

This should sound the same as it did originally, only quieter. Cutting the sound samples in half in this way reduces the amplitude of the sound waves by half. The amplitudes are at most 1 for sound data in a WAVE file. A second example file, "piano2.wav" contains more notes from the same piano as "piano1.wav". Another pair of files, "flute1.wav" and "flute2.wav" have a few notes from a flute.

10.2 DEPRECATED SOUND COMMANDS

MATLAB supported functions specifically for .wav files in previous editions. It can still read and write audio files stored with a .wav extension, however, programs from before 2012 may contain `wavread`, `wavrecord`, `wavplay`, or `wavwrite`, and these no longer work. Note that these functions only worked for Microsoft-based MATLAB installations. Languages change over time, typically adding new features while still supporting all of the old features (known as maintaining backward-compatibility). However, sometimes languages will deprecate features, meaning that they must be replaced, as in this case. In 2012, these functions generated warnings under the latest MATLAB version, indicating that they would no longer be supported. Later versions completely removed these functions.

Deprecated functions can pose problems. A program that relies upon a deprecated function may work well for years, then suddenly generate errors with the latest compiler/interpreter. While uncommon, this has real consequences for programmers, who must adapt the old software to the new way of doing things. MATLAB still performs these tasks, although you must use `audioread`, `audiorecorder`, `play`, and `audiowrite`, instead.

10.3 WRITING A SOUND FILE

MATLAB works with a variety of audio encoding formats, including Audio Interchange File Format (AIFF), Free Lossless Audio Codec (FLAC), Ogg Vorbis, MPEG-4 (MPEG stands for Moving Picture Experts Group, which uses the Advanced Audio Codec, abbreviated as AAC), and Waveform Audio File Format (WAVE). Some formats, such as .ogg, compress the data, while .wav files do not. The Free Lossless Audio Codec (FLAC) format uses loss-less compression, so the stored data will be perfectly recreated. Other compression formats, such as MP3, use lossy compression, meaning that the data read are not a perfect copy of the original data. As of 2019, MATLAB still reads .mp3 files, but no longer writes them. When done well, the listener will not hear a difference in a lossy format, while the file size will be greatly reduced. When writing a file, choose the format that works best for your application.

To illustrate how the choice of audio format affects the file size, consider the following. One of the oldest known recordings, "Au Clair de la Lune," comes from 1860, and lasts about 11 seconds. Several websites host copies of it, such as https://www.firstsounds.org/sounds/scott.php.

```
[x, fs] = audioread('1860ScottAuClairdelaLune.mp3');
sound(x, fs)
audiowrite('1860v2.flac', x, fs)
audiowrite('1860v2.ogg', x, fs)
audiowrite('1860v2.mp4', x, fs)
audiowrite('1860v2.wav', x, fs)
```

The audiowrite command wrote the data in x to several different files, each using a different format. Note that MPEG-4 (.mp4) may not be supported on all systems. Also, some MPEG-4 files use the .m4a extension.

If you need to know about a sound file's compression, the audioinfo command returns this, among several other fields. Be aware that since audioinfo returns a structure, we access the field a bit differently than we would with an object. That is, we use the field name without quotes instead of invoking a get method. Also, to see every field, use the audioinfo command without suppressing the output with the semi-colon at the end of the line.

```
>> audioStruct = audioinfo('1860ScottAuClairdelaLune.mp3');
>> disp(audioStruct.CompressionMethod)
MP3
>> audioStruct = audioinfo('1860v2.flac');
>> disp(audioStruct.CompressionMethod)
FLAC
>> audioStruct = audioinfo('1860v2.ogg');
>> disp(audioStruct.CompressionMethod)
Vorbis
>> audioStruct = audioinfo('1860v2.mp4');
>> disp(audioStruct.CompressionMethod)
AAC
```

```
>> audioStruct = audioinfo('1860v2.wav');
>> disp(audioStruct.CompressionMethod)
Uncompressed
```

The preceding commands determine the compression algorithm for each file. As the response indicates, this .mp4 file uses Advanced Audio Coding (AAC), although an .mp4 file can include video as well as MPEG audio.

Now we can compare the file sizes.

```
>> ls -l 1860*
-rw-r--r--@ 1 mweeks   staff   176994 Jul 29 18:43 1860ScottAu
ClairdelaLune.mp3
-rw-r--r--  1 mweeks   staff   635168 Jul 29 18:46 1860v2.flac
-rw-r--r--  1 mweeks   staff   229260 Jul 29 18:46 1860v2.mp4
-rw-r--r--  1 mweeks   staff   162650 Jul 29 18:46 1860v2.ogg
-rw-r--r--  1 mweeks   staff   956204 Jul 29 18:46 1860v2.wav
```

We see that the data in the .wav file takes more than five times the amount of space as the compressed .ogg file. Since the data in this example comes from an .mp3 file, it makes sense to choose a compressed file format, even a lossy one. Had this file been in an uncompressed format from the start, it would have made sense to keep it uncompressed, or at least in a loss-less compression format. Also, keep in mind that this example presents only one data point, and should not be indicative of the superiority of one file format over another. In general, an uncompressed file will require the most space, a file with lossy compression should need the least amount of space, although at the cost of lower quality, and a file stored with loss-less compression will maintain the original quality and still retain space savings.

10.4 MAKING SOUND

We can create sounds fairly easily. A wave is a sinusoid, and in general, sinusoids take the form:

$$\text{amplitude} \times \sin\left(2\pi \text{ frequency time} + \text{phase}\right).$$

The amplitude should be a value less than or equal to 1, since sound data samples have a range of -1 to $+1$. The cos function could be used in place of the sin function. You probably remember π as the mathematical constant related to the circumference of a circle, with $2\pi r$ specifying the circumference of a circle with radius r. When $r = 1$, the circumference simplifies to 2π, thus 2π can be thought of as the normalized distance around the unit circle. In other words, $2\pi\theta/360$ converts an angle θ from degrees to radians. The frequency means how fast the sinusoid repeats, while time varies. The phase is also an angle, representing the value of the sinusoid at time 0. Think of the phase as specifying where the sinusoid starts.

```
>> t = 0:0.0001:2;
>> fs = 1/0.0001
fs =
        10000
```

With the time variable t incrementing 0.0001 seconds between the samples, our sampling frequency, fs, can be defined as 1/0.0001. The cut-off at 2 for t means that it lasts for 2 seconds. Next, we create the array x with an amplitude of 0.5, a frequency of 200 Hz, and a phase of $\pi/5$. Actually, the phase could be 0 without noticeably changing this example. Once we have the x array, we can play it through the speakers with the sound command. Now we define the sinusoid, and listen to it.

```
x = 0.5 * sin(2 * pi * 200 * t + pi/5);
sound(x, fs);
```

You should hear a fairly low tone when this command executes.

Figure 10.1 shows a plot of x, defined as

```
x200Hz = 0.5 * sin(2 * pi * 200 * t + phase);
```

with a phase of 0 (top) and $\pi/5$ (bottom). As you can see, signal x200Hz repeats the same pattern over and over. The phase angle only changes the starting point.

Now let's modify the tone. We start by creating another tone, y, that has double the frequency, and a bit less of an amplitude. We keep the phase the same.

```
y = 0.4 * sin(2 * pi * 400 * t + pi/5);
sound(x+y, fs)
```

When adding sinusoids together to form sound, the data results should not exceed the minimum/maximum values to avoid clipping. In the preceding example, x has a maximum of 0.5 and y has a maximum of 0.4, so even if the maximums (or minimums) happen to line up, we do have to worry about clipping. In the following example, the resulting signal may exceed 1. We use a slightly different function, `soundsc`, which MATLAB provides to get around this issue.

Next, create another tone, `z`, similar to `y`, although again at double the frequency.

```
z = 0.2 * sin(2 * pi * 800 * t + pi/5);
soundsc(x+y+z, fs)
```

Playing `x+y` with the `sound` command makes the tones sound arguably better, and playing `x+y+z` makes it sound a bit like a pipe organ. The idea comes from studying musical instruments, where a note played on an instrument generates not only one frequency, but several multiples of that frequency as well, called harmonics. Figure 10.2 shows what these three wave forms look like when graphed.

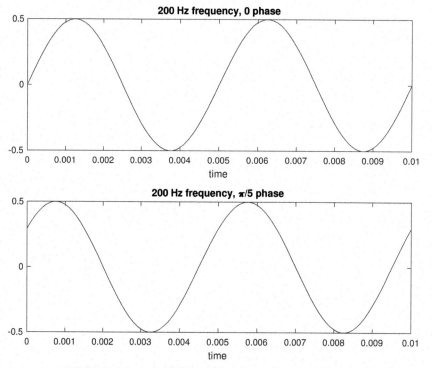

FIGURE 10.1 A graph of 200 Hz with a phase of 0, and a phase of $\pi/5$.

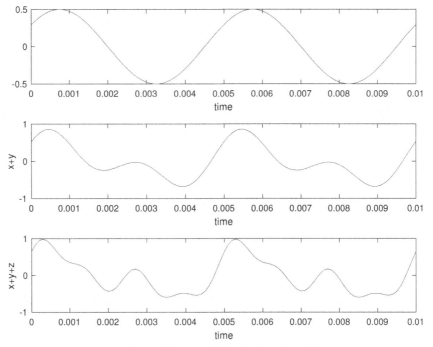

FIGURE 10.2 A graph showing three sinusoids.

10.5 PLAYING NOTES

Let's revisit the idea of creating a sinusoid to make sound. As any piano player knows, the piano has a note called middle-C. Pressing this key causes the instrument to emit a 261.6 Hz note. A real piano also generates harmonics, but we can overlook that to keep this discussion simple. The following example creates, then plays, a sinusoid with the same frequency as middle-C.

```
fs = 8192;
note = 261.6;
mynote = 0.5 * sin(2 * pi * note * (0:(fs-1))/fs);
sound(mynote, fs)
```

It first sets the sampling frequency and note's frequency. The range `0:(fs-1)` means that it has `fs` samples, ensuring that we have exactly one second's worth of data returned to the array called `mynote`. Dividing by the sampling rate has the same effect as sampling every `Ts` times, where `Ts` stands for sampling time (or time between samples), since `Ts = 1/fs`. The frequency unit, Hz, literally means 1/*second*, so frequency is the inverse of time.

We can take this a step further, and store this note, along with several others, to play in sequence. Like other instruments, pianos have octaves. The note A, a few keys to the left of middle-C, has a frequency of 220 Hz. The next A note, to the right of middle-C, has a frequency of 440 Hz. As you might anticipate, going from one octave to the next doubles the frequency. The following example makes an array of the notes between 200 Hz and 440 Hz, using whole number values. Some are "sharp" notes, corresponding to the black keys on the keyboard, and denoted by the pound-sign ("#").

```
% A A# B C C# D D# E F F# G G# A
notes = [220, 233, 247, 262, 277, 294, 311, ...
    330, 349, 370, 392, 415, 440];
for k=1:length(notes)
    % store this note
    % 0.5 is used to keep the sound from being loud
    allnotes(k, 1:fs) = 0.5 * ...
        sin(2 * pi * notes(k) * (0:(fs-1))/fs);
end
```

With the values in `notes`, we create an array, then store it as a row in `allnotes`. Looping through `allnotes`, the computer plays the notes in sequence.

```
for k=1:length(notes)
    sound(allnotes(k,1:fs))
    pause(1);
end
```

Since each note lasts for one second, we pause for one second between them, to allow the current note to finish. Now that we've verified that it works, we can play a random set of notes. Let `r` be an array of 10 values, where each has a random value between 1 and the length of the `notes` array. The `ceil` function returns a result of at least 1 for any argument greater than 0, and the `rand` function does not generate exactly zero. Therefore, values in `r` will be 1 or greater.

```
r = ceil(rand(1,10)*length(notes));
for k = r
    sound(allnotes(k,1:fs));
    pause(0.5);
end
```

In the example with sequential notes, the notes sometimes have an abrupt transition, even with a half-second overlap of notes. We will address this shortly with a revised version of the function.

Playing random notes leads to some amusing results, sometimes pleasant, and sometimes unusual. What about playing a repeatable series of notes? The function `note_play.m`, available with this text, does that. It borrows from the previous examples of creating an array of notes, using `sound` to play them, and pausing for half a second between them. Actually, the preceding example could do this if the user specifies the notes as an array of numbers from 1 for A to 13 for the A in the next octave. A more natural way to specify the notes would be to give a list as a string, like "cde". The sharp notes pose a concern; should A-sharp be specified as "a#", or "A"? A `switch` statement implements the latter easily. The code looks like the following.

```
switch (notes2play(k))
    case 'a'
        n = 1;
    case 'A'
        n = 2;
    case 'b'
    case 'B'
        n = 3;
    ...
    otherwise
        n = 13;
end
sound(allnotes(n,1:fs), fs);
```

Every character translates to an integer value, with the upper-case letters serving to specify the sharp-notes. In the case where no sharp-note exists, such as "B," the logic maps it to the same value as the regular note, i.e., "b." Anything failing to match a `case` statement gets to the `otherwise`, which maps to the "a" note in the next octave. Whatever value n resolves to, the `sound` command plays the corresponding row of data from `allnotes`. To call the function, we pass a character array to it, as follows:

```
note_play('aAbcCdDefFgG');
```

This instructs the function to play each note in sequence, but of course we could have it play the notes in any sequence.

One problem with the `note_play` function is that it does not smoothly transition from one note to the next. The software for this text also includes an improved version, called `note_play2.m`. It does not play the sound, unless you uncomment the `sound` command at the end of it. Instead, it returns an array of sound data. Using the `sound` command, pausing, and using it again causes the abrupt transitions, while using it once on all of the data produces a smooth sound. How does it work? Essentially, the structure looks like the following.

```
note_sequence = [];
for k = 1:length(notes2play)
    % set the n value according to notes2play(k)
    ...
    note_sequence = [note_sequence, allnotes(n,1:fs)];
end
```

We start with an empty matrix, then concatenate a row of `allnotes` again and again until finished.

Could we ramp the notes up at first, then ramp them down? Section 10.7 discusses how to apply ramping functions to sound data; the `note_play2` function uses this concept when passing a `true` value as the second argument. The following lines demonstrate how to use the `note_play2` function.

```
note_sequence = note_play2('CabbCeF', true);
sound(note_sequence, 8192);
```

Ramping the sound up, then down, does not smooth the transitions, but it does provide a nice effect. Looking at `note_play2`, you probably notice that it sets `fs` and does not provide an easy way for a user to change it. Yes, an advanced user could alter it by locating the assignment statement and trying a different value, however, passing it as an argument makes more sense. Better yet, make that and the Boolean variable for the ramping effect optional parameters. And since the `note_play2` function does not actually play the sound, we might desire to pass another Boolean value for that. And what if we decide to use the pound-sign to indicate a sharp note, as in "A"? Implementing these improvements is left as an exercise for the reader.

10.6 RECORDING SOUND

The following code creates an `audiorecorder` object, made with a sampling rate of 8000 samples/second, 16 bits per sample, and 1 channel. The sampling rate controls how many data values are recorded per second. On the one hand, we want many samples per second to give us a good digital copy of the sounds. On the other hand, having more samples means a larger amount of data to store and process, thus we choose the rate carefully. Theoretically, the sampling rate must be at least twice the highest frequency that we want to capture. Music CDs use the rate 44,100 samples per second, so the following example uses only about one fifth of that rate. The next argument, bits per sample, govern the size of the values used per sample. This can go as low as 8, or potentially as high as 32 bits per sample. Once again, we should choose the bits per sample in light of the conflicting goals of small data size versus good resolution. Whatever the choice, with n bits per sample, each sample has 2^n possible values. Finally, the argument 1 corresponds to a single channel. You can think of a channel as a speaker; while you only need one, a pair of earphones allows you to experience music in two channels, and some music takes advantage of the left/right channels.

```
>> audioObject = audiorecorder(8000, 16, 1);
>> whos audioObject
  Name           Size     Bytes  Class            Attributes
  audioObject    1x1          8  audiorecorder
```

Now that we have an `audiorecorder` object, we can record audio data.

```
>> record(audioObject);
>> pause(audioObject);
```

When we issue the `record` command, the computer starts sampling the microphone. Calling `pause` stops it, at least temporarily, since we could resume the recording later. The `audiorecorder` object's `pause` method looks like the `pause` command, although it has a different effect. Now let's play the recorded sound. We cannot use `sound` on the `audioObject` directly, although a command called `play` does work.

```
>> play(audioObject);
```

The following line specifies the optional argument of starting and ending samples of 700 and 30000, respectively.

```
>> play(audioObject, [700, 30000]);
```

If you are following along with your own MATLAB session, the second instance of the `play` command might not work for you, unless enough time elapsed between `record` and `pause`. Commands `resume(audioObject)` and `stop(audioObject)` continue (unpause) the recording, and finish the recording.

Next, we get the data from the `audiorecorder` object with the `getaudiodata` command. We then play it, specifying the same sampling rate that we used for the `audiorecorder` object.

```
>> audioData = getaudiodata(audioObject);
>> sound(audioData, 8000);
```

The `getaudiodata` command allows a second argument to indicate the data-type. For example, we could use `int16` instead, if desired. Data type `int16` means a signed integer value with 16 bits. Since $2^{16} = 65536$, and negative values account for half of the possibilities, the range goes from -32768 to $+32767$. Under this representation, negative zero does not exist, and we count 0 among the positive values.

Finally, we write `audioData` to a file, called "snaps.ogg."

```
>> audiowrite('snaps.ogg', audioData, 8000);
```

This audio file contains three snapping sounds, which have a very short time duration, like impulse functions. Sounds like this are interesting because they can reveal a lot about the environment. If you record an impulse-like sound in different environments, such as a large room, a hallway, and a closet, you should notice something about the environment when playing it back.

In the preceding example, you may have noticed that `sound` requires the sampling rate, unless it happens to be 8192 samples per second. However, when calling the `play` function, we do not specify the sampling rate. The reason has to do with the way we store the data. The `audioData` variable holds a `double` array, and nothing more. The `audioObject` variable refers to an object of the `audiorecorder` class. Look at what it tells us with the `get` method.

```
>> get(audioObject)
          SampleRate: 8000
       BitsPerSample: 16
    NumberOfChannels: 1
            DeviceID: -1
       CurrentSample: 87297
        TotalSamples: 87296
             Running: 'off'
            StartFcn: []
             StopFcn: []
            TimerFcn: []
         TimerPeriod: 0.0500
```

```
          Tag: ''
     UserData: []
         Type: 'audiorecorder'
```

As the output informs us, the object includes information about the sample rate, bits per sample, and so forth. Some of these are read-only, for example, trying to change `SampleRate` with a `set` command generates an error. The `UserData` property can be changed, as follows:

```
>> set(audioObject, 'UserData', 'Three snaps');
>> get(audioObject, 'UserData')
ans =
    'Three snaps'
```

Querying the property with `get` reveals that the `set` command did change the data.

10.7 WORKING WITH TWO CHANNELS

In the next example, we create an effect that uses two channels. We start with a sound file called `whistle.aiff`, stored in an uncompressed format. The free program, "Audacity," recorded and wrote this sound data. Anyone who works extensively with audio data can benefit from such a powerful tool.

We read the sound file, and store the data in variable x. The sound only lasts for about a second when played.

```
[x, fs] = audioread('whistle.aiff');
```

Next, we generate a ramping function, called `w1`. It should have the same number of samples as the sound data, start around 0, and increase until it becomes 1. Therefore, variable `increase` will be `1/length(x)` so that at the very last sample (at `length(x)`), we get 1 as the very last ramping value. To make it exactly the same length using this `increase`, we start at `increase`. It represents a percentage.

```
increase = 1/length(x);
w1 = increase:increase:1;
```

Now we have an array called `w1` with the same number of elements as one channel of x. Next, we address one important difference: MATLAB stores a channel of sound data as a column, while `w1` represents a row. We can easily fix this by transposing it. Then, we create another ramping array called `w2`. We make it a reverse copy of `w1`, so it starts at 1 and ramps down to about 0.

```
w1 = w1.';
w2 = w1(length(w1):-1:1);
```

Next, we apply the two ramping array to the sound data. The following line multiplies every element of channel 1 in x with the ramping-up function, while it multiplies every element in channel 2 with a ramping-down function. It stores the result in a new variable called y.

```
y = [w1 .* x(:,1), w2 .* x(:,2)];
sound(y, fs)
```

Finally, we use the sound command to play the newly created y matrix.

The result of applying the ramping functions can be seen in Figure 10.3. The original signal, x, has two channels, although they have little difference between them, with a maximum difference of only 0.004. We would be unlikely to notice a difference in the sound coming out of a two-speaker system. One ramping function de-emphasizes the sound in one channel at the beginning, and emphasizes it at the end. The other ramping does the opposite. Listening to this through headphones, the sound goes from right to left.

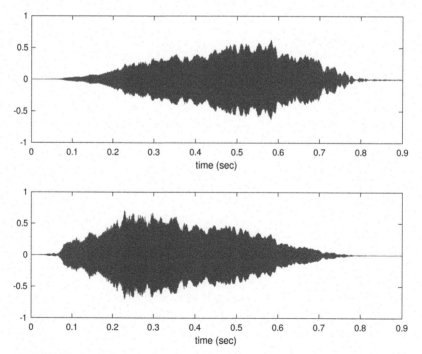

FIGURE 10.3 Combining ramp functions with two channels of sound to create a right to left audio effect.

10.8 THE KARPLUS-STRONG ALGORITHM

The Karplus-Strong Algorithm [7] generates an interesting pattern that sounds like a guitar's note. It starts with random values, then finds subsequent values based on the previous ones. We create array y as the random values, making sure that we have at least two values to use. In other words, y(N) and y(N-1) must have already been assigned, when N has a value of at least 2.

```
y(N+1) = y(N-1)*0.5 + y(N)*0.5;
```

Then, it computes the next N values from the previous N values in a loop, until it reaches at least M values in size. The effect matches the preceding line of code, except that it works on multiple values at once. The resulting array, y, typically tends toward 0. If the initial array, x, has the values [1, 1], then the next value computed will be 1 * 0.5 + 1 * 0.5 = 0.5 + 0.5 = 1, as will the next one, and so forth. Given an initial array of [2, 4], or [4, 2], the results quickly settle down to 3, not surprisingly, since the function finds an average of the previous two values. Therefore, to make a signal that we can play, the given initial array should have different values, confined to a range of −1 to +1. Seeding this algorithm with a set of random numbers means that the signal it produces will approach zero over time, but not immediately. This demonstrates the idea of feedback in a system.

See the function code in myKarplusStrongAlgo.m, along with myKarplusStrongAlgo2.m. The second version uses a digital signal processing transform, called a wavelet, to populate the feedback coefficients. That is, it replaces the values 0.5 and 0.5 from the preceding example with another averaging function, one with four values. The following code shows how to invoke these functions.

```
x = rand(1,100) - 0.5;
y = myKarplusStrongAlgo(x, 16000);
sound(y, 8000)
```

See Figure 10.4 for an example plot of the Karplus-Strong Algorithm's output.

The result sounds good. A look at the frequency magnitude response (FMR), Figure 10.5, explains why. In the figure, we see a plot of the relative frequencies that make up the sound. For this signal, these appear as spikes that get smaller as we look from left to right, mimicking harmonics. To make such a plot, convert the sound data to frequency data (with the fast Fourier Transform, fft), then show the first half of the results. We use the abs function since the fft returns complex data.

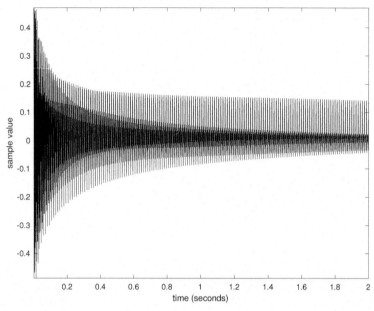

FIGURE 10.4 Samples found from random values and the Karplus-Strong Algorithm. Notice how the signal decays towards zero over time.

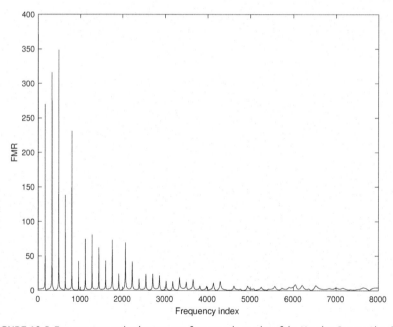

FIGURE 10.5 Frequency magnitude response for example results of the Karplus-Strong Algorithm.

```
Y = fft(y);
plot(abs(Y(1:8000)))   % since Y has 16000 values
```

The "frequency index" simply means the indices for Y, and it relates to the actual frequencies in the data. Unless you already have a background in this area, this may be confusing. The point is that we can use the fft to reveal trends in the frequencies. This discussion only scratches the surface; for more information, refer to a textbook on digital signal processing, such as [8].

Using the second version, myKarplusStrongAlgo2.m, we pass a few optional arguments. These specify clipping and scaling values. The clipping argument says whether or not to limit the produced values, while the scaling value reduces the magnitude of the feedback coefficients.

```
x = rand(1,100)-0.5;
y = myKarplusStrongAlgo2(x, 8000, true, 0.7);
sound(y, 8000)
```

Using feedback can be tricky, and if done without care, the output can approach infinity (or negative infinity). The function myKarplusStrongAlgo2 allows you to try this out. For example, the code below generates a y array that grows over time.

```
x = rand(1,100)-0.5;
y = myKarplusStrongAlgo2(x, 8000, false, 1.1);
plot(y);
title('An unstable system');
```

It oscillates, with the values getting larger and larger in magnitude. The preceding code generates 8000 values. What are their minimum and maximums?

```
>> disp(min(y(7980:8000)))
  -3.3346e+14
>> disp(max(y(7980:8000)))
  2.0104e+14
```

As reported for this particular run, the output value swings from 201 trillion to -333 trillion in less than 20 samples. Inspecting the data, in Figure 10.6, show that the output values end on an up-swing. The graph may not look too unreasonable until you notice the $\times 10^{14}$ in the upper left. If you attempt to play this array, use the soundsc(y, 8000) command. It does not produce much sound, except for a small amount at the end.

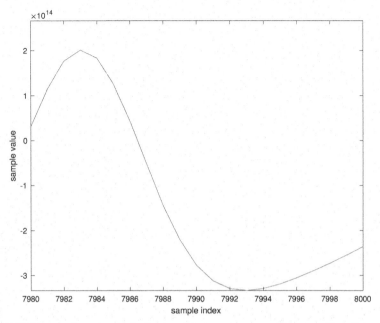

FIGURE 10.6 Purposely setting the feedback to demonstrate an unstable system. The values get larger and larger as the system produces more samples.

10.9 SUMMARY

MATLAB makes sound data easy to manipulate. For example, just as we can listen to sound data with this command:

```
sound(x, fs);
```

we can play it backwards with the following.

```
sound(x(end:-1:1), fs);
```

Sometimes we get noises in our sound data. If you tried the code to record data, then typed the `pause` command, the microphone probably picked up on the sound of the key presses. With the sound data as an array, we can easily trim the array with a command like the following.

```
start = 10000; % or whatever value
stop = 70000; % or whatever value
x = x(start:stop);
```

In the case of the microphone picking up extraneous noise before and/or after the sounds we want, a plot of the data visually indicates what the `start` and `stop` values should be.

This chapter presents the commands that allow MATLAB programs to play and record sound data, as well as read and write sound files. It covers some sound theory, and talks about how arrays of numbers represent oscillating signals, which one or more speakers turn into sound. It examines how to create sounds, including playing a series of notes, and an implementation of an algorithm that produces a decaying signal that sounds somewhat like a guitar.

EXERCISES

1. Using the `audioread` command, load an example sound file, such as "piano1.wav," and play it.

2. Using the `audioread` command, load an example sound file, such as "piano1.wav," and play it with double the sample frequency, then play it again with quadruple the sample frequency.

3. Read in the "flute1.wav" sound file, and write it out as an .ogg file.

4. Consider the following example.

   ```
   >> a = 1:9;
   >> disp(a(9:-1:1))
        9    8    7    6    5    4    3    2    1
   ```

   Applying this idea to the sound data of "piano1.wav," play channel 1 of it backwards. What does it sound like?

5. The example file "piano1.wav" has some noise at the end, from pressing a key. Make a new version of it that ends before that noise, and write it under a new name. How did you determine where to cut it off?

6. Apply a ramp-up function to the beginning of the example file "piano1. wav," and a ramp-down function at the end, and write it under a new name. How does the new version compare to the original?

7. Record a few seconds of yourself speaking, and write it to a file. Play it back to verify that it recorded correctly. Also, plot the sound samples.

PROJECT

• **Acoustic Signature**

For this project, you will need to have portable equipment, such as a laptop running MATLAB. Have you ever had a phone conversation where the other person sounds different than usual? For example, you might notice if the other person is in an enclosed space such as a car. In creating sound effects for entertainment media, sound engineers will sample different spaces to get the acoustic signature, which can then be applied to a recording, to make it sound more authentic. Record the sound in at least three different spaces, such as a closet, a medium-sized room, and a large room. First record the room tone, at least 5 seconds where you do not make any noise. Then record an impulse, which is a loud sound of short duration, such as snapping your fingers. Do your best to have the impulse the same distance from the microphone each time. Also, make sure to give sensible names; you know what "recording1" means today, but will you remember tomorrow? Something like "shoe_closet_tone" is a lot better. Next, compare the recorded sounds. Can you tell, just by playing them back, where each one was recorded? Finally, apply the sounds to an example file, like "piano1.wav." You do not want to apply the impulse itself, but the audio after it. Try both addition and element-multiplication to combine the room sound and the piano sound. How good are the results? Are you able to make a convincing combination?

11

GETTING HELP AND DEBUGGING

Is a factorial function available in MATLAB? From time to time, you may have a question like this. MATLAB comes with many useful functions, almost anything you can think of. What do you do when you do not know if a function exists?

11.1 HOW DO YOU KNOW IF MATLAB SUPPORTS A COMMAND?

Of course you can always ask someone else. However, people are prone to error, and this may be inconvenient. You could also enter the name of the function at the command line, and see how the computer responds, although a negative result can be misleading. For example, entering `exponential` at the command line results in an "undefined function" error, even though a function to find the exponential exists under the name `exp`. We need a better approach.

Try `help <function>`, and see if it responds positively (where `<function>` is a placeholder for the function to find). But if it is not available, or is available under a different name (such as `mean` instead of `average`), this method will fail. You can also try `help help`, which will give you other possibilities to search.

One command in particular is very helpful: `docsearch`. Just type this at the MATLAB prompt, press return, and a help navigation window will appear. It includes a "search for" dialog box at the top. Not only will it provide help if a function exists by that name, but it will bring up search results that *list* that keyword as well. Searching for "average" produces over 70 hits.

MATLAB provides a function called `exist`, and it can answer the question directly.

```
>> disp(exist('cos'))
     5
>> disp(exist('dwt'))
     2
>> disp(exist('cost'))
     0
```

The `exist` function can check for defined variables, files, built-in commands, and a few other possibilities. When invoked with a single parameter, it returns 0 when it cannot find a definition, as it did for "cost." Other codes represent the type of definition, such as 1 for a variable, 2 for a `.m` file, and 5 for a built-in function, such as `cos`. The `dwt` command comes with the Wavelet Toolbox, so your results may be different according to whether or not it came with your software installation.

If that fails, try searching online with a search engine. For example, *AIFF* is a standard for sound files. Until recently, MATLAB supported the *WAV* standard with the specialized command `wavread`, but there is no (as of this writing) separate `aiffread` command. Currently, the command `audioread` does read *.aiff* files, along with other standards including *WAV*. A quick search on the Internet reveals an `aiffread.m` program available from the MathWorks "File Exchange" website, `https: //www.mathworks.com/ matlabcentral/fileexchange/`.

MATLAB comes with optional *toolboxes* for specific domains, like image processing, bioinformatics, and fuzzy logic, to name a few. What if a command is part of a toolbox, one that you do not have? In this case, it may not show up in either the `help` or `docsearch` command. An Internet search should help you determine if it exists in a toolbox.

If you happen to find code that will do what you need, but it is not written in MATLAB, you may still be able to compile it and run it from MATLAB with the `mex` command. We will cover this in more detail later. If all else fails, consider writing the function yourself. If you do a good job of it, you can use it again later. By the way, `factorial` is a MATLAB command.

11.2 DEBUGGING—ABSTRACTING OUT THE PROBLEM

A student recently encountered a problem with his MATLAB program, and sought help. He was working on an assignment that required simulating a loan repayment with interest. At issue was the output line that declared, for a certain initial principle, that the loan was paid after 2 years and 1 months. Obviously, the number of months was invalid, but the number of years may be incorrect, too.

The program was over 90 lines long, but the key issue turned out to be based on only three lines. In cases like this, we can abstract the problem out and create a new, small, program with the salient features. After some initial investigation, these three lines were found to be responsible:

```
years = month_count/12;
rounded_years = floor(years);
excess_months = floor((years*12)-(rounded_years*12))-1;
```

Variable `month_count` holds the total number of months, which we want to separate out into years (`rounded_years`) and months (`excess_months`). To test these lines, we repeat them in a loop, create a table, and check the entries to see a pattern.

```
for month_count = 0:30
    years=month_count/12;
    rounded_years=floor(years);
    excess_months=floor((years*12)-(rounded_years*12))-1;
    str_month = sprintf('%d months is', month_count);
    str_years = sprintf('%d rounded_years', ...
        rounded_years);
    str_xmonths = sprintf('and %d excess_months', excess_months);
    disp(sprintf('%s %s %s',str_month, str_years, str_xmonths));
end
```

When we enter this code, MATLAB responds with a table of values. Below we have the first year's worth of outputs.

```
0 months is 0 rounded_years and -1 excess_months
1 months is 0 rounded_years and 0 excess_months
2 months is 0 rounded_years and 1 excess_months
3 months is 0 rounded_years and 2 excess_months
4 months is 0 rounded_years and 3 excess_months
```

```
5 months is 0 rounded_years and 4 excess_months
6 months is 0 rounded_years and 5 excess_months
7 months is 0 rounded_years and 6 excess_months
8 months is 0 rounded_years and 7 excess_months
9 months is 0 rounded_years and 8 excess_months
10 months is 0 rounded_years and 9 excess_months
11 months is 0 rounded_years and 10 excess_months
12 months is 1 rounded_years and -1 excess_months
```

We can see from this output that the number of excess months is always 1 less than it should be. The answer, therefore, is to remove the -1 from the excess_months calculation. See the file badMonthCount.m for the original code, and file goodMonthCount.m for the revised version. When corrected, we get the following output for the first year.

```
0 months is 0 rounded_years and 0 excess_months
1 months is 0 rounded_years and 1 excess_months
2 months is 0 rounded_years and 2 excess_months
3 months is 0 rounded_years and 3 excess_months
4 months is 0 rounded_years and 4 excess_months
5 months is 0 rounded_years and 5 excess_months
6 months is 0 rounded_years and 6 excess_months
7 months is 0 rounded_years and 7 excess_months
8 months is 0 rounded_years and 8 excess_months
9 months is 0 rounded_years and 9 excess_months
10 months is 0 rounded_years and 10 excess_months
11 months is 0 rounded_years and 11 excess_months
12 months is 1 rounded_years and 0 excess_months
```

As you can verify, the code works as expected. Note that the preceding outputs are limited to only the first 13 lines, and that the code actually generates many more lines.

11.3 USING THE DEBUGGER

The MATLAB environment comes with a debugger. You may have noticed that, if you click to the left of a line of code in the editor, a small red dot appears, reminiscent of a stop-sign. This sets a *breakpoint*, a place where

MATLAB will stop running your code. It will change the prompt to K>>, where the "k" stands for keyboard. At this prompt, you can check variables, and slowly proceed through the program.

You can also set and clear breakpoints with the pull-down menu, marked "Breakpoints" in the MATLAB editor, or "Debug" on older versions. This menu has a few other features, such as Open M-Files when Debugging. There is also Step, Step In, Step Out, and Continue. Note that you cannot set a breakpoint until you save the program in the editor, at least the first time. Also, the circle may appear gray, if you need to save the program.

A breakpoint allows you to stop a program, to check things out. Do the variables have the values you expect? What variables are defined? These are the sort of questions that you can address once the program stops. You may want the program to continue from this point, in which case you can select the Continue option from the Debug menu. Do not use the MATLAB command continue, since has a different context; it is used within while or for loops to jump to the next iteration. If you prefer to type a command at the prompt instead of using the menu, type dbcont to continue.

Another function available on the Debug menu is Step. After MATLAB stops running a program because it reached a breakpoint, you may want to continue very slowly. The Step menu option, or equivalently the dbstep command, proceeds with the next program command and stops. It also allows you to specify the number of lines to execute, such as dbstep 2 to do the next two commands.

Related menu options are Step In and Step Out, which have command equivalents of dbstep in and dbstep out. These are useful with functions. Suppose that we call a function from our program. Do we want to step through each line of the function that we call? We can use dbstep to treat the function call as one command, or we can use dbstep in to go line by line inside the function. The command dbstep out allows us to continue for the rest of the function, and return to the calling program.

When finished debugging, the command dbquit exits debug mode. This does not quit MATLAB, but instead returns the normal prompt.

```
K>> dbquit
>>
```

If you have trouble with a section of code, you may want to use a *code cell*, a group of commands that you can run from the editor. Using two percent signs in a row (%%), indicates the start of a cell. Use an additional two percent signs after the commands that you want to isolate. Actually, this will create a second cell, but you do not have to use it. The editor provides a drop-down menu called Cell. Notice how this menu appears on the editor, but not the main MATLAB window. There are several selections on this menu, the first of which is Enable Cell Mode. You must enable cell mode before you can use it. Once it is enabled, you can click on a line of code, and that code cell will appear slightly different. It will change the background of the code cell from white to pale yellow. From the Cell menu, you can then select Evaluate Current Cell. This will run the commands in that code cell. This feature is worth exploring: it has a similar effect as copying and pasting code, except that the commands do not appear in the command window.

11.4 CHECKING ASSUMPTIONS

Often, a programmer makes assumptions about the data. Hopefully, they will do a good job of conveying these assumptions to other people in the comments and program documentation. The assert command provides a way to test an assumption, a way to have a function check a condition, and generate an error when it is not met. The following line demonstrates this command simply.

```
>> assert(5 < 2)
Assertion failed.
```

The computer checks 5 < 2, but obviously that returns false. It responds with the message shown, which appears in red. Now let's see a counter-example, where we swap the numbers.

```
>> assert(2 < 5)
>>
```

In this case, the assertion holds, and the computer quietly goes on to the next command.

We can also pass a message to the assert command, to give more context to the assertion. In the following, the computer checks an assertion that fails.

```
>> assert(5 < 2, 'The first value is too small.')
The first value is too small.
```

This time, it generates the error message that we passed to the assert command. Note that this text appears in red.

In an interactive session, an assertion is not likely needed. It comes in handy when writing a function, to confirm an assumption. Consider the following program.

```
function assert_example(n)
assert(n < 100);
assert(n > 0);
disp('The value is OK.');
```

See the program `assert_example.m` for a copy of this code. As a function, it receives a value n. We check to make sure that the value is less than 100, then we check to see that it has a value greater than zero. While we could turn this into a single `assert` command by finding the AND of these two conditions, this serves the purpose of showing the behavior when we have multiple `assert` commands.

```
>> assert_example(5)
The value is OK.
>> assert_example(-1)
Error using assert_example (line 10)
Assertion failed.
>> assert_example(100)
Error using assert_example (line 9)
Assertion failed.
```

As the output shows, the function executes to the end when we pass the value 5. Giving it a value of –1, we get an error message that terminates the function. Likewise, with a value of 100, the function also generates an error. Notice how the computer indicates the line number of the failed assertion. The line numbers will be different if you type the function yourself, unless your version has the same number of comments at the top.

11.5 VALIDATING FUNCTION INPUTS

MATLAB recently introduced a way to validate inputs to a function, that also works with class methods. It uses the `arguments` keyword, after which goes the name of the argument and how the function expects it to be. Consider the following example.

```
function exampleValidation(myInput)
    arguments
        % argument name, size, class, functions = default
        % https://www.mathworks.com/help/matlab/matlab_prog/argument-
        %   validation-functions.html
        myInput (1,1) double {mustBePositive}
    end
    % The rest of the function goes here.
    disp(sqrt(myInput));
end
```

This defines a function called `exampleValidation` with a single input, `myInput`. It contains an `arguments` block, that has the pattern: variable name, expected size, expected class, functions to check the variable, and a way to specify a default value. This example says that the variable `myInput` must have a 1 × 1 size, that it must be a double type, and that function `must-BePositive` should return true. If the input does not meet these conditions, it will generate an error. The following code shows an example success and an example failure. See also the `assert` command.

```
>> exampleValidation(3)
    1.7321
>> exampleValidation(-3)
Error using exampleValidation
Invalid input argument at position 1. Value must be positive.
```

Thus, the function accepts the value 3 and computes the square root. When passing the value –3, it fails the `mustBePositive` test, and generates an error message. Note that MATLAB supports complex numbers, so asking it to find `sqrt(-3)` does not cause a problem. It could be a problem, however, if the program's output should be a real value, such as a length of wood to order for a project.

In the `arguments` section, we can assign the input a default value by adding it after the equals sign, as shown on the next line.

```
myInput (1,1) double {mustBePositive} = 2;
```

Then, when we call the function without specifying an argument, the computer will assign the default value. Copying `exampleValidation.m` to `exampleValidation2.m`, and changing the line produces the following behavior.

```
>> exampleValidation2()
    1.4142
```

As the run indicates, passing no argument means that `myInput` gets the value 2, which then results in the display of the square-root of two.

11.6 DEBUGGING AN EXAMPLE COMPARING PIXEL VALUES

Suppose that we want to automatically change an image by increasing the intensity of the red values. One can easily imagine the desire to "turn up" the red component of an image, especially with the understanding that images are composed of pixels with a mixture of red, green, and blue. As usual with a program, the details make the problem more complicated than the overview suggests.

One detail is that changing the red value of every pixel makes shades of grey look odd, where they take on a pinkish tinge. The following code, called `changeAllRed.m`, shows an example of this.

```
x = imread('streetcar.JPG');
figure(1);
imshow(x);
title('Original image');
x(:,:,1) = x(:,:,1) + 20;
figure(2);
imshow(x);
title('Image with red values increased');
```

Figure 11.1 shows the original image on the left, while the red-enhanced version appears on the right.

FIGURE 11.1 Original image of a streetcar (left) and red-increased (right).

The result of increasing the red values makes the image appear as if it were taken through a pink lens. Therefore, it would be good to leave any grey pixels alone. For this purpose, what is a grey pixel? Any pixel that has the same value for red, green, and blue appears as grey, or black or white at the extremes. Implementing this is simple enough, where the code can check to see if the red, green, and blue values are exactly the same, and leave those alone. Then a new detail becomes apparent, as some grey pixels are still becoming pink. This is where a good programmer will check their assumptions, and an implication of the grey definition having "exactly the same" values for the three color components is that it draws a sharp distinction between what is grey and what is not. If we generate an image with values of 128 (i.e., in the middle of the range) for red and green, and 127 for blue, wouldn't we describe that the image as grey? This is easy to check, with the following code.

```
x = 128*ones(256,256,3,'uint8');
x(:,:,3) = 127;
imshow(x)
```

The first line creates a 256 × 256 × 3 matrix of `uint8` values. The `ones` function returns the value 1, and multiplying it by 128 means that every value in that matrix will be 128. The second line changes all values of the third matrix plane, i.e., the blue component values, to 127. The final line shows it as a figure. Doing so reveals a square image that appears grey.

Now it should be clear that a definition of grey must have some flexibility to it. Instead of saying that the component values are "exactly the same" we can say they should be "about the same," or that they should be the same within a degree of tolerance. Here is a judgement call, one that individuals might disagree where the cut-off should be. We can set a value for this, and change it if we do not like the results.

```
CUTOFF = 8;
red = x(r,c,1);
green = x(r,c,2);
blue = x(r,c,3);
if ((abs(red - green) < CUTOFF) && (abs(red - blue) < CUTOFF))
    % grey pixel
else
    % not a grey pixel
end
```

The code above has the cut-off value (CUTOFF) set to 8. There is nothing special about the name, that is, it is just another variable to MATLAB. The variable has all capitals simply as a convention, a sort of extra piece of information from the programmer that this value is not expected to change. Typically, we put an assignment like this one at the top of the function or program, so that we can quickly change the behavior. Given r and c, indices for row and column, we can get the red, green, and blue components for the image x, and then compare them. The if statement uses the abs function to get the absolute value, so that the result of the subtraction will be positive. We do not care about whether red is bigger than green, or the other way around, we just want to know if the difference between them is more than CUTOFF. We also check the difference between red and blue. The % grey pixel is used to indicate that more code would appear at this spot, as is % not a grey pixel. With this, the code looks good, like it should work. However, testing it reveals a problem. Sometimes it gets the comparison wrong!

To simulate the problem, define a and b as in the following code. They could be the red, green, or blue value from a pixel, and when the comparison works correctly, we will iterate this over the entire image. This is why it is important to know what the difference is regardless of the order. That is, if the two are the same, the program should not alter them, but if they are different, the program will enhance the red color. The values chosen are 61 and 117, and these are completely arbitrary. You could see the same problem with any two positive, non-equal values for a and b that are less than 256.

```
>> a = uint8(61)
a =
    61
>> b = uint8(117)
b =
   117
```

Next, we compare them to a cut-off value. Since the cut-off value is not part of the bug, we use 1 in its place. With a and b set, we can test it out. The code below uses disp statements to tell us what is going on.

```
if (abs(a-b) < 1)
    disp('leave this pixel alone');
else
    disp('change the red value');
end
```

Obviously, the difference between the values 61 and 117 is much larger than 1, so we expect it to print `change the red value`. But when we run the code, it outputs `leave this pixel alone`. The next line should help clarify this problem.

```
>> abs(a-b)
ans =
    0
```

We can double-check the values for a and b, and they are 61 and 117, respectively. This is one of those bugs that makes us wonder if the computer has gone crazy. Is it the `abs` function?

```
>> a-b
ans =
    0
```

No, the `abs` function is not the problem. Going back over the code, we might even double-check the subtraction.

```
>> 61-117
ans =
    -56
```

This serves to give us hope; the computer at least agrees with us on something.

```
>> c = 61;
>> d = 117;
>> c-d
ans =
    -56
```

And we see that 61 − 117 = −56, as we expect. Why does this work for c and d, but not a and b? What is different about these variables? The `whos` command will give us some information.

```
>> whos a b c d
  Name      Size       Bytes     Class        Attributes
  a         1x1            1      uint8
  b         1x1            1      uint8
  c         1x1            8      double
  d         1x1            8      double
```

Now we should remember the difference between these variables: the class type. How is a subtraction performed on uint8 values different?

```
>> f = a-b
f =
   0
>> whos f
   Name      Size      Bytes      Class       Attributes
   f         1x1           1      uint8
```

We see that the subtraction returns 0, and that the type of value returned is also uint8. Recall that the "uint8" type means unsigned integer of 8 bits. By definition, this type cannot store a negative value. Think of it this way: what would you do if someone asked you to write down the result of 61 – 117, with the instructions that your answer must be positive? Writing 0 is not perfect, but it is closer to the result than any other positive value.

Now we have understanding of the problem, and why it occurs. Let's check the subtraction of these two variables.

```
>> f = a - b
f =
     0
>> f = b - a
f =
    56
```

Since these are uint8 values, the subtraction order matters, even if we use abs on the result. To get around this, we can convert the values to the double type, as in the following code.

```
>> f = double(a) - double(b)
f =
   -56
```

Now we can find out the magnitude of the difference, regardless of the order.

```
>> f = abs(double(a) - double(b))
f =
    56
>> f = abs(double(b) - double(a))
f =
    56
```

This is important to make the case general. The a and b values will come from an image, and we cannot know which one will be larger. Thus, converting to the `double` type allows the subtraction to work beyond the narrow range that `uint8` values support.

As with many programming problems, this is one solution of many. For example, we could compare the values (a > b) first, and switch them based on the outcome. This would work, however, it does not appear to be optimal since it requires more steps. Similarly, is converting to `double` the *best* solution? This is not an easy question to answer, and there could be an infinite number of solutions. Also, what do we mean by "best": the fastest, the one that uses the least memory, the one that is the quickest to write, or the one that will be clearest to other people?

11.7 A SPECIAL CHARACTER CREATES AN ERROR

The program `TwoMinus1is2.m` shows an interesting MATLAB problem. An equation was copied from a web page. It includes an en-dash, which looks like a minus sign, but it is not. When pasted into a MATLAB program, it causes MATLAB to generate an error.

```
??? Error: File: TwoMinus1is2.m Line: 15 Column: 3
The input character is not valid in MATLAB statements
or expressions.
```

Oddly, if copied directly into the command window, it returns a result without an error.

```
>> 2 - 1
ans =
    2
```

Obviously, the answer is wrong, or at least it is not two minus one. Even more strange is that it appears as a red dash in the MATLAB command window, and as the letter a with a circumflex (^) over it in the MATLAB editor.

So what is this character? It is a UTF-8 encoding. This is a character encoding that includes ASCII characters, which take up a single byte, but it also allows special characters which take up multiple bytes. While ASCII works well for English, encoding the upper and lower case alphabet along with numeric digits and punctuation, it cannot exceed 256 possible characters. To represent characters from other languages, such as ä, â, and à, we need more capacity. UTF-8 provides this, and as a result it is a popular choice for web pages.

To figure out what this character is, an easy way is to convert all characters of the file to hexadecimal, such as with the Unix utility program `xxd`, then locate the character by searching through the output. The file `TwoMinus1is2.txt`, included with the programs from this text, shows the output from the `xxd` utility on the program `TwoMinus1is2.m`. Doing this reveals this character to be the sequence `e2 80 93` in hexadecimal. We can directly convert each hexadecimal digit to binary, such as with a look-up table, and find that it represents 1110 0010 1000 0000 1001 0011. The next part is a bit tricky, since we have to know about UTF-8 encoding. The first 4 bits are part of the UTF-8 encoding, followed by 4 bits of data, then 2 more encoding bits, 6 bits of data, 2 more encoding bits, and 6 bits of data. In other words, we have the pattern `xxxx 0010 xx00 0000 xx01 0011` when replacing the encoding bits with x's. The data bits that remain are `0010 00 0000 01 0011` or `0010 0000 0001 0011`. Converting this back to hexadecimal results in `2013`. And a quick look-up of this code in a table of UTF-8 shows that it is the "en dash". It looks a lot like a minus sign, but it is not. The solution is simple: replace this character with the minus sign.

11.8 AN ERROR COMPARING STRINGS

Suppose that we have two strings that we would like to compare, to see if they are equal. We could use code like the following.

```
if (a == b)
    disp('strings are equal');
else
    disp('strings are not equal');
end
```

However, there is a problem. When `a` and `b` have different lengths, this code generates the following error.

```
??? Error using ==> eq
Matrix dimensions must agree.
```

To understand this problem, we must look a little deeper. Here are two example strings of equal length, and the result of the comparison.

```
>> a = 'file123';
>> b = 'file124';
```

```
>> (a == b)
ans =
     1   1   1   1   1   1   0
```

The answer has 7 values, just as the strings are 7 characters each. Comparing for equality is done character by character, and the characters are the same except for the last ones. The computer performs the comparison like we might do it ourselves: check the first character of each string, see that they match, check the second character of each, see that they match, etc. In order for us to conclude that the strings are equal, we must have a match for every pair of characters. As in this case, since the characters at the end do not match, we conclude that the strings are not equal. We could subtract one character from the other, and see if we have a match (result of 0) or not, just as we would if these were arrays of numbers. In a sense, the strings are arrays of numbers; the numbers that encode each character. The problem lies with attempting an operation like subtraction on arrays of different lengths. Unless the arrays have the same length, or one of the arrays has only one element, subtraction is not defined. Consider the following code.

```
>> c = 'a';
>> d = 'aaaa';
>> (c == d)
ans =
     1   1   1   1
```

The comparison worked, since c has only one element. Notice what this implies:

```
>> if (c == d)
      disp('equal');
else
      disp('not equal');
end
equal
```

that is, when we test for equality, MATLAB tells us that c and d are equal. We would not consider them the same, however. Also, if we continue with this example, consider the following.

```
>> e = 'aa';
>> (d == e)
??? Error using ==> eq
Matrix dimensions must agree.
```

We see that we cannot compare `'aa'` with `'aaaa'` in this fashion, even though we can compare `'a'` with `'aaaa'`.

Before we do such a comparison, we should check the lengths of the strings. If they are equal, then we can compare them with the == operation. However, there is a better alternative, the function `strcmp`.

```
>> strcmp(a,b)
ans =
     0
>> strcmp(c,d)
ans =
     0
>> strcmp(d,e)
ans =
     0
>> strcmp(a,'file123')
ans =
     1
```

As we see in the above code, `strcmp` returns a 0 indicating inequality for each of the cases, except for the last one, just as we would. In the next section, we revisit the idea of comparing strings, with the additional consideration of matching a substring. Also, Section 9.4 discusses this idea with objects of the string class. Note that there the 2019b release of MATLAB includes a special `matches` function that could be used in place of `strcmp`.

11.9 ANOTHER DEBUGGING EXAMPLE

Recently, a program that normally works crashed on a particular input. Ideally, this sort of thing would never happen; a robust program should be able to handle any data, even bad data. Fortunately, the program includes a DEBUG variable, a convention where a program gives details to help the programmer verify its behavior. Normally, that variable has the value false. When set to true, the program prints a lot of information useful for debugging and maintenance. This can be as simple as having a line like this at the top of the program.

```
DEBUG = true;
```

Then, later in the program, especially at places where there have been problems, the code can print extra information.

```
if (DEBUG)
    disp(sprintf('Creating buffers of size %d', buffer_size));
end
```

If the program is working well, we can either comment out lines like the ones above, or at least set DEBUG to false.

This is especially useful when considering the life-span of a program. We write programs for a variety of reasons. Some are disposable, used to find an answer one time, similar to scribbling notes and equations on paper. Others might start this way, then morph into a useful utility. Still others might be meant to be run on a regular basis. As long as it works, we are not likely to change it. So a program of moderate complexity typically starts with an idea or need, is developed over a relatively short time, then used for a relatively long time. As bugs are uncovered or new features are desired, we might revisit the code, change it, or add to it. Eventually, we might retire the program if we no longer have a need for it. Or we could retire it by re-writing the program in a new language. The longest part of the life-cycle is use and maintenance, so it's a good idea to leave plenty of comments and choose variable and function names well, among other good programming practices. When you first write a program, you know it very well, but that clarity fades over time. You may find yourself asking "why did I do it like that?" with only a vague memory. Is the code avoiding a serious problem that you encountered? Could it be that you started doing it one way, then changed direction? Or is it just sloppy code?

In this case, the original program was written over several months in 2005. It was updated and expanded a couple of times in 2007, then debugged again in 2012, then again in 2013. By the time this bug surfaced, the program was well over a decade old. It's actually a C++ program, but that detail is not critical to this discussion. Debugging it is easy enough: set the DEBUG variable to true, and run it with an input file that causes problems. Here are some of the relevant lines that it printed,

```
From file location 1385125 to 1385124
filePointerStart = 1385125
filePointerEnd = 1385124
Creating buffers of size 18446744073709551615
Reading 18446744073709551615 bytes from file to buffer
```

and then it crashed. It tried to allocate much more memory than the computer has, over 4 billion times the total amount of memory. That's a very large number. How did it get to be so large? Notice that the "from" location is larger than the "to" location, and a difference operation (subtraction) should produce a negative value. However, some languages like C/C++ allow "unsigned" integers, so that such variables hold a larger range of positive values, like the `uint8` `uint16`, `uint32`, and `uint64` datatypes in MATLAB, compared to the `int8`, `int16`, `int32`, and `int64` datatypes. That is, `uint8` values range from 0 to 255, while `int8` values range from –128 to 127. Guess what happens when the subtraction of two unsigned numbers results in a –1 value? In C, we get the maximum value that the datatype can represent, in this case 2^{64}. What does MATLAB do?

```
>> disp(uint8(254) - uint8(255))

0
```

In MATLAB, such a subtraction yields the value 0.

To fix the symptom, simply check that the end comes after the start. This is a good thing to do anyway. The code for that looks like the following, expressed in MATLAB syntax.

```
if (filePointerStart < filePointerEnd)
    % create the data structures and read the file
    % do the normal processing
end
```

The actual problem was a little more complicated, where it looked for a pattern and did not find it because it had a few extra characters. The search pattern consisted of 70 characters, and the pattern did appear later, although it had an extra semi-colon at the end. Machines and humans differ in their abilities, especially with a task like this. If a human looks for a string of 70 characters and finds one that matches, except that it has a semi-colon as a 71st character, he or she would think it matches well. The computer examines these two and declares them unequal. Could we make the machines "smarter," so that they compute more like humans? Of course; we call that the field of artificial intelligence.

While checking to see if the end comes after the start avoids the crash, it does not fix the problem. The code would then run without crashing, although it would not find the match, and thus not do all of its tasks. The fix involved comparing the two strings, but only up to the length of the first one. Consider the following MATLAB code.

```
>> str1 = 'abcdefghijklm';
>> str2 = 'abcdefghijklm;';
>> strcmp(str1, str2)
ans =
     0
>> maxlen = length(str1);
>> strcmp(str1, str2(1:maxlen))
ans =
     1
```

Here, we define two similar strings, str1 and str2. Notice that the second one has an extra character. When we compare them with the first strcmp command, it returns a 0 result, indicating that they are not equal. However, in this case, we desire a result of 1. Defining maxlen as the length of the first string, the second strcmp compares the first string to the first maxlen characters of the second string. These are the same, so the comparison returns a 1. Note that extra care should be taken here, to make sure that the second string is the longer of the two. Code for this extra check looks like this.

```
>> if ((length(str2) >= maxlen) && (strcmp(str1, str2(1:maxlen))))
        disp('The strings appear to be the same.');
   else
        disp('The strings appear to be different.');
   end
The strings appear to be the same.
```

What if the second string contains some of the characters of the first string, but it has a shorter length? In this code, and for the application, the two would be considered unequal. See the program stringCompare.m for the previous example.

11.10 DEALING WITH ERRORS

Suppose that variable fname holds the name of a *.png* image file, and we want to add a border to that image. A few lines of code should read it in, copy it to a new, larger, image matrix, then overwrite the image with the new data.

```
>> fname = 'plant_corner.png';
>> y2 = zeros(48*3, 128, 3, 'uint8');
>> ya = zeros(48*3, 128, 'uint8');
>> [x2, map, a2] = imread(fname);
>> y2(1:67, 1:85,:) = x2;
Subscripted assignment dimension mismatch.
```

The error stopped the interactive work. This is not a typical program, since this code will only be run once. It forms one step of a long process of working with an image to mold it into the desired image. In this case, the image needs to be enlarged, without disturbing the data that it already holds. These commands do not appear in a program file, since they are a means to an end, just one might write down a series of calculations on a piece of scrap paper. Thus, these commands contain hard-coded values like 67 and 85.

As when faced with any bug, let's check our assumptions.

```
>> y2dim = size(y2);
>> x2dim = size(x2);
>> disp(sprintf('y2 is %d x %d x %d', y2dim(1), y2dim(2), y2dim(3)));
y2 is 144 x 128 x 3
>> disp(sprintf('x2 is %d x %d x %d', x2dim(1), x2dim(2), x2dim(3)));
x2 is 128 x 128 x 3
```

Matrix x2 does not fit into a $67 \times 85 \times 3$ matrix. Those values come from the dimensions of a previous version of x2, before it was changed by another program a few minutes ago.

This problem presents no real challenge to fix. Either the size of the source matrix (x2) needs to be limited to 67 rows and 85 columns, or the destination submatrix (part of y2) should be expanded to accommodate the full size of x2. The latter choice better fits the intention of the command.

```
>> y2(1:128, 1:128,:) = x2;
>> ya(1:128, 1:128,:) = a2;
>> imwrite(y2, fname, 'PNG', 'Alpha', ya);
```

The second assignment copies the alpha plane to another variable (ya), also a larger one than the original (a2). Since the imwrite command creates a new image with 4 planes (red, green, blue, and alpha), matrices y2 and ya must match in terms of the rows and columns. This works.

11.10.1 Seeing What Is There

This example looks fine on the surface. However, the resulting image looks odd.

```
x = imread('plant.jpg');
y = x(100:200:100:200,1:3);
imshow(y)
```

The original has a square shape, and colors. Expecting the image of y to be a smaller sub-set of the image, we instead see something very narrow, and greyscale. Checking the dimensions of y reveals that it has 101 rows, as expected, but only 3 columns, and no color planes. Carefully inspecting the assignment statement for y, one might notice an error in the line, where the second colon character (":") should be a comma (","). Although MATLAB did not generate an error, the code does not do what we intended. The following code corrects the problem.

```
y = x(100:200, 100:200, 1:3);
```

This exemplifies a common condition in programming, where we might not see the problem in code that we write. It is as if we see what we meant the code to be instead of what is really there. Often, a fellow programmer can notice the issue immediately. If you run into a problem where you simply cannot find the cause, asking someone else can help.

One caveat: writing code for a business, research, or a university class will likely limit your options. In a business or research setting, allowing someone outside the company or lab to see the code, even a part of it, may violate confidentiality rules. Likewise, in a university class, you may be expected to work completely independently of other students. If you are not sure, talk to your supervisor or instructor.

11.10.2 Seeing What Is There, Part 2

Here is an error message that turned out to be a simple fix.

```
>> seeingWhatsThere2
Error: File: seeingWhatsThere2.m Line: 2 Column: 20
Unexpected MATLAB operator.
```

The error message does not indicate what the problem could be, just where it occurs. The line reads as follows:

```
scaleY = -scaleY; // correct the sign on scale.
```

To an experienced programmer, it may appear to be error-free. This line, along with many others, come from a program originally written in another language. The text after the semi-colon is intended to be a comment, so the line needs just a little modification, as follows:

```
scaleY = -scaleY; % correct the sign on scale.
```

Using two forward-slash characters denotes a comment in languages such as C, C++, Java, JavaScript, and others. Maybe a future version of MATLAB will adopt this notation, too, but for now it does not make sense to the MATLAB program.

11.11 MAKING A PROBLEM EASIER

When it comes to breaking down a problem, one approach is to consider ideal circumstances. Plan to only make it work when everything is just right, first, then turn your attention to the possible complications. For example, suppose that you want your program to work on a sub-image. Make a test image to use, and have the program work with it. You will likely want to allow the user to choose a different image, and will need to verify that it loads correctly, but these tasks can wait. Allowing the user to choose the sub-image boundaries can be done simply enough with the `ginput` command, followed by a conversion of the results to integers. If the user happens to select the upper-left corner first, then the lower-right corner, the returned values can be used as rows and columns, to copy part of the image matrix to a sub-image matrix. The code for "ideal" conditions would look something like the following.

```
fname = 'original_image.png';
[myimage, map, alpha] = imread(fname);
imshow(myimage);
[a, b] = ginput(2);
rows = floor(b);
cols = floor(a);
mysubimage = myimage(rows(1):rows(2), cols(1):cols(2), :);
imshow(mysubimage);
```

If this code is simply a means to an end, where you need a sub-image, and you type this code to select it, then this ideal-circumstance case completes the task. If you might reuse it in the future, it needs more work. Saving it as a program, comments at the top will document what it does, although it should provide some directions to the user. It does not prompt the user to select the points, except that the cursor changes to cross-hairs when moved over the figure. You cannot expect the user to know (or yourself to remember) that the first point should be the upper-left and the second in the lower-right. Even if the program says to do this, people do not always follow directions.

Therefore, some of the non-ideal cases to consider are when the user selects the points in a different order, or clicks outside of the image. What if the image file does not exist? What if a file by that name exists, but it is not an image? What if the image has no content, such as when the image file has zero bytes? What if the user selects the first point, then decides to re-do that? What if you desire to store the file, and need a properly sized alpha matrix to go with the sub-image? If MATLAB already displays the current figure, but other windows block its view, does `imshow` show it on top? (The answer to this varies by system.) Should it create a new figure for this anyway? If your program eventually overwrites the image, such as with the sub-image, should it first make a back-up copy of the original? Should it prompt the user to choose a new name? Can it expect that the user selects a new name that does not already exist?

Should it create a new name automatically, and if so, how? It would be a fairly easy task to change the string `original_image.png` to `original_image_old.png`. Although if the computer already has a file with that name, it could instead use `original_image_old1.png`, where the program changes the `1` to a `2` if needed, and re-tries with increasing numbers until it produces a unique filename. What if the image might be copied to different computers, each with their own back-up copies, so that two completely different files called `original_image_old3.png` could exist on two different computers at the same time? Would it make more sense to embed a date code, such as `original_image_old_011020.png` for a back-up file created on January 10, 2020? Suppose that a company uses your program, and they have offices in the US and Europe, where a date code of `011020` would be considered October 1, 2020? What if the user creates a second back-up copy on the same date? Addressing these questions means that the code becomes increasingly difficult, longer, and potentially bloated. The bloat creeps in when substantial changes are made, such as changing the version number to a date code. Will the programmer, or programming team, take the time to carefully remove all of the old code? Will their employer or manager encourage this, or pressure them to move on to the next task?

By the way, you may have noticed that variables have names starting with "my," such as "`myimage`" and "`mysubimage`." This convention of prepending variable names assures us that those names do not conflict with other variables or functions. In MATLAB, both `image` and `subimage` are commands.

11.12 SUMMARY

We began this chapter with a discussion on how to get help with MATLAB. Then we looked at abstracting out a problem, illustrated by an example of months and years. Next, this chapter presented the debugger. Also, we examined a few problems where programs did not work as expected. One example showed how an equation copied from a web page resulted in a very unusual error, since it appeared like a normal subtraction, although a detailed look revealed it to contain a character MATLAB did not recognize as an operator. Experience helps in trouble-shooting programs.

No one writes perfect code, especially not the first time. Debugging is an important part of programming. Sometimes we fix the symptom, although the problem remains. We must understand what the code does, and figure out why it fails. Often problems come from invalid assumptions, such as an incorrect formula, using data types that do not support what the code needs to do, or that a match will be found when it is not exactly the same. Abstracting out the problem helps, that is, make the problem behavior show up with the fewest amount of lines. Having the program verbosely give output can help debug and maintain that code. Also, MATLAB comes with debugging tools to help you inspect variables, by setting breakpoints and allowing you to step through the code a little at a time. This chapter presents some debugging problems. The next chapter explores this, along with writing application specific software, in more detail.

EXERCISES

1. What is the difference between using `help` and `docsearch`?

2. Using the example program `badMonthCount.m`, set a break-point at the line defining `excess_months`. Inspect the variable `rounded_years` the first time through, and step though the loop a few times (with `dbstep`). Then use `dbcont` a couple of times to continue, and finally use `dbquit`.

3. Make a function to return the division result of one parameter by another. Use the `assert` command to check the second parameter, to make sure that it is not zero. Test it out to make sure that it works as expected. It should allow the second parameter to be negative.

4. Alter the `exampleValidation` function to check to see if the parameter is nonnegative, instead of positive. What is the difference?

5. How would you alter the `exampleValidation` function to check if the parameter is real, non-zero, and an integer?

6. What value does `a = uint8(250) + 6` return, and why?

7. What values does `a = uint8(4) - 6` return, and why?

8. What does the comparison (`'ab' ~= 'cde'`) generate an error, and how would you fix it?

9. What is the purpose of having a line like `DEBUG = false;` at the beginning of a program?

PROJECT

- **Related Help Files**

  If you write several functions to do different, but related, things, it would be nice to have a repeated set of help instructions. For example, suppose that you have programs to combine two images (creating a new image with image 1 on the left and image 2 on the right), convert a jpeg to a png image (or viceversa), double the size of an image along the rows and columns, and shrink an image along the rows and columns. All of them work with images, and later you might remember one of the names, but not the one that you want to use.

  Make a set of comments to briefly document several related programs. Along with realistic filenames, include comments for each individually, then add a "See also" section with a list of similar commands (the related functions), along with a description in a few words.

12

PRACTICAL MATLAB PROGRAMMING AND DEBUGGING CASE STUDIES: HOMEBREWING DATA

To master a computer programming language, you must practice it. This means writing programs to achieve a goal. What should the programs do? That is not the question to ask; that's the question to answer! Involve programming as part of a hobby, and use it to automate, analyze, or solve problems. In this chapter, we examine MATLAB code centered on the theme of homebrewing. Prior knowledge about homebrewing does not matter for this discussion. The process involves temperature control and analysis, gravity measurements, conversions from one unit to another, measurement corrections, dealing with faulty data, and data processing.

A liquid increases in density as one adds sugar to it. A device called a hydrometer measures this. It floats in liquid, like a bobber on a fishing line, and with pure water, it reads 1.0000 at the water line. In water with sugar mixed in, it floats higher, and calibrated markings on it indicate the amount relative to pure water, in a dimensionless reading called the gravity. You might see this as SPG for specific gravity, or simply SG. Variations on this include OG for original gravity, the gravity of the liquid before yeast are introduced, and FG for final gravity, the gravity reading after the yeast finish. These two important measurements allow us to calculate the percentage of alcohol in the solution.

The degrees Brix also specify the amount of sugar in water, with one degree corresponding to 1 gram of sugar in 100 grams of water. The idea of water measured in grams might seem strange, except that the original definition of a liter comes from the weight of water. Winemakers tend to use Brix, while American homebrewers tend to use specific gravity, although both Brix and specific gravity measure the same thing. Sometimes we might need to convert from one to the other.

12.1 BREAK IT DOWN, ALSO KNOWN AS DIVIDE AND CONQUER

The following example comes from a program called BB133plot. It reads in a data file, "BB133temps.csv," which contains seven columns of numeric data from a "mash." A mash means the heat-sensitive process of allowing enzymes to convert starches to sugars. Crushed, malted grain steeps in hot water for about an hour, and different enzymes work on it. The enzymes work well at certain temperatures, but shut down when the environment exceeds their range. Therefore, we desire to keep the temperatures at the proper values as accurately as possible.

The comma separated value (.csv) file looks like the following.

```
154.1,  155.0,  0,  165.6,  165.0,  0,  0
154.1,  155.0,  0,  165.6,  165.0,  0,  0
154.0,  155.0,  1,  165.6,  165.0,  0,  0
154.1,  155.0,  1,  165.6,  165.0,  0,  0
154.1,  155.0,  1,  165.5,  165.0,  0,  0
```

The columns represent the measured temperature of the mash, the mash's target temperature, the status code for mash's heating device, then the measured temperature of the water around the heat exchanger, the target temperature for it, and the heating status code. The final value represents the stage, meaning that we might have several targets. For example, we might want to start with a temperature of 155°F for 60 minutes, then raise it to 165°F for 10 minutes. Using an indirect heat source helps avoid overshooting the target temperature. Rather than heat the grain and water directly, this system pumps the liquid through a heat exchanger, which sits on an electric burner. Thus, the pump serves as the mash's heating device, since turning it on means the liquid flows through a heated tube. The heating status code represents the state of the burner. For simplicity, think of the status codes as 0 for off and 1 for on. Examining the data, we see the measured mash temperature get to be a full degree below the target, and the pump turns on. Meanwhile, the heat exchanger's water has overshot the target by 0.6 degrees, which is not a concern. It would be a lot better to see a graph of this data, rather than examine the thousand-plus lines. That's what the BB133plot program should do.

12.1.1 Debugging a Script

When you have an error on a complicated looking line, see if you can break it down into smaller parts. When writing the program, it generated the following error message.

```
>> BB133plot
Index exceeds matrix dimensions.
Error in BB133plot (line 23)
plot(x1(1:k), y2(1:k,7)-15.0, 'g');
```

First of all, the program line number allows us to narrow down the problem. The program may even work if we comment the line out. No, it will not likely do everything as intended if we make that line a comment, however it is reassuring to have a program that runs to completion even if it does not fully do its job. In more severe cases, we can put the keyword return before the line that causes the error, making a program that works up to that command, and exit gracefully.

The plot line that causes the error looks complicated. Keep in mind that it has three parameters, x1(1:k), y2(1:k,7)-15.0, and 'g'. We can safely ignore the last parameter; the program generates the same error with the line below.

```
plot(x1(1:k), y2(1:k,7)-15.0);
```

We can also eliminate the -15.0 since the line still fails without it. This means we should focus on x1(1:k) and y2(1:k,7).

What if we plot x1, but not y2?

```
>> plot(x1(1:k))
```

This results in a plot, without an error. Now we can try plotting y2 by itself.

```
>> plot(y2(1:k,7))
Index exceeds matrix dimensions.
```

Apparently, the problem has to do with y2. Let's examine variable k.

```
>> k
k =
      1234
```

Checking the variable `y2` by looking at the workspace window reveals that `y2` has 2000 rows, so the `1:k` part is not the issue. Instead, the problem is the `7:` there are only 4 columns to this matrix.

How did this happen? The program loads data into a variable called `y1`, which has 7 columns, each representing a signal from an experiment. Later, `y2` is assigned a subset of `y1`, but only 4 columns. Thus, `y2` is 2000 × 4, not the expected 2000 × 7. The solution turns out to be very simple, replacing the problematic line with the following.

```
plot(x1(1:k), y2(1:k,4)-15.0, 'g');
```

After this minor change, the program works well.

The point of this example is that an error might seem overwhelmingly complex, but it can be broken down into smaller pieces. When faced with a problem like this, take away as much as you can (like the `'g'` parameter and the `-15.0`) and reduce the problem to its core. You might also reduce the program down to as few lines as possible, that still generate the error. Then check your assumptions. Often, when the non-essential things have been eliminated and the error-producing code is at its simplest, the reason for the error becomes apparent. This method also works when faced with a logic error, like when one or more variables have non-sensical values.

12.1.2 Debugging a Function

This debugging effort worked easily, because a script generates the error. What if the problem had been embedded in a function? Consider the function `BB133plot_fn.m`, which copies the script, and adds the following line to the top.

```
function BB133plot_fn(filename)
```

Instead of expecting the user to know what to change for a different data file, this version accepts the filename as an argument. Arguably, it improves on the script, even though both contain an error.

```
>> BB133plot_fn('BB133temps.csv');
Index exceeds matrix dimensions.
Error in BB133plot_fn (line 26)
plot(x1(1:k), y2(1:k,7)-15.0, 'g');
>> whos
>>
```

Calling the function results in an error. We might try to examine the variables, but as the `whos` command reveals, we have no variables defined! Let's start by viewing the function in the editor.

```
>> edit BB133plot_fn
```

From the editor, click on the dash next to line 26, to set a breakpoint. Figure 12.1 shows the editor with the breakpoint set, where we observe the circle. Clicking on it a second time clears that breakpoint. After setting the breakpoint, we run the function again.

```
>> BB133plot_fn('BB133temps.csv');
26  plot(x1(1:k), y2(1:k,7)-15.0, 'g');
K>>
```

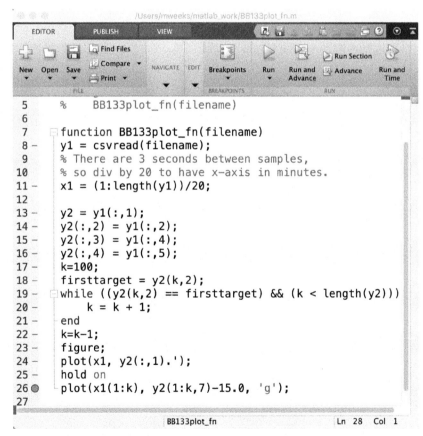

FIGURE 12.1 Setting a breakpoint in the editor.

Now we see a different response. First, it did not generate an error since it did not have the chance; the breakpoint stopped execution right before the error. Remember that the K>> prompt means debug mode. Now we can examine the variables.

```
K>> whos
  Name              Size          Bytes  Class     Attributes
  filename          1x14             28  char
  firsttarget       1x1               8  double
  k                 1x1               8  double
  x1                1x1442        11536  double
  y1                1442x7        80752  double
  y2                1442x4        46144  double
K>>
```

We know what line causes the problem, and we also know that the line uses arrays x1 and y2, and that the "[i]ndex exceeds matrix dimensions."

Yes, the problem's cause and solution are the same as in the preceding example, but we will pretend not to know that since this example uses a different technique. Variable k might have something to do with it.

```
K>> disp(k)
      1234
K>> disp(x1(k))
   61.7000
```

Examining variable k, we see that it has a positive value less than the maximum element of x1. The access of x1(k) verifies that the code does not exceed the limits of the x1 array. Next, we check array y2.

```
K>> y2(k,7)
Index exceeds matrix dimensions.
K>> y2(1,7)
Index exceeds matrix dimensions.
```

The problem appears with and without variable k, so we can eliminate that as the cause. Let's check the dimensions of y2.

```
K>> [MAXR, MAXC] = size(y2)
MAXR =
        1442
MAXC =
     4
```

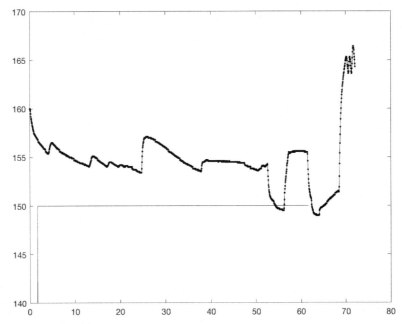

FIGURE 12.2 The fixed version of the "BB133plot" function produces this graph, with measured temperature data as a dash-dot line, and a variation of the target temperature as a straight line, to illustrate where the stage begins and ends.

Now the real cause of the problem should be clear: the column index (7) has a larger value than the maximum column. We can quit the debugger.

```
K>> dbquit
>>
```

At this point, we would fix the function, and clear the breakpoint before saving the file. Figure 12.2 shows the graph made by the fixed version of this function. The graph simply shows the measured temperatures with the straight line marking where the stage starts and stops.

12.2 A PROBLEM WITH ROUNDING, WHERE 1.1179999999999999 SHOULD BE 1.118

This problem comes from a Javascript application. While MATLAB does not have this problem, it helped to understand the difficulty. After some calculations, a number shows up as 1.1179999999999999, which is not desired. It should have 3 digits past the decimal. Actually, the fourth digit is at the limits of measurement accuracy, so 1.117 or 1.118 would be fine.

The code is as follows: As stated, it comes from Javascript, where the `console.log` command acts similar to `disp`.

```
console.log(' round EstPts is ' + Math.round(EstPts));
approxOG = 1 + Math.round(EstPts)/1000;
console.log('   update approxOG is ' + approxOG);
```

It prints some text, and rounds some floating point numbers. The variable `EstPts` could be set to 118, to see the problem. Obviously, the `round` function of 118 should be 118. If we then divide by 1000, then add 1, we should have 1.118.

MATLAB code to do this same task appears below.

```
EstPts = 118;
disp(sprintf(' round EstPts is %d', round(EstPts)));
approxOG = 1 + round(EstPts)/1000;
disp(sprintf('   update approxOG is %8.5f', approxOG));
```

This code has been included for completeness; it actually works as intended. The reader can find the Javascript version included in the program files, called `estPoints.html`, and it shows the output as the following.

```
round EstPts is 118
update approxOG is 1.1179999999999999
```

A way exists to display it with 3 digits after the decimal, i.e., without changing the value, although the program specifications ask for rounding or truncating.

Changing the code to this

```
approxOG = Math.round(1000 + EstPts)/1000;
```

makes the output

```
round EstPts is 118
update approxOG is 1.118
```

which works. The reason has to do with precision. The number 118 does not really need to be rounded, and once it is divided by 1000, the result will be a floating point value (0.118). Then we did another floating point operation, that is, adding 1 to it. The resulting number (1.118) might not be stored exactly in binary.

Part of the problem lies with JavaScript. MATLAB does not have this problem, as the following interaction shows.

```
>> EstPts = 118;
>> a = 1 + round(EstPts)/1000
a =
    1.1180
```

We see that **MATLAB** gets the number with the desired precision in the first attempt. **MATLAB** allows us to easily see the hexadecimal pattern for variables, which could be converted to a binary pattern.

```
>> disp(sprintf('%tx', a))
3f8f1aa0
>> disp(sprintf('%bx', a))
3ff1e353f7ced916
>> format long
>> a
a =
    1.118000000000000
```

Note how the number a, stored internally, uses all the hexadecimal digits of storage, even the right-most digits. This indicates that the number is not represented compactly, and may be an approximation.

Let's try the second way of finding the number in **MATLAB**.

```
>> approxOG = round(1000 + EstPts)/1000
approxOG =
    1.118000000000000
>> disp(sprintf('%bx', approxOG))
3ff1e353f7ced917
```

Interestingly, the two values a and approxOG are not the same! We can confirm this with the following code.

```
>> a
a =
    1.118000000000000
>> approxOG
approxOG =
    1.118000000000000
>> if (a == approxOG)
  disp('equal');
```

```
else
  disp('not equal');
end
not equal
```

They appear to be exactly the same to us, as they should. Internally, they have slightly different representations.

The fix to this code is not satisfying. It should work either way in JavaScript, just as it works both ways in MATLAB. However, we have no control over how a language like JavaScript does things. So the program keeps this "fix" even though it is more of a "hack." It may have to change again if a future case comes along where the number would work better done the first way.

Another way to fix this is to fake the floating point number. That is, with EstPts as the 3 digit value to display, it could be rounded to an integer, then shown with 1. before it. The code below accomplishes this.

```
document.writeln(' EstPts is 1.' + Math.round(EstPts));
```

However, this solution glosses over an important detail: how do ensure that EstPts has exactly three digits? The code should check the value, and append zeros after the 1. text. A corresponding MATLAB command appears below.

```
disp(sprintf(' EstPts is 1.%3d', round(EstPts)));
```

The MATLAB code does not have a problem when EstPts has fewer than three digits, since the %3d specifier takes care of this. Although rare, a problem that exists in one computer language, but not in another, does come up. This problem exists in Javascript, and we used MATLAB to confirm that it comes from the language, not the algorithm. We also saw the way the computer represents the floating-point number internally. Although we did not get into how that pattern represents a floating-point number, we saw that it used all of the available space. For more information on this, see a reference about the IEEE 754 standard, such as [8].

12.3 FIXING A PROBLEM WITH APPARENT ATTENUATION

This section discusses another JavaScript program, one that calculates the apparent attenuation. But its example value is incorrect: although it should be 65, the program reports 6 instead. This seems like an easy-to-fix, ordinary bug. Let's find out.

First, here is a bit of background. When yeast are present in a sugary solution, they will consume the sugar, producing alcohol and carbon dioxide. We can measure the specific gravity of the sugary solution before the yeast are mixed in, called the original gravity (OG), and again after the yeast are finished, called the final gravity (FG). Here is the equation, expressed in JavaScript.

```
apparent_attenuation = Math.round(100*(OG - FG)/OG);
```

We can set up a MATLAB program to use the example values, as below. Why do this? This bug seems to be independent of the language, and this will verify that suspicion. If it does not, this would drastically change how to go about this problem, and we would need to shift focus to exactly what JavaScript is doing.

```
OG = 1.110;
FG = 1.038;
apparent_attenuation = round(100*(OG - FG)/OG);
```

Just like in the JavaScript program, the answer is 6. The original JavaScript program is over 3000 lines long, and now we know that the problem is reproducible in only three lines!

Calculating the answer by hand results in 65. What is the difference? The calculation-by-hand uses the values without the leading 1, and multiplied by 1000. This description makes it sound more complicated than it is; what it means is that it uses 110 and 38 instead of 1.110 and 1.038, respectively. What would happen if we use these values instead?

```
>> OG = 110;
>> FG = 38;
>> apparent_attenuation = round(100*(OG - FG)/OG)
apparent_attenuation =
    65
```

Good, this is the expected value. And it makes sense, too: if you had 110 grams of sugar, and your roommate ate some of it, and the remainder weighed 38 grams, you would say that your roommate ate 65% of it.

Thus, we have a solution: express the gravities as "points" instead, as below.

```
OG = 1.110;
FG = 1.038;
```

```
OGpoints = (OG - 1.0)*1000;
FGpoints = (FG - 1.0)*1000;
apparent_attenuation = round(100*(OGpoints - FGpoints)/OGpoints)
```

We have to modify the last line slightly to make it work as a JavaScript command, but that is trivial. The bug is fixed.

We are not quite done, though. Sometimes when programming we run into a bug and find a solution without really understanding the problem or why the fix works. This is like hitting an old TV to get a clear picture: we don't understand what the problem is or why hitting it works, but it may solve the problem for the moment. Won't the problem happen again? The issue here is that we have a fix, and it seems to work, but we've only tested it with one example. And if we do not understand what the problem is, how do we know it will not happen again with a different set of values?

One thing to notice is that we appear to be off by a decimal: maybe if we multiplied the original answer by 10 before we round it, we would get the correct answer.

```
>> OG = 1.110;
>> FG = 1.038;
>> apparent_attenuation = round(10*100*(OG - FG)/OG)
apparent_attenuation =
    65
```

OK, that works. What if we multiply the gravities by 1000 first?

```
>> OG = 1110;
>> FG = 1038;
>> (OG - FG)/OG
ans =
    0.0649
```

The issue here goes back to the definition. As we can see from above, 1038 is only a 6% difference from 1110, just as 1.038 is only a 6% difference from 1.110. If we had these two measurements without any further information, we would find the missing percentage in this way. For example, if we had 1.110 pounds of sugar before our roommate ate some, and we had 1.038 pounds left, we would say the roommate ate 6% of it.

So should 6% be the correct answer? No. The gravities tell us the amount of sugar in the solution, but indirectly. If we have pure water with no sugar, the gravity would be 1.000. We must subtract the 1, because otherwise our measurements do not start at 0. In other words, if 1.110 represents water plus sugar, and 1.000 represents the pure water by itself, the difference in sugar between them is 100%, not 9.9%. To continue with the example from above, we might start with a bowl of sugar that weighs 1.110 pounds, then see that it weighs 1.038 pounds after the roommate ate some. If the bowl weighs 1 pound when it is empty, we must subtract 1 from both measurements before we calculate the percentage. Otherwise the roommate could eat all of the sugar then claim that he only ate 9.9% of it.

Therefore, the part that made the solution work is the subtraction from 1, not the multiplication by 1000. The code below shows an equivalent way to find the correct percentage.

```
OG = 1.110;
FG = 1.038;
% Subtract the 1 from each gravity
% to give us relative measurements from 0
% instead of from 1.
OGwithout1 = (OG - 1.0);
FGwithout1 = (FG - 1.0);
apparent_attenuation = round(100*(OGwithout1 - ...
    FGwithout1)/OGwithout1)
```

This is better than the first solution, since it makes the needed correction (subtracting the 1) without additional code (multiplying by 1000) that does not make a difference. Even more importantly, it improves the code with a comment.

12.4 CORRECTING A REFRACTOMETER READING

A homebrewer will typically make 5 gallons at a time, although some people make batches as small a 1 gallon, for a variety of reasons. One-gallon equipment takes only a modest amount of space, it is light and easy to move, and allows indoor operation on a kitchen stove-top during bad weather. Producing a small quantity means that it will not last a long time, so it allows the brewer freedom to experiment.

In beer making, we often measure the specific gravity. Given readings before and after fermentation, we can use the difference to calculate the alcohol percentage. It can also be used to determine when the fermentation is finished, i.e., when the gravity readings over several days remain the same. Thus, a brewer will typically take at least two readings.

For convenience, a homebrewer might use a device called a refractometer to measure the specific gravity of a beer. This works well before fermentation. After fermentation, the refractometer reading must be corrected to compensate for the presence of alcohol. Equations to correct the reading exist, however, for one particular beer, the corrected value did not seem possible. The calculated correction indicated that the gravity increased. What caused this?

12.4.1 Converting Specific Gravity to Degrees Brix

The specific gravity and degrees Brix are both measures of the sugar content of a liquid. They are used among homebrewers to indicate things like the amount of sugars extracted during the mash process, how much alcohol is produced, and even how well a beer matches a specific style. Sometimes it is necessary to convert from one measurement to the other, such as when correcting a refractometer's reading due to the presence of alcohol. Here, we discuss the conversion of specific gravity to degrees Brix.

Function `grav2brix_approx.m` shows the first, simple attempt, using the formula $y = mx + b$, the equation for a line. We can find the slope (m) and the y-intercept (b) based on a couple of points. The problem with this approach is that the relation is not a line, so it does not give accurate results. After some experimentation, this approximation was found to be too inaccurate to be useful. A better function, called `grav2brix.m`, took its place.

An online search revealed an authoritative reference that provides a table of gravities and Brix values, and contains more information than we need, such as "grams of sucrose per 100 ml weight in vacuo" [9]. It also goes well beyond the maximum measurement shown on Figure 12.3 of 1.120. The refractometer shown in Figure 12.6 only goes to 1.130, and the hydrometer shown in Figure 12.5 has a maximum mark of 1.170, while the table goes up to 1.519 [9]. At first, this data was used to refine the conversion function. But why do that, when it would be easier just to use it as a look-up table? Copying the desired columns of data proved to be a tiring effort, although a rewarding one. Data up to a specific gravity of 1.178 were included, which may seem arbitrary except that it corresponds to 39.9 Brix, i.e., all data below 40 Brix are present. Of course, the needed range depends on the application. Wort (the technical term for unfermented beer) has a gravity of about 1.050, although typical values range between 1.030 and 1.100 depending on the desired style. Wine making or candy making could benefit from a higher maximum than shown on Figure 12.3. Since the original table has the specific gravities to 5 places beyond the decimal, the computerized table keeps this precision, too, even though 4 places beyond the decimal would be sufficient. The program `Brix2SPGTable.m` creates a matrix with 2 columns, with the Brix values in column 1 and the corresponding specific gravities in column 2. To use it, find the value in column 2 that most closely matches the given specific gravity, and return the value in that row's column 1. This method is exact, not based on an approximation.

A second version of this data is worth mentioning, since the `grav2brix.m` function uses it. Program `Brix2SPGTable_v2.m` defines an array of specific gravities. It is the same as column 2 of the matrix created by `Brix2SPG-Table.m`. The trick is that the Brix values are implicit. If we know the row, we can find the Brix value by subtracting 1 from it and dividing by 10. First, consider a special case of the very first line, where we have the gravity 1.00000. This is on row 1, so (row-1)/10 gives us 0, the correct Brix value. Now suppose we have the gravity 1.009, found on row 24. Finding (24-1)/10 results in 2.3, the correct Brix value. To use this array, find the closest value in it to the given specific gravity, and use the row index as shown above.

12.4.2 Comparing the Approximate and Exact Answers

How much error is in the `grav2brix_approx` function? This program calculates it.

```
Brix2SPGTable_v2
spg = SPGarray(1:282);
m = 1;
for k=spg
    approx(m) = grav2brix_approx(k);
    exact(m) = grav2brix(k);
    % Print a few of the exact values, to double-check them.
    if ((k > 1.050) && (k < 1.060))
        disp(sprintf('exact Brix for %8.6f is %4.2f',k,exact(m)));
    end
    m = m + 1;
end
```

First, it generates an array of specific gravities called `SPGarray`, then it defines `spg` as a smaller array. The loop repeats for every value in the smaller array, and stores the approximate and exact values given by `grav2brix_approx` and `grav2brix`, respectively. Notice that the code stores the values into arrays, but that it uses `m` as the index, instead of `k`, since `k` has non-integer values like 1.0004. The code also prints the `exact` array's values for a subset of the specific gravities. The resulting output appears below.

```
exact Brix for 1.050050 is 12.40
exact Brix for 1.050470 is 12.50
exact Brix for 1.050900 is 12.60
exact Brix for 1.051320 is 12.70
exact Brix for 1.051740 is 12.80
exact Brix for 1.052160 is 12.90
exact Brix for 1.052590 is 13.00
exact Brix for 1.053010 is 13.10
exact Brix for 1.053430 is 13.20
exact Brix for 1.053860 is 13.30
exact Brix for 1.054280 is 13.40
exact Brix for 1.054700 is 13.50
exact Brix for 1.055130 is 13.60
exact Brix for 1.055560 is 13.70
exact Brix for 1.055980 is 13.80
exact Brix for 1.056410 is 13.90
exact Brix for 1.056830 is 14.00
exact Brix for 1.057260 is 14.10
exact Brix for 1.057690 is 14.20
exact Brix for 1.058110 is 14.30
exact Brix for 1.058540 is 14.40
exact Brix for 1.058970 is 14.50
exact Brix for 1.059400 is 14.60
exact Brix for 1.059820 is 14.70
```

Next, we plot the exact versus the approximate Brix values. The command `figure()` creates a new figure, where we plot the `exact` array in black (`'k'`). Since we will show another graph on this figure, `hold on` tells the computer to allow more plots on top of the current graph. With the second plot command, the `approx` array values also appear in black, as a dash-dot line (`'k-.'`). The other commands enhance the graph's presentation.

```
figure();
plot(spg, exact, 'k');
hold on
plot(spg, approx, 'k-.');
axis('tight');
title('Exact Brix values (solid) versus approximate ones (dash-dot)');
xlabel('gravity');
ylabel('Brix');
```

The resulting plot appears in Figure 12.3. This shows that the two signals are not exactly the same. If you look closely at the figure, you can see that the plots cross each other twice. Therefore, the data cannot be approximated well with a line. The next graph, Figure 12.4, shows this idea even better, since it plots the differences.

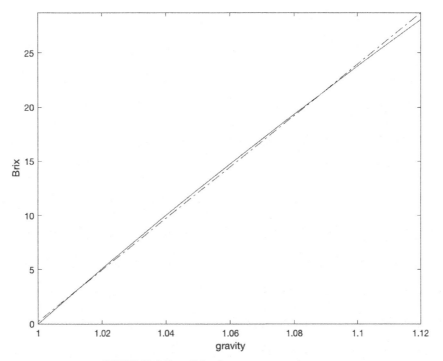

FIGURE 12.3 Exact Brix values versus approximate ones.

The next line finds the differences between them.

```
diff = exact - approx;
```

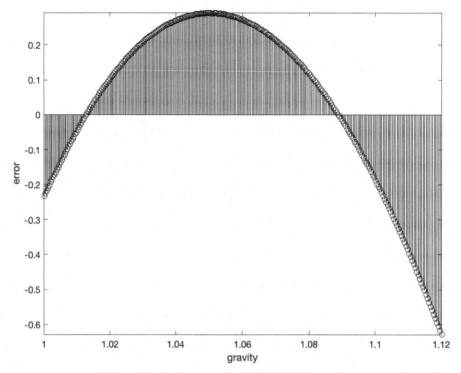

FIGURE 12.4 Errors between approximate and actual Brix values.

Now we can plot the differences. The following code makes such a graph. It invokes the `stem` command that creates a plot of circles for each data point, with a line segment connecting to the axis. Here, it plots the differences between the approximate and actual Brix values, in a way that accentuates them.

```
figure();
stem(spg, diff, 'k')
title('Errors between approximate and actual Brix values');
axis('tight');
xlabel('gravity');
ylabel('error');
```

As can be seen in Figure 12.4, the differences between the approximations from the line formula and the actual values appear as a parabola. The errors are significant, too, since we can see a difference of 0.1 Brix with a good refractometer. Thus, approximating this conversion with a line does not work well, and trying to improve it, perhaps with a more complex equation, at best would match a look-up table in accuracy.

12.4.3 Refractometer and Hydrometer

FIGURE 12.5 A hydrometer, floating in water. Dissolving sugar into the water causes the hydrometer to float higher.

Measuring the SPG with a hydrometer, such as the one shown in Figure 12.5, requires over 4 ounces of liquid. With 1 gallon batches (128 ounces), we would lose 3% of the batch every time, or 8 to 9 ounces just for 2 readings.

This is too much. In contrast, a refractometer like the one shown in Figure 12.6 only needs a few drops per reading. Figure 12.7 shows what you would see when looking through the refractometer's eye-piece. However, unlike the hydrometer, it does not give an accurate reading after fermentation has started, because the liquid contains a mix of water, alcohol, and other chemicals, making it lighter than the original solution. The density of the liquid changes as the yeast consume the sugars and turn them into alcohol and carbon dioxide (CO_2). Most of the CO_2 in fermentation bubbles up and escapes, just like it does with a soda poured into a glass. See programs `correctRefract.m`, `correctRefract2.m` and `correctRefract3.m`, as well as section 12.5.

For example, one beer, a Belgian Tripel, started with an original gravity (OG) of 1.097, or 23.2 in Brix. The refractometer reading for the final gravity (FG) is 1.045, or 11.2 in Brix. The refractometer reading, corrected by the formula from `HomeBrewStuff.com`, is 1.012. The refractometer reading, corrected by the formula from `SeanTerrill.com`, is 1.014. Both values are similar, and close enough for most purposes.

Another beer, a Belgian Dark Strong Ale, started with an original gravity of 1.117, or 27.5 Brix. When measuring the final gravity with the refractometer, it reads 1.075. The correction formula maps this to 1.108. This does not make sense, because any correction should be lower than the reading.

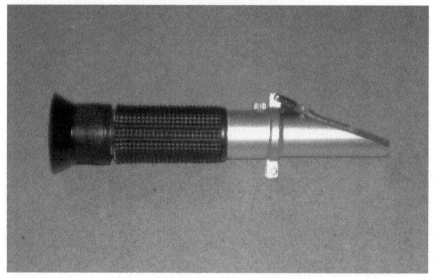

FIGURE 12.6 A refractometer. A small liquid sample goes under the plastic flap on the right, then a person looks through the eye-piece on the left.

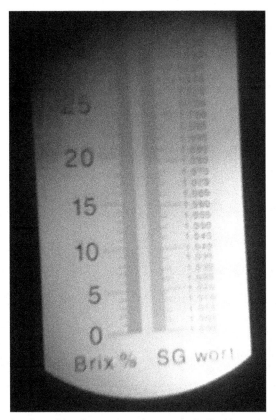

FIGURE 12.7 The view through a refractometer. The sugar in the liquid sample affects the refraction, and we look for the line where the shaded area (near 20) meets the white. Here we read that value as 20 Brix. This refractometer also includes a scale for specific gravity.

This is from `morebeer.com`, an online retailer:

"*Brix*(P lato) = $-676.67 + 1286.4 \times SG - 800.47 \times (SG^2) + 190.74 \times (SG^3)$

$SG = 1.001843 - 0.002318474(OB) - 0.000007775(OB^2) - 0.000000034(OB^3) +$
$0.00574(AB) + 0.00003344(AB^2) + 0.000000086(AB^3)$

where SG = Specific Gravity, OB = Original Brix, AB = Apparent Brix (Brix Readings During Fermentation)" [`https://www.morebeer.com/images/file.php?file_id=6161`, Refractometer Alcohol Correction Spreadsheet].

Given OB = 27.5 Brix (1.117) and AB = 18.18 Brix (1.075), this spreadsheet indicates that it has: Actual SG 1.049 and Actual Brix 12.0. Let's compare correction formulae. Note that the formula on `HomeBrewStuff.com` is the same one as provided by `MoreBeer.com`. The following function, `comparing_` corrections, takes the original gravity and final gravity as arguments, then returns a correction for the final gravity. It assumes that the final gravity argument comes from a refractometer, and thus needs to be corrected.

```
function [bestFG] = comparing_corrections(bestOG, bestFG)
x = grav2brix(bestOG);
y = grav2brix(bestFG);
c = [ 1.001843, 0.002318474, 0.000007775, ...
    0.000000034, 0.00574, 0.00003344, 0.000000086 ];
d = [ 1.0000, -0.0044993, 0.00027581, ...
    -0.0000072800,  0.011774, -0.0012717, 0.000063293 ];
% Could also use the ^ operator
w = c(1) - c(2) * x - c(3) * x * x - c(4) * x * x * x ...
        + c(5) * y + c(6) * y * y + c(7) * y * y * y;
v = d(1) + d(2) * x + d(3) * x * x + d(4) * x * x * x ...
        + d(5) * y + d(6) * y * y + d(7) * y * y * y;
s1 = strcat('Refractometer reading corrected', ...
    ' (formula from HomeBrewStuff.com) is ');
disp(sprintf('%s %7.4f ', s1, w));
s2 = strcat('Refractometer reading corrected', ...
    ' (formula from SeanTerrill.com) is ');
disp(sprintf('%s %7.4f ', s2, v));
if (v < w)
    % v Seems OK
    bestFG = v;
else
    % v is too large! So use w instead.
    bestFG = w;
end
disp(sprintf('Using %7.4f ', bestFG));
```

With two possibilities, it simply picks the lower of the two. Calling the function with the previous example values shows that it gives reasonable estimates of the final gravities.

```
>> comparing_corrections(1.097, 1.045)
...
Using   1.0120
```

```
>> comparing_corrections(1.117, 1.075)
...
Using   1.0476
```

This function generates extraneous information that the output omits.

Figure 12.8 shows how the two correction formulae work. The original gravity is arbitrarily fixed at 1.090, just to make the relation easier to visualize. The dashed line shows the uncorrected final gravities, the values that we might read from a refractometer. For this problem, the final gravities that we read are likely to start at the original gravity, perhaps when a brewer first introduces the yeast, and drop over the following days as the yeasts consume the sugars and produce alcohol. Eventually, the yeasts will stop, typically because the sugars that they can consume run out. (There are many different types of sugars, and there may be sugars left that the yeasts cannot consume.) So the dashed line represents what we might expect to see from a refractometer over time, essentially working from right (the beginning) to left (the stopping point). Also note that the dashed line rises from left to right the same amount as it rises from the bottom to the top; it is a reference line that tells us that if we have a gravity such as 1.040, we can draw a vertical line up from 1.040 on the *x-axis* to the line, then a horizontal line from that intersection over to the *y-axis* to read the actual value, in this case 1.040. For the dashed line, every value that we choose along the *x-axis* gives us the same value on the *y-axis*. The dash-dot and dotted plots function in a similar manner: if the OG is 1.090, we can take a reading with a refractometer, find that value along the *x-axis*, draw a vertical line to the dash-dot (or dotted) plot, then draw a horizontal line to the *y-axis* to get the corrected reading.

Examining Figure 12.8 we can see a problem with the dash-dot curve: around 1.060, the dash-dot curve intersects with the dashed line, and beyond this point the dash-dot curve is above it. In other words, for refractometer readings above 1.060, the corrected value is larger than the reading, at least for the example starting gravity of 1.090. However, this does not make sense with the process. We start with a solution of sugar and yeast. As the yeasts consume the sugar, they produce alcohol which is lighter than water, along with carbon dioxide, which bubbles out. A refractometer reading thus may overestimate the amount of sugar, but it will not under-estimate it. So a correction for a refractometer reading should not be higher than the reading.

How can we resolve this? On the one hand, the dash-dot curve appears to do a better job of correcting the reading (at least according to the author's observations), but on the other hand, the dotted plot does not ever return an erroneous correction. The simple solution, although perhaps not ideal, is to calculate both corrections. We will use whatever correction has the lower of the two values.

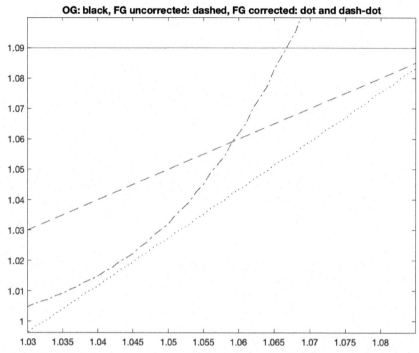

FIGURE 12.8 Two ways to correct a refractometer's reading for the presence of alcohol.

Also noteworthy is the formula by Petr Novotný ["Revisiting the refractometer," *Zymurgy*, Vol. 40, No. 4, July/Aug 2017, pages 48–54]. Using the same x and y as defined in `comparing_corrections`, we can calculate the refractometer correction as follows:

```
u = -0.002349 * x + 0.006276 * y + 1;
```

This surprisingly simple method gives results comparable to the other two formulae, if not superior to them. How do we choose between three values? Since this correction allows us to approximate the alcohol by volume, choosing the smallest value is the safest assumption, so that in the worst case we get an overestimation of the alcohol content, rather than an under-estimation.

Figure 12.9 shows a mesh plot of the first refractometer correction formula, using different starting and finishing gravities. Similarly, Figure 12.10 plots the second refractometer correction formula. From these two plots, we see that the two correction approaches differ considerably. Which one is best? This may not be a fair question; perhaps each performs better under certain circumstances. Many parameters could affect the result, such as the yeast strain, and the types of sugars present. Perhaps these other parameters should be present in the correction equation.

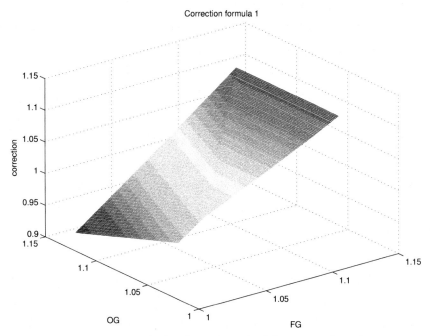

FIGURE 12.9 A mesh plot of correction 1 for different OG and FG values.

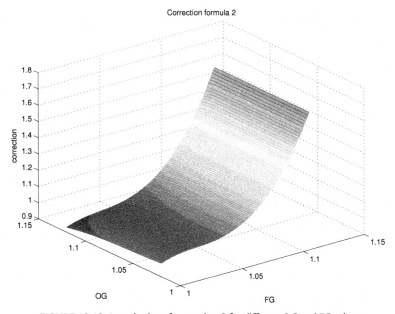

FIGURE 12.10 A mesh plot of correction 2 for different OG and FG values.

12.5 A BUG CREATES AN APPARENT DISCONTINUITY

Another problem comes from a function called `correctRefract3`. It produces a plot of a function of the form

$$c_0 + c_1 x + c_2 x^2 + c_3 x^3 + c_4 y + c_5 y^2 + c_6 y^3,$$

where the c_n values are constants, and some are negative. One plot has a discontinuity, a sudden jump in value, which does not make sense, shown in Figure 12.11. Given an original gravity reading, the program calculates a correction to possible final gravity readings, according to a formula. Essentially, a liquid's sugar content (original gravity) can be measured with a refractometer, but once yeast consume the sugars, later readings by that device are incorrect. To compensate, we can use a program like this.

For the purposes of illustrating the bug, the code has been changed. The programmer took out everything that he could without getting rid of the bug, and reduced it down to the following 7 lines. The mathematical function is now simply $x - y$. The following code creates an array, w, which stores the difference between x, a constant, and y, which governs the `for` loop.

```
x = input('Please enter a number higher than 30: ');
i = 1;
for y = 30:5:x
    w(i) = x - y;
    i = i + 1;
end
plot(1:length(w), w, 'b');
```

This version is called `correctRefract3b`. Below are a couple of example runs.

```
>> correctRefract3b
Please enter a number higher than 30: 100
>> correctRefract3b
Please enter a number higher than 30: 80
>>
```

This produces the plot we see in Figure 12.12.

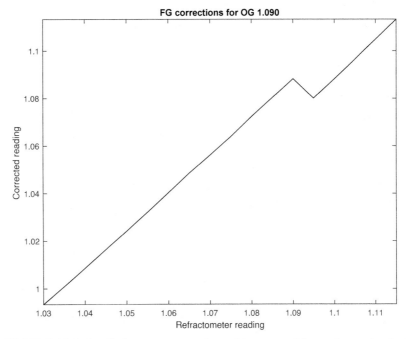

FIGURE 12.11 A plot of refractometer corrections, with an unusual feature due to a bug in the program.

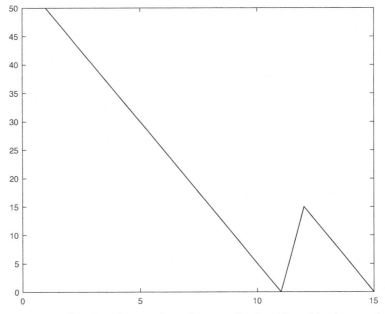

FIGURE 12.12 A plot of $x - y$ for an x value and a range of y values. The sudden rise around $x = 11$ should not be there, and is due to a bug.

This bug is easier to see with the shortened code. We can inspect the w values, to confirm that the plot command is not the source of the problem. (It is not.) The `input` line works, the assignment for variable i works, and the `for` loop functions normally. So our suspicion should fall on the assignment of array w. An unusual thing about this bug is that it does not always show up. That is, if we had entered 80 the first time and 100 the second time, it would have worked well. If you do not yet see the bug, consider this: what is the difference for w when we give x the value 80 and when we give it the value 100?

When we specify 80, the w array will have 11 values. When we specify 100, w will have 15 values. And here is the key to the bug: if w already has more values than we use, the ones that we do not re-assign are still there. The bug shows up when we specify 100, creating 15 values for w, then when we run the program again with 80, it overwrites the first 11 values. The last 4 are still defined, and still part of w, so when we do the plot, we see the new w array with some of the previous w values.

What seemed to be a complex bug turned out to have a simple, almost comical, explanation. Often with software problems, understanding the set of conditions and assumptions that lead to the error takes much longer than correcting it. To fix this particular bug, we can add the command `clear w` before the `for` loop, in case w already has a definition.

12.6 MASH-STEP ANALYSIS FROM TEMPERATURE DATA

As mentioned earlier, an important aspect of homebrewing is controlling temperatures for the mash, a temperature sensitive process where enzymes convert starch in malted barley to sugar. With a lot of temperature data, it would be good to use MATLAB to do mash-step analysis, where it tells us what the target steps are (e.g., 145°F for 30 minutes, 155°F for 20 minutes, etc.), how long it took to transition between steps, and what the average temperature is (e.g., 144.2°F average for the first step). The target temperatures should appear along with the actual temperatures. These were recorded with several other signals, so one of the first steps will be to separate out the signals of interest from the rest. Here is an example of results to get from the data.

```
phase 1:  starting at 145 hold at 145  for 30 minutes
phase 2: heating from 144   to    158 took 40 minutes
phase 3:  starting at 157 hold at 158  for 30 minutes
phase 4: heating from 157   to    165 took 22 minutes
phase 5:  starting at 164 hold at 165  for 10 minutes
```

12.6.1 Reading and Writing Comma Separated Value Files

Suppose that we have some data files that we would like to get information from. Each file should have two signals: the measured temperature in column 1 and the desired temperature in column 2. How long did it take to reach the desired temperatures, and how long was that desired temperature held?

The first file is fairly simple, containing only the measured temperatures. First, the program reads the data and stores it in a variable called y. The data come from a comma separated value (.csv) file, which is a simple type of spreadsheet.

```
y = csvread('bb92c.csv');
plot(y)
```

The plot shows the temperatures, and you may notice that, for the "bb92c. csv" file, measurements appear in centigrade. Some files have temperatures in degrees centigrade and some are in Fahrenheit. To make it consistent, we will convert it to Fahrenheit. This is not an easy choice, since most of the world uses centigrade. However, Americans are the intended users for this application, and most people have an intuitive "feel" for temperatures in the units used in their home country. For example, an American homebrewer might see a temperature of 70°C, and have to think about whether that is too hot or too cool for this process. With a temperature reading of 158°F, on the other hand, they would immediately know that it is on the high-end of the acceptable range for the process.

Notes on this batch indicate that the system targeted 67°C as the desired temperature. Before going further, we set a second column of y to be 67.0.

```
y(:,2) = 67;
```

Now we can convert the centigrade temperatures to Fahrenheit. You probably remember the necessary formula:

$$f = c \times 9/5 + 32.$$

To apply this to variable y using MATLAB, type the following.

```
f = y * 9/5 + 32;
plot(f)
```

The plot shows the data as expected. For the moment, this is a good step forward, so we can write the data to a new file.

```
csvwrite('data92revised.csv', f);
```

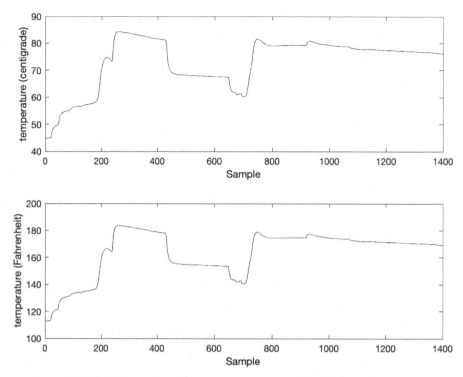

FIGURE 12.13 Plot of temperatures in centigrade (top) and Fahrenheit (bottom).

Notice that we wrote the variable f to the file, since y still contains the original (centigrade) temperatures.

In Figure 12.13, we see the example signal plotted in degrees centigrade (top), while it also shows the same data plotted in degrees Fahrenheit (bottom). As we should expect, the figures look exactly the same, except for the numbers on the *y-axis* (on the left).

12.6.2 Making and Correcting Data Files

Some of the data files are missing. Log files exist that can re-create them, so this is not a serious problem. The following lines show an example log.

```
0:12:0 104.5 F,   Target: 122.0 F   Burner off, status 0
0:12:3 104.6 F,   Target: 122.0 F   Burner on,  status 3
0:12:6 104.7 F,   Target: 122.0 F   Burner on,  status 3
0:12:9 104.8 F,   Target: 122.0 F   Burner on,  status 3
```

Each line of the log starts with a time stamp, followed by the temperature reading and units, some text, the target temperature and units, then other information regarding heating. Not every line has temperature information, though; system information like "Low temp—turning on the burner" may appear, and files may be double-spaced. However, every line with temperature information contains a colon, and none of the other lines do, by design. This allows us to easily collect only the temperature lines with the Unix utility `grep`. That is, the command below could be typed in a terminal window of a computer running a Unix, Linux, or Macintosh operating system.

```
grep : logfile1.txt > logfile2.txt
```

It uses the `grep` utility and passes : and `logfile1.txt` to it. The first parameter is the pattern to find. The second parameter specifies the file. The greater than sign specifies that the results should be put into a file, with a filename of `logfile2.txt`. This utility program pulls out only the lines with temperature information, and puts them in the new file.

How do we get only the temperature values from these lines? Another Unix utility can help, called `awk`. We can tell it to print only certain columns. It does not really care what the columns contain; it groups letter and digits together and views the spaces as separators. Considering the time-stamp to be column 1, the temperature sensor reading is column 2, the degree units (`F,`) are in column 3, the word `Target:` is column 4, the target temperature is column 5, and we can ignore the rest of the line. Thus, we want columns 2 and 5.

The command below uses the `awk` command to print columns 2 and 5. The less-than sign specifies the file to use as input, and the greater than sign specifies the output file, just like before. It literally prints text between the double quotes, too. As with the `grep` command, this is a command for the operating system's shell, not a MATLAB command.

```
awk '{ print $2", "$5 }' < logfile2.txt > datafile.csv
```

It prints the characters forming the temperature reading, then a comma and a space, then the characters forming the target temperature. We use `.csv` for the extension of the new file, so that we (as well as the computer) will know that it contains data in comma separated value format. Performing this command on the example log shown above results in the following.

```
104.5, 122.0
104.6, 122.0
104.7, 122.0
104.8, 122.0
```

Now we have just the signal data that we need.

12.6.3 How Did It Get So Cold?

With this temperature data, we can make a plot using MATLAB.

```
y = csvread('bb96f.csv');
plot(y)
```

This data reveals something unexpected, as Figure 12.14 shows. The measured temperature sometimes appears to be −1768.0°F. How did it get to be so cold? It did not get that cold, not to mention that this is less than absolute zero, making it a physical impossibility.

A quick inspection of the data, along with some knowledge about the environment, reveals that there are some bad measurements. The data come from a sensor placed in a pot, on top of an electric burner, inside a typical kitchen. This is not some trick environment like the surface of a distant planet. Nor is there enough time for the temperature to change rapidly. The data are recorded either every 3 seconds or every second, depending on the data set. There may be sharp rises in the measured temperature, maybe a room temperature probe is placed inside a pot of hot water. The measured temperature could even fall quickly, too, perhaps the probe is pulled out of the pot. While the *sensed* temperature could change dramatically, the actual temperature does not change quickly.

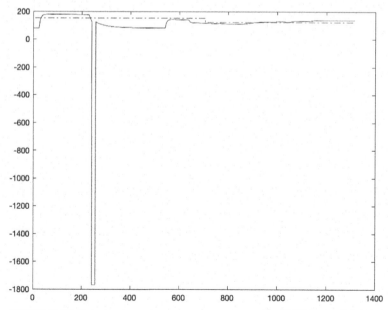

FIGURE 12.14 Plot where some temperatures are supposedly −1768 degrees Fahrenheit.

Any negative measurement is just a bad value, at least in these sets of data. It makes these values even more suspicious when we realize that –1768.0°F is the same as – 1000.0°C, a nice, round number, like the kind of value a programmer might use to indicate a problem. The probes will give these readings when a wire becomes disconnected. In fact, loose wiring was an on-going problem with the early data sets, later fixed by getting better connections, along with soldering.

Thus, whenever we find a bad value, we should not allow it to remain in the data. We do not necessarily want to remove the line, although since each line corresponds to a time value, so throwing out lines makes the elapsed time seem shorter. For the purposes of this study, a better way to handle bad data is to replace it with the previous value. The time scale is short enough that we can be assured that any missing value must be close to the value before and after it. To fix the bad data points, we replace them by repeating good data points, as in the function fixCSV.m. The program looks like the following. It takes two filenames, one to read and one to write, so that it does not overwrite the original data. It makes the assumption that the very first reading will be good. If that is not the case, the worst possible outcome would be that it does not fix a sequence of bad values starting at location 2. The function reads a .csv file, scans the data for bad values, starting with the second measured temperature, and copies the previous value when it finds one. Once the loop ends, the function writes a new .csv file.

```
y1 = csvread(filename);
for k=2:length(y1)
    if (y1(k, 1) <= -1000)
        y1(k,1) = y1(k-1,1);  % Copy the temp.
        y1(k,3) = y1(k-1,3);  % Copy the heat status
    end
end
csvwrite(fname2, y1);
```

Suppose that the data contain several bad values in a row, starting at position n, where $n >= 2$. To keep it simple, imagine that the data are {152, -1768, -1768, -1768, 153}, and let $n = 2$. The function will fix the first bad value at n by copying the previous good value from index $n - 1$. Then it will fix the second bad value at $n + 1$ by copying in the value from the first bad value's index (n). Since that has already been fixed, the good value will repeat again. Next, it will copy the $n + 1$ value to $n + 2$. Finally, the value at $n + 3$ does not need correcting. When finished, the data will be {152, 152, 152, 152, 153}.

Note that this solution works for this particular application, but it may not be acceptable for every data set.

12.6.4 Downsampling

Most of the logs are in 3-second intervals, meaning that there are 3 seconds between each line. However, there are a few that have 1 second intervals. While a 1 second interval provides 3 times as much data, it is not better quality. The temperature does not change rapidly enough to make this sampling rate worthwhile; instead we just have 3 times as much data to store and process. The 3-second interval should not be assumed to be optimal, however. Perhaps an interval of 2 seconds or maybe one of 5 seconds would be a better compromise between the conflicting goals of saving memory and good signal resolution.

To make all resulting signals uniform in timing, we need a way to reduce the signals with 1-second intervals. An easy way to accomplish this is to keep only 1 of every 3 samples. The technical name for this process is *downsampling*. The command below accomplishes this.

```
newy = y(1:3:length(y),:);
```

This may seem a little confusing—remember that `length(y)` gives the number of rows, since that size dominates the dimensions.

Variable `y` holds the array of signal values with a 1-second interval. The range `1:3:length(y)` makes a new array starting at 1 and counting by 3. Suppose that the length happens to be 10. The output below demonstrates how this range works.

```
>> 1:3:10
ans =
     1     4     7    10
```

Thus, we generate an array of rows starting with 1 up to the end, counting by 3. We store the result in `newy`. Doing this allows us to convert data sampled every second to data sampled every 3 seconds. Incidentally, an *upsampling* operation also exists, allowing us to stretch out a signal. Like the previous example of replacing bad data values, upsampling fills in missing information by repeating values.

12.7 ANALYZING THE TEMPERATURE DATA

With the data files available in a pre-processed form, we can now get to solving the problem. In each experiment, the system raises the temperature until it reaches a target, then it keeps the temperature at this level for a set amount of time. However, the problem is not so simple as turning on the heat until the temperature is met, then turning it off. The environment is much cooler than the target temperatures, by as much as 100°F. So the system must periodically re-apply the heat to keep it within range. We know the target temperatures, and can figure out, just by inspecting a plot, where the target temperature changes. Therefore, we know when the heating stages end. But where do they begin?

Our first step is to determine when the target is met, and use this for our start. Then we can figure out how many sample are between the beginning and end, and can calculate the time.

What do we name the function? This has a reverberating affect for later. If we choose a good name, a short one that accurately describes its purpose, there will be no doubt when we run across it later. If we can make its operations general, we might be able to use it in the future for a different application. Just as important, if we choose a name well, we might be able to easily find it at some point in the future when we need it, long after we've forgotten about the problem we are trying to solve now.

Yes, we could rename the function after we name it. This becomes much more difficult once we start using it, however. That is, once we start calling the function from other programs, we would need to make sure to rename it everywhere that we use it. Also, we would want to rename the backup copies and any older versions of it.

When writing a new function, we should write comments for it: What is the function for, what does it do, what inputs and outputs does it have, and how to use it. The first objective is to get a count of the samples when the measurement temperature matches the target. To begin, we have the filename stored in a variable. Since this code will be run over and over again with different filenames, it makes sense to display the filename. Then, load the data.

```
% Set and display a filename
fname = 'data139.csv';
disp(sprintf('Data set is %s', fname));
% Read the .csv file
y = csvread(fname);
% Isolate column 1, and make it a row.
measured = y(:,1).';
% Isolate column 2, and make it a row.
target = y(:,2).';
```

Variable y stores a matrix containing the data from one experiment. Each column represents a different signal, and the number of rows depends on how many samples were recorded. To make things a bit easier, we can copy the first and second columns to variables `measured` and `target`, respectively, representing the temperature that the system measured and the temperature to which it was set.

Next, we need to know when the measured temperature meets the targets. A function called `locateOverlap` was written for this purpose. The target changes infrequently, typically between 2 and 5 times for each data file. Also, the system moves to a new target only after holding the previous target for a set period of time. Thus, we can assume that a changing target temperature means that the stage is complete. It provides us with an end, and implies that the target must have been met at some point before then. So the `locateOverlap` function finds where the target changes, which tells us the end of the previous hold time as well as the start of the transition time. From the transition's start, we can scan along until we find a match between the measurement and the target. All that we really need is the first match after every transition; like a heating system in a home, once the temperature reaches the thermostat's set temperature, it may deviate from that temperature but it will remain close to it. For this data, a "match" occurs when there is 1 degree of difference or less. The `locateOverlap` function returns an array, in this case we store it in the variable z.

```
z = locateOverlap(measured, target);
```

What does z contain? It has the same length as `measured` and `target`. Since it only needs to tell us when the measurement and target overlap, it is a binary signal: it has a 0 for each sample where the measurement has not yet reached the target, and a 1 for every sample after that until the target changes.

Next, we form an array called x that simply indicates the sample number. We plot the `measured` data in blue, then plot `target .* z` on the same figure, as red asterisks. Either the target has not yet been met, and the asterisk for that sample will appear along the *x-axis*, or it has been met and will appear over top of the measured temperature.

```
x = 1:length(measured);
plot(x, measured, 'b');
hold('on');
plot(x, target.*z, 'r*');
```

This way, we can visualize the measured temperature data, as in Figure 12.15.

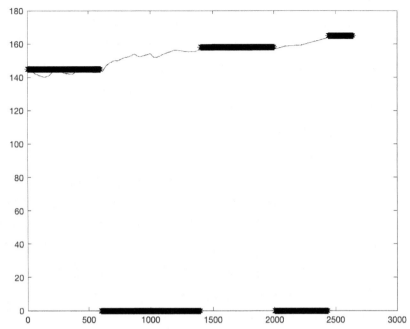

FIGURE 12.15 The measured temperatures (thin) and whether the target has been met (thick). Later, we set the axes to only show the top portion. The $x-axis$ shows the sample numbers, while the $y-axis$ shows the temperature in degrees Fahrenheit.

Now that we have z to tell us what samples correspond to transitions and which ones correspond to hold periods, we can summarize each group. We just need to count the number of samples where z is 0, then count the number of samples where it is 1, then count the number of samples where it is 0 again, etc. We will develop an array called count: every time two consecutive z values are the same, we add to the current index of count. If the values are different, we append a new value onto the count array, initializing it to 0. Variable j is the index to the count array.

It might not be clear why count must be an array. We want it to store the number of repeats in a row, for each set of repeats. We do not know in advance how many repeats will be included. At worst case, every value could be different, so there could be as many repeats (of zero) as there are in the input. Perhaps a couple examples will clarify this. Suppose that we have input of 5, 5, 6, 7, 7. We have 5 in the input twice, then 6 appears only once, then 7 repeats, thus the count array should be 2, 1, 2. It does not matter how many times a value appears in the array as a whole, we need to parse out how many times a value repeats. In other words, input of 5, 5, 6, 5, 5, should generate the same count as before, i.e., 2, 1, 2.

The code to do this appears next. We will examine it in greater detail soon.

```
j = 1;
count(j) = 0;
% Find sum of each stage
for k=2:length(z)
    if (z(k) == z(k-1))
        % Increase count
        count(j) = count(j) + 1;
    else
        % This is a transition
        j = j + 1;
        count(j) = 0;
    end
end
```

Notice that we start k, the index into z, with the value 2. This makes it easy to compare to the current value z(k) with the one to the left of it, z(k-1). When the two values are different, we start a new count. First, we create an example signal, z. Here is an example run.

```
>> z(1:3) = 1;
>> z(4:8) = 0;
>> z(9:12) = 1
z =
  Columns 1 through 9
     1    1    1    0    0    0    0    0    1
  Columns 10 through 12
     1    1    1
```

We see that signal z is a series of 1's, followed by a series of 0's, followed by another series of 1's.

```
>> j = 1;
count(j) = 0;
```

How many of the same values in a row do we have? The following code counts each run. We may only have one run of values, i.e., if all z's values are the same. We start by initializing count(1) to zero. Maybe there will be many elements of count, or maybe not. We can safely assume that there will be at least one element of count. We also assume that z has at least one value. If it does not, the value count(1) will not change from zero. Now we compare every element of z to the element before it, and either add one to the current count, or begin a new count.

```
>>    % Find sum of each stage
      for k=2:length(z)
          if (z(k) == z(k-1))
              % Increase count
              count(j) = count(j) + 1;
          else
              % This is a transition
              j = j + 1;
              count(j) = 0;
          end
      end
```

To recapitulate, we should have an array called count that contains the number of times a value repeated in the array z. Whenever two z values in a row are the same, we increment the count. Otherwise, we start a new count.

```
>> count
count =
     2    4    3
```

We see that we have 2 repeats, then 4 repeats, then 3 repeats. There is one caveat to the above approach, that the counts will always be one lower than they should be. This comes from starting the index at 2, so we never count the first 0 or 1, and again when we switch from counting 1's to counting 0's (or vice-versa) we do not count the first one of the series. Therefore, in the example above that starts with 3 1's, 5 0's, and 4 1's, count is 2, 4, and 3. An easy fix is to simply add 1.

```
>> count = count + 1
count =
     3    5    4
```

The approach that we have, using a for loop to examine each z value, could be done differently. However, we need more information from the z array which makes this approach a good one. We get the count of each series of 0's and 1's, but we do not know whether we started with a 0 or 1, we do not know the starting measured (or target) temperature of each series, and we do not know what index started the series. The z values in the series tell us if we are in a heating phase, or a holding phase (where the system periodically turns on the heat to keep the temperature consistent). To remember all of this, we can alter the code to create several arrays: one for the target temperature of this phase (temp), one for the measured temperature of this phase (mtemp), one to indicate whether it is a holding or heating phase (holding), and finally one to remember where the series starts (index).

```
count(1) = 0;
temp(1) = target(1);
holding(1) = z(1);
% mtemp is the measured temperature
mtemp(1) = measured(1);
index(1) = 1;
% Find sum of each stage
for k=2:length(z)
    if (z(k) == z(k-1))
        % Increase count
        count(j) = count(j) + 1;
    else
        % This is a transition
        j = j + 1;
        count(j) = 0;
        temp(j) = target(k);
        mtemp(j) = measured(k);
        holding(j) = z(k);
        index(j) = k;
    end
end
index(j+1) = length(measured);
```

We add a final entry to index so that it specifies the start and end indices of each phase.

Another detail is that each sample represents 3 seconds of time. Thus, we can convert the `count` array from a number of samples to how many minutes each phase lasted.

```
% Convert count to minutes.
count = count * 3 / 60;
```

With these arrays, it is easy to get and summarize the information we set out to find. The code below completes the task.

```
stage = 1;
for k=1:length(count)
    if (holding(k))
        str=sprintf(...
            ' phase %d: starting at %d hold at %d  for %d minutes', ...
            stage, round(mtemp(k)), round(temp(k)), ...
            round(count(k)));
    else
        str=sprintf(...
            ' phase %d: heating from %d  to  %d took %d minutes', ...
            stage, round(mtemp(k)), round(temp(k)), ...
            round(count(k)));
    end
    disp(str);
    stage = stage + 1;
end
```

It prints a line about each stage, based on whether it is heating to a target temperature, or holding the temperature.

Here is the output when we run the entire program, called `countStageTime`.

```
>> countStageTime
Data set is data139.csv
   phase 1:  starting at 145 hold at 145   for 30 minutes
   phase 2: heating from 144   to      158 took 40 minutes
   phase 3:  starting at 157 hold at 158   for 30 minutes
```

```
phase 4: heating from 157  to     165 took 22 minutes
phase 5:  starting at 164 hold at 165  for 10 minutes
```

Also included with the examples for this text is a program called countStageTimeFromTemps.m, which makes several improvements, including a flag to allow LaTeX output (see Section 14.2 for information about LaTeX). Internally, it stores data using structures/fields.

Later, another program averages information about the different systems that produce the data. In the print-out below, the first word is a description of the pump used, i.e., a larger pump has a higher throughput, and will circulate liquid through the heat exchanger faster, potentially leading to a faster rise in temperature. "Indirect" means that a heat exchanger is used, providing indirect heat. Direct means that the monitored vessel (a steel pot) is directly on a burner. It is possible to not use a pump, if it utilizes a stirring mechanism or a person to stir it. Also, using a large pump does not make sense on the smaller volumes; it would be too powerful.

```
medium direct rose on avg 1.4 deg F / min 13.7 F in 10 min
no_pump direct rose on avg 1.2 deg F / min 12.3 F in 10 min
small direct  rose on avg 1.2 deg F / min 11.5 F in 10 min
large indirect rose on avg 0.9 deg F / min  9.3 F in 10 min
medium indirect rose on avg 0.6 deg F / min  6.4 F in 10 min
small indirect rose on avg 0.5 deg F / min  5.2 F in 10 min
sm/med indirect rose on avg 0.3 deg F / min  3.2 F in 10 min
```

Not every experiment went as planned. Sometimes a pump would clog, leading to it being replaced, which is why at least one experiment used both small and medium pumps.

The data analysis with MATLAB allows us to draw conclusions about the process. Does a larger pump help raise the temperature more quickly? It does: the data consistently show this. Another thing that helps raise the temperature quickly is to use direct heat. The problem with that is that it is harder to control, and there is overshoot. A final consideration is the noise produced by the pumps; the large pump is loud, the medium pump is annoying, and the small pump is often inaudible. So if the planned temperature adjustments are few, the small pump may be the preferred one to use.

12.8 SUMMARY

This chapter deals with problems arising from programming for a particular application, in this case, homebrewing. Sometimes the errors appeared to be daunting, and turned out to be simple mistakes. Other cases showed alternate approaches, such as abandoning an imprecise calculation by using a look-up table instead. Overall, this chapter looked at getting things done, using MATLAB to process data, trouble-shooting some problems, and dealing with the problems as they arose. If homebrewing is not a hobby of yours, what is? One point of this discussion is to encourage you to find your own reasons to use the MATLAB language. Only with experience from trial and error will you master it.

EXERCISES

1. Given a comma separated value such as "BB133temps.csv," make a MATLAB program to plot the average error between the measured temperature (first column) and the target temperature (second column).

2. The `fixCSV.m` program assumes that the first value is OK. What if this assumption is wrong? How would you change that program to deal with that possibility?

3. Assuming that any temperature below freezing or above the boiling point of water must be incorrect, alter a copy of the `fixCSV.m` program to fix those, too.

4. Downsampling and upsampling have applications in other areas, like signal processing. How would you use downsampling to shrink an image? What would an image look like if you upsample it?

PROJECT

- **Specific Gravity**
  The specific gravity (SPG) measures how thick a fluid is, with a reading of 1.000 for water. As sugars such as malt (maltose) are added to a liquid, the SPG reading increases. This measurement is important in beer brewing, since a difference in readings before and after fermentation indicates the alcohol content.

A beer brewer has 4 gallons of wort (unfermented beer), with a specific gravity of 1.060. The brewer adds 1 gallon of water to the wort, which obviously lowers the SPG. After fermentation is complete, the beer measures an SPG of 1.020.

a. Using MATLAB commands, write a small program to calculate the wort's SPG after the water is added.

b. During fermentation, the SPG drops by 0.008 for every one percent of alcohol by volume (as sugars are converted to alcohol and CO_2). Using MATLAB commands, what is the alcohol content of this beer?

c. If the water were not added, the beer would have a stronger alcohol content. Write MATLAB commands to compute the alcohol by volume that the beer would have had, if the water were not added.

d. Write MATLAB commands to display the above results nicely.

13

ADVANCED PROGRAMMING CONCERNS

This chapter discusses solving a few problems, to demonstrate how a problem can grow. We think of computers as fast, and they are, but computation speed is not the only factor to finding a solution quickly. Just as crossing the continent in a car takes many hours regardless of how fast the car is, a computing task that requires many operations is not going to be solved instantly. While we might often ignore the time that a program takes, what do we do when we come back to the computer to find that the program is still not done? If we give it just a few more minutes, will it complete? Or, maybe it will be done after lunch. Should we just leave it running overnight and check back in the morning? Or leave it running over the weekend? Will it ever end, or could it be stuck in an infinite loop? We will look at a few examples.

Imagine that you need to know the maximum value from a list of numbers. For example, if you are making a monthly budget, you might have a list of payments that are seemingly random. A home's natural gas bill is an example, where the amount you pay is based on the amount you use in cooking, heating the house, and heating water in the hot water tank. The amount that you use might vary considerably from month to month. To come up with a maximum payment, you could look through all past payments, and remember the largest one. The worst case in terms of operations for you to find the maximum value is N. That is, if you have a stack of N receipts from the gas company in front of you, you would look through all N of them. If there are 12 of them, you would examine all 12. If there were 100 of them, you would look at all 100. As the problem grows, the worst case in terms of the number of things that you need to do grows at the same rate. For example, if you repeat this for the water bill and have twice as many receipts, you expect it to take about twice as much time. It certainly would not take 10 times as long. In this example, the growth rate is dominated by the number of receipts, N.

13.1 HOW A PROBLEM GROWS

Program `brains.m` finds a partial solution to a puzzle from the television show *Futurama*[1]. The story goes like this: two people switch brains with the aid of a machine, then realize that they cannot switch back, at least not directly. Supposedly, with two more people, they can switch brains between people and end up back in their original bodies.

To represent this, we have an array. The index (position in the array) represents the "body" of the individual, while the array value denotes the "brain." Initially, we start this with 2, 1, 3, 4, ..., representing the condition that people 1 and 2 have switched brains. The goal is to have the indices match the values, meaning the array becomes 1, 2, 3, 4, ...

During an iteration, we can only swap two values, and the swap cannot occur more than once. That is, for any given m and n indices, we can make the swap at most one time. In a problem like this, visualizing how it works allows us to understand it well. Here is an example. Suppose that initially, we have 1, 2, 3 for the array. The problem states that a swap occurs with the first two, resulting in 2, 1, 3. For simplicity, assume that we already have a function called `swap` that will carry out the operation for us, given the array and the two indices. A call to that function would look like the following.

```
myarray = 1:3;                  % 1, 2, 3
myarray = swap(myarray, 1, 2);  % 2, 1, 3
```

At this point, the goal is to find a way to use `swap` to make the array 1, 2, 3 again. (Actually, we could think of this either altruistically or selfishly. For this problem, an altruistic solution means that every value matches its index when finished. A selfish solution would have a much lower bar, where if we find a way to switch the first two back, we declare it a success. If we can find a selfish solution, does this mean that we could also find an altruistic one?) With the array 2, 1, 3, we cannot swap the first two again, so the options for the next swap is limited to `swap(myarray, 1, 3)`, and `swap(myarray, 2, 3)`. Notice that we are dealing with combinations, not permutations. In other words, we cannot consider `swap(myarray, 2, 1)` as an option, since it does exactly the same thing as `swap(myarray, 1, 2)`. As a convention, we will write the lower index first.

---

[1] *Futurama*© 2017 Comedy Partners

Let's consider the possibilities. We could do this.

```
myarray = 1:3;                    % 1, 2, 3
myarray = swap(myarray, 1, 2);    % 2, 1, 3
myarray = swap(myarray, 1, 3);    % 3, 1, 2
myarray = swap(myarray, 2, 3);    % 3, 2, 1
```

At this point, we cannot continue since no valid options remain. And it did not solve the problem. Instead, we could do this, choosing to swap 2 and 3 before swapping 1 and 3.

```
myarray = 1:3;                    % 1, 2, 3
myarray = swap(myarray, 1, 2);    % 2, 1, 3
myarray = swap(myarray, 2, 3);    % 2, 3, 1
myarray = swap(myarray, 1, 3);    % 1, 3, 2
```

This fails to lead us to a solution. We cannot find a solution with an array size of 3, but what if we have size 4, or more? See if you can find a way.

How could the computer know which path to take? It would not. It could, however, try to find a solution, and if it does not work, try another one, and keep trying until it finds a solution or exhausts all possibilities.

How much does the search space change for larger arrays? For the moment, ignore the first swap since it happens automatically as part of the problem. To swap values in an array, the array must have at least 2 values, in which case it performs 1 swap. With 3 values, like the previous example with `myarray`, we can swap (1,2), (1,3), and (2,3) for a total of 3 options, or 1 + 2. Going to 4 values means we can swap (1,2), (1,3), (2,3), (1,4), (2,4), and (3,4), where the next step options become 6, or 1 + 2 + 3. Going from 4 to 5 values means we can swap (1,5), (2,5), (3,5), and (4,5), giving an additional 4 possibilities, 1 + 2 + 3 + 4. Let N be the total number of values in the array. We observe that every time we let the array size (N) increase by 1, we add another $N - 1$ options, i.e., increasing the size from 3 to 4 added ($4 - 1 = 3$) new options, and 4 to 5 added ($5 - 1 = 4$) new options. The total options (number of possible swaps) are thus $1 + 2 + 3 + ... + (N - 1)$. A summation allows us to express this compactly.

$$\text{possible swaps} = \sum_{n=1}^{N-1} n$$

A well-known identity for a similar sum looks like this:

$$\sum_{m=1}^{M} m = \frac{M(M+1)}{2}.$$

If we replace M with $N - 1$, and m with n, we can re-write the number of possible swaps.

$$\text{possible swaps} = \sum_{n=1}^{N-1} n = \frac{(N-1)(N)}{2}$$

We can use a bit of code to verify this.

```
str = '';
for N=2:7
    swaps = (N-1)*N/2;
    str = strcat(str, sprintf(' %d',swaps));
end
disp(str);
```

Running this code generates the following output.

```
1 3 6 10 15 21
```

From this, we can conclude that the expression `(N-1)*N/2` does tell us the number of possible swaps, and agrees with the preceding analysis. This information comes in handy when we "scale" the problem by allowing it to grow to a large size. The number of possible swaps gives us a worst-case scenario, namely, if a solution exists, but it happens to be the very last one that we try, how many calculations must we do to find it? Given an array length of N, we can quickly calculate the worst case. With some knowledge of how long our computer takes to perform a swap, we could even get an approximate time to completion. Be aware that some problems grow at an unsustainable rate. In that case, the computer will attempt to carry out all of the operations, even if it would need years to finish. Here, we have an expression for the number of operations, and could use it to find an approximation of the run time, or at least whether the program needs a reasonable time to complete.

13.2 FINDING A VALUE IN A SORTED LIST

Now consider a problem of finding data in a sorted list. Before computers and cell-phones became house-hold items, people had home phones. If you needed to call a business, you could find the number to dial in the business phone book: a large book provided by the phone company with every phone number listed in alphabetical order according to the name of the business. Finding a business in the phone book is an example of finding data in a sorted list. Assuming that you know the name of the business, you could look in the book to get their phone number. If you've never done this before, you might turn to the very first page and scan the names on it to find the one you are looking for. However, you would quickly realize that the names on the first page all start with the letter "a," and the book might be hundreds of pages. If the business you want starts with an "s," you would quickly adapt by skipping to a page around the middle, and looking at the first entry on it. If it starts with a letter before "s," then you know that you do not need to look further in any page before this one. Now pick a page in the middle of the remaining ones, and compare the first entry to the name you want. If it begins with a letter after "s," you can eliminate the pages after it. With every comparison, we are able to narrow our focus to half of the remaining pages. Suppose that the phone book is 512 pages long. We could open it to the middle, compare the name at the top of the page to the name we are searching for, and know whether it is in the 256 pages on the left or the 256 pages on the right. So now the search space is half of what it was: with one comparison, we narrowed it down to 256 pages. Repeating this process, we jump to the middle of the remaining 256 pages, compare to what we want, and eliminate half of them, bringing the search size down to 128 pages. With another comparison, we eliminate another 64 pages. Then we eliminate 32 pages, then 16, then 8, then 4, then 2, then 1. We are left with only 1 page to search. Thus, with only 8 comparisons, we can find the page the contains the name of the business from a phone book of 512 pages. It may take a few more operations to find the name on the page, but we could use the same algorithm by comparing to the one in the middle, then eliminating the top half or the bottom half, and repeating this process. To keep things simple, you can just imagine that every business has their own full-page entry in the book. The point is that the worst-case number of operations is based on N, the number of entries in the list, where we eliminate $N/2$ entries with the first comparison, then $(N/2)/2$ with the next one, then $(N/2/2)/2$ with the next one, and continue until we are left with 1. With three comparisons, we narrow the search list down to

$$(N/2/2)/2 = N/2^3.$$

With a fourth comparison, we are left with $N/2^4$ values to consider, then $N/2^5$ after the fifth comparison. Generalizing, we can say that after p comparisons, we have $N/2^p$ entries left in our search space. How many comparisons do we need? We need to keep doing this until there is only one entry left. In other words:

$$N/2^p = 1,$$

or

$$N = 2^p.$$

In asking how many comparisons, we want to know the value of p. The value for N should already be given to us, for example, we could simply look at the page number of the last page in the phone book. To get p by itself, we use the logarithm identity that

$$a = b^c$$

is equivalent to

$$c = log_b a,$$

and substituting our variables in, we can say that

$$N = 2^p$$

is equivalent to

$$p = log_2 N.$$

Now we can talk about the worst case, where we know how many operations we need to find an entry in a sorted list. Given $N = 512$, we can narrow down the phone book to a single page in

```
>> log2(512)
ans =
     9
```

operations. This is a very efficient algorithm, called a *binary search*, and the worst-case number of operations is $log_2 N$.

In discussing the worst-case growth, the idea is to talk about the number of operations in an approximate fashion. If there are N numbers in our data set, and it takes, perhaps 473 operations when N is 400 and, say 873 operations when N is 800, we represent this as $N + 73$. We broadly speak of the worst case as N operations, and denote it as $O(N)$, spoken as "order of N," in what we call "big-O" notation. The growth rate should give us an idea of the number of operations of the algorithm; it does not have to give a precise time estimate.

13.3 SORTING

Sorting is an iconic $O(N^2)$ problem. To sort a list of numbers, we can scan the list, and switch any two values appearing out of order. After scanning all values, repeat the scan, until no switches need to be made. We call this the "bubble-sort" algorithm, since any large value will move up the list like a bubble rising in water. The worst possible case occurs when the list has all values in the reverse order. We scan the data $N - 1$ times, and each scan takes $N - 1$ comparisons. Thus $(N - 1) \times (N - 1) = N^2 - 2N + 1$ or just $O(N^2)$. Actually, we can save some comparisons if we realize that the largest value will be at the end of the list after the first scan. So the necessary comparisons reduce by one every scan. However, this does not really help. We must do $(N - 1)$ comparisons, then $(N - 2)$, then $(N - 3)$ and so forth, down to $(N - (N - 1)) = 1$. The sum of all those comparisons becomes $(N - 1)$ down to 1, or equivalently, 1 up to $(N - 1)$. A sum from 1 to M can be computed by the formula $M(M + 1)/2$, so if we let $M = N - 1$, we get

$$(N - 1)(N - 1 + 1)/2 = (N^2 - N)/2.$$

The N^2 term still dominates the number of operations.

The bubble sort is the kind of solution that a programmer would think of first. Can it be improved? This question was an active area of algorithm research in the early days of computing. Yes, many other sorting algorithms out perform the bubble sort. We use it here for illustrative purposes.

13.4 THE TRAVELING SALESMAN PROBLEM

Now let's consider the problem of planning a trip with many different stops. Suppose that we plan to travel to Atlanta, Boston, Chicago, Denver, El Paso, and Fort Lauderdale. Although the order does not matter, we want to minimize the cost. Given the prices to travel from any city to any other city, how many comparisons do we need to make to find the cheapest possible route?

The city names are purposefully chosen to be representable by the first letter. If we visit them in alphabetical order, which is one possible solution, these are ABCDEF. To keep things simple, we assume that we only visit each city once. Also, there may not be any logical reason for the pricing. Before we get to figure out how many possible solutions there are, let's look at a subset to see how it grows. With 2 cities, we have only 2 solutions: AB or BA. With 3 cities, we have 6 solutions: ABC, ACB, BAC, BCA, CAB, and CBA. With a fourth city, the pattern for the number of solutions emerges. Considering just the solution of ABC with D added gives us DABC, ADBC, ABDC, and ABCD. Realizing that ABC is just one of 6 possible solutions, and that we got 4 solutions from it when including D. In other words, going from 3 cities to 4 means that the number of potential solutions grows by a factor of 4. We already saw that going from 2 cities to 3 means that potential solutions grew from 2 to 2 × 3. Going from 3 to 4 means we now have 2 × 3 × 4 potential solutions. The pattern should be clear that every time we add a new city, the number of potential solutions grows by the new total number of cities. That is, for N cities, there are N ! possible solutions. With 6 cities, there are 720 possibilities to check to find the cheapest one. While this is a reasonable amount, what happens if we want to visit one city in every state? For fun, see how long it will take your computer to check every one of these possible solutions, assuming that it does not have to do anything else, and can check a potential solution in every clock cycle. (For reference, a 1.4 GHz clock speed is 1.4 × 10^9 cycles per second.) This problem is a generalization of the traveling salesman problem, and program `TSPcentury.m` gives details about it.

13.5 EVALUATING INTEGRALS

Suppose that you want to paint a wall. A trip to the hardware store inevitably leads to the question "how much paint do you need?" According to a well-known paint maker, "One gallon can of paint will cover up to 400 square feet" [https://www.glidden.com/how-much-paint-do-i-need]. A rectangular surface is straightforward; we just multiply the height by the width to get the area in square feet. What if it's more complicated than that, like what if you work with an artist who paints a curve on the wall, centered at five feet from the floor, and requests paint for the area from the curve to the floor? He says that the unpainted section is the area under the curve, which can be approximated by a function. How do you figure out the area, given a reasonably good description of the curve and length of the wall? If we know (or can find) the area under the curve, centered at $y = 0$, we can add the rectangular area (5 times the length), and determine how much paint to get. Yes, this example is far-fetched, although it illustrates how something can be solved by an integral.

13.5.1 MATLAB's Integral Function

Sometimes solving a problem requires advanced mathematics, like evaluating integrals. MATLAB can certainly accomplish this. Suppose that we want to evaluate the integral

$$\int_0^\infty \frac{sin(x)}{x} dx.$$

For this particular example, a good calculus source will give us the analytical answer, i.e.,

$$\int_0^\infty \frac{sin(x)}{x}\,dx = \frac{1}{2}\,\pi.$$

Let's imagine that we do not know this. Can we get MATLAB to calculate it? MATLAB has an `integral` function that can help.

```
>> help integral
integral  Numerically evaluate integral.
    Q = integral(FUN,A,B) approximates the integral of function
    FUN from A to B ...
```

To use it, we must define a *function handle*, as in the following line.

```
>> f = @(x) sin(x)./x
f =
    function_handle with value:
      @(x)sin(x)./x
```

The `@(x)` indicates that this function has x as a parameter. Notice that we use `./` for the division, since we want sin(*x*)/*x* for each individual x value, not as an array of `sin(x)` values divided by an array of x values. In other words, it will not work with a `/` instead of `./` in this example. Now, we can pass this function handle to the `integral` function. We also use `Inf` for infinity, a special number of type `double`. Let *myArea* be the integral's result.

```
>> myArea = integral(f, 0, Inf)
Warning: Reached the limit on the maximum number of intervals in
use. Approximate bound on error is  4.9e+00. The integral may
not exist, or it may be difficult to approximate numerically to
the requested accuracy.
> In integralCalc/iterateScalarValued (line 372)
  In integralCalc/vadapt (line 132)
  In integralCalc (line 83)
  In integral (line 88)
myArea =
    3.4497
```

This does not appear to have worked, but it gave us an answer. Is it close to the known value?

```
>> pi/2
ans =
    1.5708
```

No, the computed value does not match the analytical one. Let's try another approach. Instead of evaluating to `Inf`, use another large number.

```
>> myArea = integral(f, 0, 100000)
myArea =
    1.5708
```

Comparing to the analytical value, we see that this works well.
Let's try this again, checking the precision.

```
>> format long
>> disp(pi/2)
    1.570796326794897
>> disp(integral(f, 0, 100000))
    1.570806320400103
```

We see that this gives a fairly good result, up to 4 digits beyond the decimal point. What if we use a slightly smaller or larger end value?

```
>> disp(integral(f, 0, 100000-3))
    1.570786382438481
>> disp(integral(f, 0, 100000+3))
    1.570786483957630
```

Interestingly, both of these answers are not quite as good as the previous one. In the next section, we will see why this happens.

13.5.2 Calculating This Result Ourselves

Next, let's examine how we could calculate it ourselves.

```
>> x = 0:1000;
>> r = sum(sin(x) ./ x)
r =
    NaN
```

The problem is that when $x = 0$, we divide by it, resulting in `NaN`. It actually only affects the first value, as the following code demonstrates.

```
>> z = sin(x) ./ x;
>> z(1:4)
ans =
        NaN    0.8415    0.4546    0.0470
```

Once we have NaN, anything added to it also produces NaN.

Now, let's visualize this. Since $f(0)$ is a bit of a problem, because we cannot divide by 0, let's use something really close, like $f(0.001)$ instead.

```
>> t = 0.001; sin(t)/t
ans =
    1.0000
```

What if we get even closer to 0, say 0.000001?

```
>> t = 0.000001;  sin(t)/t
ans =
    1.0000
```

We could even plot this function for very small values of t. It should be clear that our answer for $f(t)$ should be 1 when t is very small.

```
f = @(x) sin(x) ./ x;
x = 0.001:0.1:1000;
fx = f(x);
plot(x, fx)
title('plot of sin(x)./x');
xlabel('x');
ylabel('f(x)');
```

Notice that the code computes fx as f(x), as if we had defined a function called f within a file called f.m. MATLAB treats "anonymous" functions such as f a lot like a regular function.

We can get a good sense of what this function does by plotting it. To see only the first 200 values (corresponding to $x = 20$, since the range defining x uses 0.1 for the step size), we plot only a subset.

```
plot(x(1:200), fx(1:200));
```

Then, to view the last 200 values, we plot fx, and use the axis command to restrict what we see.

```
plot(x, fx);
axis([980, 1000, -0.01, 0.01]);
```

Now, we can find the sum. Figure 13.1 shows the plot of sin(x)/x for values from almost 0 to 1000. Next, Figure 13.2 presents a close-up of the first values, up to $x = 20$, and Figure 13.3 shows the last values. We see from the plots that function sin(x)/x rapidly approaches 0, but does not settle down. It oscillates back and forth across the x-axis, changing the sum a tiny amount every time, as Figure 13.3 shows.

If we calculate the sum of fx, we get the following.

```
>> sum(fx)
ans =
    16.191933139703821
```

This does not look correct, because it is 10 times what it should be. Remember that we use an increment of 0.1, meaning that a sum will have 10 values by the time we get to 1. Think of it this way: if we have a piece of paper 2 feet tall and 1 foot wide, we say that it has an area of 2 square feet. If we cut the paper to produce 10 strips, each 2 feet tall, the pieces still have a combined area of 2 square feet. Cutting the paper does not change its area, and likewise, dividing a function into smaller units does not alter the area under the curve, although it may give us a better approximation. Thus, the value should be 1.61919, close to pi/2, but not quite the same. Figure 13.4 shows the sum of the sin(x)/x function as x gets larger. We observe that it hovers around 1.61919.

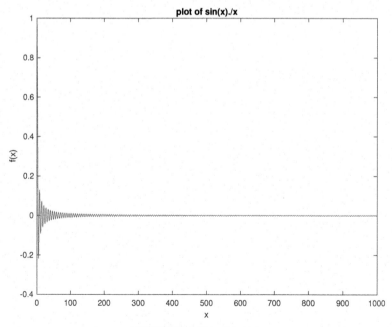

FIGURE 13.1 Plot of sin(x)/x.

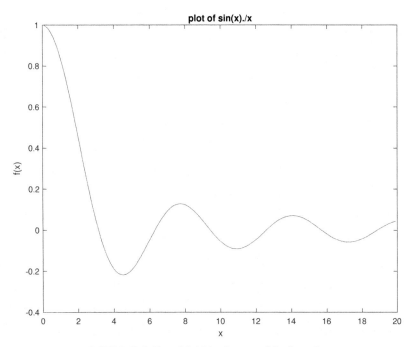

FIGURE 13.2 Plot of sin(x)/x, close-up of the first values.

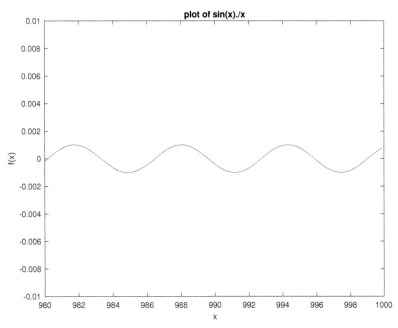

FIGURE 13.3 Plot of sin(x)/x, close-up of the last computed values.

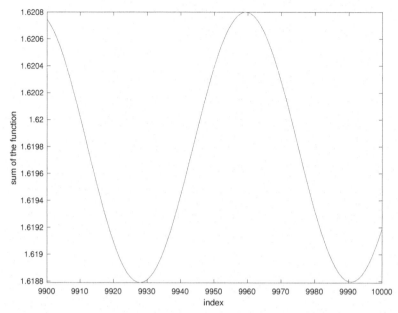

FIGURE 13.4 The sum of sin(x)/x, for positive x values with an increment of 0.01, changes a bit but does not grow.

Can we do better at approximating the area under the integral? Obviously, adding more values to the end does not help in this case, since the function approaches zero. As we saw in Figure 13.2, this function looks interesting at the beginning. What if we utilize a finer increment value?

```
>> N = 100;
>> x = 0.001:1/N:1000;
>> fx = f(x);
>> sum(fx/N)
ans =
    1.574229818598277
```

With 100 samples of the function per unit, we divide the sum by 100. The result is pretty good. What about 1000 samples?

```
>> N = 1000;
>> x = 0.001:1/N:1000;
>> fx = f(x);
>> sum(fx/N)
ans =
    1.569733535455312
```

This gives a better approximation. If we go beyond this, we also need to examine where to start as the initial x value. In other words, the gap between 0 and 0.001 suddenly becomes an important detail.

```
>> N = 10000;
>> x = 1/N:1/N:1000;
>> fx = f(x);
>> sum(fx/N)
ans =
   1.570183163313190
```

As we see, the answer does get closer to the analytical solution.

13.5.3 A Slow and a Fast Way to Find the Change

This discussion hinges on the way that the function's sum changes over time. To visualize it, it makes sense to evaluate the function many times, and to find the sum each time. We can start this with a few definitions.

```
f = @(x) sin(x) ./ x;
x = 0.001:0.1:1000;
N = length(x);   % 10000;
fx = f(x);
```

This sets up a function handle, f, along with the range x, and the variable N to remember the range's length. Then it evaluates the function for each x value, and stores the results in fx. From this, we can find the sum of fx, which gives us an approximation of the integral. How does this approximation change?

MATLAB can calculate that readily. We can set up a new array, called mysum, that contains the sums of all fx values up to that point. In other words, mysum(2) has the value sum(fx(1:2)), mysum(3) has the value sum(fx(1:3)), mysum(4) has the value sum(fx(1:4)), etc. With this array, we can look for the trend; do the values get larger, smaller, or stay about the same? Here we have a straightforward way to implement the mysum array.

```
>> clear mysum
   tic
   for last=1:length(fx)
       mysum(last) = sum(fx(1:last));
   end
   toc
Elapsed time is 0.168471 seconds.
```

The first line, `clear mysum`, is not needed if the array does not exist. However, allocating memory for the variable takes some time, and this creates a fair basis for comparison. We use the `tic` and `toc` functions to find the elapsed time. As we observe, this particular run took 168 ms.

Now let's try this again. The straightforward approach wastes time re-computing the same things again and again. As mentioned previously, `mysum(4)` has the value `sum(fx(1:4))`, but we can re-state this as `sum(fx(1:3)) + fx(4)`, or even as `mysum(3) + fx(4)`. Why re-compute `mysum(3)`? This key insight means that we can re-write the loop as follows:

```
>> clear mysum
   tic
   mysum(1) = fx(1);
   for last=2:length(fx)
       mysum(last) = mysum(last-1) + fx(last);
   end
   toc
Elapsed time is 0.009962 seconds.
```

When run, we get the result within 10 ms, a small fraction of the time compared to the first implementation. And, as we saw with the growth of algorithmic complexity, this more efficient way looks more and more appealing as the number of inputs (N) increase. By the way, examining the values in `mysum` reveals that they do stay about the same.

13.5.4 Evaluating Our Own Function as an Integral

In an earlier example, we saw that we could set a function handle, then call the `integral` function to evaluate it. Could we do this with a function that we define? Yes.

Suppose that we have the following function defined.

```
function result = g(x)
if (x < 0)
    result = 0;
elseif (x > 5)
    result = 0;
else
    result = 2;
end
```

We can set up a function handle to it, with the next line.

```
f = @g;
```

Notice that this omits the `(x)`, since the computer already has this information specified in the line with the `function` keyword. Now we can pass that function handle to the `integral` function.

```
integral(f, -100, 100, 'ArrayValued', true)
```

Like before, this evaluates the integral from the starting to the ending values. As one of several, optional parameters, `ArrayValued` informs the `integral` function that we want to set it to `true`, which means it will call the function with a scalar argument.

Could we rewrite the function to work with non-scalar inputs? Of course, and that would look something like the following.

```
function result = g2(x)
result = ((x >= 0) & (x <= 5)) * 2;
```

Now we can call it with an array. The two function calls below illustrate the difference between the functions `g` and `g2`.

```
>> disp(g(-1:6))
    2
>> disp(g2(-1:6))
    0    2    2    2    2    2    2    0
```

Clearly, the latter one works properly for an input array. Now we find the integral of it, without having to pass the extra parameters to the `integral` function.

```
f = @g2;
integral(f, -100, 100)
```

The computer returns the value 10.0000 in either case. Realizing that the function simply defines a rectangle 5 units long and 2 units high, the integral gives us the area.

Finally, consider the following function, `g3`. It finds the area under the curve, for two functions added together. The first is simply a rectangular area, perhaps 5 by 10, although we do not specify the length (e.g., 10) here. The second is the $\sin(x)/x$ function, where we assume units of feet for x instead of time.

```
function result = g3(x)
result1 = (x >= 0) * 5;
% define x2 to be 0.0001 any place where x is 0
```

```
x2 = (x == 0) .* 0.0001;
% Now redefine x to be 0.0001 wherever it was 0.
x = x + x2;
% result2 should not have a NaN value
result2 = sin(x)./x;
% Add the two results, to return.
result = result1 + result2;
```

The first part, result1, appears much like the previous examples except for a height of 5 and an implied length. The second part defines a temporary variable x2 to be the same length as x, and zero value, except where x itself is zero. In that case, we give it the value 0.0001. This approximates zero and yet does not introduce a divide-by-zero error. Next, it redefines x to add x2, meaning that x changes to 0.0001 only in the case where it has a zero value. An example should help to clarify this idea.

```
>> x = -1:1
x =
    -1    0    1
>> x2 = (x == 0) .* 0.0001;
>> x = x + x2
x =
   -1.0000    0.0001    1.0000
```

Here, we can see that the first and last values of x do not change, but the zero value becomes 0.0001. With the input x guaranteed to contain non-zero values, we use it in the sin(x)./x calculation, and store the result in result2. Finally, we return the sum of those two results.

Now let's compute the area. Notice that the integral has bounds of 0 and 10, since we assume that the wall has 10 feet in length. Actually, the g3 function defines result1 as non-zero only after 0, while result2 could stretch from negative infinity to positive infinity. While we could evaluate this with a lower bound less than zero, the function would not work for this purpose without some editing.

```
>> f = @g3;
>> disp(integral(f, 0, 10))
    51.6583
```

We get the result of about 52. Returning to the idea of finding the area for paint, a gallon would provide seven times more that the amount we need. A smaller, and cheaper, quart-sized can should do the job.

13.6 SUMMARY

Is a software solution scalable from a small number of test cases to a real-world data set that could easily have millions of entries? We can time the execution of a MATLAB program with commands like `tic`, `toc`, and `cputime`, to know how long it takes on test data. However, sometimes we need to analyze a program's performance in more depth than simply timing it. Algorithmic analysis enables us to study how growing data affects our software, giving us an upper bound on the number of operations. If it runs slowly, why not add more processors? MATLAB supplies a `parfor` command that can split a work-load among many processors, and the `gpuArray` allows MATLAB to work with graphical processing units (GPUs, see `help gpuArray` for more information). But parallel processing only divides the number of operations by a constant. In other words, a program that takes years to complete still has an unacceptable run-time even when split between hundreds of processors. Can the algorithm be made more efficient? That approach makes more sense than just adding hardware in the form of processors, memory, graphics cards, etc. A famous example of an algorithm is the fast Fourier Transform, which cleverly rearranges calculations to find the equivalent of the discrete Fourier Transform, while bringing the number of operations down from $O(N^2)$ to $O(N \log N)$. See the `fft` function's help text for more information.

Algorithmic growth is an important topic, and an advanced programming concern. When we demand a solution to a problem, we implicitly desire it to be as fast as possible. Sometimes data grows in such a way that a program does not scale, and to deal with this, the programmer must understand why. The traveling salesman problem presents a classic example of extreme growth. While we could easily write a program to solve the problem, the number of potential solutions quickly grows, so that a test of 6 cities completes in a reasonable time, but a test of 600 cities does not, as the following analysis shows.

```
>> disp(factorial(6))
   720
>> disp(factorial(600))
   Inf
```

In situations like these, we may be able to narrow the search space. Or we may use another algorithm to find a good, fast solution, even if it may be suboptimal.

EXERCISES

1. For a given string of several unique characters, like "abc," make a function that outputs all unique permutations of the characters. How many lines does it output with a 3-character input? How many lines does it output with a 4-character input, a 5-character input, and an N-character input? What is the growth rate?

2. For a given string of several characters that might not be unique, like "aba," make a function that outputs all unique permutations of the characters. For example, "aba" as input should result in "aba," "aab," "baa." What is the growth rate? Is it different than the worst-case growth rate when all of the characters are unique?

3. The Fast Fourier Transform (FFT) uses $n \, log_2(n)$ operations, compared to the Discrete Fourier Transform (DFT) which has n^2 operations. Both of these give the same results. MATLAB has a function for the fft, as shown below.

    ```
    >> a = rand(1, 1000000);
    >> tic; c = fft(a); toc
    Elapsed time is 0.052091 seconds.
    ```

    The elapsed time on your computer will likely be different. Find how long this takes on your computer, by repeating the computation 10 times, and finding the average elapsed time. Based on this time, consider what it would be like if your computer were to use a DFT function instead. How much longer would the elapsed time be?

PROJECT

*   **Growth of a Problem**
    What is the maximum amount of money you can have without being able to make change for a dollar? (This problem has been circulating on-line since at least 2000, but is likely much older.) E.g.:

    3Q 3D 0N 0P = 105 cents, cannot make change

    3Q 2D 2N 0P = 105 cents, can make change

    Write a program, with related functions as needed, to solve this.

Historically, the United States has had other coins, such as the half cent, the two-cent piece, and the three-cent piece. Suppose that the US starts minting a three-cent piece again, causing you to revise your solution. How many comparisons does the solution make now? How much would the problem grow with the addition of a three-cent piece?

14

OTHER USEFUL COMPUTING TOOLS

MATLAB is an accessible programming language, and scientists often use it in research, both inside and outside of computer science. For some students, a MATLAB programming class may be the only exposure to computer science outside of a "literacy" type of survey course. This chapter covers a few other technologies that you may need to use with MATLAB. Among other things, it covers Unix, which has been the predominant operating system for scientific applications. If you go to work in a bio-informatics lab, there is a good chance that you will work with a Unix/Linux-based workstation.

14.1 LINUX AND OTHER TOOLS

Linux is a version of the Unix operating system, developed for the Personal Computer (PC) architecture. To fully appreciate this, we first need a bit of history. When computers first made their way into the home, there were many different possibilities. Computer makers included Apple, Atari, Texas Instruments, Commodore Business Machines (CBM), Timex/Sinclair, International Business Machines (IBM), and Tandy Radio Shack (TRS), among others. Each had their own hardware design and software, and were incompatible with each other. For example, the (optional) diskette drive for the Commodore 64 might work with the Commodore VIC-20 or Commodore Amiga, but it would not work with a TRS-80. IBM did a great job selling their computers, to the point where their "PC" became standard. The term had been used before this to describe computers for the individual, as opposed to the very large and expensive computers that a business might buy. The hardware designs were proprietary, meaning that one company could not copy the same design that another company used without risking serious legal problems. But IBM did something innovative; they licensed other companies to copy their hardware, and the "IBM PC Compatible" market became very popular. Software and even hardware parts were compatible, instead of being locked in by only a single vendor. As the market evolved, some computer makers quit completely, while others copied the PC architecture: Commodore and Tandy both had their version of the IBM PC compatible. These days, only Apple is left making computers. Companies like Dell, Hewlett Packard, and Compaq continue to make IBM PC compatible computers, even though IBM does not. Interestingly, Apple started making computers based on the Intel microprocessor in 2006. Intel microprocessors formed the "brains" in the PC architecture since the first IBM PC.

Classes in computer science, even in the 1990s, talked about the different types of computers: super-computers, mainframes, minicomputers and microcomputers, ordered in terms of power and price. The lowly microcomputer, once essentially a toy, grew drastically in power while keeping a low price. The distinctions between computer types blurred and became obsolete. Unix was the predominant operating system for the power computers of the past, and is still used today for high-end servers, workstations, and parallel processing machines. As the microcomputers gained in power, a college student named Linus Torvalds developed a project to make a version of Unix for the PC, and thus Linux came about.

Richard Stallman developed the free software movement in the 1980s. Free software like "gcc," a compiler for the C language, was developed under the GNU Project. It is licensed under the GNU Project's philosophy, allowing people to liberally use, examine, modify, and share copies. The famous saying is that "you should think of 'free' as in 'free speech,' not as in 'free beer'," [http://www.gnu.org/philosophy/free-sw.html]. Yes, it is possible to charge money for "free" software of this nature. For example, why spend the night downloading code and trying to configure it to work properly, if someone already did it and is willing to sell a DVD with all necessary software, including step-by-step instructions, for a reasonable price? Or perhaps the purchase of free software from a company comes with a year's worth of customer support. The GNU Project and Linux are tightly linked, for example, the "gcc" program comes with most Linux installations.

Linus Torvalds did a couple of revolutionary things with his project. He released his code for free, like Richard Stallman's GNU Project. Second, the source code was made available on the Internet allowing people from all over the world to add to his project. In keeping with the free software philosophy, improvements to this open-source code are made available to all. The Linux kernel (the core part of the operating system) has been packaged with utility programs and nice user interfaces, and released for sale by companies like Red Hat. Sun has its own Linux distribution, which is interesting since they also are well know for their Solaris (Unix) operating system. Other big companies like IBM have come to back Linux.

Apple has an interesting operating system. With the release of OS X, they incorporated the Unix version called Berkeley Software Distribution (BSD). While this is technically not Linux, there are many similarities. A user who is familiar with one will find the other almost identical when it comes to commands typed at the terminal.

There are some nice features of Linux/Unix systems, such as access permissions enforced by the operating system. For example, the system can easily be set up to keep an inexperienced user from deleting important system files. This also makes it much harder for computer viruses to do damage or spread. As an example, a recent "virus" for OS X required the user to enter his password before it could spread. In summary, Linux is an operating system that runs on the PC architecture, meaning that home users can have a Unix-like operating system.

14.1.1 Libre Office (also Apache Open Office)

A major concern for anyone who buys a computer is what the computer can do for him. A few applications are prominent, namely word processors, spreadsheets, and presentation makers. Collectively, we call these products an office suite since they are typically used in the workplace. As the name suggests, Libre Office is an open-source collection of these programs.

The word processing program (Writer) reads and writes Microsoft Word files, the presentation software (Impress) reads and writes Microsoft Powerpoint files, and the spreadsheet software (Calc) can work with Microsoft Excel files. Libre Office's native storage formats are open, which means that any programmer with enough skill and patience can write a program to read and write these files. The state of Massachusetts recently proposed requiring all state documents to be in an open format [William M. Bulkeley, "Massachusetts Proposes Open Document Format," The Wall Street Journal, September 1, 2005, online: `https://www.wsj.com/articles/SB112561152150829537`]. This makes sense from a citizen's point of view;

the state should not require that citizens have a particular, proprietary software package to read and write state documents.

By the way, Adobe's portable document format (PDF) is an open standard. Libre Office (along with the former Open Office, and the related StarOffice) allow people running Linux/Unix to have an open-source office suite. These applications do the sorts of tasks you might expect to find in the typical office: word processing, spreadsheets, and presentations.

14.1.2 Firefox and JavaScript

The first web browsers ran on the X Window System, on Unix systems. A browser called Mosaic was later developed into Netscape, which was developed into Mozilla's Firefox. This open-source software has some configurable features, such as extensions that disable Flash programs. While Macromedia/ Adobe Flash allows interesting content including animation and games, this can be quite distracting when automatically downloaded and displayed, not to mention security concerns. Autoplay of other video or audio can be disabled, too. Instead, the user will see an icon that can be clicked to download and display it. Firefox, like most modern browsers, runs JavaScript, a language that web pages invoke to configure the appearance, or respond to user's interactions. Even games have been written in JavaScript, accessible through web pages (one example can be found at `http://hallertau.cs.gsu.edu/~mweeks/balloons/balloons3.html`).

14.1.3 Shell Programming

The Linux/Unix environment provides a great deal of flexibility with the command line interface (CLI), as well as the better known graphical user interface (GUI). Both provide a way to interact with the computer. An analogy to imagine for the command line interface is verbally giving orders, where you specify what to do followed by any parameters. A graphical user interface is more like using your hand to signal the commands. Some tasks are easier to do with one interface than the other.

A command line interface (also called a terminal window) allows you to execute commands, much like the MATLAB interface. In fact, on some systems you might start MATLAB from the command line interface. You can put several commands in a file called a shell script. The *shell* refers to the terminal's interpreter, for example, `echo $SHELL` shows which shell (such as `bash`) the terminal uses. Shell scripts allow for variables and have some input and output capabilities, similar to MATLAB programs. There are many powerful programs available to a shell script, much like the functions that come with MATLAB. The guiding philosophy behind the programs available at the command line is to do one thing, but do it quietly and well. Examples include `sort`, `grep`, `sed`, and `awk`, which respectively sort data, look for a pattern, find and replace, and pattern processing. For more information, try the built-in help feature `man` *command* at the prompt, short for consulting the "manual." Note that a shell script can have variables, conditional (`if`) statements, loops (`while` and `for`), input, output, and even user-defined functions.

Other examples of available command line programs include file editing (`vi` and `emacs`), electronic mail (`mail` or `pine`), and access to remote computers with secure file transport protocol (`sftp`) and secure shell (`ssh`). The `sftp` program is great for moving files from one computer to another. The related `ssh` program allows you to remotely connect to a computer and execute commands on it, as long as it is on the network (or Internet). With *X Windows* forwarding set up correctly, you can access the remote computer graphically. The X Window System is a way for programs to specify graphics to the computer, developed at the Massachusetts Institute of Technology in the mid-1980s. For more information, see the X.Org Foundation (`https://X.Org`). That is, you can have the remote computer display graphics on your local computer, and accept keyboard and mouse input as if you were in front of the remote machine. This may be slow, depending on your network connection. The `sftp` and `ssh` programs effectively replace the much older and non-encrypted file transport protocol (ftp) and telnet programs, respectively.

14.1.4 An Example Using Shell Commands

You might wonder why someone would interact with the computer's operating system through a terminal window, when a graphical user interface could be used instead. The following code shows an example. It utilizes the vertical bar to "pipe" the output from one command into the input of the next command. The dollar sign ("$") represents the terminal's command prompt.

```
$ ls */*pdf | grep "_ " | awk '{ print "mv -i "$1"\\ "$2" "$1$2
}' > foo
$ chmod 700 foo
$ ./foo
```

This paragraph describes what the commands do step by step, although the important point is what these commands accomplish together. The `ls` command finds all files that match the pattern `*/*.pdf`, meaning every file-name in the first level of subdirectories that ends with the ".pdf" extension. The `grep` command takes this as input, and outputs only the ones that match the pattern of an underscore followed by a space ("_ "). Next, `awk` receives the input, and prints the text "`mv -i`" followed by the first string on the line passed to it, then a backslash (using two in a row to indicate that it's a special case), and a space, then the second string, another space, and then the first two strings together. Given the input `filename_ .pdf`, this results in the string `mv -i filename_\ .pdf filename.pdf`, a command instructing the operating system to move (rename) a file, but inform us if one by the new name already exists. The backslash must be there, so that the computer knows that space following it should be included as part of the filename. Otherwise, since a space works as a delimiter, it would treat "`filename_`" as the first file-name, and ".`pdf`" as the second one, then generate an error when it gets to what appears to be a third one. These `mv` instructions are stored in a file called "foo," a place-holder typically used alongside the name "bar," both deriving from an acronym meaning messed up beyond all repair (or alternately, recognition). Although the expression is not one to use in polite company, "foo" and "bar" have found their way into countless examples in programming documentation since at least the 1960s.

Once the file called "foo" has been created, we set the permissions with `chmod` to allow execution. In a case like this, check the contents to make sure that it will not do anything unexpected before running it. The third line does run it, using the `./` before the name to indicate that the computer should look in the current directory (abbreviated as a period) to find it, rather than the places where it usually stores executable programs. This example comes from a session on a computer running macOS Mojave, and it also works under Ubuntu. However, a Linux OS sometimes has differences in how commands work compared to a macOS.

What does it do? The problem comes from a collection of `.pdf` files in many (17 to be exact) subdirectories. Each subdirectory has as many as 20 or 30 such `.pdf` files, which come from different sources. Some have a name such as "name4_5.pdf", while others are called something like "name4_ 6.pdf", and the project manager prefers to have them without the space. While we could click on each file individually a few times, then carefully back-space over the blank, this approach is tedious, time consuming, and error-prone. Instead, those three lines in the preceding example changed the names of over 230 files in a matter of seconds!

14.1.5 Running MATLAB from a Terminal Window

It is possible to run MATLAB from command line in a terminal window. For example, the following invokes MATLAB on a Macintosh computer.

```
/Applications/MATLAB_R2016b.app/bin/matlab -nodesktop
```

The `desktop` or `nodesktop` option turns on or off the command environment's main window, respectively. Either of them also invokes the Java Virtual Machine. Several other options exist, to tailor the experience to your needs. Option `nodisplay` refers to the lack of a graphical output under Linux, but should invoke the Java Virtual Machine. Some commands rely on the Java Virtual Machine, such as `plot`. Option `nojvm` means no Java Virtual Machine, `nosplash` says to suppress the graphical "splash screen," which you normally see for a few seconds after invoking MATLAB, but before it shows the main window. The `-r` argument means run, interactively, and the string after it specifies the commands.

In the following example, the shell command `alias` defines `matlab` as a short way to refer to the MATLAB program, which exists a few sub-directories under the `/Applications` directory. Of course, a different computer, or even a different version of MATLAB, mean that the exact location of the software will be different. With the alias defined, we can invoke it as a command.

```
cascade:~> alias matlab='/Applications/MATLAB_R2016b.app/bin
/matlab'
cascade:~> matlab -nodisplay -nojvm -nosplash -nodesktop -r
"disp(cos(0.5)); exit(0);"
                        < M A T L A B (R) >
              Copyright 1984-2016 The MathWorks, Inc.
               R2016b (9.1.0.441655) 64-bit (maci64)
                        September 7, 2016
For online documentation, see http://www.mathworks.com/support
For product information, visit www.mathworks.com.
    0.8776
cascade:~>
```

As the output shows, it runs MATLAB, and carries out the `disp(cos(0.5))` instructions. Then it executes the `exit` command, and control returns to the shell, which shows the terminal prompt.

Next, we have another example of running MATLAB from a terminal window. Notice that the lack of an `alias` command; that command can be placed inside a file such as `.bashrc`, which executes when the "bash" shell starts. The terminal program, when properly configured, does it automatically. This instance does not include the `-r` argument, so it runs interactively.

```
cascade:~> matlab -nodisplay -nojvm -nosplash -nodesktop
                      < M A T L A B (R) >
               Copyright 1984-2016 The MathWorks, Inc.
                 R2016b (9.1.0.441655) 64-bit (maci64)
                         September 7, 2016
For online documentation, see http://www.mathworks.com/support
For product information, visit www.mathworks.com.
>> t = 0:0.02:1;
>> x = sin(2*pi*t + 3*pi/2);
>> whos
   Name        Size        Bytes  Class      Attributes
    t           1x51          408  double
    x           1x51          408  double
>> t(10)
ans =
     0.1800
>> plot(t, x)
Error using plot
This functionality is no longer supported under the -nojvm
startup option. For
more information, see "Changes to -nojvm Startup Option" in
the MATLAB Release
Notes. To view the release note in your system browser, run
web('http://www.mathworks.com/help/matlab/release-notes.html
#btsurqv-6', '-browser').
>> exit
cascade:~>
```

As we see from the output, the MATLAB application started, it accepted a few commands, then gave an error. The error stems from the `nojvm` option;

we need the Java Virtual Machine to see the figure created by the `plot` command. Although it generates an error, it does not quit, behaving just like the graphical command window. The `exit` command quits MATLAB.

To run this example successfully, invoke MATLAB with the following.

```
cascade:~> matlab -nosplash -nodesktop
```

This leaves out the `-nojvm` and `-nodisplay` arguments. Running MATLAB like this, and copying the commands for `t`, `x`, and `plot` as shown in the preceding example, generates a graphical window for the plot.

14.2 LATEX

L^AT_EX, pronounced as if the "x" were a "k," is a powerful typesetting program. You are likely familiar with word-processing programs like OpenOffice Writer or Microsoft Word. Another possibility that you may not be aware of is text-processing. Examine the source of a web page the next time you use a browser, typically with the "View" menu then the "Page Source" option. (On FireFox v68, this now appears under "Tools," "Web Developer," then "Page Source.") The HyperText Markup Language (HTML) for the page will be shown, with specifications on how to display it. These display commands are enclosed within angular brackets, to distinguish them from the normal text. You will see things like `<b>Introduction</b><br>`, which says to the browser to "turn bold on," then "show the word Introduction," then "turn bold off," then "break this line and start at the beginning of the next one." You can change a web page with a simple text editor, such as `vi`. This is an example of text-processing.

L^AT_EX also does text processing. There are some very good "front end" programs available that allow you to use pull down menus and the typical graphical user interface interactions. One example is `TeXShop`, so named because L^AT_EX is built on top of T_EX. Of course, you could use any text editor that you like, as long as it will save the file without extraneous data. The L^AT_EX environment is a bit like the MATLAB environment. You have your text in an editor, and then run the L^AT_EX program to see the output. L^AT_EX uses your text like a MATLAB runs a `.m` file, since both your text and a MATLAB program specify what you want to do. L^AT_EX is not a programming language, though.

One advantage of L^AT_EX is the ability to use a style-file from a conference, journal, or academic department, with formatting commands like the boundaries already set up. This way, you can concentrate on what you want to say, knowing that the program will make it look right. When doing text-processing for the first time, you should take a deep breath and relax. You no longer need to specify where things go in detail. Instead, the program will take care of this for you. It will take your suggestions, but ultimately it will put things on the page as it sees fit. For example, you may have a table that you include below a particular paragraph. The L^AT_EX processor may include it right below that paragraph, or it may move it to the next page, or even the page after that. Try not to let this bother you; your paper will look great when it is finished.

It can do things like automatically generate a table of contents, table of figures, index, and bibliography. It allows you to specify complex mathematics, two columns of text, tables, figures, and references. Labels can be defined, so that the user does not have to remember what order things have. That is, you can refer to a figure, table, equation, reference, or section by an identifier that you set up, and the program will automatically put the number in for you. If you move it later, the numbers will be updated.

14.3 GIT EXAMPLE

The following shows a session using `git`. A project called "Weeks_MATLAB" exists on a remote computer called `hallertau.cs.gsu.edu`. That server also hosts web pages, such as `http://hallertau.cs.gsu.edu/index.html`, although not all servers with git repositories host web pages, and vice-versa. Details of how to set up a remote `git` repository are omitted here. For this example, assume that the server has an account set-up for user `mweeks`, and that the account has permissions to modify the project. Further, the local computer, `cascade`, has a copy ("clone") of the project stored on it already.

First, we do a "pull" request, to make sure the local copy of the files has the latest updates.

```
cascade:Weeks_MATLAB> git pull
mweeks@hallertau.cs.gsu.edu's password:
Already up to date.
```

Notice that it asks for a password, since the local machine (called `cascade`) requests private information for the project hosted on the remote computer (called `hallertau`). It informs us that we already have an up-to-date copy. If not, it would download the new file versions.

Next, we edit one of the project files, although we could edit as many files as needed. While the following line uses the `vi` editor, it simply represents editing the file, and using the `edit` command in MATLAB also would work. After changing the file, the `git status` command informs us of local changes.

```
cascade:Weeks_MATLAB> vi other_tools/pascal5.m
cascade:Weeks_MATLAB> git status
On branch master
Your branch is up to date with 'origin/master'.
Changes not staged for commit:
  (use "git add <file>..." to update what will be committed)
  (use "git checkout -- <file>..." to discard changes in working
directory)
    modified:   other_tools/pascal5.m
no changes added to commit (use "git add" and/or "git commit -a")
```

As it indicates, we have a modified file, but we have not yet told it to commit the file. Here, we would typically test out the changed files to make sure that we really want to keep them.

The next `git` example invokes a `diff` utility to compare the changes between the committed version (represented by the keyword HEAD) and the version that we changed. This applies to the current branch, although a project might have several branches. You can think of a branch as a copy, such as an experimental version, that may be later merged back into the main version.

```
cascade:Weeks_MATLAB> git diff HEAD other_tools/pascal5.m
diff --git a/other_tools/pascal5.m b/other_tools/pascal5.m
index 1b172bd..ddcfaa8 100644
--- a/other_tools/pascal5.m
+++ b/other_tools/pascal5.m
@@ -74,6 +74,7 @@ function pascal5(varargin)
      % plot(1:iterations, p(row,:), colorArray(colorIndex));
      pause(1);
  end
+title('Bar chart showing each iteration in a different color');
  % Output the data graphically.
  %figure();
```

The git diff utility tells us a lot, and at the same time, does not include unnecessary information. It compares two copies of the same file, the last one from the repository, and the one changed with the vi editor. It shows the differences between the two, indicating the affected lines, i.e., line 74 in this case. It shows a few lines around the changes, too, to give it context.

Assuming that the changes look good, we can "commit" them, which updates the local repository (i.e., on your computer).

```
cascade:Weeks_MATLAB> git commit -am "Added a title, pascal5.m"
[master a0c2808] Added a title, pascal5.m
1 file changed, 1 insertion(+)
```

The -a argument means that the commit should apply to all modified files, while the m argument means that the message, following in quotes, will be saved in the log.

Next, we "push" the updates to the remote repository. Notice that it asks for a password; it connects to the remote git server, authenticates the user, sends the updated information, and quits.

```
cascade:Weeks_MATLAB> git push
mweeks@hallertau.cs.gsu.edu's password:
Enumerating objects: 7, done.
Counting objects: 100% (7/7), done.
Delta compression using up to 4 threads
Compressing objects: 100% (4/4), done.
Writing objects: 100% (4/4), 435 bytes | 435.00 KiB/s, done.
Total 4 (delta 3), reused 0 (delta 0)
To hallertau.cs.gsu.edu:/srv/git/Weeks_MATLAB.git
   b61235d..a0c2808  master -> master
```

There can be multiple people working with a project, and the "push" command makes your changes available. Even if no one else works on the project, this allows you to move from one computer to another.

If the git pull command does not work, try git pull origin master, which specifies the destination repository and source. Similarly, git push origin master may be what you need if the git push command does not work. There is also a git grep command, among many others.

Finally, we view the change log with the git log command.

```
cascade:Weeks_MATLAB> git log
commit a0c2808bb5c13b605e9e65dc32883fc5cb425b9d (HEAD -> master,
```

```
origin/master, origin/HEAD)
Author: M. Weeks at Cascade <myemail@address.com>
Date:   Mon Sep 9 10:00:34 2019 -0400
    Added a title, pascal5.m
```

This shows who made the change, when it occurred, and the comment. Although only the last comment appears in the preceding text, the log contains more data, including an entry for each commit.

The `git` program includes many powerful features to aid programmers in code versioning. It can help coordinate between multiple people on large projects, merge different versions, track changes, and even allow a programmer to go back to an earlier copy. Two different people working on the same project might change the same files, and use the provided tools to resolve the differences. People sometimes have a bad day, and a programmer may come to the realization that a program was actually better before the changes made that day, especially if a newly introduced bug cannot be figured out. With large projects, a programmer might find that a seldom-used feature no longer works, while remembering it that it worked well in a previous version. For these reasons and more, a code versioning system like `git` can make project management easier.

14.4 SCILAB

We have seen several open source, free software packages available. But what about a free version of MATLAB? Yes, there are programming languages similar in syntax to MATLAB, available for free, for example, "Scilab" (https://www.scilab.org/). Scilab uses two forward slashes in a row for comments. Another difference is the file extension. Instead of `.m`, Scilab uses other extensions such as `.sci`.

Let's start with an example MATLAB program, `simple_example.m`.

```
% An example summation of 10 to 97,
% in increments of 2.718
startvalue = 10;
endvalue = 97;
increment = 2.718;
% Initialize the sum
mysum = 0;
counter = startvalue;
```

```
% Loop until finished
while (counter <= endvalue)
    mysum = mysum + counter;
    % add the increment
    counter = counter + increment;
end
disp(sprintf('The sum from %d to %d with ', ...
    startvalue, endvalue));
disp(sprintf('increment %4.2f is %8.2f', ...
    increment, mysum));
```

Let's test the program. From the editor's menu, select Debug then Run.

```
The sum from 10 to 97 with
increment 2.72 is  1765.10
>>
```

Now we will copy the program to a new file, simple_example.sci. Next, we change the percent signs to two forward slashes, being careful not to do a global replace, since we only want to do this for comments. Scilab also uses the percent sign for formatting output in sprintf statements, just like the programming language C. You may have noticed that the two forward slashes is the way to tell the C compiler to ignore the rest of the line, also.

```
//
// An example summation of 10 to 97,
// in increments of 2.718
startvalue = 10;
endvalue = 97;
increment = 2.718;
// Initialize the sum
mysum = 0;
counter = startvalue;
// Loop until finished
while (counter <= endvalue)
    mysum = mysum + counter;
    // add the increment
    counter = counter + increment;
end
```

```
disp(sprintf('The sum from %d to %d with ', ...
    startvalue, endvalue));
disp(sprintf('increment %4.2f is %8.2f', ...
    increment, mysum));
```

Now, let's run the program to see what we get. To do this, select `Execute` from Scilab's editor's menu, then select "Load into Scilab."

```
-->
 The sum from 10 to 97 with
 increment 2.72 is  1765.10
```

Sure enough, the program ran and gave us the same answer as MATLAB.

SciLab is one of several free alternatives to MATLAB, however, it is not completely compatible. Other open-source projects have a similar syntax to MATLAB, such as "Octave" [10] and "FreeMat." These might work for some purposes, such as for students learning MATLAB and desiring to work on their own computer. Keep in mind that there may be other options available. Many university bookstores sell student editions of MATLAB for a fraction of the cost of the full version of MATLAB. Also, some universities make the MATLAB software available to students. Using X Window forwarding, a Unix, Linux, or Macintosh computer can remotely connect to a server running MATLAB, provided that the network connections are fast enough to make this approach feasible. In a similar fashion, a virtual machine can run a MATLAB session.

14.5 SIMULINK

Simulink is another product from the MathWorks, and it often comes packaged together with MATLAB. Simulink allows the user to drag and drop icons (design blocks) to a model (drawing), and facilitates connecting them, so that the design can be simulated. If you have this software installed, you can invoke it from MATLAB with the following command.

```
simulink
```

Design blocks include electronic parts, logic gates, and signals. Simulink uses the ".mdl" or ".slx" extension for the model files that the user creates.

An example model, "SRlatch_simfile.mdl" is included in the supplementary material. This model appears in Figure 14.1. The word "latch" means a memory element that remembers a zero or one for half of a clock signal. We can "set" it to logic one, or "reset" it to logic zero, thus the name. Program

"SRlatch.m" runs this model. It uses the MATLAB command `sim` to start the simulation.

```
sim SRlatch_simfile
```

Once the simulation completes, the results are available via variables named `simout`, `simout1`, `simout2`, etc. The rest of the `SRlatch.m` program extracts the data and plots it. In the next few lines, we copy the data from `simout1` to a new variable called `R`, to give it a more convenient name. The code does the same for `Clock` and `Q`.

```
R = simout1.signals.values;
Clock = simout2.signals.values;
Q = simout3.signals.values;
```

How do we know which `simout` goes with what variable? The model shown in Figure 14.1 conveys this: looking at the top, left corner, we can see that `R Input` splits off to output `simout1`. The plots from the `SRlatch.m` program can be seen in Figure 14.2.

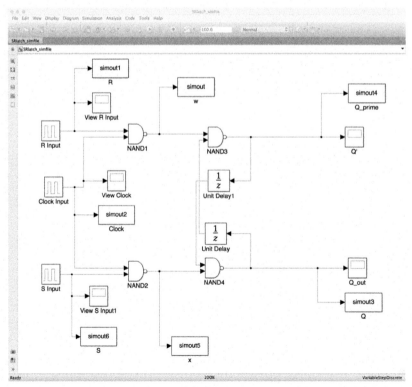

FIGURE 14.1 A Simulink model of an SR latch.

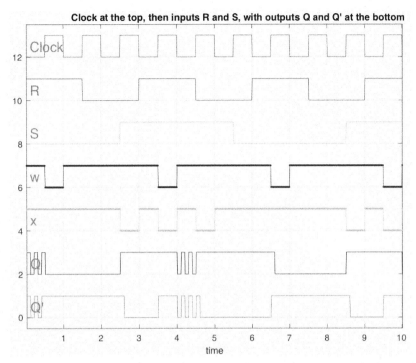

Clock at the top, then inputs R and S, with outputs Q and Q' at the bottom

FIGURE 14.2 Output from the SR latch Simulink model.

Simulink contains a powerful set of simulation tools. It has a "drag and drop" interface for creating models from design blocks, and an intuitive graphical tool to make connections between components. It can then run simulations based on the diagrams, so users can analyze their designs before implementing them in hardware.

14.6 MEX—INTERFACING WITH C

MATLAB has a command called `mex` that allows the environment to work with programs developed in other languages. A programmer can use `mex` to compile a program written in the language C, C++, or even FORTRAN. Once compiled, the program can be called from MATLAB, as if it were a MATLAB function.

For example, the code below sets up the `mex` program, then compiles an example C program that comes with MATLAB.

```
mex -setup
mex /Applications/MATLAB7/extern/examples/mex/yprime.c
```

The directory "/Applications/.../mex/" depends on your system setup. You may need to search for `yprime.c` with your operating system's file search feature, then alter the `mex` command's argument to match your system. Finally, we run the program as if it were a built-in MATLAB function.

```
>> yprime(1,1:4)
ans =
     2.0000     8.9685     4.0000     -1.0947
```

Besides `yprime.c`, other examples come with the `mex` function. These show how to extend MATLAB with C code. What do you do when you have a C program already, and desire to get it to work from MATLAB? Consider the following C language program. Do not worry if the code does not make sense, after all, it is written in a different computer language. The rest of this section is intended for those who have some familiarity with C. The following shows a simple example of a C program that computes $2 \times x + 1$, where x represents a value that we pass to it.

```
#include <stdio.h>
#include <stdlib.h>
int main(int argc, char *myinputs[]) {
    if (argc < 2) {
        printf("Expecting an input argument.\n");
        exit(-1);
    }
    int c;
    double currentInput;
    double myoutput;
    // For each input(c), calculate the output(c).
    for (c=1; c<argc; c++) {
        currentInput = atof(myinputs[c]);
        // calculate output = 2*input + 1
        myoutput = 2 * currentInput + 1;
        printf("%5.2f \n", myoutput);
    }
    return 0;
}
```

The parameters to the `main` function specify the number of arguments (`argc`) and the arguments themselves (`myinputs`). This program expects the user to pass at least one number to it. It converts the number from an ASCII string to a floating-point value with the `atof` function. It performs the calculation and prints the result. It works with multiple arguments. Notice that the `for` loop initializes variable `c` to the value 1. Arrays in the C language start with element 0, but the first element passed the `main` corresponds to the name of the program, something that we ignore in this example.

From the computer's command line, such as in a "Terminal" window, we can compile this program. This is different from the MATLAB command window. The one shown in the following example is on a Macintosh; look under the "Applications" folder, then under "Utilities" to find a program called "Terminal". If you are using Unix or Linux, there should be an icon for it under the main applications list. The Microsoft Windows equivalent is the `command.exe` program. Note that you must also have a C compiler, like the GNU C Compiler (`gcc`), available and installed for this to work. Also, your computer might have a window-based integrated design environment for the C language, although we do not need something that complex and powerful for this example.

The following command uses `gcc` to compile the `Cexample.c` program. The output from the compiler, specified with `-o` will be stored in a file called `Cexample`. The text "`mweeks$`" simply indicates the prompt for the terminal, much like MATLAB uses >> in the command window.

```
mweeks$ gcc Cexample.c -o Cexample
mweeks$
```

We see the computer prints the prompt again after the command. It did not complain, so the compilation must have worked. Now let's try it out with a simple example. The command `./Cexample` says to run the program called `Cexample` that the compiler created. Including a period and forward-slash tells the computer to look for it in the current directory. By default, the operating system looks in places where commands normally belong (e.g., `/bin`), and may not check the current directory.

```
mweeks$ ./Cexample 1.0
 3.00
mweeks$
```

We passed the value 1.0 to `Cexample`. The program received it as a string, then converted it to a floating-point data type. Then it multiplied it by 2, and added 1. As expected, this produces the value 3.0. Now let's try a few other examples.

```
mweeks$ ./Cexample 3.1
  7.20
mweeks$ ./Cexample 3.1 1.0 14.2 10
  7.20
  3.00
 29.40
 21.00
mweeks$
```

Passing 3.1 to the program works as expected. Then we pass four values to it, and see that it finds the calculation on each one. At this point, we have a C program that we know compiles correctly, and we tested the executable version of it. Now we convert it to a form that we use with mex.

To interface MATLAB with a C program, we must use some MATLAB-specific C commands. The mex function understands them, thanks to the header file "mex.h". The C language uses header files to define constants, structures, function declarations, and other things that the program may need. Function declarations give some information about the C functions, namely the function name, its inputs and output. A C program uses a directive called "#include" to get the necessary header files. Therefore, if a C program will be called from MATLAB, then

```
#include "mex.h"
```

should be one of the first lines.

A C program has a function called "main" that the computer calls to start executing the program. The main function specifies how the operating system connects to it, such as what labels it uses for the arguments passed by the operating system. In a C program written for MATLAB, we use the name mexFunction instead of main. Similar to main, the mexFunction also labels the arguments passed to and from the calling program, in this case, MATLAB. In other words, the computer's operating system passes arguments to a C program via the main function, which typically returns a value indicating success or failure. When calling a C program through MATLAB, MATLAB passes arguments to the C program via the function called mexFunction, and it can return multiple arguments back to MATLAB.

The following line shows the start of an example mexFunction definition. The yprime.c program has an identical line; besides the variable names nlhs, plhs, nrhs, and prhs, there is not much else that can be changed. The names nlhs and plhs likely come from the number of the left-hand side's arguments and pointer to left-hand side's arguments, respectively. Similarly, we can surmise that `nrhs` and `prhs` stand for the number of the right-hand side's arguments and pointer to right-hand side's arguments. For consistency, we will use the same variable names in this example.

```
void mexFunction(int nlhs, mxArray *plhs[],
                 int nrhs, const mxArray *prhs[]) {
```

Consider that a single line even though it is split into two lines for formatting. Note that in C, we do not use an ellipsis to continue a line.

We might want to check that the number of arguments matches what the program expects. Compare variable `nrhs` to the expected number of inputs, and variable `nlhs` to the number of outputs. While the program has not yet computed the outputs, MATLAB informs it about the call to the program. For example, `nlhs` indicates one when the call is `a = myCfunction()`, and two for the call `[a,b] = myCfunction()`. Thus, your function can generate an error message as appropriate. Or it could use this information to alter its behavior, like a MATLAB function can with the `nargout` keyword. As one would expect from the name, `mexErrMsgIdAndTxt` can be used to indicate an error.

C and C++ define `size_t` as a positive integer type. MATLAB defines `mwSize` for the same purpose. We can think of them as being interchangeable, and to your computer, they could be exactly the same. However, we will shortly convert from `size_t` to `mwSize`, to guarantee code compatibility for all computers. In other words, `size_t` and `mwSize` could be different on some platforms, and we should not assume that it will work for everyone just because it works for us. The next few lines are very similar to lines from `yprime.c`. They get the size of the input argument using the functions `mxGetM` and `mxGetN`.

```
size_t m, n;
m = mxGetM(prhs[0]);
n = mxGetN(prhs[0]);
```

People speak of matrices as m by n, referring to the size in a general way. Pointer `prhs` refers to memory, and the topic of pointers is arguably the most difficult concept that students have when learning C. Wherever the computer stores the input arguments in memory, the variable `prhs` points to it. The arguments appear one after another, as an array. What do the memory contents look like? It will appear as numbers, so the computer needs to know how to interpret them. The `mexFunction` declaration defines the arguments as an `mxArray`. Therefore, `prhs[0]` represents the first input argument, since C starts counting at zero. Function `mxGetM` gets the number of rows of `prhs[0]`, and `mxGetN` gets the number of columns of it. If the program has more arguments of matrices, it would need to get their dimensions in a similar fashion, i.e., using `mxGetM(prhs[1])` and `mxGetN(prhs[1])` for the second matrix.

In C, we must declare variables before using them. The variable's declaration typically reserves memory for it, although in the case of pointers, we can allocate and deallocate memory using special functions (`malloc` and `free`, respectively). We want the `twoXplus1` function to return a matrix with the same dimensions of the input, so we need to specify this. The following line creates an `m×n` matrix of double values.

```
plhs[0] = mxCreateDoubleMatrix( (mwSize)m, (mwSize)n, mxREAL);
```

The pointer for the first output stores the spot in memory where the computer places the matrix. Remember that `mwSize` is a positive, integer data type that has a definition within the header files provided by MATLAB (file "tmwtypes.h" defines it). Putting a data type in parentheses *casts* the variable following it to be that type, so the line converts variables m and n from `size_t` to `mwSize`, to match the parameters that `mxCreateDoubleMatrix` expects.

Now that we know the size of the input matrix, and we have allocated memory for the output matrix, we are almost ready to use the inputs and outputs. To make this intuitive, we create two new variables, `myinputs` and `myoutputs`. Both variables likely refer to multiple values. Defining them as pointers to double values means that we can use these variables like arrays. After declaring the variables, we use the `mxGetPr` function, provided by MATLAB, to return a pointer to real data.

```
double *myinputs;
double *myoutputs;
myinputs = mxGetPr(prhs[0]);
myoutputs = mxGetPr(plhs[0]);
```

As the preceding code shows, `myinputs` gets a pointer to the memory for the right-hand side, and `myoutputs` gets ones for the left-hand side. The example does not need the C function `atof`, since the inputs come from MATLAB instead of as string parameters from the operation system. We can now use the inputs to assign the outputs.

We know that the inputs could be a matrix, and that variable m and n contain the dimensions. Therefore, we need to access each input row and column, and variables r and c serve this purpose. Under MATLAB, we would start at 1 and count to m for the rows, but C starts arrays at index 0, so the following code loops with index r with from 0 to m−1 instead of 1 to m. Likewise, variable c ranges from 0 to n−1 in a nested loop.

Before continuing with this example, consider the following MATLAB session.

```
>> B = [10, 20, 30; 40, 50, 60];
>> B(1:6)
ans =
    10    40    20    50    30    60
```

Accessing matrix B with a single index shows a different order than you might expect. The second value, 40, reveals that the internal order goes along rows instead of along columns. That is, getting the sequential values of matrix B gives us the first column, then the second column, and then the third column, instead of the first row followed by the second row. Knowing this ordering comes in handy when we access MATLAB data outside of the MATLAB environment.

One way to make memory work like a two-dimensional structure is to convert the row and column into an index, like the following code does with the expression c*m + r. Since m represents the number of rows, c*m gives us the index position at the first row for the column c. Then we add the row, r, and we have the correct index for that row and column.

```
for (r=0; r<m; r++) {
    for (c=0; c<n; c++) {
        // calculate output = 2*input + 1
        myoutputs[c*m + r] = 2 * myinputs[c*m + r] + 1;
    }
}
```

The example code ends after the nested loops. We do not need to signal the values to return, since the earlier code already set this up.

The following shows the complete example. File twoXplus1.c, in the supplementary material, contains this example.

```
/*
    twoXplus1.c
```

```
   Simple example of a C program: find 2 * x + 1.
   -Michael Weeks
   This code contains some lines from YPRIME.C, which
   is an example provided by MATLAB. Some variable
   names (m, n, nlhs, plhs, nrhs, prhs) are the same
   as in YPRIME.C.
*/
// Start of lines from YPRIME.C.
#include "mex.h"
void mexFunction(int nlhs, mxArray *plhs[],
                 int nrhs, const mxArray *prhs[]) {
    size_t m, n;
// End of lines from YPRIME.C.
    int r, c;
    double *myinputs;
    double *myoutputs;
    // The next line is from YPRIME.C, and the following lines
    // are similar to lines in that program.
    /* Check for proper number of input and output arguments */
    if (nrhs != 1) {
        mexErrMsgIdAndTxt("MATLAB:mexevalstring:nInput",
           "Expecting an input argument.");
    }
    if (nlhs > 1) {
        mexErrMsgIdAndTxt("MATLAB:mexevalstring:nOutput",
           "There should be zero or one output argument.");
    }
    // Get the size of the input argument.
    // Lines are similar to YPRIME.C
    m = mxGetM(prhs[0]);
    n = mxGetN(prhs[0]);
    // Comment below is from YPRIME.C
    /* Create a matrix for the return argument */
    // Make the return argument the same size as the
```

```
        // input argument.
        plhs[0] = mxCreateDoubleMatrix( (mwSize)m, (mwSize)n, mxREAL);
        // Get the input and output parameters as pointers.
        myinputs = mxGetPr(prhs[0]);
        myoutputs = mxGetPr(plhs[0]);
        // For each input(r,c), calculate the output(r,c).
        for (r=0; r<m; r++) {
            for (c=0; c<n; c++) {
                // m rows by n columns
                myoutputs[c*m + r] = 2 * myinputs[c*m + r] + 1;
            }
        }
}
```

Next, we compile it with `mex`.

```
>> mex -setup
MEX configured to use 'Xcode with Clang' for C language compilation.
...
```

For the sake of brevity, only the first output line appears. The output from the command `mex -setup` may differ somewhat, depending on your computer's compiler. Now we compile the program. If the compiler finds any errors, it will stop and let us know.

```
>> mex twoXplus1.c
Building with 'Xcode with Clang'.
MEX completed successfully.
>>
```

This looks good so far. Next, we test it.

```
>> twoXplus1(1)
ans =
     3
>> twoXplus1([1, 2, 3])
ans =
     3     5     7
>> twoXplus1([4, 5, 6; 1, 2, 3])
```

```
ans =
     9    11    13
     3     5     7
```

It seems to work when passing a scalar value, an array, and a matrix. What about assigning the results to a variable?

```
>> a = twoXplus1(7)
a =
    15
```

This appears to work. What if we assign the results to two variables?

```
>> [a,b] = twoXplus1(7)
Error using twoXplus1
There should be zero or one output argument.
```

Note that this error message comes from the `twoXplus1.c` program itself. It checks the number of outputs, and prints this error when the user expects more than one output. Suppose that the user does not know what to expect, and requests information with the `help` command.

```
>> help twoXplus1
twoXplus1 not found.
Use the Help browser search field to search the documentation, or
type "help help" for help command options, such as help for methods.
>>
```

Since we have no `twoXplus1.m` file, we do not have an automatic place to find comments for the program. The C program contains some comments, and that would be a good place to start. To improve this situation, we could create a file called `twoXplus1.m` that documents the C program, and gives usage examples.

14.7 MEX—INTERFACING WITH C++

The C++ language grew from the C language. The following example closely matches the earlier example of `Cexample.c`. Like the earlier example, it converts any strings passed to it to numbers, then multiplies these by 2 and adds 1. It can be found in the supplementary material under the name "CppExample.cpp."

```cpp
#include <iostream>
using namespace std;
int main(int argc, char *myinputs[]) {
    if (argc < 2) {
        cout << "Expecting an input argument." << endl;
        exit(-1);
    }
    int c;
    double currentInput;
    double myoutput;
    // For each input(c), calculate the output(c).
    for (c=1; c<argc; c++) {
        currentInput = atof(myinputs[c]);
        // calculate output = 2*input + 1
        myoutput = 2 * currentInput + 1;
        cout << myoutput << endl;
    }
    return 0;
}
```

Much of the syntax and structure found in C is also understood by a C++ compiler. The C++ language has some conceptual enhancements, such as the idea of streams of input and output, and the object-oriented paradigm. In C++, we can define classes, and objects inherit methods. The preceding code does not include any class definitions, and it does not define any objects. Although it does not contain the things that set C++ apart from C, it still has the elements that any C++ program that you wish to interface with MATLAB will contain.

First, we compile it with the g++ compiler, then run it, as the following session from a terminal shows.

```
mweeks$ g++ CppExample.cpp -o CppExample
mweeks$ ./CppExample
Expecting an input argument.
mweeks$ ./CppExample 1
3
mweeks$ ./CppExample 2 7
5
15
```

The first run shows that it prints an error message when we call it by itself. Running it again and passing the number 1 gives us a result of 3, as expected. The third run shows it work on two values on the command line.

Now that we see that it works, we turn our attention to making it something that mex will process. MATLAB provides some examples, such as the mexcpp.cpp program. In terms of the differences between this and the twoXplus1.c program, the C++ version, called "twoXplusplus.cpp," includes the lines

```
#include <iostream>
using namespace std;
```

like any other C++ program would. Like the C example, it defines a function called mexFunction in place of the main function. It likewise gets the number of arguments, the dimensions of the first argument, and sets up an output matrix of double values. From there, it maps the inputs to the outputs.

Let's try this example with mex. We have to let MATLAB know that we want to interface with a C++ program, and the line mex -setup C++ does that. It may produce more lines than just one, as noted by the ellipsis. Next, we use mex to compile the program.

```
>> mex -setup C++
MEX configured to use 'Xcode Clang++' for C++ language compilation.
...
>> mex twoXplusplus.cpp
Building with 'Xcode Clang++'.
MEX completed successfully.
>>
```

This looks good so far. Now to test it out.

```
>> twoXplusplus
Error using twoXplusplus
Expecting an input argument.
>> twoXplusplus(1)
ans =
     3
>> twoXplusplus([1, 4; 0, 2])
ans =
```

```
3    9
1    5
```
>>

Calling it with no parameters generates the error message, like the code says to do. Giving it one value has it compute the result, as expected. Then we test it with a 2×2 matrix, and see that it returns a 2×2 matrix of results, as it should.

14.8 INTERFACING WITH JAVA

Java is a popular, object-oriented programming language, often taught at universities. MATLAB allows the creation of Java objects, and the running of Java methods. This section gives an example of how to do that.

14.8.1 An Example Java Program

To get started, we need an example Java program. A typical initial exercise in any language is the "Hello World" program, one that simply prints a message. Here is an example with a little more complexity, setting up a `HelloExample` object. It defines and initializes an integer variable called `Count`, then defines the `main` method that prints the text "HelloExample initialized." It also defines a method called `sayHello`. When called, `sayHello` increments the `Count` variable and then prints one of three possible strings, depending on `Count`.

```java
public class HelloExample {
  public static int Count = 0;
  public static void main(String[] args) {
    Count = 3;
    System.out.println("HelloExample initialized");
  }
  public static void sayHello() {
    Count++;
    if (Count > 2)
      Count = 0;
    switch (Count) {
      case 0:
```

```
        System.out.println("Hello World!");
        break;
     case 1:
        System.out.println("Bonjour le Monde!");
        break;
     case 2:
        System.out.println("Hallo Welt!");
        break;
     }
   }
}
```

We cannot run this program directly in MATLAB. The Java syntax is similar to, but different from, MATLAB's. Of course, we could re-write this program in MATLAB, which would only take a few minutes for something this simple. What if such a program were to take months to re-write? If it already works as a Java program, we would have very little motivation to re-write it. As we will soon show, we can instead run it from MATLAB.

To use this program, we need to compile it, then run it. The following text comes from a terminal program, common in a Unix environment. Similar to the >> prompt in the MATLAB environment, the text `cascade:~/ Desktop>` is the prompt for this terminal, indicating the computer's name ("cascade") and the current directory (" /Desktop"). Note that such a prompt is easily customizable, and may be different even for the same person on a different computer.

```
cascade:~/Desktop> ls HelloExample.*
HelloExample.java
cascade:~/Desktop> javac HelloExample.java
cascade:~/Desktop> ls HelloExample.*
HelloExample.class HelloExample.java
```

It the above log, we see that there is a program called "HelloExample.java" listed. It contains the `HelloExample` class, the same one shown earlier. Next, the command `javac` compiles it. After this, we see a new file listed, called "HelloExample.class," that contains the compiled version of the code. Now we can run it.

```
cascade:~/Desktop> java HelloExample
HelloExample initialized
```

When we ran the program, it set up a `HelloExample` object, and called the main function. It did not call the `sayHello` method, however. We will do this from MATLAB.

14.8.2 Using a Java Program from MATLAB

First, we can see the current path for Java files with the `javaclasspath` command. Your output will vary, depending on your version of MATLAB and where it is installed on your computer.

```
>> javaclasspath
        STATIC JAVA PATH
/Applications/MATLAB_R2011a.app/java/patch
/Applications/MATLAB_R2011a.app/java/jar/util.jar
/Applications/MATLAB_R2011a.app/java/jar/widgets.jar
..
/Applications/MATLAB_R2011a.app/toolbox/javabuilder/jar/
javabuilder.jar
        DYNAMIC JAVA PATH
        <empty>
>>
```

The two periods (..) above are not actually MATLAB output, but mark where lines were removed for the sake of brevity. Next, suppose that we want to add a directory, which we can do with the `javaaddpath` command.

```
>> dynPath = '/Users/mweeks/Desktop';
>> javaaddpath(dynPath)
>>
```

This tells the computer to look in the `/Users/mweeks/Desktop` directory for Java programs, too. Note that `mweeks` is the author's username, and you can substitute your username here.

```
>> javaclasspath
        STATIC JAVA PATH
/Applications/MATLAB_R2011a.app/java/patch
/Applications/MATLAB_R2011a.app/java/jar/util.jar
/Applications/MATLAB_R2011a.app/java/jar/widgets.jar
..
```

```
/Applications/MATLAB_R2011a.app/toolbox/javabuilder/jar/
javabuilder.jar
            DYNAMIC JAVA PATH
/Users/mweeks/Desktop
>>
```

Viewing the preceding output from the `javaclasspath` command, we see that the path that MATLAB uses for Java has been appended. Next, we can create a Java object with the `javaObject` command, specifying the name of the class, followed by any number of arguments that we need to pass to it. In the following example, we do not pass any arguments.

```
>> myJavaObj = javaObject('HelloExample');
>> sayHello(myJavaObj);
Bonjour le Monde!
>> sayHello(myJavaObj);
Hallo Welt!
>> sayHello(myJavaObj);
Hello World!
>> sayHello(myJavaObj);
Bonjour le Monde!
```

Notice that it did not print anything when we invoked the `javaObject` command, because it did not run the `main` method. Something else to notice is how it started with the *second* message ("Bonjour le Monde!") instead of the first ("Hello World!"). This has to do with the `Count` variable's value. It is initialized to 0 when the computer creates the variable, but in the `main` method it is set to the value 3, i.e., large enough to trigger the reset to 0 in `sayHello`. Thus, if we call the `main` method first, we can have it start with "Hello World!"

We can call the `main` method just like we called `sayHello`, right? No.

```
>> main(myJavaObj)
??? No method 'main' with matching signature found for class 'HelloExample'.
>>
```

The Java program has a parameter of arrays of the String type for the `main` method, meaning that we cannot call it without including a String, even though it is ignored in this example.

```
>> main(myJavaObj, 'this is ignored')
HelloExample initialized
>>
```

To finish this example, here is a session showing the MATLAB commands from a fresh start.

```
>> javaaddpath('/Users/mweeks/Desktop');
>> myJavaObj = javaObject('HelloExample');
>> main(myJavaObj, 'this is ignored')
HelloExample initialized
>> sayHello(myJavaObj)
Hello World!
>>
```

Note that the String "this is ignored" happens to be ignored by the "HelloExample.java" program's main method, although this is not true in general. We could have the Java program make use of it.

14.8.3 Using the "main" Parameter

Typically, Java programs include a main class definition similar to the one in the preceding example, allowing Strings to be passed to it. This comes in handy when we want to run a Java program from the terminal prompt, passing in parameters to customize the experience. Let's consider a similar program, "HelloName," to demonstrate using the parameter.

```
public class HelloName {
  public static int Count = 0;
  public static String name = "";
  public static void main(String[] args) {
    Count = 3;
    System.out.println("HelloName initialized");
    if (args.length > 0)
      name = args[0];
  }
  public static void sayHello() {
    Count++;
    if (Count > 2)
```

```
        Count = 0;
      switch (Count) {
        case 0:
          System.out.println("Hello " + name);
          break;
        case 1:
          System.out.println("Bonjour " + name);
          break;
        case 2:
          System.out.println("Hallo " + name);
          break;
      }
    }
  }
```

One of the key differences between this and the "HelloExample" program is the variable called `name`, that starts off as an empty String. If the user passes an argument to the `main` function, then it will set this variable to whatever the argument is.

Assuming that the Java program has been compiled and located in a directory that MATLAB will search, we can call it.

```
>> myJavaObj = javaObject('HelloName');
>> sayHello(myJavaObj)
Bonjour
>> sayHello(myJavaObj)
Hallo
>> sayHello(myJavaObj)
Hello
>> sayHello(myJavaObj)
Bonjour
>>
```

Again, notice that it cycles through the three greetings, starting with the second one. Now let's call the `main` function and call the `sayHello` method again.

```
>> main(myJavaObj, 'Jim')
HelloName initialized
```

```
>> sayHello(myJavaObj)
Hello Jim
>> sayHello(myJavaObj)
Bonjour Jim
>> sayHello(myJavaObj)
Hallo Jim
>>
```

This time, it customized the greetings based on the parameter that we passed to the `main` function.

14.9 MCC, THE MATLAB COMPILER

There are ways to compile programs in other languages, to use with MATLAB. What about going the opposite direction and compiling MATLAB programs? The `mcc` command does this. It compiles programs written in MATLAB so that a user can run them outside of MATLAB.

To illustrate the compiler, let's start with an example MATLAB program called "`pascal2.m`", available in the supplementary material. MATLAB already has a function called `pascal`, which returns a matrix of values. The example program `pascal2.m` instead prints strings of characters that correspond to Pascal's triangle. For example, Pascal's triangle has the following sequence.

```
   1
  1 1
 1 2 1
1 3 3 1
```

Each subsequent row can be found from the row above it, by adding the two values directly above each position. In the last row, we start with 1, since the only value above it is a 1. Then we have a 3, since there is a 1 and a 2 above it. The next value has 2 and 1 above it, so it results in 3 as well. And the final value on the row has a 1 above it, so it becomes a 1. The MATLAB command `pascal(4)` gives the same data, if you ignore the values under the diagonal. The following example shows this.

```
>> disp(pascal(4))
     1     1     1     1
     1     2     3     4
     1     3     6    10
     1     4    10    20
```

The `pascal2.m` program outputs alphabetic letters instead of numbers. Next, we have first four lines of the output from it.

```
>> pascal2
a
aa
aba
acca
```

All numbers map to characters, first a space, then lower-case alphabetic characters, then upper-case, in a circular fashion such that it repeats. In other words, after "z," we start over with the space, then "a," "b," etc. An abbreviated program listing appears in the following code block.

```
% pascal2.m
iterations = 21;
% Form a matrix q of Pascal's triangle entries.
q = zeros(iterations, iterations);
q(1,1) = 1;
for row=2:iterations
    q(row,1) = q(row-1, 1);
    for col=2:iterations
        q(row, col) = q(row-1, col-1) + q(row-1, col);
    end
end
% Now map the numbers to lower-case letters.
chars2print = ' abcdefghijklmnopqrstuvwxyzABCDEFGHIJKLMNOPQRSTUVWXYZ';
chars2printLength = length(chars2print);
% Make a new matrix with just the values we can print.
p = mod(q, chars2printLength) + 1;
for row=1:iterations
    str = '';
```

```
for col=1:iterations
    % Add a character to the string.
    str = strcat(str, sprintf('%c', chars2print(p(row, col))));
end
disp(str);
end
```

Matrix q actually contains the Pascal's triangle values. Then the code creates matrix p, made from q, but using the mod function to ensure that the values map to the range 1..53. This way, we can turn the values into a character from the chars2print array. Notice that chars2print intentionally starts with a blank space. Each row thus becomes a character string represented by the variable str.

Next, we compile the pascal2.m program using the mcc command. The "-m" parameter signals that it should create a standalone executable.

```
>> mcc -m pascal2.m
>>
```

This may take a while to run; on a Macintosh manufactured in 2016, it takes about 28 seconds. Notice that it did not generate any output to the command window. It did, however, make some new files. The following gets the list of files with pascal2 in the filename.

```
>> ls *pascal2*
pascal2.m run_pascal2.sh
pascal2.app:
Contents
```

We know about the pascal2.m program, although the file "run_pascal2.sh" and directory "pascal2.app" are new. The files on your computer may be different. The extension ".sh" indicates that this is a shell script, meaning that we can run it as a command in a terminal window.

Before we can run the run_pascal2.sh program, we need to know a bit about the MATLAB installation. Like other computer languages, MATLAB provides *libraries* to its functions. Instead of an executable program containing everything that it needs, it will access some things from the operating system as it needs them, that is, *dynamically*. This way, the computer only needs to have one copy of the function. If you have heard of a dynamically linked library, this is exactly what that means. Without this ability, every executable program would need to have a copy of the same functions. Imagine a commonly used function like `disp`: conceptually, it seems simple, but it needs to know a lot of details, like the width and height of the window, how many lines have already been shown, how many lines the current argument will take, and so forth. Therefore, such a function might take up a lot more space than you expect. How many programs on your computer use this command? If every one of them were to store its own copy of the function, there would be many redundant copies of it, and a lot of wasted space. Thus, libraries allow for efficient programs.

Since our compiled programs rely on libraries, the computer must know where to find the libraries. However, libraries could be placed in different locations, even on very similar computers. To run a MATLAB compiled program, we need the help of the MATLAB Command Runtime (MCR), and the `mcr` command gives us some information.

```
>> mcr
The MACI64 MATLAB Runtime Installer, version 9.1, is:
    /Applications/MATLAB_R2016b.app/toolbox/compiler/deploy/maci6
4/MCRInstaller.zip
MATLAB Runtime installers for other platforms are located in:
    /Applications/MATLAB_R2016b.app/toolbox/compiler/deploy/<ARCH>
<ARCH> is the value of COMPUTER('arch') on the target machine.
Full list of available MATLAB Runtime installers:
/Applications/MATLAB_R2016b.app/toolbox/compiler/deploy/maci64/MC
RInstaller.zip
>>
```

The important part appears at the beginning: "`/Applications/MATLAB_R2016b.app`" tells us the root of the MATLAB application, at least for this particular computer and software version. Related commands include `mcrversion` and `mcrinstaller`. Command `mcrversion` returns the major version number. Optional outputs minor version number and update can be used.

```
>> disp(mcrversion)
     9
>> [mj, mi, up] = mcrversion;
>> sprintf('MCR version is %d.%d.%d', mj, mi, up)
ans =
MCR version is 9.1.0
```

The command `mcrinstaller` gives information about the MATLAB compiler's run-time installer.

```
>> mcrinstaller
ans =
/Applications/MATLAB_R2016b.app/toolbox/compiler/deploy/maci64/MC
RInstaller.zip
```

The installer allows other computers to run compiled MATLAB programs, even if they do not have MATLAB. That is, other people can put a copy of the run-time files on their computer. Command `matlabroot` tells us where MATLAB is installed.

```
>> disp(matlabroot)
/Applications/MATLAB_R2016b.app
```

We can use this information when running the compiled program. If we run the compiled program on the same machine, this provides the most direct way to get the run-time root.

At this point, we switch to a terminal window. The prompt "`cascade:matlab_work>`" reminds us that the current working directory is `matlab_work`, on a computer called `cascade`. The next command gets a list of the files related to `pascal2`.

```
cascade:matlab_work> ls -l | grep pascal2
drwxr-xr-x  3 mweeks  staff   102 Dec 6 18:05 pascal2.app
-rw-r--r--@ 1 mweeks  staff  1334 Dec 6 17:37 pascal2.m
-rwxr--r--  1 mweeks  staff   843 Dec 6 18:05 run_pascal2.sh
```

To run the compiled program, we must tell it the location of the root of the MATLAB Command Runtime directory.

```
cascade:matlab_work> ./run_pascal2.sh /Applications/MATLAB_R2016b.app
-----------------------------------------
Setting up environment variables
---
DYLD_LIBRARY_PATH is .:/Applications/MATLAB_R2016b.app/runtime
/maci64:/Applications/MATLAB_R2016b.app/bin/maci64:/Applicatio
ns/MATLAB_R2016b.app/sys/os/maci64
a
aa
```

```
aba
acca
adfda
aejjea
afotofa
aguIIuga
ahBcqcBha
...
cascade:matlab_work>
```

The output actually continues on for several more lines before the computer returns with the prompt. From the result of matlabroot, which we must pass to the run_pascal2.sh script, it is able to figure out where the run-time libraries are.

So far, the example code takes no input, and generates text output. It always prints the same number of lines, and having a parameter to specify the amount to print would clearly be an improvement. To accomplish this, we make a few, minimal changes. First, we copy the script pascal2.m to a new file called pascal3.m. Then, we declare it to be a function, which means we can specify an input variable iterationsString. The program needs a number, but it receives the argument as a string, so the str2num command converts it. This way, it has the variable iterations, like before.

```
function pascal3(iterationsString)
iterations = str2num(iterationsString);
% iterations should be an odd number.
if (mod(iterations, 2) == 0)
    % This number is even, so make it odd.
    iterations = iterations + 1;
end
% The rest is the same as in pascal2.m.
```

The user should pass this value, and it should be an odd number. Can we trust the user to only give it odd numbers? Instead, we check it out, and add 1 to it if needed. From this point, the code should be the same as in pascal2.m.

Next, we test it out under a MATLAB session. Since we plan to compile this and run it from the computer's command line, and the parameter will be a string, we give it a string to test it.

```
>> pascal3('10')
a
aa
aba
acca
adfda
aejjea
afotofa
aguIIuga
ahBcqcBha
aiJEttEJia
ajSnYNYnSja
>>
```

As the output shows, the program generates 11 lines of output. The correction to an odd number appears to work. Next, we compile it with `mcc`.

```
>> mcc -m pascal3
```

Switching back to a terminal window, we can run this program outside of a MATLAB session. Since this is the same computer, the MATLAB Command Runtime is the same as before.

```
cascade:matlab_work> ./run_pascal3.sh /Applications/MATLAB_R2016b.app 10
-------------------------------------------
Setting up environment variables
---
DYLD_LIBRARY_PATH is .:/Applications/MATLAB_R2016b.app/runtime/maci64:/Ap
plications/MATLAB_R2016b.app/bin/maci64:/Applications/MATLAB_R2016b.app/s
ys/os/maci64
a
aa
aba
acca
adfda
aejjea
afotofa
aguIIuga
```

```
ahBcqcBha
aiJEttEJia
ajSnYNYnSja
cascade:matlab_work>
```

We observe that it works here, too.

Do you find the extra output about environment variables off-putting? This comes from the shell script, and we can change it. Under a shell, the echo command prints information. The following shows a couple of quick examples.

```
cascade:matlab_work> echo Hello.
Hello.
cascade:matlab_work> #echo Nothing, since this is a comment.
cascade:matlab_work>
```

Notice that the first line printed the text "Hello.", while the second echo line did not print anything. Technically, the second one is not an echo command, since the number-sign that precedes it indicates that the computer should ignore the rest of the line, just like %disp('Nothing'); would be considered a comment in MATLAB. This means that we can have the shell script print more things, if we like, or we can comment out the lines that prints things we do not want to see. With this in mind, here is an altered version of run_pascal3.sh, called run_pascal3_quiet.sh. In a case like this, making a copy before making changes is a really good idea. For example, the very first line looks like a comment, and you might expect to be able to delete it. However, it serves the special purpose of letting the computer know how to interpret the rest of the file. Having a backup allows us to recover from an error like deleting that line would cause.

```
#!/bin/sh
# script for execution of deployed applications
#
# Sets up the MATLAB Runtime environment for the current $ARCH
# and executes the specified command.
#
exe_name=$0
exe_dir=`dirname "$0"`
# echo "-------------------------------------------"
```

```
if [ "x$1" = "x" ]; then
  echo Usage:
  echo   $0 \<deployedMCRroot\> args
else
  # echo Setting up environment variables
  MCRROOT="$1"
  # echo ---
  DYLD_LIBRARY_PATH=.:${MCRROOT}/runtime/maci64 ;
  DYLD_LIBRARY_PATH=${DYLD_LIBRARY_PATH}:${MCRROOT}/bin/maci64 ;
  DYLD_LIBRARY_PATH=${DYLD_LIBRARY_PATH}:${MCRROOT}/sys/os/maci64;
  export DYLD_LIBRARY_PATH;
  # echo DYLD_LIBRARY_PATH is ${DYLD_LIBRARY_PATH};
  shift 1
  args=
  while [ $# -gt 0 ]; do
      token=$1
      args="${args} \"${token}\""
      shift
  done
  eval "\"${exe_dir}/pascal3.app/Contents/MacOS/pascal3\"" $args
fi
exit
```

Notice that the `echo` statements after the `else` are commented out. The ones before the `else` remain the same, since those could help someone who does not provide the MCR information. Note that this shell script does not contain the `pascal3.m` commands. Instead, it sets up some parameters, and calls the compiled `pascal3` code in the `eval` line. Something else to observe is that this line sets the variable `MCRROOT` to the first argument to the shell script.

```
MCRROOT="$1"
```

We could alter this to make things even easier. For example, if we expect this program to be run on the same computer every time, we could set it to the output of `matlabroot` automatically, so that the user would not need to specify it. Or we could check to see if the user passed an argument, and try to guess the correct location if they did not. However, such refinements are out of scope here, and should only be done by someone who understands shell scripts well. For example, allowing the user to skip the MCR information means the `shift 1` line should be commented out, but the other `shift` line should remain intact. This might seem confusing, although we can appreciate how the shell script shares similarity to MATLAB scripts.

Let's return to the quiet version of the shell script. When we run it, we get the following output.

```
cascade:matlab_work> ./run_pascal3_quiet.sh /Applications/MATLAB_
R2016b.app 10
a
aa
aba
acca
adfda
aejjea
afotofa
aguIIuga
ahBcqcBha
aiJEttEJia
ajSnYNYnSja
cascade:matlab_work>
```

As we can see, this version of the shell script does not print any extraneous information.

We invoked the previous examples from the command line. What if we want to run the program from a graphical user interface? We can click on the applications to run them, just as we run other applications. For this example, we create a new version of the example, called "`pascal4.m`." It can take an argument, but does not require one. To do that, we use the `varargin` keyword, along with `nargin` to set the `iterations` variable. If the number of input arguments (`nargin`) is one or more, then we set `iterations` to the number given in the argument string. It would be good addition to check the type of `varargin` value. If the user passes no arguments, then we assume a value of 21 for `iterations`.

```
function pascal4(varargin)
% Get the number passed, or use a default value.
if (nargin >= 1)
    iterationsString = varargin{1};
    iterations = str2num(iterationsString);
else
    iterations = 21;
end
% Lines defining p and q are the same as before.
% Lines printing the string are commented out.
% Output the data graphically.
figure();
mesh(1:iterations, 1:iterations, p);
```

This code listing leaves out the definitions of matrices p and q, since they appear in the `pascal2.m` code, shown previously. Also, this version (`pascal4.m`) does not output text, so the `disp` statements have been removed. Finally, it opens a figure and displays the output with the `mesh` command.

We can run this from the MATLAB command window.

```
>> pascal4('11')
```

We can compile it, as follows:

```
>> mcc -m pascal4.m
```

Then, we can run the program from a terminal window, through the shell script.

```
cascade:matlab_work> ./run_pascal4.sh /Applications/MATLAB_R2016b.app 10
------------------------------------------
Setting up environment variables
---
DYLD_LIBRARY_PATH is .:/Applications/MATLAB_R2016b.app/runtime/maci64:/Ap
plications/MATLAB_R2016b.app/bin/maci64:/Applications/MATLAB_R2016b.app/s
ys/os/maci64
cascade:matlab_work>
```

The operating system allows us to run the program directly. Open a file browser, navigate to the directory where the computer stores your MATLAB files, and click on the `pascal4.app` icon. It should open the figure window, like the one shown in Figure 14.3. By the way, you might have tried these examples with an open MATLAB session. However, you do not need to have MATLAB running when executing these compiled programs through the command line or GUI.

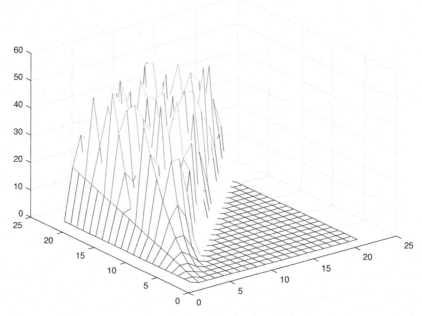

FIGURE 14.3 A mesh plot of Pascal's triangle, from a compiled program.

14.10 MATLAB AND HTML

MATLAB can publish your code to a variety of formats, include LaTeX and HTML. We briefly discuss the latter. To do this, use the `publish` command. We start off with a short program, called `plotSin`, that creates a new figure, a plot of a sine wave.

```
% Plot a sin wave
x = 0:0.01:2*pi;
y = sin(2*pi*x);
plot(x,y,'m');
```

Next, we use the `publish` command.

```
>> publish('plotSin.m')
ans =
/Users/mweeks/matlab_work/html/plotSin.html
```

It creates an HTML file with the name that it returns. This will be different for you, depending on your computer's operating system and your account name. In this case, it creates the `html` subdirectory. By default, the `publish` command creates an HTML file of the same name as the MATLAB program, although other options exist. To view the page created with the `publish` command, you can a browser. Figure 14.4 shows a screen-capture of the page displayed with FireFox.

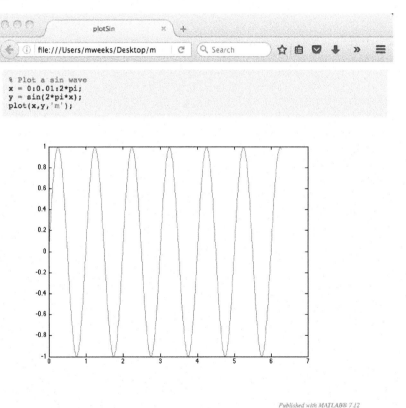

FIGURE 14.4 The web page created by MATLAB for the "plotSin.m" program.

This brings us to another interesting MATLAB command, web. As you might guess from the name, it displays a web page. While you could certainly view the pages created by the publish command, it can show regular HTML files, too. Included with the programs, you will find a file called "helloMAT-LAB.html." To view it with the web command, enter the following command.

```
web('helloMATLAB.html')
```

It produces a window like that shown in Figure 14.5. Notice that this example has a button on the page, labelled "say Hi," as well as text that reads "This page has loaded" in the left corner. The computer automatically generates both the button and the text. The button comes from a document.write command, a bit of Javascript embedded in the page. And when the browser completes loading the page, it in turn calls a Javascript function for the text to appear. Thus, not only does the web function understand HTML, it executes Javascript, allowing the user to interact with the page. If you click on the button, it changes the text in the bottom-left corner to "hello!," responding to the event like the MATLAB figures do.

Hello MATLAB. Greeting...

This page has loaded.

FIGURE 14.5 MATLAB can show other web pages, too.

Related to the web command are the urlread and urlwrite commands. The acronym URL stands for universal resource locator. In other words, you can read a web page into a string with a command like the following one.

```
>> y = urlread('http://yahoo.com');
```

The returned string contains the data from the requested page, including the HTML and Javascript. You could potentially edit the string, or process it, then view the results. However, you may find this slow compared to viewing the page in a web browser. The urlwrite does a similar job as urlread, since they both connect to an external website and fetch the contents. Whereas urlread puts the results in a string, urlwrite creates a file on your computer with the contents. Here is an example.

```
>> urlwrite('https://yahoo.com', 'ycopy.html');
```

The urlwrite command makes a file, called "ycopy.html" in this case. If you type these two commands in yourself, you may have noticed that the URLs are not exactly the same: the first uses "http" while the second uses "https," a secure version with an encrypted data transfer.

Many websites have moved from "http" to "https," including the one in these examples. In fact, if you examine the string `y` from the previous `url-read` command, you will see text indicating that the page has moved. In other words, Yahoo now longer supports unencrypted web traffic. From a privacy point of view, this protects people. For example, using a web browser on a cell phone or laptop via a free Wifi connection means that anyone else nearby can eavesdrop. With unencrypted traffic, it does not take much skill to monitor or record this traffic. Of course, someone could also listen to encrypted traffic. The key difference is that the encrypted communications should be unintelligible. Unencrypted communications would be as easy for the listener to see as it is for the intended recipient.

14.11 WORKING WITH AN ARDUINO

An Ardiuno is an open-source board with a microcontroller. You can think of it as a little computer, since it can be programmed, and the board can fit in the palm of your hand. It has limitations compared to a desktop computer, such as limited memory, fewer input and output capabilities, and a slow processor. That is, a desktop computer typically comes with a keyboard, mouse, and monitor, while an Arduino does not. However, it does have analog and digital pins that can easily connect wires, and a USB port to allow it to connect to another computer. Due to its ability to program, its ease of connecting to sensors, and its inexpensive cost, many projects include an Arduino. They could be put in devices like garage door openers, microwave ovens, digital thermostats, and security systems: a field called *embedded systems*. You may even own a few embedded systems and not realize it.

Recent MATLAB versions allow you to connect and control an Arduino through a MATLAB session. Plug the Arduino into your computer by a USB cable, then set up an object to refer to the Arduino. In the following example, variable a will be used for this purpose. The Arduino may come with a power connector, however, the USB cable provides enough power for it to run the examples in this section.

```
>> a = arduino()
Updating server code on board Uno (/dev/tty.usbmodem1461). Please
wait.
```

```
a =
  arduino with properties:
                          Port: '/dev/tty.usbmodem1461'
                         Board: 'Uno'
                 AvailablePins: {'D2-D13', 'A0-A5'}
                     Libraries: {'I2C', 'SPI', 'Servo'}
```

While we do not go further with this, the listArduinoLibraries command gives information about the libraries available for the Arduino.

```
>> disp(listArduinoLibraries())
  'Adafruit/MotorShieldV2'
  'I2C'
  'SPI'
  'Servo'
  'ShiftRegister'
```

The "Servo" library, for example, allows the control of servo motors.

The serial command creates an object for MATLAB to communicate with the serial port. Here, we connect to the Arduino through the serial port, instead of using the arduino command. The Arduino board should already be physically connected to the computer through the USB cable. Note that text /dev/tty.usbmodem1461 specifies the serial port for this example, which you would need to change to match your system.

```
>> arduinoSerial = serial('/dev/tty.usbmodem1461');
>> fopen(arduinoSerial);
>> arduinoSerial
Serial Port Object : Serial-/dev/tty.usbmodem1461
Communication Settings
   Port:                /dev/tty.usbmodem1461
   BaudRate:            9600
   Terminator:          'LF'
Communication State
   Status:              open
   RecordStatus:        off
Read/Write State
   TransferStatus:      idle
   BytesAvailable:      1
```

```
   ValuesReceived:      0
   ValuesSent:          0
>> fclose(arduinoSerial)
```

This opens the connection and later closes it, just like we would do for a file. Other file commands, such as `fprintf` and `fscanf`, would work here, too. This would be useful if the Arduino already has a program on it to read from the serial input, and respond back through the serial output. Arduinos store their programs in non-volatile flash memory, meaning that it does not lose the contents when the power goes out, and that it can overwrite this memory. A "flash drive," "thumb drive," or "USB key" based on the same technology allows file storage.

The following command gives us another piece of information. The `which` command tells us where the constructor can be found, and the location will vary according to where your MATLAB installation stores its files.

```
>> which arduino
/Users/mweeks/matlab_work/SupportPackages/R2016b/toolbox/matlab/
hardware/supportpackages/arduinoio/arduino.m  % arduino constructor
```

If you want to see what methods it makes available, looking through that file will reveal them.

Let's try reading a few inputs from pins. These are not connected to anything. If you are following along with the previous serial connection code, make sure to use `fclose` before the `arduino` command.

```
>> a = arduino();
>> disp(a.AvailablePins)
  Columns 1 through 8
    'D2'   'D3'   'D4'   'D5'   'D6'   'D7'   'D8'   'D9'
  Columns 9 through 15
    'D10'   'D11'   'D12'   'D13'   'A0'   'A1'   'A2'
  Columns 16 through 18
    'A3'   'A4'   'A5'
>> v = readDigitalPin(a, 'D7')
v =

    0
>> v = readDigitalPin(a, 'D2')
v =

    0
```

Note that the "AvailablePins" lists D2 through D13 for this board. What if we try to read a pin outside of this range?

```
>> v = readDigitalPin(a, 'D1')
Invalid pin number. Valid pin numbers for this board Uno are D2,
D3, D4, D5, D6, D7, D8, D9, D10, D11, D12, D13, A0, A1, A2, A3, A4,
A5
```

What if we decide to write a value to a pin?

```
>> writeDigitalPin(a, 'D7', 1)
Pin D7 was previously configured for 'DigitalInput'. To complete
this operation, use 'configurePin' with mode 'DigitalOutput', or
'Unset' to allow arduino to automatically set the pin mode.
```

To use it as an output, we have to set it up to be an output first.

```
>> configurePin(a, 'D7', 'DigitalOutput');
>> writeDigitalPin(a, 'D7', 1)
```

While this did not do anything observable, since nothing is connected to the pins, it did not generate an error. Shortly, we will see how we can interact with other devices connected to the board.

14.11.1 Technical Difficulties

Using equipment like this can sometimes be difficult. For example, consider this attempt, and remember that your experience will likely vary. The computer has an Arduino connected through a serial port. First, we can try to use it the easy way, letting the computer do the work.

```
>> a = arduino()
Cannot detect Arduino hardware. Make sure original Arduino
hardware is properly plugged in. Otherwise, please specify
both port and board type. For more information, see arduino
function reference page.
```

We have to specify more information. The `arduino` command takes optional parameters, the first two being the port and the board.

Which serial port? On a computer running Microsoft Windows, this would be a *com* port, such as "com1." Under Linux, this would be a virtual file under the "/dev" directory. Since the computer in this example is a Macintosh, it will have a port under /dev, too. From a terminal window, we get a list of devices connected, but filter the results with `usb` in an to attempt to get only the relevant information. (The `/dev` directory contains over 300 entries.) First, we see the results when the Arduino is not connected.

```
cascade:~> ls /dev | grep usb
cascade:~>
```

After plugging in the Arduino, the same command reveals a different result.

```
cascade:~> ls /dev | grep usb
cu.usbserial-A700ewnJ
tty.usbserial-A700ewnJ
cascade:~>
```

With this information, we turn to MATLAB to make a connection with the board, an Arduino Duemilanove, apparently named for the Italian word for 2009. (Google Translate renders the words "two thousand nine" individually to "due mille nove" in Italian, or "duemilanove" when put together.)

```
>> a = arduino('/dev/tty.usbserial-A700ewnJ', 'Duemilanove')
'Duemilanove' is not recognized as a supported board.
Possible board values are:
Uno, Nano3, Pro328_5V, Pro328_3V, ProMini328_5V, ProMini328_3V,
Mega2560, MegaADK, Due, DigitalSandbox, Fio, Mini, Leonardo,
Micro.
```

Although this did not work, it did give some additional information. Let's try again. Of the listed boards, the "Due" seems closest—could it be a shortened name for the "Duemilanove"? Actually, no, these are two different boards, with the Due coming out 3 years after the Duemilanove. What if we try it anyway?

```
>> a = arduino('/dev/tty.usbserial-A700ewnJ', 'Due')
Updating server code on board Due (/dev/tty.usbserial-A700ewnJ).
Please wait.
Cannot program board Due (/dev/tty.usbserial-A700ewnJ). Please
make sure the board is supported and the port and board type are
correct.
```

This time, the command took a minute before giving the error message. Another project uses this particular board, so it has some additional things connected to it, including external switches wired to it. Apparently, the computer did communicate with the Arduino; after issuing this command, the Arduino toggled the external switches, causing them to make a clicking sound, as they normally do when turning off or on.

Connecting an Arduino Duemilanove has resulted in a problem like this before, where additional software called a "virtual COM port driver" fixed it. If you are attempting to connect an Arduino and run into a similar problem, this may solve it. However, it did not help in this case. Note that connecting the board to the computer and programming it with the Arduino *integrated design environment* (IDE, also called an *integrated development environment*) may be challenging, although once it works, connecting it via MATLAB should be easy, assuming that MATLAB supports the board. In this case, however, the Arduino IDE does work with the Duemilanove board, yet MATLAB does not appear to support it. In this case, switching to a more recent Arduino fixed the problem.

Usually, textbooks give examples as simply and elegantly as possible. Cleaning them up hides the mistakes, however, and it can create a false impression that things work easily and well the first time. Sometimes we get lucky, and change the hardware or software almost effortlessly. Other times, making an insignificant-looking change causes a cascade of problems. This example shows how things can go wrong in an unexpected way. Interestingly, it comes from using a particular board, in a lab with plenty of different equipment. Originally, this example used an Arduino Uno, and it worked well. Choosing the board sitting next to it, an Arduino Duemilanove, caused the technical difficulties in this counter-example. The lesson here is not which board to use, since a different environment might work well with the Duemilanove and have some issues with the Uno. Instead, this example illustrates that challenges that often come with doing something new with electronic devices, and it signifies that we should expect some difficulties along the way.

14.11.2 Working with an External Sensor

An Arduino can interface with many different devices, such as proximity sensors, light sensors, sound sensors, temperature sensors, accelerometers, RFID readers, flex/pressor sensors, humidity sensors, heart rate sensors, and potentially even brain wave scanners. Here, we use a simple float sensor. It has a lightweight cylinder with a rod going through it. The cylinder can easily move along the rod, though barriers prevent it from going beyond a centimeter or two. It has two wires, and the cylinder's position either connects the wires or not. Thus, it serves as a simple, digital sensor. If the cylinder rests against one barrier, it will form a connection, and if it touches the other barrier, it will not have a connection. Typically, this sensor would go in a wet environment, such that a rising water level causes the cylinder to float and thus change its connection status. Which barrier makes the connection depends on the sensor's orientation. Using electrical devices around water can be dangerous, but this experiment can be done in a dry environment.

To get started, we connect the circuit shown in Figure 14.6. A bread board appears in the upper left corner of the figure. These come in handy when making physical connections between wires, although you do not have to have one. The design shows a 4700 Ohm resistor, connected to one wire of the float sensor. Here, a wire from digital pin 2 connects to both the resistor and the float sensor wire. The other wire from the float sensor connects to the ground. Another wire connects digital pin 3 to the other end of the resistor. We will instruct the Arduino to put a logic 1 on digital pin 2 (D2), then read the logic level on digital pin 3 (D3).

With the circuit connected, we next set up the Arduino.

```
>> a = arduino()

a =

   arduino with properties:

                      Port: '/dev/tty.usbmodem1461'
                     Board: 'Uno'
             AvailablePins: {'D2-D13', 'A0-A5'}
                 Libraries: {'I2C', 'SPI', 'Servo'}
```

This example uses the following lines multiple times. It writes a logic 1 value to the pin connecting to the sensor. It then reads the value on a connected pin, after a brief delay. The other sensor's wire connects to a ground pin, so one of two things happen. If we read the pin and get a logic 0, we know that the sensor connects to the ground. If the sensor does not make the connection, then we should be able to read the pin's value as logic 1.

```
configurePin(a, 'D2', 'DigitalOutput');
configurePin(a, 'D3', 'DigitalInput');
```

Now we can try this code to set a default value of logic 1, then read whether it changed.

```
writeDigitalPin(a, 'D2', 1);
pause(0.001);
disp(readDigitalPin(a, 'D3'));
```

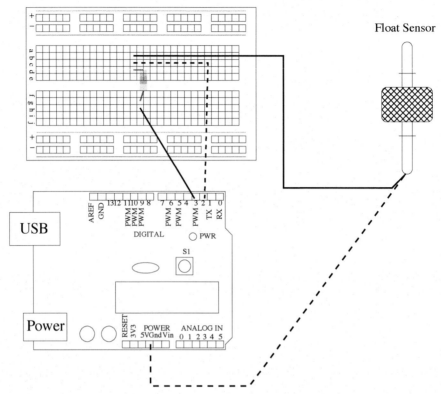

FIGURE 14.6 An Arduino connected to a float sensor via a bread board. It uses a 4700 Ohm resistor. The float sensor has a freely moving float, shown in the hatched pattern, which will typically rest against one of the two barriers, i.e., due to gravity or a rising water level.

Putting the float against one barrier and running the code gives this output.

```
>> writeDigitalPin(a, 'D2', 1);
   pause(0.001);
   disp(readDigitalPin(a, 'D3'));
      1
```

We see that we get a logic 1, so there is no connection through the sensor. Now, we do the same thing, after moving the float against the other barrier.

```
>> writeDigitalPin(a, 'D2', 1);
   pause(0.001);
   disp(readDigitalPin(a, 'D3'));
      0
```

This time, we get a logic 0, indicating that the float has changed state. When done, we can clear the a variable and disconnect the Arduino.

This section should give you an idea about how you can read and write binary values to Arduino pins. If you want to control a large device, such as a desk lamp, pump, or electric burner, you will need a power switch that can be controlled by a small device like an Arduino. For example, the "Power-Switch Tail II" provides a safe way for an Arduino to turn a large device on or off. It plugs into a standard wall outlet, and the device to control plugs into it, as shown in Figure 14.7, except that the "PowerSwitch Tail II" works with three-pronged plugs. The Arduino (or other controller) sends a signal to turn the switch on or off via a couple of wires, and the signal can be sent with the same command to write a logic value as we saw in the preceding example.

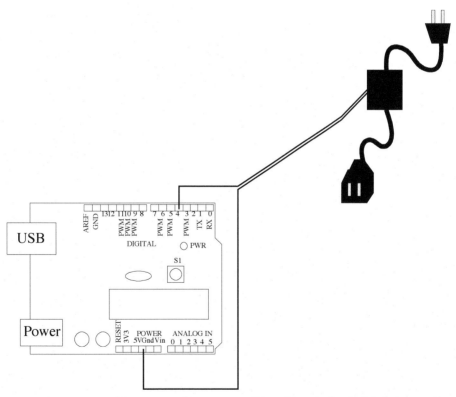

FIGURE 14.7 An Arduino connected to a power switch. Writing a logic 1 to digital pin 4 would allow a larger device plugged into the switch to get power, while writing a logic 0 to that pin would shut it off.

14.12 SUMMARY

The theme of this chapter is working with other software and hardware. It covers open-source software tools, working with other languages, compiling a MATLAB program, and controlling an Arduino. The intent is to provide you with an overview of the tools (besides MATLAB) that you are likely to see in a scientific or engineering laboratory. You are highly encouraged to get the software mentioned in this chapter, and try it out for yourself. You may be very happy with what you find. And if you are not happy with it, there's always the possibility that you can change it!

EXERCISES

1. Set up a program of yours on a git repository, such as GitHub (`https:// github.com/git`). Make a change or two, commit it, and update it, to see how it works.

2. Try compiling the `yprime.c` program with the `mex` function.

3. Make a copy of the `HelloExample.java` program to `HelloExample2.java`, then make a small change to the copy by replacing "HelloExample" with "HelloExample2," and compile it. Then run it like the following.

   ```
   myJavaObj = javaObject('HelloExample2');
   sayHello(myJavaObj);
   ```

4. Try the `mcc` command on a program of yours, and verify that you can run it from the command-line interface of your computer's OS.

PROJECT

- **Parsing Website Data**
  Given a list of data available as a table on a website, isolate some of the data. Use that data in a calculation. Your program should be given a URL, and it should get the webpage, parse the relevant data from it, and present the calculated result. For example, the Center for Disease Control provides data on the influenza. At the time of this writing, the webpage at `https://www.cdc.gov/flu/weekly/index.htm` lists cumulative

numbers for "positive specimens by type" for Influenza A and Influenza B. How do the numbers compare to the numbers from the previous two years? Of course, the program must be tailored to the specific webpage, and will need to look for a key word or phrase. Also, some understanding of HTML tags will be helpful, such as `<th>`, `<tr>`, and `<td>`, for table header, table row, and table data, respectively.

SOLUTIONS TO SELECTED PROBLEMS

SOLUTIONS FOR CHAPTER 1

1. `disp('hello John Doe');`

3. Character vector is not terminated properly.

In other words, we need a single quote after "Hello" to indicate the end of the string.

5. The line defines a variable called "`intrest`," then uses "`interest`." Either one would work, but they have to match.

```
intrest = 5; sprintf('Rate is %d per year', intrest)
```

Also, the semi-colon after the `sprintf` command means that nothing is displayed. The created string is available in `ans`, though.

7. This is asking for an algorithm. I assume that a "a list of unique numbers" means that every number in the long list of values must appear in the output exactly once, so a list like "1, 2, 2, 3" should output "1, 2, 3." Does the output list need to be in the same order? If we assume that it can be out of order, then a list like "1, 2, 3, 2" could be sorted to find "1, 2, 2, 3," which makes the process easy: the first value is OK, then the next value is OK if it does not match the one preceding it.

```
1. Sort the input
2. Copy the first number to an "OK" list
```

3. Set an index to 2

4. If the value at (index) is not equal to the value at (index-1), copy it to the OK list.

5. Add 1 to index

6. If index is less than or equal to the end of the list, go to step 4

7. Output the OK list

If we assume that the output should be in the same order as the input:

1. Copy the first number to an "OK" list.

2. Set an index to 2

3. If the value at (index) is already on the OK list, go to step 5

4. Copy the value at (index) to the OK list

5. Add 1 to index

6. If index is less than or equal to the end of the list, go to step 3

7. Output the OK list

A complete answer should do a better job of defining what happens in step 3:

3a. Set index2 to 1

3b. If the OK list's value at (index2) is the same as the input value at (index), go to step 5

3c. Add 1 to index2

3d. If index2 is less than or equal to the end of the OK list, go to step 3b

9. The data from the US Census is updated periodically. The website https://www.census.gov/data/tables/2018/demo/education-attainment/cps-detailed-tables.html contains a table for both sexes that has "Labor Force Status" at line 44. The raw data from this spreadsheet looks like this.

```
Employed 135,851 3,510 5,935 34,152 21,121 15,102 34,943
         15,318 2,401 3,368
Unemployed 4,941 209 462 1,652 948 434 860 280 37 59
```

Putting this into a way that we can use in MATLAB, we delete the commas, then replace the tab characters with commas to separate the values.

```
empl= [135851, 3510, 5935, 34152, 21121, 15102, 34943, ...
15318, 2401, 3368];
unemp= [4941, 209, 462, 1652, 948, 434, 860, 280, 37, 59];
```

The other lines can be the same.

11. An algorithm is a set of instructions providing a plan to solve the problem, written in pseudo-code. A program is an instance of the algorithm, expressed in a particular programming langauge, such as MATLAB.

13. The `disp` command displays the value of a variable, including a string. The `sprintf` command creates a string, from a specification and often one or more variables.

15. This depends on the version of MATLAB being used. Older versions do not support using double-quotes to define a string. The following works on any version.

```
disp('hello')
```

17. The meaning of this statement is not clear. Assuming that the person who wrote it meant for b to have the value 2 added to it, the following shows how that should be done.

```
b = b + 2
```

19. These comments describe what the line below them does.

```
% Set the number of hours worked to 60 hours
hoursWorked = 60;
% Rate of pay for this person is $8.75
payRate = 8.75;
% The tax rate is 20 percent
taxRate = 0.20;
% Charge for (monthly) parking is $30
parking = 30;
% Figure out the amount due to the employee for this
% pay period, after subtracting the parking charge
subtotal = hoursWorked * payRate - parking;
% Calculate taxes based on the amount earned, after parking
taxes = subtotal * taxRate;
```

```
% Calculate the pay amount in Dollars after taking out taxes
pay = subtotal - taxes;
```

21. The simple answer would be something like "scan the list and find the largest value," then "write it down," next "cross it off of the list," and "repeat until there are no values left." Each of these steps should be expanded to be more specific. How do we really scan the list for the largest value? That would be something like compare the first two values, and remember whichever one is larger, then compare that with the next value, remember whichever one is larger... until we have reached the end of the list. Even "cross it off of the list" requires a bit of fore-thought: how do we handle the case where a value appears more than once? Should we cross off all of repeats, or only the first one? We assume here that we cross off only the one found to be the largest.

```
1. Copy input to list
% Scan the list and find the largest value
2. Set largest to list(1), and location to 1
3. Set index to 2
4. If index is greater than the list length, go to step 8
5. If list(index) is greater than largest,
      set largest to list(index)
      and remember location by setting location = index
6. Increment index
7. Go to step 4
% write it down
8. Write largest to the output
% cross it off of the list
9. Copy input(1 to location-1), input(location+1 to end)
   to list
% repeat until there are no values left
10. If the list is not empty, go to step 2
11. End
```

SOLUTIONS FOR CHAPTER 2

1.
```
function [y,z] = SortTwo(a,b)
    if (a < b)
        y = a; % a,b in order already
        z = b;
    else
        y = b; % copy in order
        z = a;
    end
end % This last end is not required for a function
```

3.
```
n = 1; % initial, non-zero value
clear mylist; % In case we already have this defined
next_index = 1;
while (n ~= 0)
    n = input('Enter a number, or 0 to exit: ');
    if (n ~= 0)
        % Add it to the list
        mylist(next_index) = n;
        next_index = next_index + 1;
        % Print some statistics
        disp(sprintf('Sum is %5.2f', sum(mylist)));
        disp(sprintf('Mean is %5.2f', mean(mylist)));
        disp(sprintf('Median is %5.2f', median(mylist)));
        disp(sprintf('Variance is %5.2f', var(mylist)));
    end
end
```

5. The code below presents a simple solution. We define `side_len` to be the total length of the side, and since we have a square piece, we only define one side. Next, we define our x as a range between 0 and half the side length, the two possible extremes. Then we calculate the volumes of all the possible three-dimensional surfaces, and plot the results.

```
side_len = 100;
x= 0:0.01:50;
```

```
volume = (side_len - 2*x) .* (side_len - 2*x) .* x;
plot(x, volume)
```

With bounds of 0 to 50 and an increment of 0.01, we have 5001 values for x. We can visually tell that the maximum volume occurs between 15 and 20. For more precision, we can find the index with the max function, as below.

```
[value, index] = max(volume);
```

The maximum value corresponds to index 1668; now we need to determine what this index means in terms of the value x. Fortunately, we still have the x array in memory.

```
>> disp(x(index))
    16.6700
```

This answer agrees well with the analytical answer of 16.6̄6.

7.
```
% loop
for k=1:5
    disp(k);
end
% conditional flow
if (k < 3)
    disp('less than three');
end
% error control
try
    n = input('Enter a number: ');
    s = 1/n;
catch
    % If user only presses return
    disp('Try a different number');
end
```

9. The input command expects a number. Pass 's' to it to specify a string.

```
name = input('What is your name?', 's');
```

It's a nice idea to put a space after the question mark, but this is not required.

11. A syntax error generates an error message from the computer, indicating that it does not understand what to do. Thus, an infinite loop is a logic error, since the computer understands what to do, but it is not really what the programmer wants.

13.
```
day_of_month = 0; % initial value
while ((day_of_month < 1) || (day_of_month > 31))
    day_of_month = input('Please enter a day of the month: ');
end
```

15. The range specifies the values from 7 to 9, but there are only three of them (7, 8, and 9). Attempting to access `myarray(7)` results in an error. Assuming that the user means the first value, it could be:

```
>> myarray = 7:9;
>> myarray(1)
```

Alternately, we could define `myarray` differently.

```
>> myarray = 7:9;
>> myarray(4:7) = 0;
>> myarray(7)
```

17. The variables `count` and `maxV` are not changed inside the loop, so the comparison's result never changes. Updating `count` would fix this.

```
count = 1;
maxV = 4;
while (count < maxV)
    disp('hello');
    count = count + 1;
end
```

19. The first one is an access to a variable (or perhaps a script) called `a`. The second is a call to the function named `b`, with the value `a` as an argument.

SOLUTIONS FOR CHAPTER 3

1. It suppresses output. The default for most commands is to echo the result back to the command window, even a trivial one like the result of an addition.

    ```
    >> a = 5 + 1
    a =
          6
    >> b = 5 + 1;
    >>
    ```

    When we place the semi-colon at the end, the same evaluation is performed, but the result it not displayed.

3. Variable m must be a two dimensional matrix, and m(:,n) selects all rows of it with a column specified by n. (Technically, this also works for an n value specifying a range of columns.) The .' notation causes the resulting column (or columns) to be transposed. The .* notations means element-by-element multiplication, so the number of items on the left of it should match the number of items on the right. This would still work if the values on the left, right, or both sides were 1.

    I assume that m is a two dimensional matrix, and b is a one dimensional matrix (array), where the number of rows in m match the number of columns in b.

5. Recent versions of MATLAB now give a suggested fix.

    ```
    Did you mean:
    >> x = ((12-15)/(4+(2-1)))
    x =
        -0.6000
    ```

    This does give a working line, but does it do what it should? To check it out, let's examine it with the original above it. Using a mono-spaced font, the point(s) where they differ will be easily visible.

    ```
    x = ((12-15)/(4+(2-1))
    x = ((12-15)/(4+(2-1)))
    ```

The proposed change adds a parenthesis to the end. This looks reasonable. It is also possible that this is meant:

```
x = ((12-15))/(4+(2-1))
```

However, the numeric result is the same.

7. To start, we need to define a value for `userEntry`. Next, we can check out both halves of the condition.

```
userEntry = 1;
disp(userEntry ~= 1);
disp(userEntry ~= 2);
```

This displays the values 0 and 1. Since 0 OR 1 results in 1, the condition evaluates to true. In fact, there is no value for `userEntry` that will cause the condition to be false, since it will always be unequal to 1 or unequal to 2 (or both). The condition should use an AND operation instead of an OR operation.

9. The statement a * b means to multiply the values in a with those in b, where each variable could be scalar, vector, or matrix. The statement a .* b means to do an element-by-element multiplication, where where each variable could be scalar, vector, or matrix, but they should have the same number of elements if both are vectors or matrices.

11. Multiplication is a binary operation, meaning that you must specify two operands to perform it. Something like `mytime = mytime * mytime;` would be valid.

SOLUTIONS FOR CHAPTER 4

1. The `sort` command actually does this.

```
>> x = [ 3.32 2.91 2.55 2.55 2.95;
            1    2    3    4    5 ];
>> [y, z] = sort(x(1,:))
y =
    2.5500    2.5500    2.9100    2.9500    3.3200
z =
    3    4    2    5    1
```

However, while MATLAB often provides easy ways to do things, knowing how to do this yourself has value, too. Here is a program to do that.

```
% Sort matrix x along row 1
%
% First, define x
x = [ 3.32 2.91 2.55 2.55 2.95;
        1    2    3    4    5 ];
% Build a new matrix, x2
% copy row 1 to a new variable
y = x(1, :);
% Remember the largest value, to use as a replacement
largest = max(y) + 1; % Make it larger than the largest
n = 1; % index for sorted array
% Find the smallest value, note where it is, replace
% it with something larger than the largest.
% Repeat for every value in the array
for k = 1:length(y)
    % What is the smallest value?
    [v, loc] = min(y);
    % Remember where it is
    sorted_cols(n) = loc;
    n = n + 1;
    % Replace the smallest value with largest
    y(loc) = largest;
end
disp('After sorting to preserve row 2:');
% sorted_cols now has the order of the columns
newx = [x(1, sorted_cols);
        sorted_cols]
```

3.
```
%
% Given an array of numbers, output an array that
% only contains the ones that are repeated.
%
% For example, [4, 7, 2, 3, 2, 4, 2, 5] should
```

```
% return [4, 2, 2, 4, 2].
function outArray = noUnique(inArray)
% Initialize output array
outArray = [];
for k=1:length(inArray)
    if (isUnique(inArray(k), inArray))
        outArray = [outArray, inArray(k)];
    end
end
% Determine if the value appears more than once
% in the array
function moreThanOnce = isUnique(value, array)
% Count the number of times value appears in array.
EqCount = sum(value == array);
moreThanOnce = (EqCount > 1);
```

5. Grayscale image data is simpler to use than color, since there is only one "color" plane, so we start by defining a grayscale image.

```
% Create an example image
N = 200;
x = 255*ones(N, N, 'uint8');
s = floor(99*sin(2*pi*(1:N)/N) + 100);
for k=1:N
    x(floor(s(k)), k) = 0;
end
% Now x is a black sinusoid on a white background.
% Create a new image, y, as x reversed along rows
% (columns in reversed order)
% This forms a mirror image along the right edge.
y = x(1:N, N:-1:1);
% We can put these together, and
% form a new matrix of twice the width
z = 255*ones(N, 2*N, 'uint8');
% copy x, then y
z(1:N, 1:N) = x;
```

```
z(1:N, N+1:N+N) = y;
% Show the new image to verify
imshow(z)
```

7. Let's use an example image like the right-edge mirror solution.

```
% Create an example image
N = 200;
x = 255*ones(N, N, 'uint8');
s = floor(99*sin(2*pi*(1:N)/N) + 100);
for k=1:N
    x(floor(s(k)), k) = 0;
end
% Now x is a black sinusoid on a white background.
```

Assume that the diagonal is the one from the upper-left corner to the bottomright. Anything above the diagonal will be mirrored under the diagonal. So a simple case like [1 2; 3 4] should output [1 2; 2 4], since 3 is the only value below the diagonal.

```
% First, copy x to y
y = x;
for k=1:N
    % Copy the columns of x to the rows of y
    y(k+1:end, k) = x(k, k+1:end);
end
% Show the result
imshow(y);
```

9. Let's use an example image like the right-edge mirror solution.

```
% Create an example image
N = 200;
x = 255*ones(N, N, 'uint8');
s = floor(99*sin(2*pi*(1:N)/N) + 100);
for k=1:N
    x(floor(s(k)), k) = 0;
end
```

```
% Now x is a black sinusoid on a white background.
% To reverse the image values, use 255 minus the original.
y = 255 - x;
% Show the result
imshow(y);
```

11. Sometimes it is easier to worry about the "edges" of the problem later. We will do that here. The problem boils down to knowing if the current value is the same as the last value. The following `if` statement does this.

```
% Start with example input
a = [2, 1, 1, 1, 1, 7, 3, 8, 2, 2, 7];
n = 2;
count = 1;
out = ''; % Empty string
while (n <= length(a))
    % for the current value (n), is it repeated?
    if (a(n) == a(n-1))
        % repeat of the previous
        count = count + 1;
    else
        % not a repeat
        % report previous run
        out = sprintf('%s, %d - %d', out, count, a(n-1));
        count = 1;
    end
    n = n + 1;
end
disp(out);
```

This solution has a few remaining problems. One is that it always starts the output with a comma. This is a trivial issue, and can be fixed by adding an `if` statement around the `out = sprintf...` command. The second problem is that the final run of values is not included. A way to fix that is to add the `out = sprintf...` command before the final `disp` command. Last, while the code works for character strings, the output puts the characters as decimal values, e.g. "A" becomes 65. The solution is to change the `%d` specifier in the `sprintf` command to `%c` when needed. A call to `ischar(a)` returns true when the input (a) has the character class.

13. The first value will always be kept. The next value will be kept only if it does not already appear on the "kept" list.

```
% Start with example input
a = [2, 1, 1, 1, 1, 7, 3, 8, 2, 2, 7];
kept(1) = a(1); % keep 1st value
k = 2; % index of next kept value
for n = 2:length(a)
    % Is a(n) already on kept list?
    % find (a(n) == kept), a logical array
    % if the sum of it is 0, it is not on the list
    if (sum(a(n) == kept) == 0)
        % Not on kept list yet
        kept(k) = a(n);
        k = k + 1;
    end
end
disp(kept);
```

This solution uses a trick: comparing a value to an array, which results in an array of zeros and ones. If the results are all zeros, we know that there is no match in the array.

15. This is a simple syntax error. We use square brackets to define an array.

```
>> a = [1, 2, 3]
```

Alternately, the range `a = 1:3` would also work.

SOLUTIONS FOR CHAPTER 5

1. The structure should have fields like `value` and `repetitions`. This question does not explicitly state that we have to parse the sequence string, though this answer will. Parsing the string is likely to be the most difficult part. This answer assumes that all numbers are integers.

```
input_str = '1 - 2, 4 - 1, 1 - 7, 1 - 3, 1 - 8, 2 - 2, 1 - 7';
% Find the numbers in the string as an array. There are
% more compact solutions, but should be easy to follow.
```

```
% Make note of the commas and dashes in the input.
digits = ((input_str >= '0') & (input_str <= '9'));
count = 1;
k = 1;
% Simple way to loop until we've processed
% all digits in input
while (sum(digits(k:end)) > 0)
    % Find the first 1 (digit)
    while ((k <= length(digits)) && (digits(k) ~= 1))
        k = k + 1;
    end
    start = k;
    % Find the next 0 (meaning end of this digit sequence)
    while ((k <= length(digits)) && (digits(k) ~= 0))
        k = k + 1;
    end
    stop = k - 1;
    % Now start, stop define the substring holding a number.
    numbers(count) = str2double(input_str(start:stop));
    count = count + 1;
end
% Now we have an array, numbers, that contains all values
% from input. Assume first is value, second is repetitions,
% third is value, fourth is repetitions...
count = 1; % re-use this for a different purpose
for k=1:floor(length(numbers)/2)
    mystruct.value = numbers(count);
    count = count + 1;
    mystruct.repetitions = numbers(count);
    count = count + 1;
    runlengths(k) = mystruct;
end
% Finally, print it to make sure it's correct
disp('Original input:');
disp(input_str);
```

```
    disp('Structure of values and repetitions');
    for k=1:length(runlengths)
        disp(sprintf(' %d value %d repetitions', ...
            runlengths(k).value, runlengths(k).repetitions));
    end
```

3. This question has a potential trap to it: using `csvread` on the file will generate an error, since it has text in it, too. The solution is to use `readtable`.

```
    employee_table = readtable('example_table.csv');
    employee_table{1,2} = employee_table{1,2} + 1;
    writetable(employee_table, 'example_table_new.csv');
```

5. This answer starts as a copy of `bmi_object6.m`, with the word "active" appended. Here are a few other changes. If the `am_active` flag is true, then we subtract 5 from the BMI.

```
    % in the constructor
    if (nargin > 2)
        obj.am_active = varargin{3};
    end
    % in getBMI
    if (obj.am_active)
        bmi = bmi - 5;
    end
```

The example below shows this new class in use.

```
    bmi_object6active1 = BMI_class6active(70, 175);
    bmi_object6active1.getBMI(); % without active
    bmi_object6active2 = BMI_class6active(70, 175, true);
    bmi_object6active2.getBMI(); % with active
```

It shows a difference of 5 for the second one.

SOLUTIONS FOR CHAPTER 6

1. A file containing e-mails can be thought of as text. Each message has a header, including who sent it, when, the subject, and who the receiver is. It may have a lot of other information, like the path of computers it traveled

through to get to you. After the header is a blank line, then the body of the message. For this solution, the first line of the header is assumed to be the word "From," followed by a space. To see how this works, put together a simple set of example messages in a file called myemails.txt. Function fgetl might be useful, too, except that it omits the end of line character, meaning that finding a blank line is difficult.

```
filename1 = 'myemails.txt';
    % Open files, check that it worked.
infile = fopen(filename1, 'r');
if (infile < 0)
    error('Could not open the input file');
    return
end
% Read the whole file in.
temp = fgets(infile);
linecount = 0;
while (ischar(temp))
    % disp(temp);
    linecount = linecount + 1;
    lines{linecount} = temp;
    temp = fgets(infile);
end
fclose(infile);
% Look through the lines, isolating the subjects
LF = 10; % linefeed, end of line
em = 0; % email index
for k=1:length(lines)
    temp = lines{k};
    % Note the space after the m in the next line
    foundStatus = strfind(temp, 'From ');
    if ((~isempty(foundStatus)) && (foundStatus == 1))
        % This is the start of a new message
        header = true;
```

```matlab
        if (em > 0)
            % This is not our first email,
            % so remember stop
            email(em).stopLine = k-1;
        end
        em = em + 1;
        email(em).startLine = k;
    end
    if ((temp(1) == LF) && (header))
        % Found start of message body
        header = false;
        email(em).startBody = k;
    end
    foundStatus = strfind(temp, 'Subject');
    if ((~isempty(foundStatus)) && (foundStatus == 1) ...
        && header)
        % Found the subject
        % If input is malformed, em could be 0.
        email(em).subjectIndex = k;
    end
end
% Remember last stop line
email(em).stopLine = k;
% Put all subjects together
for k=1:length(email)
    si = email(k).subjectIndex;
    subjects{k} = lines{si};
end
% Sort the subjects
[sorted, indices] = sort(subjects);
% Print e-mails in sorted order
% This could be done to a file.
for m=1:length(indices)
    % Show emails in sorted order
```

```
        em = indices(m);
        for k=email(em).startLine:email(em).stopLine
            % On the screen, this prints an extra LF
            % after each line
            disp(lines{k});
        end
    end
```

3. The base64 encoding takes 6 bits at a time from binary values and translates them to characters. The 64 characters are A to Z, then a to z, then 0 to 9, then + and /. The character = is used for padding, when the binary sequence does not end on an even boundary. Here is a program to encode it.

```
filename1 = 'somebinaryfile';
filename2 = 'somebinaryfile.txt';
base64 = strcat('ABCDEFGHIJKLMNOPQRSTUVWXYZ', ...
    'abcdefghijklmnopqrstuvwxyz0123456789+/=');
% Open files, check that it worked.
infile = fopen(filename1, 'r');
outfile = fopen(filename2, 'w');
if ((infile < 0) || (outfile < 0))
    error('Could not open the files');
    return
end
% Process the input
binvals = [1, 2, 4, 8, 16, 32];
[ch, notdone] = fscanf(infile, '%c', 3);
while (notdone == 3)
    % Every 3 chars read in is 4 out
    a = uint8(ch); % convert to uint8
    % Isolate bits.
    bits1 = bitget(a(1), 1:6);
    bits2 = [bitget(a(1), 7:8), bitget(a(2),1:4)];
    bits3 = [bitget(a(2), 5:8), bitget(a(3),1:2)];
    bits4 = bitget(a(3), 3:8);
    % Convert bits to index (0 to 63) + 1
    v1 = sum(binvals .* double(bits1)) + 1;
```

```
        v2 = sum(binvals .* double(bits2)) + 1;
        v3 = sum(binvals .* double(bits3)) + 1;
        v4 = sum(binvals .* double(bits4)) + 1;
        % Form a new set of base64 chars
        outchars = [ base64(v1), base64(v2), ...
                     base64(v3), base64(v4)];
        fwrite(outfile, outchars);
        % Get more
        [ch, notdone] = fscanf(infile, '%c', 3);
end
% Process the last few chars
a = uint8(ch);
a(notdone+1:3) = 0;
bits1 = bitget(a(1), 1:6);
bits2 = [bitget(a(1), 7:8), bitget(a(2),1:4)];
bits3 = [bitget(a(2), 5:8), bitget(a(3),1:2)];
v1 = sum(binvals .* double(bits1)) + 1;
v2 = sum(binvals .* double(bits2)) + 1;
v3 = sum(binvals .* double(bits3)) + 1;
v4 = 65;
if (notdone < 2)
    v3 = 65;
end
outchars = [ base64(v1), base64(v2), ...
             base64(v3), base64(v4)];
fwrite(outfile, outchars);
% Close the files
fclose(infile);
fclose(outfile);
```

Here is a program to decode.

```
filename1 = 'somebinaryfile.txt';
filename2 = 'somebinaryfile2';
base64 = strcat('ABCDEFGHIJKLMNOPQRSTUVWXYZ', ...
    'abcdefghijklmnopqrstuvwxyz0123456789+/=');
% Open files, check that it worked.
```

```
infile = fopen(filename1, 'r');
outfile = fopen(filename2, 'w');
if ((infile < 0) || (outfile < 0))
    error('Could not open the files');
    return
end
% Process the input
binvals2 = [1, 2, 4, 8, 16, 32, 64, 128];
[ch, notdone] = fscanf(infile, '%c', 4);
while (notdone == 4)
    % Every 4 chars read in is 3 out
    a = uint8(ch); % convert to uint8
    % Convert to indices
    v1 = strfind(base64, a(1)) - 1;
    v2 = strfind(base64, a(2)) - 1;
    v3 = strfind(base64, a(3)) - 1;
    v4 = strfind(base64, a(4)) - 1;
    % Indices are 0..64
    bits1 = [bitget(v1, 1:6), bitget(v2, 1:2)];
    bits2 = [bitget(v2, 3:6), bitget(v3, 1:4)];
    bits3 = [bitget(v3, 5:6), bitget(v4, 1:6)];
    % Convert bits to 0..255
    v1 = uint8(sum(binvals2 .* double(bits1))) ;
    v2 = uint8(sum(binvals2 .* double(bits2))) ;
    % This appends a 0 if the file is encoded then decoded.
    % For files that need an exact decoding, this is a problem.
    v3 = uint8(sum(binvals2 .* double(bits3))) ;
    fprintf(outfile, '%c%c%c', v1, v2, v3);
    % Get more
    [ch, notdone] = fscanf(infile, '%c', 4);
end
% Assume we end on an even boundary of 4.
% This might not be true for other encoders.
% Close the files
fclose(infile);
fclose(outfile);
```

SOLUTIONS FOR CHAPTER 7

1. Here is a function to do that.

```
function rsum = recursive_sum(n)
if (n <= 1)
    % If we get bad input, like -1, this will give a bad result
    % but it will work.
    rsum = 1;
else
    rsum = n + recursive_sum(n-1);
end
```

To test it out, call `disp(recursive_sum(4))`.

SOLUTIONS FOR CHAPTER 8

1. Here is a program to solve it.

```
x = imread('redBottleCap3.jpg');
figure();
imshow(x);
% Convert to grayscale
y = rgb2gray(x);
figure();
imshow(y);
```

3. Using `help edge`, we see a variety of edge detection techniques. Here is a program to use four of them.

```
x = imread('redBottleCap3.jpg');
y = rgb2gray(x);
edges1 = edge(y, 'canny');
edges2 = edge(y, 'log');
edges3 = edge(y, 'prewitt');
edges4 = edge(y, 'sobel');
% Show the results
figure();
```

```
subplot(2, 2, 1);
imshow(edges1);
title('Canny');
subplot(2, 2, 2);
imshow(edges2);
title('Laplacian of Gaussian');
subplot(2, 2, 3);
imshow(edges3);
title('Prewitt');
subplot(2, 2, 4);
imshow(edges4);
title('Sobel');
```

5. This solution has two parts: the first is straightforward, to show an image, get `ginput` coordinates, translate them to a row and column, and get the corresponding image's pixel color values at that location. Turning that pixel blue is also easy, it's just a matter of changing the color values. The second part is more difficult, even though we can imagine it easily. By checking the neighboring pixels, and changing them, then checking their neighboring pixels, and so on, it grows quickly. From the first pixel, we have 8 neighbors to check. Each of those neighbors also have 8 neighbors, including the first pixel, and at least two other repeats. We need a way to remember which neighbors to check, and to know if we've already checked a location.

Here is a function to handle the first part. The second part will be handled by a function called `blue_image`.

```
v = imread('redBottleCap3.jpg');
x = rgb2gray(v);
imshow(x);
[mousex, mousey] = ginput(1);
r = round(mousey);
c = round(mousex);
% Set the neighbors blue, too
y = blue_image(x, r, c);
% Show the result
imshow(y);
```

Changing the neighbors takes a bit of work. One way to handle this is to create a matrix the same size as the image. We can code the matrix with values 0 meaning unchecked, 1 meaning checked. So we set the first pixel's coordinates on the check matrix to 1, and change the image's pixel to blue. We then add the row and column to a checklist array.

We process the checklist array until we reach the end of it, indicating that there is nothing left to check. From the current entry on it, we check all neighbors, and if they are 0, we change them to 1. We then check to see if they have the same pixel value as the original, and if so, we make it blue and add all of its neighbors to the checklist array.

```
% Given original image and r,c,
% set the pixel at r,c blue, and
% set every neighbor blue, too,
% if it matches the first pixel.
function x = blue_image(original, r, c)
% Copy original to color
x(:,:,1) = original;
x(:,:,2) = original;
x(:,:,3) = original;
originalR = x(r, c, 1);
originalG = x(r, c, 2);
originalB = x(r, c, 3);
% Make this pixel blue
blue1 = 0;
blue2 = 0;
blue3 = 200;
x(r, c, 1) = blue1;
x(r, c, 2) = blue2;
x(r, c, 3) = blue3;
[MAXR, MAXC, MAXD] = size(x);
checkMatrix = zeros(MAXR, MAXC);
k = 1;
checkedIndex = 0;
checklist(k).row = r;
checklist(k).col = c;
```

```
checkMatrix(r, c) = 1;
% Offsets to neighbors
roffset = [-1, -1, -1, 0, 0, 1, 1, 1];
coffset = [-1, 0, 1, -1, 1, -1, 0, 1];
while (checkedIndex < length(checklist))
    checkedIndex = checkedIndex + 1;
    % get the next thing, process it
    r1 = checklist(checkedIndex).row;
    c1 = checklist(checkedIndex).col;
    % Check each of the 8 neighbors
    for m=1:8
        r2 = r1 + roffset(m);
        c2 = c1 + coffset(m);
        % Make sure this row,col is good
        if (isRCinbounds(r2, c2, MAXR, MAXC))
            % Have we been here before?
            % If so, go on to next
            if (checkMatrix(r2, c2) == 0)
                checkMatrix(r2, c2) = 1; % Mark it
                % Is this pixel the same as the original?
                if ((x(r2, c2, 1) == originalR) && ...
                    (x(r2, c2, 2) == originalG) && ...
                    (x(r2, c2, 3) == originalB))
                    % Make it blue
                    x(r2, c2, 1) = blue1;
                    x(r2, c2, 2) = blue2;
                    x(r2, c2, 3) = blue3;
                    % Add neighbors to check list
                    for m=1:8
                        r3 = r2 + roffset(m);
                        c3 = c2 + coffset(m);
                        if (isRCinbounds(r3, c3, MAXR, MAXC))
                            % Add this neighbor to the list
                            % to check
```

```
                              k = length(checklist) + 1;
                              checklist(k).row = r3;
                              checklist(k).col = c3;
                          end
                      end
                  end
              end
          end
      end
  end
  function OK = isRCinbounds(r1, c1, MAXR, MAXC)
  if ((r1 > 0) && (r1 <= MAXR) && (c1 > 0) && (c1 <= MAXC))
      OK = 1;
  else
      OK = 0;
  end
```

The sub-function `isRCinbounds` is used to make the code a bit easier.

SOLUTIONS FOR CHAPTER 9

1. Here is a program to set up the GUI.

```
global x;
% A few of these globals are not used
global startR;
global stopR;
global startC;
global halfR;
global halfC;
global MAXR;
global image_handle;
startR = 1;
startC = 1;
x = imread('redBottleCap3.jpg');
```

```
[MAXR, MAXC, MAXD] = size(x);
halfR = floor(MAXR/2);
halfC = floor(MAXC/2);
fighandle = figure();
% Slider 1
sl = uicontrol('Parent', fighandle, ...
    'Style', 'slider');
set(sl, 'Position', [180, 110, 200, 50]);
set(sl, 'Callback', {'figslider_callback', 1});
set(sl, 'MAX', halfC);
set(sl, 'Value', startC);
set(sl, 'SliderStep', [1/halfC 0.1]);
% Slider 2
sl2 = uicontrol('Parent', fighandle, ...
    'Style', 'slider');
set(sl2, 'Position', [360, 170, 50, 200]);
set(sl2, 'Callback', {'figslider_callback', 2});
set(sl2, 'MAX', halfR);
set(sl2, 'Value', startR);
set(sl2, 'SliderStep', [1/halfR 0.1]);
% Show the initial view
stopR = 201;
stopC = startC + halfC;
image_handle = axes('Parent', fighandle, ...
    'Position', [.25 .4 .5 .5]);
imshow(x(startR:startR+200, startC:startC+200, :));
```

We also need a callback function, `figslider_callback`.

```
function figslider_callback(object, ignoreme, num)
global x;
global startR;
global startC;
% global MAXR;
global image_handle;
% disp('get object');
```

```
% get(object)
V = round(get(object, 'Value'));
% disp(V);
if (num == 1)
    disp(sprintf('Changing startC from %d to %d', ...
        startC, (V+1)));
    startC = V + 1;
else
    disp(sprintf('Changing startR from %d to %d', ...
        startR, (V+1)));
    startR = V + 1;
end
axes(image_handle);
imshow(x(startR:startR+200, startC:startC+200, :));
```

3. There is a function called `uigetfile` that could be used, though this question asks for something with more programmer control. So we will show text, an input box, and a push-button. This code sets up the GUI.

```
% 100 random integer values up to 50
mydata = round(50*rand(1,100));
save mydata.mat
clear
% Only need to do the above once.
global fname
global fighandle
fighandle = figure();
text_handle1 = uicontrol('Parent', fighandle, ...
    'Style', 'text', ...
    'String', 'Enter a filename', ...
    'Position', [30 70 100 20]);
editText_handle = uicontrol('Parent', fighandle, ...
    'Style', 'edit', ...
    'String', '', ...
    'Position', [30 50 130 20], ...
    'Callback', {'getfilenameGUI_callback', 1});
```

```
button_handle = uicontrol('Parent', fighandle, ...
    'Style', 'pushbutton', ...
    'String', 'Load', ...
    'Position', [300 10 100 100], ...
    'Callback', {'getfilenameGUI_callback', 2});
```

The callback function handles both interactions, either setting the filename, or loading the file. Use parenthesis around the filename in the `load` command, or it will generate an error.

```
function getfilenameGUI_callback(object, ignoreme, num)
global fname
global fighandle
if (num == 1)
    % filename is set
    fname = get(object, 'String');
else
    % button is pressed
    try
        load(fname);
        % x = imread(fname);
        plot(mydata);
        set(fighandle, 'Color', [0, 1, 0]); % green
    catch
        disp('File does not exist');
        set(fighandle, 'Color', [1, 0, 0]); % red
    end
end
```

SOLUTIONS FOR CHAPTER 10

1. These two lines accomplish this.

```
>> [x, fs] = audioread('piano1.wav');
>> sound(x, fs)
```

3. These two lines accomplish this.

```
>> [x, fs] = audioread('flute1.wav');
>> audiowrite('flute1.ogg', x, fs);
```

5. First, we read the audio file and play it. To determine how long the sound plays before the noise, we can use a plot of the data.

```
[x, fs] = audioread('piano1.wav');
sound(x, fs);
plot(x);
```

Looking at the plot, we can see the data suddenly get larger near the end. By restricting the range, we can view it well, and listen to only the first part.

```
plot(x(450000:end,1));
sound(x(1:450000), fs);
audiowrite('piano1b.ogg', x(1:450000), fs);
```

Since it sounds good, we write it out under a new name.

7. Commands `record`, `pause(3)`, and `pause(audioObject)` are entered on the same line, so that the computer will do one after the other without waiting for more input.

```
audioObject = audiorecorder(8000, 16, 1);
record(audioObject); pause(3); pause(audioObject);
play(audioObject);
```

Since the play-back sounds good, it can be written to a file.

```
audioData = getaudiodata(audioObject);
audiowrite('speaking1.ogg', audioData, 8000);
```

SOLUTIONS FOR CHAPTER 11

1. The command `help` gives helpful, text information about a command. When you know the command's name, and need some quick documentation, such as what arguments to pass to it, the `help` command works well. Command `docsearch` calls up a window that allows you to search for a term regardless of whether it is a command, and it will display a list of all documents that include it. For example, `help average` tells us "average not found," and suggests using `docsearch`. Using `docsearch average` brings up a browser window that has over 800 results.

3.
```
% Return the division of a by b.
% Usage:
%    c=mydivision(a,b);
function c = mydivision(a, b)
assert(b ~= 0, 'Second parameter must not be zero.');
c = a/b;
```

Now we test it.

```
>> mydivision(3, 2)
ans =
    1.5000
>> mydivision(3, 0)
Error using mydivision (line 5)
Second parameter must not be zero.
>> mydivision(3, -2)
ans =
    -1.5000
```

5. It includes the following line.

```
myInput double
```

The webpage for argument validation at the MathWorks lists `mustBeReal(value)` and `mustBeInteger(value)` as two possibilities. However, the second one also includes a check to make sure it is real, so we do not need the first one. Another function is `mustBeNonzero(value)` which completes the checks. Thus, we change the line to the following.

```
myInput double {mustBeInteger, mustBeNonzero}
```

This shows how it works with those changes.

```
>> exampleValidation2(4)
    2
>> exampleValidation2(-4)
    0.0000 + 2.0000i
```

```
>> exampleValidation2(0)
Error using exampleValidation2
Invalid input argument at position 1. Value must not be zero.
>> exampleValidation2(4.1)
Error using exampleValidation2
Invalid input argument at position 1. Value must be integer.
>> exampleValidation2(4 + 1j)
Error using exampleValidation2
Invalid input argument at position 1. Value must be real.
```

7. It returns 0. The `uint8(4)` part specifies that the value returned is an unsigned, 8-bit value. MATLAB uses this data type for the result of the expression, and subtracting 6 from 4 results in 0, the closest `uint8` value to –2 that it has.

9. Assuming that periodically within the code there are checks to this variable,and additional/verbose information printed when it is true, this makes the programmer's job easier when the program needs to be updated. This can happen when new functionality is added, or after discovering that the program fails for certain input.

SOLUTIONS FOR CHAPTER 12

1. We can read the data and plot the first two columns easily.
```
x = csvread('BB133temps.csv');
plot(x(:,1),'b')
hold on
plot(x(:,2),'g')
```

To find the error, we subtract one column from the other. Next, plot this on a separate figure.
```
% Find the error
y = x(:,1) - x(:,2);
figure();
plot(y, 'r');
```

The plots the error between the measured and set temperature, but what about the "average error"? We can keep a running sum of the error, where the value at sample n is the total up to that point. Then we can find the average error as the sum of all error divided by the number of measurements.

```
err_sum(1) = y(1);
for k=2:length(y)
    err_sum(k) = err_sum(k-1) + y(k);
end
avgerr = err_sum./(1:length(y));
plot(avgerr);
```

We then plot the average error.

3. The fixCSV.m program has a couple of lines to be changed.

```
if (y1(k, 1) <= -1000)
...
if (y1(k, 4) <= -1000)
```

Since the −1000 is much smaller than 0, we can simply look for values below 0 or above 100. This assumes the measurements are in Centigrade; use 32 and 212 for Fahrenheit.

```
if ((y1(k, 1) < 0) || (y1(k, 1) > 100))
...
if ((y1(k, 4) < 0) || (y1(k, 4) > 100))
```

Better yet, define the freezing and boiling values instead of hard-coding them.

SOLUTIONS FOR CHAPTER 13

1. The function perms can be used, though it is more instructive to write a program that does this yourself. For example perms(1:3) gives a matrix where every row corresponds to one permutation of the values 1, 2, and 3.

```
N = length(str);
% Get matrix of permutations for values 1, 2, .. N
```

```
p = perms(1:N);
% Apply p to character string
[MAXR, MAXC] = size(p);
for k=1:MAXR
    disp(str(p(k, :)))
end
```

For 3 characters, it prints 6 lines. For 4 characters, it prints 24 lines, or 4×(6). For 5 characters, it prints 120 lines, or 5×(4×(6)). From this, we can see that N characters generates $N!$ lines. This is a growth rate of $O(N!)$.

3.
```
a = rand(1, 1000000);
t = zeros(1, 10);
for k=1:10
    tic;
    c = fft(a);
    t(k) = toc;
end
```

From this, one computer gives the average as 47 ms.

```
>> t1 = sum(t)/10;
>> disp(t1)
    0.0468
```

Assuming that this represents $n \, log_2(n)$ operations, where n is 1,000,000, this is 19,931,568 operations (op1). Doing the DFT would take n^2 or 1,000,000,000,000 operations (op2).

```
>> op1 = 19931568;
>> op2 = 1000000 ^ 2;
>> t2 = t1 * op2 / op1;
```

With a simple ratio of t2 = t1 * op2 / op1, we find t2 is 2348 seconds, or 2347.9872 seconds longer.

SOLUTIONS FOR CHAPTER 14

1. You can also set up a git repository on your own machine. Here is an example of committing and updating a project.

```
cascade:js> git status
On branch master
Changes not staged for commit:
  (use "git add <file>..." to update what will be committed)
  (use "git checkout -- <file>..." to discard changes in
  working directory)
 modified:  brew4.html
 modified:  brewUpdateOther.js
 modified:  ingredients_list.xml
no changes added to commit (use "git add" and/or
"git commit -a")
cascade:js> git commit -am "Added timing functionality
to boil start and end."
[master 819dc94] Added timing functionality to boil start
and end.
 3 files changed, 83 insertions(+), 3 deletions(-)
cascade:js> git push origin master
Password:
Enumerating objects: 9, done.
Counting objects: 100% (9/9), done.
Delta compression using up to 4 threads
Compressing objects: 100% (5/5), done.
Writing objects: 100% (5/5), 1.41 KiB | 720.00 KiB/s, done.
Total 5 (delta 4), reused 0 (delta 0)
To cascade.local:/Users/git/js.git
    2bcb24f..819dc94 master -> master
cascade:js>
```

3. The work might look something like this, though these can also be done via a GUI. Command `cp` copies the file, `vi` edits it, and `javac` compiles it. This is done through a terminal window, not through MATLAB.

```
cascade:matlab_work> cp HelloExample.java HelloExample2.java
cascade:matlab_work> vi HelloExample2.java
cascade:matlab_work> javac HelloExample2.java
```

Under MATLAB, this can be executed by the following.

```
javaaddpath('/Users/mweeks/matlab_work/');
myJavaObj2 = javaObject('HelloExample2');
sayHello(myJavaObj2);
```

Running it looks gives this output.

```
>> javaaddpath('/Users/mweeks/matlab_work/');
>> myJavaObj2 = javaObject('HelloExample2');
>> sayHello(myJavaObj2);
Bonjour le Monde!
>> sayHello(myJavaObj2);
Hallo Welt!
>> sayHello(myJavaObj2);
Hello World!
```

BIBLIOGRAPHY

[1] B. Goodman, "3 arrested in plot to sell Coca-Cola secrets to rival," *Business - International Herald Tribune, New York Times,* July 6 2006.

[2] R. Shah, J. Kesan, and A. Kennis, "Implementing open standards: A case study of the Massachusetts open formats policy," in *Proceedings of the 2008 International Conference on Digital Government Research,* dg.o '08, pp. 262–271, Digital Government Society of North America, 2008.

[3] PROMETEUS Professor Meuer Technologieberatung und Services Gmbh, "Top 500 the list." `https://www.top500.org/statistics/sublist/`, 2017. [Online; accessed 14-November-2017].

[4] S. J. Vaughan-Nichols, "Linux totally dominates supercomputers." `http://www.zdnet.com/article/linux-totally-dominates-supercomputers/`, 2017. [Online; accessed 14-November-2017].

[5] C. Moler, "The origins of MATLAB." `http://www.mathworks.com/company/newsletters/articles/the-origins-of-matlab.html`, 2004. [Online; accessed 05-September-2016].

[6] M. Dunham, "Object oriented programming in MATLAB," *Computer Science website hosted by the University of British Columbia,* December 2008.

[7] K. Karplus and A. Strong, "Digital synthesis of plucked-string and drum timbres," *Computer Music Journal,* vol. 7, pp. 43–55, Summer 1983.

[8] M. Weeks, *Digital Signal Processing Using MATLAB & Wavelets, Second Edition.* USA: Jones and Bartlett Publishers, Inc., 2nd ed., 2010.

[9] F. J. Bates and Associates, *Polarimetry, Saccharimetry and the Sugars.* Circular of the National Bureau of Standards, 1942.

[10] J. W. Eaton, D. Bateman, S. Hauberg, and R. Wehbring, *GNU Octave version 5.1.0 manual: a high-level interactive language for numerical computations,* 2019.

INDEX